Contents

Preface		iv
Acknowledgements		vi
Abbreviations and Glossary		vii
Introduction		x
1	The Prehistory of *Fallschirmjäger Regiment 1*	13
2	Commanding Officers of *Fallschirmjäger Regiment 1* during the Winter Campaign of 1942–1943	17
3	The Organisation of *Flieger Division 7*	24
4	Operation MARS	31
5	Transfer of the Paratroopers to Smolensk	38
6	To the Frontline	45
7	Partisans	58
8	Aggressive Reconnaissance	62
9	The Raid at Durnevo	65
10	The Offensive Hits Others	71
11	Rearrangements	77
12	Skirmishes before Christmas	84
13	Christmas and New Year	93
14	*III. Bataillon* at Velikiye Luki	100
15	*I. Bataillon* 11 January–8 February 1943	123
16	*II. Bataillon* 11 January–8 February 1943	127
17	The Crisis in the South	135
18	The Transfer of *Fallschirmjäger Regiment 1* to Orel (9–14 February 1943)	143
19	*Fallschirmjäger Regiment 1* (without *I. Bataillon*) 14 February–4 March 1943	152
20	Schulenburg's *I. Bataillon*, 13–28 February	193
21	*I. Bataillon* at Dmitrovsk-Orlovsky	200
22	*Fallschirmjäger Regiment 1* in the sections of *12. Panzer* and *216. Infanterie Division*	234
23	The Failed Offensive of the Central Front	258
24	The Last Days on the Eastern Front	263
25	Losses	272
26	Conclusion	277
Appendices		
I	Combatant Strengths	280
II	Awards	282
III	Approved Close Combat Actions of *Fallschirmjäger Regiment 1* during Winter 1942–1943 at Smolensk, Velikiye Luki and Orel	284
IV	Subordinations	286
Bibliography		288

Preface

Much has been written about the actions of the German paratroopers during the Second World War. Most of these sources deal with airborne operations in Norway, Belgium, the Netherlands and Crete, and the fighting around Monte Cassino. Less has been written about their infantry combat missions on the Eastern Front. My father was a veteran of *Fallschirmjäger Regiment 1* which he joined as a volunteer in the autumn of 1941. He saw action during the campaigns in Russia 1942–1943, Italy 1943–1945, and Austria 1945. Although he received full parachute training, he never took part in an airborne operation. In editing his memoirs, I had to do extensive research into the history of the regiment. This was not an easy task as most of the primary sources, such as the regimental and divisional war journals, had been destroyed. Particularly scarce were the published and unpublished sources relating to the deployment in Russia 1942–1943.

In his standard work, Hans-Martin Stimpel devoted only a few pages to this mission, partly because of the aforementioned lack of sources available to him.[1] He wrote only one page about the deployment of *Fallschirmjäger Regiment 1* in Orel. *III. Bataillon/Fallschirmjäger Regiment 1* at Velikiye Luki gets about the same amount of space, while he devotes a total of eight pages to the more isolated partisan fighting. Stimpel made use of the existing files in the Bundesarchiv-Militärarchiv in Freiburg, in particular the war diaries of *Fallschirmjäger Regiment 3* and *4*. Those of *Fallschirmjäger Regiment 1* no longer exist. Files from other units and formations were only consulted in individual cases. The scope of the work probably did not allow a more detailed approach. The files of the *Fallschirmtruppe* were destroyed on 12–15 February 1945 by order of their commander-in-chief, *Generaloberst* Student, carried out by his first orderly officer, *Major i.G.* Hans Teusen.[2] The Luftwaffe files preserved in the Bundesarchiv-Militärarchiv are estimated at 2–3% of the original volume of files.[3]

The division's superior commands, such as the *9. Armee* or *Heeresgruppe Mitte*, are only dealt with in detail in the literature about the battles around Rzhev and the so-called BÜFFELBEWEGUNG ('Buffalo Movement') – the retreat of *9. Armee* from Rzhev. The winter battle for Orel of *2. Panzer Armee* has so far received little attention in military-historical studies. Even in the comprehensive work *Das Deutsche Reich und der Zweite Weltkrieg* these events are only marginally examined.[4]

---

1 Hans-Martin Stimpel, *Die deutsche Fallschirmtruppe 1942–1945 – Einsätze auf Kriegsschauplätzen im Osten und Westen* (Hamburg: Mittler, 2001), pp.66–88.
2 Hans-Martin Stimpel, *Widersinn 1945* (Göttingen: Couvillier, 2003), 4th extended edition, p.VII and by the same, *Die deutsche Fallschirmtruppe 1936–1945 – Innenansichten von Führung und Truppe* (Hamburg: Mittler, 2007), p.247.
3 Andreas Kunz, *Wehrmacht und Niederlage: Die bewaffnete Macht in der Endphase der nationalsozialistischen Herrschaft 1944 bis 1945* (Munich: Oldenburg, 2007), 2nd edition, p.17, fn.41.
4 Bernd Wegener, 'Der Krieg gegen die Sowjetunion 1942/43' in *Das Deutsche Reich und der Zweite Weltkrieg* (Stuttgart: DVA, 1990), vol.6, pp.1082–1089.

I researched mainly the primary and secondary sources of other formations and memoirs to get an overview of the regiment's deployment and got lucky in the archive of the *Bund Deutscher Fallschirmjäger*. Unfortunately, I could not use all my newly acquired knowledge for my father's memoirs, as only the broader context was needed. So, the next step for me was to go into more detail.

This book is not about emphasizing heroics, but aims to describe as accurately as possible what happened and how the soldiers perceived it. Some of the paratroopers' recollections have created a number of myths, which I hope I have been able to put into perspective.

German defensive actions are mentioned a lot, which implies that the attacking side is the aggressor. It is clear and undisputed that the German side was the aggressor in this war, and the Soviet army was defending its country. The German soldiers themselves had a different view, they thought they were defending Germany against the aggression of Bolshevism. In the end – as always – the soldier was fighting for his comrades next to him and for their own survival. The question of 'why' cannot and will not be answered in this study, as much has been written on the subject already and would distract from the focus.

The photos have mostly been chosen for their documentary value and are therefore sometimes of poor quality. The majority are from private collections and have been taken by paratroopers of the regiment or the division. Despite my best efforts, in many cases it was not possible to determine exactly who took the photos, as they are private. Infringements on anybody's rights are not intended. If you feel that your rights have been infringed, please contact the author.

For the sake of readability, the use of abbreviations has been kept to a minimum. German ranks, formation and unit names have been kept in German and are in *italics*, while abbreviations are in normal script. In the German *Wehrmacht*, a division or corps was called a *Verband* (formation) and a regiment, company or platoon an *Einheit* (unit). This distinction is used in this book. Soviet ranks, formations and units are given in English and normal script.

The Germans' usage of the term '*Gruppe*' might be confusing. A platoon had several groups or sections of eight to 10 men. I use the term 'group' for this kind of unit. But it could also mean a combat group, a reinforced formation or unit, usually named after its commander (e.g., '*Gruppe Häring*', '*Kampfgruppe von der Chevallerie*'), or simply an undefined gathering of a few people. A 'group' is divided into squads (*Trupps*).

As I worked on this study and delved deeper into the subject, I realised that data protection could become an issue. I have therefore tried to include only data that is of historical significance or publicly available. The generals' and senior officers' data are given in full, those of junior officers only the year of birth, as it is important to show how young the protagonists were in some cases. The non-commissioned officers' or enlisted men's data – although known to me – have not been given. However, the data of those who received the Knight's Cross have been given in full, as these data are publicly available. Where a recipient of the German Cross in Gold was a non-commissioned officer, I have given the year of birth as age is relevant to this award for exceptional bravery. Every fallen soldier had a story, an identity and a family – they deserve to be not just a number, but a reminder that war is not heroic, it is destruction. To make a point here, it was necessary to give data of selected fallen paratroopers in full. I have taken the possible wish of families not to be identified as having had a relative who was a paratrooper seriously and have tried my best to strike a balance between historical interest and the protection of their interests. If anyone still feels that I have gone too far, I have to say I am sorry, I have done my best.

During my research I came into contact with several descendants of paratroopers who took part in this campaign. Almost all of them had in common that they wanted to know more about the actions and circumstances in which their relatives had fought, been wounded, or even killed. In order to make my knowledge available to these and other interested parties I decided to write this study. It is also intended to fill a gap in the combat history of *Fallschirmjäger Regiment 1*.

Acknowledgements

As always with works like this one, over the years lots of people were involved who helped me along. It is impossible to name everybody, but I am grateful to all. Of the few I would like to mention, Ingo Apel helped me outstandingly with his extensive knowledge and encouragement. My thanks go also to one of the last 'old eagles' still alive, the impressive Heino Niehaus, whose invaluable guidance I cherish. The Bund Deutscher Fallschirmjäger – foremost Steffen L. Rhode, Dieter Nell, Manfred Müller and Michael Rackebrandt – was of invaluable help and support as I got unrestricted access to their archives. I owe special thanks to Florian Franz, who kindly provided me with Willi Wagner's letters from his collection. Siegfried Baier gave me the permission to use the estate of Walter Heinkelein and Folker Förtsch of the Archive of Crailsheim was very helpful in providing the files. The family von Oppen was also very friendly.

What would a book be without photographs? Among others, I am very grateful to Paul Bernhard, Paul Dekkers and Stephan Janzyk for their kind support and for kindly providing me with photos from their collections. Also, I would like to thank the staff of the Bildarchiv/Bundesarchiv who were very patient and forthcoming, especially Hermann Gerhardt. Peter Bedenk also gave me permission to use some photographs of his collection.

Thanks to Tom Cooper for linking me up with Helion, Rob Griffith for being a very supportive editor, Hans Holmer for proof reading and rectifying my English, Johannes Windisch-Graetz for invaluable technical advice, and – last but not least – to my wife Marieke for her patience and support.

Abbreviations and Glossary

German

Abbreviation	German	English
Ia	Erster Generalstabsoffizier	First General Staff Officer – chief of operations of a division. Responsible for operative and tactical leadership of a division
Ib	Zweiter Generalstabsoffizier	Second General Staff Officer – quartermaster. Responsible for supply of a Division
Ic	Dritter Generalstabsoffizier	Third General Staff Officer – chief intelligence officer. Responsible for intelligence gathering on the enemy
IIa	Divisionsadjutant	Divisional Adjutant, responsible for personnel matters at division headquarters
Abt.	Abteilung	Units up to battalion strength (signals, reconnaissance, artillery…)
	Armee	Army (nominal body of several army corps and led by an AOK)
AK	Armee Korps	Army corps (consisting of several divisions)
AOK	Armeeoberkommando	Army high command (leads an army).
Art.	Artillerie	Artillery
AR, ArtRgt	Artillerie Regiment	Artillery regiment
Btl.	Bataillon	Battalion
BDF	Bund Deutscher Fallschirmjäger	Association of German Paratroopers (founded 1949)
DKiG	Deutsches Kreuz in Gold	German Cross in Gold, awarded for repeated acts of bravery in combat
EK I	Eisernes Kreuz I. Klasse	Iron Cross 1st Class
EK II	Eisernes Kreuz II. Klasse	Iron Cross 2nd Class
FJR	Fallschirmjäger Regiment	Paratrooper regiment
FJD	Fallschirmjäger Division	Paratrooper division
GFM	Generalfeldmarschall	Field Marshal
Flak	Fliegerabwehrkanone	Anti-aircraft gun
Fl.Div.	Flieger Division	Air division
Fsch.	Fallschirm	Parachute

Abbreviation	German	English
GJ	Gebirgsjäger	Mountain troops
GenObst	Generaloberst	Colonel General
GR, GrRgt	Grenadier Regiment	(Heavy) Infantry regiment
GrW, Gr.W.	Granatwerfer	Mortar
Hptm	Hauptmann	Captain
HGr	Heeresgruppe	Army group (consisting of several armies)
HKL	Hauptkampflinie	Main line of defence/resistance
ID, Inf.Div.	Infanterie Division	Infantry division
i.G.	im Generalstab	of the General Staff
I.G.	Infanteriegeschütz	Infantry gun
JägerBtl	Jägerbataillon	Light infantry battalion
K 98	Karabiner 98	Carbine Model 98, the standard German rifle
Kfz	Kraftfahrzeug	Motor vehicle
KG	Kampfgeschwader	Bomber wing
Kp.	Kompanie	Company
KrKw	Kranken-Kraftwagen	Ambulance car/truck
KTB	Kriegstagebuch	War diary
l.G.	Leichtgeschütz	Recoilless gun
Lt.	Leutnant	Second Lieutenant
LW, Lw	Luftwaffe	German air force
Lw.F.Rgt./Div.	Luftwaffen Feld Regiment/Division	Luftwaffe Field Regiment/Division, an infantry unit of the *Luftwaffe*
m.	mittel	Medium
MG	Maschinengewehr	Machine gun
MPi	Maschinenpistole	Submachine gun
Nb.W.	Nebelwerfer	Rocket launcher
NSDAP	Nationalsozialistische Deutsche Arbeiterpartei	National Socialist German Worker's Party (Nazi-Party)
Oblt.	Oberleutnant	First Lieutenant
Obst	Oberst	Colonel
ObstLt	Oberstleutnant	Lieutenant Colonel
OKH	Oberkomanndo des Heeres	High command of the *Heer*
OKL	Oberkommando der Luftwaffe	High command of the *Luftwaffe*
OKW	Oberkommando der Wehrmacht	High command of the armed forces
Pak	Panzerabwehr Kanone	Anti-tank gun
Pi	Pionier	Engineer, sapper
Pz	Panzer	Tank
PzAOK	Panzer Armeeoberkommando	Panzer army high command
PzGrRgt	Panzergrenadier Regiment	Mechanized infantry regiment

Abbreviation	German	English
PzDiv	Panzer Division	Panzer division
RGG	Regiment ‚General Göring'	
Rgt.	Regiment	Regiment
RK	Ritterkreuz	Knight's Cross
SA	Sturmabteilung	lit. Storm department, paramilitary organisation of the Nazi party
s.	schwer	Heavy
sFH	Schwere Feldhaubitze	Heavy field howitzer
SFL	Selbstfahrlafette	Self-propelled (anti-tank) gun
z.b.V.	zur besonderen Verwendung	For special purpose

English

Abbreviation	
GRD	Guards Rifle Division (Soviet)
GTR	Guards Tank Regiment (Soviet)
KIA	Killed in action
MDL	Main line of defence
MIA	Missing in action
NCO	Non-commissioned officer
POW	Prisoner of war
RD	Rifle Division (Soviet)
RR	Rifle Regiment (Soviet)
TR	Tank Regiment (Soviet)
WIA	Wounded in action

Introduction

'Solid as a Rock' (in German *'Fels in der Brandung'*) has often been used to describe the heroic actions of the German *Fallschirmtruppe* and it is also an expression of the times.[1] Its definition is 'staying reliable and calm in a crisis, but also 'being very strong and not likely to break'.[2] In a military context it also means standing your ground and successfully defending against a superior attacking force. Those who were addressed by this expression felt that they belonged to an elite, that they were heroes.

Fallschirmjäger Regiment 1 fought successful defensive battles in the winter of 1942 to 1943, hence the title of this book. The study will show that the rock was partly washed away: 428 dead and missing and 1,016 wounded speak a clear language. This figure includes the missing and those who died of their wounds shortly afterwards. In relation to the combatant strength of the regiment this represents a casualty rate of 18.6% dead and 44.2% wounded – not counting the casualties who suffered from illness or frostbite.

Military historians tend to focus on the Battle of Stalingrad and the annihilation of *6. Armee* during the winter of 1942 to 1943. The successful Soviet operation URANUS, aimed at encircling *6. Armee* in Stalingrad as well as the subsequent offensive operation LITTLE SATURN aimed at splitting *Heeresgruppe A* and *Heeresgruppe B* almost led to the defeat of the whole southern sector of the German front. The Germans were unable to relieve the forces trapped in Stalingrad, but were able to mount a counteroffensive, Manstein's famous 'backhand blow', which halted the Soviet advance and brought Kharkov back into German hands. The German *Ostheer* was saved for the time being and total collapse was averted.

As *Heeresgruppe Mitte* was eventually able to successfully repel Soviet offensives on the Rhzev salient (operation MARS) and others on the southern flank towards Kursk and then turning north towards Bryansk and Orel. The aim of these Soviet offensives was the complete destruction of *Heeresgruppe Mitte*. Not much has been written about the battles in this sector.

The defeats suffered by the Red Army during operation MARS were long downplayed or ignored by Soviet post-war historiography. It was only after the breakdown of the Soviet Union and the subsequent opening of the Russian archives, that Russian and international historians were able to research these events, at least in part. The process is ongoing, as some files are still inaccessible.

There is also little to be found in *Fallschirmjäger* specialist literature and memoirs about the operations of *Flieger Division 7* in Russia and even less about *Fallschirmjäger Regiment 1*. The time north of Smolensk is usually only touched upon cursorily and Orel is mentioned at best in passing. In particular, memoires or diaries of members of *Fallschirmjäger Regiment 1* are rare.

---

1 Stimpel, *Fallschirmtruppe – Osten und Westen*, p.76.
2 <macmillandictionary.com>, accessed 18 April 2022. The German expression has the same meaning.

Gerhard Broder *(6. Kompanie)* gives a very brief account of the mission in Russia, as he was recovering from wounds and only heard about the Orel mission through stories.³ Walter Fricke *(10. Kompanie)* remembered the actions more vividly and emotionally but was only able to cover the period up to January 1943 as he was wounded near Velikiye Luki. The diary of Ernst Germer *(3. Kompanie)*, later to be awarded the Knight's Cross, gives a clear and direct account of events up to the first days of the Orel mission when he was also wounded, but little is known of how he felt. Walter Heinkelein *(5. Kompanie)* describes his experiences very vaguely. The attack on Alekseyevka and the trench warfare north of Smolensk are only rudimentarily mentioned. Rüdiger von Zimburg *(2. Kompanie)* – the author's father – describes his experiences more accurately, but occasionally makes mistakes – especially in the case of the Orel mission – in dates and locations, as he wrote down his experiences later.

Events are often blurred and intermingled in the individual's memory, so that only a superficial account is usually given. Places and dates were often confused if the diaries were not written at the same time. Freezing temperatures, wetness and exhaustion are the constants that everyone mentions. Rolf Kratzert,⁴ a battalion commander of *Fallschirmjäger Regiment 3* described this pointedly: 'This vastness and monotony of the Russian landscape blurs all details, distorts and confuses memories and one is only able to recognise the coherences as if seen through a fog. Of these snow-covered places of action, these wooden huts that are always the same, only the names remain without a clear image of what they really looked like.'⁵ Kratzert devoted less than two pages of his 191-page memoir to this winter's campaign.

Significant – because they are the most immediate – are the field post letters of *Hauptfeldwebel* Willi Wagner,⁶ the '*Spieß*' (company sergeant major) of *3. Kompanie*, who for example wrote a euphoric letter to his wife on 1 March after the first successful attack on Promklevo, but on 3 March reports the death of his friend *Leutnant* Hans Thede somewhat more quietly and sadly. After that, his letters are either brief – just a sign of life – or else an indulgence in thoughts of home, his wife, his child, and concerns about their living conditions. He mentally escaped from the events around him and reported nothing back home, probably so as not to worry his wife. His relief when the transfer to the West finally took place is very palpable. Sadly, he did not survive the war.

There are comparatively more published records from other units of *Flieger Division 7*.⁷ This also has something to do with the fact that there is more archival material for *Fallschirmjäger Regiment 3* and *4*.⁸ These units also had a more cohesive veterans' organisational structure than the veterans of

---

3   Gerhard Broder (Havelberg, 13 October 1919–20 March 2016), *Leutnant*. After the war he pursued a career as a mechanical engineer. Bernhard, Paul (ed.), Gerhard Broder, *Guerre Mondiale contre moi* (Dornstadt: Hess, 2013), 3rd expanded edition.
4   Rudolf 'Rolf' Johann Kratzert (Karlsburg, 25 April 1898–Vienna, 16 January 1996), *Major*, RK 9 June 1944, DKiG 27 October 1943.
5   Rolf Kratzert, *Vom k.u.k. Offizier zum Ritterkreuzträger* (self-published, 1991), p.86.
6   Willi Wagner (Hirzweiler,16 May 1912–KIA Laterza, 16 September 1943), *Oberfeldwebel*.
7   Johannes Hönscheid (ed.), Martin Pöppel, *Himmel und Hölle – Das Kriegstagebuch des Fallschirmjägers Martin Pöppel* (Munich: Internationaler Kulturdienst, 1985); Anon., *Rot scheint die Sonne – Eine Kompanie schreibt ihre Geschichte (Fallschirm-, Transport-, Kradschützen- und Aufklärungskompanie)* (self-published, no year); Dr Ludwig Müller, *Damals* (Würzburg: self-published, 1981); Klitzing, *Die Geschichte des Fasch.MG.Btl/Fsch.Gr.Werferbtl. 1* (self-published, no year); Rudolf Donth, *Die Geschichte des Fallschirmjägerregiments 4* (self-published, no year); Kratzert, *Ritterkreuzträger*; Klaus J. Peters, *Fallschirmjägerregiment 3 – Eine Chronik in Bildern* (San José: Bender, 1992 and 1995), vol.1 and 2.
8   The Bundesarchiv-Militärarchiv holds parts of the surviving war diaries of FJR 3 and FJR 4 for the winter campaign 1942–1943.

Fallschirmjäger Regiment 1, which allowed a more organised approach to writing the history of their units.

Memoirs of the generals are also scarce. Heidrich wrote short unfinished memoirs but died soon after the war. They were only published in a veterans' magazine. Heilmann, the commander of *Fallschirmjäger Regiment 3* never published his memoirs, the manuscript is in an archive in the United States.

Why were these very intense experiences so easily forgotten? Was it because of the numbness, the total exhaustion in which state one no longer perceived anything, or also because many of the participants did not survive the war? Neither the surviving regimental commander, Karl-Lothar Schulz, nor the surviving battalion commanders of *Fallschirmjäger Regiment 1*, Karl-Heinz Becker and Kurt Gröschke, published memoirs. There is also little to be found in the magazine of the Association of German Paratroopers (*Bund Deutscher Fallschirmjäger*) in which many former paratroopers wrote about their experiences.

What these battles did to the psyche of those involved is difficult to comprehend.

Hardly anyone felt like a hero after these battles. As successful as they were officially portrayed, the casualties were very high and hardly anyone had escaped without being wounded or being forced to fall out due to frostbite or illness. All had lost friends and close comrades. The impression of a tired, numb soldier, happy to have survived these hardships and more or less in one piece, is pervasive.

1

The Prehistory of *Fallschirmjäger Regiment 1*

Fallschirmjäger Regiment 1 (FJR 1)[1] was established on 1 April 1938 as part of the establishment of a large new formation, *Flieger Division 7*, with *Generalmajor* Kurt Student as its commander. According to the *Luftwaffe*'s system, it should have been designated as *7. Flieger Division*, which is why this variant is often found in files of higher-level commands and has occasionally been adopted in literature. This designation was initially chosen to disguise the fact that it was a paratrooper formation. The name was retained – although the secrecy was no longer necessary – until the spring of 1943 when it was finally renamed *1. Fallschirmjäger Division*.

IV. Bataillon of the *Regiment General Göring* was formed in Stendal as *I. Bataillon* of this new regiment. The *Regiment General Göring* originally consisted of policemen, who were not transferred to the army like other such formations, but instead to Göring's *Luftwaffe*. The origin of the German *Fallschirmtruppe* is generally seen in a reorganisation order issued by the *Oberkommando der Luftwaffe* (OKL) before mid-November 1935. A battalion of the *Regiment General Göring* was to be converted into a battalion of paratroopers. Parts of the personnel were then trained in parachuting from 1936,[2] under command of *Oberstleutnant* Bruno Bräuer.[3] An NCO in the First World War he was later promoted to *Leutnant* in the *Reichswehr* and joined the police force in 1920. From 1 January 1939 he was appointed commander of *Fallschirmjäger Regiment 1* with the rank of *Oberst*. Bräuer retained his command until summer 1942 and was later transferred to the island of Crete as military commander. After the war he was tried in Athens for war crimes, sentenced to death and hanged.

This *IV. Bataillon/Regiment General Göring* experienced its first operational deployment as paratroopers on 13 March 1938 during the occupation of Austria. It was not a classic airborne mission but took place as part of an air lift by *Kampfgeschwader z.b.V. 1* to Graz. Another operational airborne mission was planned for the same year as part of the occupation of the Sudentenland. This was cancelled as a result to the Munich Agreement and was converted into a training mission in the Freudenthal area on 7 October 1938.

---

1   The abbreviation 'FJR' for *'Fallschirmjäger Regiment'* used in this book was not officially used by the *Wehrmacht*, it became more common only after the war. In contemporary German documents the abbreviation *Fallsch.Jg.Rgt.* and other variations were used.
2   Karl Heinz Golla, *The German Fallschirmtruppe 1936–41* (Solihul: Helion, 2013), p.29.
3   Bruno Oswald Bräuer (Willmansdorf 4 February 1893–Athens [executed] 20 May 1947); *General der Fallschirmtruppe*; RK 24 May 1940, DKiG 13 April 1942.

As early as 1 April 1937, the army also formed a company of parachute infantry in Stendal, which was expanded to a battalion from 1 June 1938.[4] The battalion was transferred to Braunschweig on 4 November 1938 where it was presented with an infantry standard and thus took over the tradition of the German *7. Sturmbataillon* from the First World War. *Major* Richard Heidrich the battalion commander,[5] received the standard. Heidrich, a Saxon and First World War veteran, took command of *Flieger Division 7* in November 1942. He was nicknamed '*Granit Heidrich*' by his soldiers because of his reputation as a tough, feared, and respected commander. Senior officers referred to him behind his back as the '*Ideenmops*' (Idea Pug) because of his appearance and inventive methods.

On 1 January 1939, the battalion was transferred to the *Luftwaffe* and renamed *II. Bataillon/Fallschirmjäger Regiment 1*. The base for *III. Bataillon* was formed by the *Luftlandebataillon* of *Regiment General Göring*, a process that lasted well into 1939.[6]

Richard Heidrich as an *Oberst* with his newly awarded Knight's Cross for Crete, July 1941. (BArch, Bild 183-L19501/CC-BY-SA 3.0)

The formation of *Regiment 1* – the regimental staff was established in the early months of 1939 – faced acute personnel problems. As that year's conscripts had already been allocated to other formations, *Generalmajor* Student arranged for 1,200 volunteers from the *SA Standarte Feldherrnhalle* to be accepted.[7]

In March 1939, as part of the occupation of Czechoslovakia, the paratroopers were again deployed, landing in Prague on transport planes.

In terms of personnel, the parachute force consisted at that time of a mixture of volunteers: former members of the police force, the army, the *SA Standarte Feldherrnhalle* and others. This group quickly bonded during their missions. At first, during the Polish campaign, the regiment was used only sporadically and as part of a ground mission (*I. Bataillon*: no combat operations; *II. Bataillon*: combat at Wola Gułovska, 24 September 1939; *III. Bataillon*: combat at Radom, 14 September 1939).

This was followed by airborne operations in Norway and Denmark as part of operation *WESERÜBUNG* April–May 1940 (staff of *I. Bataillon, 2. Kompanie*: Oslo-Fornebu Airport; *3. Kompanie*: Stavanger/Sola Airport; *4. Kompanie*: Storström Bridge and Aalborg Airfield, Denmark; *1. Kompanie*: Dombås). The units not deployed in Norway saw action in the Netherlands in May 1940 (*I. Bataillon*: Dordrecht; *II. Bataillon*: Moerdijk; *III. Bataillon*: Rotterdam-Waalhaven). After its mission in the Netherlands *I. Bataillon* parachuted again at Narvik in Norway.

---

4   The order was issued on 15 March 1938.
5   Richard Heidrich (Lewalde, Saxony, 28 July 1896—Military Hospital Hamburg-Bergedorf, 22 December 1947), *General der Fallschirmtruppe* 16 November 1943 with effect from 1 November 1942 Commander of *Flieger Division 7*; 15 June 1943 with effect from 1 May 1943 Commander of the *1. Fallschirmjäger Division*, 31 October 1944 with effect from 16 November 1944 commanding general of the *I. Fallschirm Korps*. DKiG 4 April 1942, RK 14 June 1941, Oak Leaves 5 February 1944, Swords 25 March 1944.
6   *11. Kompanie* specified 1 June 1939 as its date of formation. Alfons Wanderwitz, *Treffen der 11./Fsch.Jg.Rgt. 1* (Neustadt a.d.Aisch: Wanderwitz, 1978), p.13.
7   Golla, *Fallschirmtruppe*, p.45.

After these operations the regiment was assigned to the following garrison towns: regimental command and staff, *13.* and *14. Kompanie* as well as *I. Bataillon* in Stendal, a newly formed *II. Bataillon* in Tangermünde, *III. Bataillon* in Gardelegen. The original *II. Bataillon* – the former *Fallschirm Infanterie Bataillon* of the army – served as the base from which *Fallschirmjäger Regiment 3* under *Oberst* Heidrich was formed.

This was followed by the airborne operation MERKUR to capture the island of Crete in May 1941, which resulted in very high losses. Hitler declared this the end of airborne operations. Thus, from this moment on, with a few notable exceptions, the German parachute troops fought only as infantry. *Fallschirmjäger Regiment 1* did not see any more airborne missions for the rest of the war.

A platoon of *III. Bataillon/Fallschirmjäger Regiment 1* parades through the German town of Tangerhütte in March 1942. (Private Collection)

After Crete, *Flieger Division 7* had to be restaffed and reorganised. During this process the deployment order for the autumn and winter of 1941/1942 was issued, with various parts of the division being transferred to different theatres on the Eastern Front. From about September to December 1941 *Regiment 1* and *3*, along with other divisional units, were deployed to *Heeresgruppe Nord* in the area east of Leningrad, where they saw heavy action on the Neva and near Shlisselburg. Again suffering heavy losses of 40 percent,[8] the division was gradually withdrawn until January 1942 and relocated back to Germany. In late December 1941 *Fallschirmjäger Regiment 2* was transferred to the Eastern Front (Mius and Volkhov), never to rejoin *Flieger Division 7.*[9]

In Germany the division not only received replacements but was also completely reorganised. Among other divisional units, *Fallschirmjäger Regiment 4* and *Fallschirm MG Bataillon* were formed, with experienced personnel from the other regiments of the division. *III. Bataillon/Fallschirmjäger Regiment 2* became *III. Bataillon/Fallschirmjäger Regiment 4*, of which one company was transferred to *I. Bataillon/Fallschirmjäger Regiment 4*. A second company from *I. Bataillon/Fallschirmjäger Regiment 3* joined this battalion as did other personnel for *13.* and *14. Kompanie*. This *Fallschirmjäger Regiment 4* consisted of only two battalions at the outset of autumn 1942. Within the other remaining regiments further reshuffles took place, mixing experienced battle-hardened *Fallschirmjäger* with young recruits who just had finished their basic training, and volunteers from *Luftwaffe* ground personnel or anti-aircraft units. Thus, for example, *Oberleutnant* Paul Ernst Renisch of *Flak Abteilung 99 (mot/*

---

8   Stimpel, *Fallschirmtruppe – Osten und Westen*, p.33.
9   The so called *Kampfgruppe Sturm* stayed on the Eastern Front until July 1942. The regiment became part of *Fallschirmjäger Division 2*.

Paul Ernst Renisch as *Hauptmann* in autumn 1944. (Private Collection)

6. Kompanie outside of Argentan in August 1942. (Private Collection)

gl.) volunteered and became a platoon commander in *2. Kompanie/Fallschirmjäger Regiment 1*.[10] Renisch, an officer mostly disliked by his men later commanded *9. Kompanie, I.* and *III. Bataillon/ Fallschirmjäger Regiment 1* and was awarded the Knight's Cross and the German Cross in Gold in Italy. After his release from British captivity, he became a tax advisor.

At the end of March, the division was sent to Normandy, France, as an intervention reserve against a possible Allied landing. *Fallschirmjäger Regiment 1* was stationed in the area of La Ferté-Macé and Bagnoles-de-l'Orne. There were also plans for the division to attack the island of Malta, which, however, were soon abandoned by Hitler.

In Normandy, the soldiers were not allowed to rest. Ongoing combat and parachute training was the basis for the creation of a division with a very high combat value. Thus, this new and quite diverse group grew into tight-knit units.

On 19 August 1942 the division was alerted, Allied forces had landed at Dieppe. Parts of the division were already on their way when the all-clear was given and the men were allowed to return to their quarters.

At the beginning of October 1942, *Flieger Division 7* relocated to Germany to prepare for an airborne operation in the Caucasus, starting from the Crimean peninsula (Kerch). After this mission was abandoned, the division was soon transferred to the Eastern Front.

---

10   Paul Ernst Renisch (Brussels/Belgium, 2 July 1917–Ettlingen, 25 January 1998), *Major*; RK 31 October 1944, DKiG 22 April 1944.

2

Commanding Officers of *Fallschirmjäger Regiment 1* during the Winter Campaign of 1942–1943

Karl-Lothar Schulz

Oberstleutnant Karl-Lothar Schulz took command of *Fallschirmjäger Regiment 1* on 28 August 1942, shortly before the regiment left France.[1] His love for cognac, which he developed during the war, earned him the nickname 'Cognac-Schulz'. He was considered a daredevil and the best regimental commander in the division.[2] Heidrich, in his positive assessment, described him as an outspoken leader with a straightforward, clean character and emphasized his military skills as 'agile, with a clear, sober judgement' and 'good tactical ability and understanding'.[3] Even the commanding general, *General der Flieger* Kurt Student, supported this in his assessment of 16 July 1942 and highlights Schulz's 'personal bravery, readiness for action and infectious drive, as well as superior leadership qualities' which 'make him one of the best leaders' of the parachute force.[4]

Unteroffizier Gerhard Nebel – a writer and humanist who rejected and criticised the Nazi regime, the war and its proponents – described him as a 'tall East Prussian, with bold, alert, charming masculinity', who was 'adored by all the ladies as a martial hero.' Nebel 'realised in the first half hour that [Schulz] is a leader – not only is he himself unshakable, but he also spreads security around

Karl-Lothar Schulz, the commander of *Fallschirmjäger Regiment 1* as *Oberst*, April 1944. (BArch, Bild 146-2006-0105/ Stocker, Dr./CC-BY-SA 3.0)

---

1 This section is based on Franz Thomas and Günter Wegmann, *Die Ritterkreuzträger der Deutschen Wehrmacht 1939–1945, Teil II. Fallschirmjäger* (Osnabrück: Biblio, 1986), pp.277–280.
2 Gerhard Nebel, *Unter Partisanen und Kreuzfahrern* (Stuttgart: Deutscher Bücherbund, no year), p.168; Magnus Pahl, *Monte Cassino* (Paderborn: Brill, 2021), p.78.
3 Recommendation for early promotion dated 8 September 1943; Bundesarchiv-Militärarchiv (BA-MA), Pers 6/1916, p.4.
4 Recommendation for early promotion dated 16 July 1942; BA-MA, Pers 6/1916, p.9.

him.'⁵ Nebel criticised the fact that Schulz (in August 1944) condemned the attempt on Hitler's life on 20 July and at the same time still believed in miracle weapons. On the other hand, Schulz no longer believed in the possibility of a German victory and saw an Anglo-Saxon victory as the salvation of Europe, but continued to fight against it. According to Nebel, 'His cynicism is a mask; his cognac intoxication an asylum of helplessness.'⁶

Schulz was born in Königsberg on 30 April 1907, the son of a Protestant cantor. He completed his military training in the *Reichswehr* from 1924 to 1925, starting in the artillery (*II. Abt./1. Preussisches Artillerie Regiment*). Shortly afterwards, in 1925, he became a police officer and attended the police academy in Brandenburg-Havel. Later, in 1935 he was promoted to *Oberleutnant* and commanded *15. (Pionier) Kompanie* of *Regiment General Göring* (RGG), which was formed from the paramilitary Brandenburg police force. A paratrooper from the very beginning, he completed the paratrooper course in Stendal in 1936, and from 1 September 1937 he was again – now as *Hauptmann* – commander of *15. (Pi.) Kompanie/IV. Bataillon* of RGG. In this capacity, he took part in the first operational deployment of the German parachute force during the occupation of Austria (Graz) in March 1939. After this mission, he became leader of *12. Kompanie* of the newly formed *Fallschirmjäger Regiment 1*. As such, Schulz took part in skirmishes near Wola Gułovska during the Polish campaign in 1939.

During the 1940 campaign in the Netherlands, Schulz participated in the airborne attack on Rotterdam-Waalhaven airport as commander of *III. Bataillon/Fallschirmjäger Regiment 1*, where he was wounded in action. For this mission, Schulz was awarded the Knight's Cross on 24 May 1940. On 19 July 1940 he was also promoted to *Major* with effect from 1 August 1940 (with rank from 1 January 1941).

After recovering from his wound, Schulz and his battalion took part in the airborne assault on Crete-Heraklion, and in the ground combat mission in the Leningrad-Shlisselburg area during the following winter. For the latter he was awarded the German Cross in Gold (DKiG) on 26 February 1942.⁷

Originally intended by his divisional commander *Generalleutnant* Petersen as a general staff officer, Schulz was given command of *Fallschirmjäger Regiment 1* on 28 August 1942 but was not appointed full commander until 10 August 1943 (with rank of 5 June 1943) after the mission described in this book.⁸ While en route to Vitebsk he received an early promotion to *Oberstleutnant* on 26 October 1942.

During the Italian campaign of 1943 Schulz led his regiment in the fighting retreat from Taranto to the Sangro River. For this successful defensive performance, he was promoted to *Oberst* on 21 October 1943 (with rank from 1 May 1944). His effective leadership at Monte Cassino in February 1944 earned him the Oak Leaves to the Knight's Cross on 20 April 1944.

For his regiment's significant contribution to stopping the advance of the 5th US Army on Bologna in the autumn of 1944, Schulz was awarded the Swords of the Knight's Cross on 18 November 1944. On the same day, he was put in charge of *1. Fallschirmjäger Division* and promoted to *Generalmajor* on 17 January 1945.

---

5 Nebel, *Unter Partisanen*, pp.167, 173. Also cited in Pahl, *Monte Cassino*, p.78 and Magnus Pahl and Armin Wagner (eds), *Hitlers Elitetruppe? – Mythos Fallschirmjäger* (Dresden: Militärhistorisches Museum, be.bra, 2021), p.194.
6 Nebel, *Unter Partisanen*, p.168.
7 Klaus Patzwall, Veit Scherzer, *Das Deutsche Kreuz 1941–1945* (Norderstedt: Patzwall, 2001), p.429. Thomas & Wegmann, *Ritterkreuzträger – Fallschirmjäger*, p.278, mentions the date 9 March 1942.
8 See *Generalleutnant* Petersen's recommendation for early promotion of Schulz, from about July 1942; BA-MA, Pers 6/1916, p.10.

After the surrender of *Heeresgruppe Süd* on 2 May 1945, Schulz was taken prisoner of war by the British and spent the next two years in the Caserta POW camp until his release on 17 October 1947.

His wife is said to have prevented him from rejoining the army after the war and he became a real estate agent instead.[9] Karl-Lothar Schulz died in Wiesbaden on 26 September 1972 at the age of 65.

Wolf-Werner Graf von der Schulenburg

Wolf-Werner Graf (Count) von der Schulenburg was a descendant of a Brandenburg-Prussian noble family, born in Muskau on 14 September 1899.[10] His parents were the Prussian *General* Friedrich Bernhard Graf von der Schulenburg (1865–1939), later an NSDAP member of the *Reichstag*, and Freda-Marie Countess von der Schulenburg, née Countess von Arnim (1873–1939). Wolf Werner grew up with four siblings, most notably his brother Fritz-Dietlof,[11] who was one of the masterminds of the assassination attempt on Hitler on 20 July 1944 and who was executed on 10 August 1944.

His sister Elisabeth 'Tisa' was married to a Jewish businessman and was a fervent anti-Nazi.[12] When Hitler came to power, she and her husband emigrated to London. After their divorce in 1938 she came back to Germany on a short visit but was not allowed to return to Britain. She knew of and supported her brother's plans to assassinate Hitler. After her second divorce she became a Catholic nun and continued to work as an artist.

According to Tisa, Wolf-Werner believed in the political 'cause'. His brother Fritz-Dietlof's attempts to win him over to the resistance in the winter of 1943/1944 were unsuccessful, he only wanted to 'devote himself, sacrifice himself' and perish. He said: 'I feel like the rider on Lake Constance. I'm not allowed to look around. If I looked around, I would drop dead.'[13]

Von der Schulenburg was respectfully called '*der Graf*' (the Count) and was greatly admired by his subordinates:

Wolf-Werner von der Schulenburg, commander of *I. Bataillon/ Fallschirmjäger Regiment 1* in 1943, after having received the Knight's Cross (Archive BDF/Dahm)

> They really took him to their hearts, their Count. Wherever there was trouble, he was to be found. When there was no progress, he would suddenly appear. With a fatherly smile, he would conjure up a bottle of cognac and cigarettes from the depths of his coat. They all trusted him, the officers,

---

9   Pahl & Wagner, *Hitlers Elitetruppe?*, p.194.
10 Sources: Thomas & Wegmann, *Ritterkreuzträger – Fallschirmjäger*, pp.274–276. Franz Schenkel, 'Unser Graf', *Der Deutsche Fallschirmjäger* [DDF], (1957), vol.7, p.11.
11 Fritz-Dietlof Graf von der Schulenburg (London, 5 September 1902–executed, Berlin, 10 August 1944).
12 Elisabeth 'Tisa' Gräfin von der Schulenburg (Tressow, 7 December 1903–Dorsten, 8 February 2001).
13 Tisa von der Schulenburg, *Ich hab's gewagt – Bildhauerin und Ordensfrau – Ein unkonventionelles Leben* (Husum: Husum, 2013), p.147.

the NCOs, the men. He was a cavalier in the best sense of the word, a gentleman, and yet his soldiers' best comrade and friend.[14]

Like his father, Wolf-Werner pursued a military career at the beginning. He served in the First World War as a volunteer and *Leutnant* of the reserve, which he survived seriously wounded. He studied in Göttingen, joined the NSDAP on 1 November 1930 and the SA on 1 February 1931. He worked as a businessman in Brazil until 1933. When Hitler came to power that year, he returned to Germany and started work as a civil servant in the public sports sector, the *Reichssportamt*. A few years later, in 1936, he became *Gauführer* of the *Gau Ausland* of the *Deutscher Reichsbund für Leibeserziehungen* (German *Reichsbund* for Physical Education). He became close to *Reichssportführer* Hans von Tschammer und Osten, who put him in charge of his office and the foreign department.[15]

At the outbreak of the Second World War, Schulenburg was drafted into *Fallschirmjäger Regiment 1* on 15 August 1939 as a *Leutnant* and orderly officer. Although doctors declared him unfit for parachute jumping because of his wounds from the First World War, Schulenburg parachuted into action in 1940 near Dordrecht and later on Crete with the regimental staff without any prior training. He was quickly promoted: on 1 April 1940 to *Oberleutnant*, on 1 November the same year to *Hauptmann*, and on 19 December 1941 to *Major*. On 23 May 1940, shortly after the campaign in the Netherlands, he was awarded the Iron Cross, both 2nd and 1st Class (*Eisernes Kreuz II*. and *I.Klasse* – EK II and EK I).

On 20 February 1942, *Major* Graf von der Schulenburg was entrusted with command of *I. Bataillon/ Fallschirmjäger Regiment 1*. He and his battalion excelled in the campaign at Orel described in this book. He was dubbed the 'Saviour of Dmitrovsk' by his commanders.[16] The commander of the *78. Sturm Division*, *Generalleutnant* Völkers recommended Schulenburg for the Knight's Cross, which was awarded to him on 20 June 1943.[17]

On 1 October 1942 he was awarded the *Erdkampfabzeichen der Luftwaffe* (Ground Combat Badge of the *Luftwaffe*) and from 20 May 1943 he was also entitled to wear the Crete Armband.

In the autumn of 1943, he saw action in Italy during the fighting retreat from Taranto to the river Sangro and after Christmas 1943, the battles at Ortona, during which he was given temporary command of the regiment from 15 November 1943 to early/mid-January 1944. Shortly thereafter, the regiment was transferred to the Cassino front, where his battalion was very successful in defence. Appointed full commander of the battalion on 20 February 1944, Schulenburg had to take leave of the regiment at the same time and was transferred to Normandy in France, where he took command of the newly formed *Fallschirmjäger Regiment 13* (5. FJD) on 21 April 1944. After the invasion he fell in fierce fighting at Les Champs-de-Losque (now part of Remilly-les-Marais), 15 kilometres north-west of Saint-Lô on 14 July 1944 – just days before the failed assassination attempt on Hitler. He rests in the Marigny War Cemetery.

Count von der Schulenburg was posthumously appointed *Oberstleutnant* of the reserve. He was married to Gisela von Stralenheim but had no descendants.

---

14 Franz Schenkel, 'Unser Graf', in DDF (1957) vol.7, p.11.
15 Hans-Joachim Teichler: *Internationale Sportpolitik im Dritten Reich – Wissenschaftliche Schriftenreihe des Deutschen Sportbundes vol.23* (Schorndorf: Hofmann 1991), p.111.
16 BA-MA, BW 57-84: special order of regimental commander *Oberstleutnant* Schulz at the end of the winter campaign in the east 1942/43, dated 17 April 1943, p.3.
17 Paul Völkers (Kiel, 15 March 1891–Vladimir, 23 January 1946), *General der Infanterie*; RK 11 December 1942; DKiG 1 April 1942. Taken prisoner by the Red Army in July 1944, he later died in Soviet captivity.

Many years later, in the 1990s, when the subject of war crimes in Italy was being dealt with in a very emotional but historically inconclusive way, his name was mentioned in connection with a massacre that was possibly carried out by paratroopers in Pietransieri on 21 November 1943. Schulenburg was accused of responsibility without further evidence. According to the latest research, however, the 'suggested direct involvement of the regimental commander [ad interim] Wolf-Werner Graf von der Schulenburg […] is more than questionable.'[18]

Kurt Gröschke

One of Gröschke's subordinates described him as very vain, as a 'peacock, dazzling, always stilted, intent on effect', but did not display any 'exaggerated stiffness or snappiness'. He knew how to use situations to his advantage but was not a man for 'spectacular heroics'. His soldiers were not deployed 'unnecessarily or imprudently', which proved very reassuring and was appreciated by his men.[19]

Born on 17 July 1907 in Berlin-Charlottenburg, Kurt Gröschke joined the Berlin police force in October 1927 after successfully completing school.[20] After attending the Higher Police School in Eiche near Berlin, he became a member of the *Landespolizeigruppe Hermann Göring*. On 1 October 1935, he was transferred to *I. Bataillon/Regiment General Göring*, where he was promoted to *Oberleutnant* and was to lead *1. Kompanie* from 10 May 1937. On 1 April 1938 he became commander of *2. Kompanie/Fallschirmjäger Regiment 1* and took part in the campaign in Poland 1939. Promoted to *Hauptmann* on 1 February 1940 he saw action in the Netherlands, Crete, and Russia. On 20 October 1939 Gröschke was awarded the Iron Cross 2nd Class (Poland), on 22 May 1940 the Iron Cross 1st

Kurt Gröschke, commander of *II. Bataillon/Fallschirmjäger Regiment 1* as *Oberstleutnant* in 1944. (BArch, Bild 146-1981-104-07/CC-BY-SA 3.0)

Class. During the reorganisation of the regiment in spring 1942, he was appointed commander of *II. Bataillon* of the regiment on 5 March and promoted to *Major* (1 April). He remained in this position during the campaign in Russia – described in this book – and later in Italy.

Gröschke was awarded the German Cross in Gold for his performance in the defensive battles for Orel on 11 August 1943. He was later awarded the Knight's Cross on 9 June 1944 for his services at Cassino when he commanded the regiment from 22 January to 11 February 1944. There, on 8 February his leadership, prudence, and personal commitment prevented an Allied breakthrough.

---

18 Carlo Gentile, *Wehrmacht und Waffen-SS im Partisanenkrieg: Italien 1943–1945* (Paderborn: Schöningkh, 2012), p.49. Klaus Hammel questions the involvement of paratroopers (Klaus Hammel, *Krieg in Italien* (Bielefeld: Osning, 2017), 2nd edition, pp.406–407). The case was still being discussed in an Italian court in 2018. As no one directly responsible could be identified, the court case was filed against the Federal Republic of Germany.
19 Bernhard & Broder, *Guerre Mondiale*, pp.13–14.
20 Thomas & Wegmann, *Ritterkreuzträger – Fallschirmjäger*, pp.89–91; Schütze, 'Kurt Gröschke', DDF (1996), vol.3, p.25.

On 24 July 1944, as *Oberstleutnant* (1 June 1944), he became commander of the newly formed *Fallschirmjäger Regiment 15*, part of *5. Fallschirmjäger Division*, which he also commanded towards the end of the war. He distinguished himself as commander of this regiment at Saint-Lô-Lessay in July 1944. He also proved his mettle during the Ardennes offensive. On the evening of 16 December 1944, the advance party of his regiment reached the Diekirch-Hosingen road and on 18 December the Bourscheid river crossing was captured undamaged. At Harlange and Villiers-La-Bonne-Eau, the regiment successfully defended its sector until 10 February, for which Gröschke was awarded the Oak Leaves on 9 January 1945. On 10 February 1945 he received his promotion to *Oberst* with effect from 1 January 1945. After his release from British captivity on 26 February 1946, he became a businessman.

Gröschke passed away on 26 March 1996 at the age of 88 in Odenthal, near Bergisch Gladbach, North Rhine-Westphalia.

Karl Heinz Becker

Karl-Heinz Becker was greatly admired by his comrades.[21] He was considered by the enemy to be 'one of the most outstanding paratrooper officers.'[22] To distinguish him from two namesakes, he was called 'the black Becker'. He led his troops prudently and successfully, with drive, wisdom, and energy, but he also had the gift of 'improvising small and large celebrations, with which he contributed to relaxation and constant enthusiasm.'[23]

Karl Heinz Becker was born in Schwedt near Frankfurt an der Oder on 2 January 1914. At the age of 20, on 10 October 1934, he joined the *Landespolizeigruppe General Göring*, where he was destined for an officer's career and completed the second ensign course in Eiche on 1 July 1935. From 1936 until the outbreak of war he rose steadily through the ranks of the *Regiment General Göring*, becoming a company commander and *Leutnant* in the *Luftlandebataillon*. On 1 January 1939 he joined *Fallschirmjäger Regiment 1* and was promoted to the rank of *Oberleutnant* on 1 June 1939.

Karl-Heinz Becker, commander of *III. Bataillon/Fallschirmjäger Regiment 1* as *Oberleutnant* in 1941. (BArch, Bild 183-L19502/ CC-BY-SA 3.0)

At the same time, he took over *11. Kompanie/Fallschirmjäger Regiment 1*, a command he held for almost three years, and which was to define his military career. He developed it into his trademark, so that later people spoke of 'Becker and his eleventh' or like a soccer team, of 'Becker-11', even when they meant *III. Bataillon* or later *Fallschirmjäger Regiment 5*.[24]

He took part in the operations in Poland (Stawiszyn-Sucha 1939), Holland (Dordrecht and Rotterdam 1940), Crete (1941), Russia (1941 and 1942–1943) and Italy (1943–1944) as well as on the invasion front in France and in the *Westwall* area (1944–1945).

---

21 Thomas/Wegmann, *Ritterkreuzträger – Fallschirmjäger*, pp.12–14; Josef Reischl, 'Fallschirmjäger der ersten Stunde', DDF (1999), vol.1, p.31; Eberhard Boerger, 'Nachruf auf Karl Heinz Becker', DDF (2000), vol.6, p 12.
22 Roger Edwards, German Airborne Troops, cited in DDF (1978), vol.6, p. 30.
23 Anon., 'Karl-Heinz Becker – ein Fünfzigjähriger' in DDF (1964), vol.1, p.7; 'Schwarzer Becker – 70 Jahre' in DDF (1984), vol.6, pp.5–6.
24 DDF (1978), vol.6, p.30.

He was awarded the Iron Cross 2nd Class for his service in Poland and the Iron Cross 1st Class for Holland. In the latter campaign he was under the battalion command of *Hauptmann* Karl-Lothar Schulz and took part in the airborne assault on Waalhaven airfield near Rotterdam.

The Crete mission earned him the Knight's Cross. *III. Bataillon* was able to take the city of Heraklion for a short time, after which the important Hill 491, on which the enemy's artillery positions were located, was taken. Becker distinguished himself in these actions. The award ceremony took place on 9 July 1941. He continued to excel in Russia (Chernaya, Velikiye Luki, Nagorniy) and Italy (Abruzzi, Ortona, Anzio-Nettuno).

During the reorganisation of the regiment in 1942, he had to relinquish command of *11. Kompanie*, was promoted to *Hauptmann* (1 March 1942) and became adjutant to the regimental commander, *Generalmajor* Bräuer, only to take command of *III. Bataillon* on 21 November 1942. He was wounded during the fighting at Velikiye Luki on 16 January 1943 but remained with his troops. Shortly afterwards he took part in the battles at the Orel salient. His regimental commander had already proposed him for the first assignment for the Oak Leaves, but this was rejected because, according to Hitler, there would be no reward for a failed attack. However, on 1 June 1943 Becker was promoted to *Major* with effect from 1 May 1943 (ranking seniority 1 December 1943).

Becker and his battalion were assigned to liberate Il Duce on the island of Maddalena in August 1943, but this mission was cancelled when Mussolini was relocated to Gran Sasso. On 29 June 1944, Becker was awarded the German Cross in Gold for his conduct in Italy at Salerno, Ortona, Anzio-Nettuno and in the Abruzzo region.

On 15 June 1944, he was appointed commander of *Fallschirmjäger Regiment 5 (3. Fallschirmjäger Division)*, its base consisted of his old *III. Bataillon*. His regiment particularly distinguished itself during the fighting in Normandy near Saint-Lô-Lessay in July 1944. Later that year in September, he distinguished himself once again as commander of the combat group *3. Fallschirmjäger Division* near Nymegen and Arnhem, in the defence against the Allied airborne landings. This earned him rapid promotion to *Oberstleutnant* on 1 October 1944. However, as the regiment was almost wiped out during the fighting in Normandy, it had to be re-formed at Oldenzaal in the Netherlands in October 1944.[25] On 30 November 1944, his regiment regained lost ground west of Merode, and during the Ardennes offensive, Becker's regiment also successfully advanced to the Malmedy-Saint Vith road. In early January, despite being hopelessly outnumbered, his regiment put up a fierce resistance to the attacking 1st US Infantry Division near Faymonville. Becker was awarded the Oak Leaves on 12 March 1945. He was also awarded the *Nahkampfspange (LW)* (Close Combat badge) in silver.

On 4 April 1945, Becker took over command of *3. Fallschirmjäger Division*, which he had previously led on a temporary basis on three occasions, and was promoted to *Oberst* on 20 April 1945. By the end of the war, Becker was 31 years old and had participated in a relatively large number of combat missions, partly because he was never seriously wounded – except at the very end of the war – or was absent for any other reason.

On his return from captivity, Becker found his family in Schleswig-Holstein, where he set up a farm, the Birkenhof in Soholmbrück. For a time, he was also mayor of his home town. He was also the centre and pivot of the veteran's community of his *III. Bataillon, Fallschirmjäger Regiment 1* and *5*. Karl Heinz Becker passed away on 3 October 2000 at the age of 86.

---

25 Christian Zweng, *Die Truppen und Verbände der Deutschen Wehrmacht 1939–1945* (Osnabrück: Institut für deutsche Phaleristik und Militärgeschichte, 2015), vol.3c, p.25.

3

The Organisation of *Flieger Division 7*

Divisional Command

During the period covered by this study, the division was still code-named *Flieger Division 7*. It was only after the mission described in this book, during the period of rest and refit in France, that it was renamed *1. Fallschirmjäger Division* on 1 May 1943. There are several inaccurate and incorrect statements circulating in the literature, ranging from 'early 1942' through 'February 1943' and 'between March and April 1943'. Hildebrand states that *Generalmajor* Heidrich relinquished command of *Flieger Division 7* on 30 April 1943 and took command of *1. Fallschirmjäger Division* on 1 May 1943.[1]

The division commander from 1 October 1941 was *Generalleutnant* Petersen,[2] originally an infantry officer in the *Heer,* who had commanded the division during the first deployment in Russia 1941. He was recalled at the start of the mission on 1 November 1942, transferred to the *Reichsluftfahrtministerium* in Berlin, and promoted to *General der Flieger*. Petersen was later appointed commanding general of *IV. Luftwaffen-Feldkorps* and *LXXXX. Armee Korps* on the western front. At the end of the war, he went into French captivity, was tried for war crimes, acquitted, and released on 18 January 1950.

Petersen was officially replaced on 16 November 1942 (with effect from 1 November) by *Generalmajor* Heidrich, previously commander of *Fallschirmjäger Regiment 3*. From 1 August 1942, *Oberst* (*Generalmajor* from 4 August 1942) Richard Heidrich was assigned to command the division *ad interim* in France. Petersen was originally due to be promoted to *General der Flieger* by 1 October 1942. As there was no suitable post for his new rank available by the end of September, Göring decided to simply postpone the promotion until one became available.[3] Petersen therefore resumed command and accompanied his division to Smolensk. He is mentioned in a war diary of *VI. Armee Korps* as attending a meeting on 1 November 1942, and he also personally signed the divisional order to move to the front.[4] During the first week of November 1942 Heidrich formally commanded a brigade but seems to have taken effective command of the division from about 7 November 1942.

---

1   Karl Friedrich Hildebrand, *Die Generale der Deutschen Luftwaffe 1935–1945* (Osnabrück: Biblio, 1991), vol.2, p.48.
2   Erich Petersen (Heidelberg, 25 August 1889–Allmannshausen, 14 July 1963), *General der Flieger*; DKiG 27 March 1942.
3   BA-MA, Pers 6/296.
4   The National Archives of the United States of America (NARA), T-314 R-310: VI. A.K., KTB No. 3, vol.25, Abt. Qu., 1–30 November 1942.

The commander of *Luftflotte 3* in France, *Generalfeldmarschall* Hugo Sperrle inspects *Fallschirmjäger Regiment 1* in July 1942. From left to right: An unknown *Oberleutnant*, *Generalleutnant* Petersen, commander of *Flieger Division 7*, *Hauptmann* Zuber, commander of *6. Kompanie*; unknown, Sperrle. (BArch, Bild 101I-543-0561-17A/Helmuth Pirath)

Order of Battle of the Division

The division consisted of *Fallschirmjäger Regiment 1* (*I., II.* and *III. Bataillon*), *Fallschirmjäger Regiment 3* (*II., III., IV. Bataillon*) and *Fallschirmjäger Regiment 4* (*I.* and *III. Bataillon*), *I. Bataillon/Luftlande Sturm Regiment* and various divisional units, including *Fallschirm Pionier Bataillon, Fallschirm MG Bataillon, I.* and *III. Abteilung/Fallschirm-Artillerie Regiment 1*, and *Fallschirm Panzerjäger Abteilung* as well as support units like *Fallschirm Luftnachrichtenabteilung 7, Fallschirm Sanitätsabteilung, Nachschubführer Flieger Division 7*. In addition, *13.* and *14. Kompanie* of *Fallschirmjäger Regiment 5* came with the division from Germany while their regiment was deployed to Africa. The former – equipped with mortars – was attached to Heidrich's *Fallschirmjäger Regiment 3* and the latter equipped with heavy machine guns to Schulz's *Fallschirmjäger Regiment 1*. Last but not least *1. Kompanie/Fallschirm Fliegerabwehr-MG Bataillon* was attached to the division. The division was organised as follows:

Division commander: *Generalmajor* Richard Heidrich
    Ia: *Oberstleutnant i.G.* Adolf Häring[5]
    Ib: *Major* Hermann Götzel[6]
Fallschirmjäger Regiment 1: *Oberstleutnant* Karl-Lothar Schulz[7]
    I. Bataillon: *Major* Wolf-Werner Graf von der Schulenburg[8]
    II. Bataillon: *Major* Kurt Gröschke[9]
    III. Bataillon: *Major* Ernst Rolschewski[10] (until 21 November 1942),
        Hauptmann Karl-Heinz Becker[11] (from 21 November 1942)
Fallschirmjäger Regiment 3: at first *Generalmajor* Heidrich, then his successor (effective 16 November) *Oberst* Sebastian Ludwig Heilmann[12]
    II. Bataillon: *Major* Eberhard Rau
    III. Bataillon: *Hauptmann* Rudolf Kratzert
    IV. Bataillon: *Hauptmann* Rudolf Böhmler
Fallschirmjäger Regiment 4: *Oberst* Erich Walther[13]
    I. Bataillon: *Major* Reinhard Egger
    III. Bataillon: *Hauptmann* Franz Graßmehl
    I. Bataillon/Luftlande Sturm Regiment: *Hauptmann* Kurt Reinhardt
Fallschirm MG Bataillon: *Major* Werner Schmidt
I. Abteilung/Fallschirm Artillerie Regiment 1: *Major* Bruno Schram
III. Abteilung/Fallschirm Artillerie Regiment 1: *Hauptmann* Siegfried von Bültzingslöwen
Fallschirm Panzerjäger Abteilung: *Hauptmann* Gerhard Brückner
Fallschirm Pionier Bataillon: *Major* Egon Liebach
Fallschirm Luftnachrichten Abteilung 7: *Major* Ernst Schleicher

---

5 Adolf Häring (28 March 1903–?), *Oberst i.G.* (by 1 January 1943); DKiG; since 28 August 1942 first general staff officer (Ia) of the *Flieger Division 7*.

6 He was later as *Oberst* part of the staff of *Generaloberst* Student and ghost-wrote and edited Student's memoirs, which were published in 1980.

7 See above. He took command from his predecessor *Oberst* Bräuer in July 1942. Before that Schulz was commander of III./FJR 1, with *Major* Rolschewski as his successor.

8 See above. He took command of the battalion from his predecessor *Oberstleutnant* Walther in spring 1942. The latter was entrusted with the leadership of FJR 4.

9 See above.

10 Ernst Rolschewski (3 July 1906–20 May 1984), *Oberstleutnant*.

11 See above.

12 Sebastian Ludwig Heilmann (Würzburg, 9 August 1903–Kempten, 26 October 1959), *Generalmajor*; RK 14 June 1941, Oak Leaves 2 March 1944, Swords 15 May 1944, DKiG 26 February 1942; tasked with the leadership of FJR 3 as Heidrich's successor on 15 November 1942, full commander of the regiment on 5 June 1943. As *Generalmajor* and commander of 5. *Fallschirmjäger Division*, he was taken prisoner of war by the British on 5 March 1945.

13 Erich Walther (Gorden, 5 August 1903–Weimar, 26 December 1947), *Generalmajor*; RK 24 May 1940, Oak Leaves 2 March 1944, Swords 2 February 1945, DKiG 13 April 1942. He commanded I./FJR 1 until spring 1942 when *Major* Count von der Schulenburg took over. Entrusted with leadership of FJR 4 from 17 September 1942, he was full commander from 1 April 1943 until 24 September 1944, then leader and later commander of the *Fallschirm-Panzer-Grenadier-Division Hermann Göring*, was taken prisoner by the Soviets at the end of the war, sentenced to 25 years in prison and died in the Soviet prison camp Buchenwald near Weimar on 26 December 1948. He was officially rehabilitated by the Russian Federation in 1996.

The Strength of the Division

The division consisted of well-trained soldiers not all of whom had combat experience. Most had served at least nine months with their respective units, while the rest were drawn from veterans of Crete and the first Russia deployment of the previous winter. The actual strength (*Ist-Stärke*) of *Flieger Division 7* on 1 November 1942 was 19,649 men, with a combatant strength of 5,891 men reported on 14 November. The officials, supply troops and drivers, but also the regimental staff units, as well as *13.* and *14. Kompanie*, were not included in the combatant strength of the battalions, while the actual strength included all the troops belonging to the division: staff, combat, and supply troops, from officers to enlisted men, from officials, and engineers, to cooks and bakers. On 8 November 1942 the *Fallschirmjäger Regiment 1* reported an actual strength of 3,684 men and combatant strengths of the battalions of 644 (I.), 635 (II.) and 662 (III.) men respectively. Including the regimental staff troops as well as the bicycle platoon, the engineer platoon, *13.* and *14. Kompanie*, the total combatant strength of *Fallschirmjäger Regiment 1* should have amounted to approximately 2,500 men.[14] This number seems low, as *Fallschirmjäger Regiment 3* reported in its after-action report dated 1 June 1943 a combatant strength of 2,807 men while having a lower actual strength than the former.[15] This shows the difficulties when comparing strength numbers of the regiments which have been reported at different times and under different circumstances.

The following is a list of the divisional units and their respective actual strength at the beginning of the mission taken from the monthly actual strength report of *Flieger Division 7* of 10 November 1942:[16]

Actual strength of *Flieger Division 7* (10 November 1942)

	Officers	Officials	NCOs	Soldiers	Total
Divisional staff	23	4	93	249	369
FJR 1	78	7	916	2,683	3,684
FJR 3	92	8	703	2,695	3,498
FJR 4	86	9	870	2,560	3,525
Fsch.Pz.Jg.Abt.7 (anti-tank bn.)	22	4	205	906	1,137
Fsch.Pi.Btl. 7 (engineer bn.)	23	4	158	902	1,087
I./Fsch.Art.Rgt. 1 (artillery bn.)	25	3	154	822	1,004
III./FschArtRgt. 1 (artillery bn.)	11	3	61	380	455
Fsch.MG.Btl. 7 (machine-gun bn.)	23	4	159	1,004	1,190
Fsch.Ln.Abt. 7 (signals bn.)	15	3	88	559	665
Div.NachschubFhr. 7 (supply bn.)	30	3	173	1,035	1,241
Medics	49	8	189	1,031	1,277
1./Fla.MG.Btl. (anti-aircraft bn.)	4	1	53	150	208
Div. Transportstaffel (transport comp.)	4	1	34	62	101
Total	485	62	3,856	15,038	19,441

---

14 BA-MA, RH 24-6/287: Compilation of weekly reports (*wöchentliche Führermeldung*).
15 BA-MA, RL 33/57: After action report of FJR 3, 1 June 1943 (*Fallschirmjäger Regiment 3 – Gefechtsbericht über den Wintereinsatz an der Ostfront vom 1.11.42-1.4.43*).
16 BA-MA, RH 24-6/287.

The following divisional units appear later in the division's actual strength reports:[17]

	Officers	Officials	NCOs	Soldiers	Total
13./FJR 5 (5 December 1942) to FJR 3	3		29	161	193
14./FJR 5 (5 January 1943) to FJR 1	2		43	143	188
Kradsch.Kp. (5 January 1943) (motorcycle comp.)	4		28	203	235
Div. Intendant (4 February 1943) (commissary)	4	2	32	61	99

Strangely enough, the *Fallschirmjäger Ski-Bataillon*, created by the division in mid-November 1942, does not appear in these lists, but in the combatant strength reports of *VI. Armee Korps*: first on 5 December 1942 with a strength of 539 men and then on 12 December of 742 men. Each of the regiments had to surrender one company, *1. Kompanie* of this battalion was provided by *Fallschirmjäger Regiment 1* (see below).

There were also various temporary subordinate units, such as *Jägerbataillon 4* and *8*.

Equipment

The soldiers were better prepared for the winter of 1942 to 1943 than for the previous one. Although some of the promised equipment was still missing in early December, the situation for the soldiers was not critical. There was a shortage of winter equipment, particularly of mittens, woollen scarves, and hats. Additional equipment such as felt boots – particularly useful for sentry duty in cold weather – were initially in extremely short supply, mittens with gauntlets were almost non-existent, and mountaineering boots and fur hats were not available at all. The only adequate supplies were fur jackets and *Zwischenhosen* (warm under-trousers worn under the uniform trousers).[18] Some soldiers also received warm clothing from home. *Gefreiter* Rüdiger von Zimburg of *2. Kompanie/Fallschirmjäger Regiment 1* was very happy to receive mittens from his father for Christmas 1942.[19]

Armament

The quantity of infantry weapons was more or less as planned. As far as light infantry weapons were concerned, the division reported on 1 February 1943:[20]

Rifles (*Karabiner 98*)	14,126
Self-loading rifles (Most probably *Gewehr 41*)[21]	216
Telescopic sight rifles (*K 98* with mounted scope *Zielfernrohr 41*)	514

---

17 BA-MA, RH 24-6/287 and 288.
18 BA-MA, RH 24-6/124 in BW 57-38: *Anlage zur Zustandsmeldung der Fl.Div.7*, 1 December 1942.
19 Albrecht Zimburg (ed.), Rüdiger Zimburg, *Kriegserlebnisse eines Fallschirmjägers* (Salzburg: Milizverlag, 2018), p.66.
20 BA-MA, BW 57-39: *Zustandsmeldung Flieger Division 7* dated 2 February 1943 and *Schematische Darstellung der Flieger Division 7* dated 1 February 1943. Earlier lists have lower numbers but are incomplete as only special weapons are listed.
21 Chris MacNab, *German Automatic Rifles* (Oxford: Osprey, 2013), p.17.

Pistols	9,229
Submachine guns	2,180
Combat pistols[22]	840
Schießbecher 30 (Rifle grenade launcher)	784
Schießbecher 40	994
MG 42	none
MG 34	1,252

The division reported the following heavy infantry weapons on 5 December 1942:

2.8 cm Schwere Panzerbüchse 41 (Pz.Büchse 41) light anti-tank gun	72
Schwerer Granatwerfer 25 (s.Gr.W. 25), heavy mortar	65
10 cm Nebelwerfer 35 (Nb.W. 10,5)[23]	36
3.7 cm anti-tank gun (le.Pak 3.7 cm)	28
4.2 cm anti-tank gun (le.Pak 41 4.2 cm)	64
5 cm anti-tank gun (m.Pak)	17
7.5 cm self-propelled heavy anti-tank gun mounted on a *Marder II* (s.Pak 40 [s.SFL])	18
7.5 cm anti-tank gun, drawn by motorized vehicles (s.Pak 40 [mot.])	11
Leichtgeschütz 41 (L.G. 41), 10.5 cm recoilless gun	24
Infanteriegeschütz 18 or *37* (I.G. 7.5 cm), infantry support gun	2
2 cm anti-aircraft gun (Fla.MG 2 cm)	17
Fsch.Art.Rgt.1 (10.5 cm)[24] (*Leichtgeschütz 40*)	24

In addition, there were heavy weapons from units temporarily attached to the division, such as the *Artillerie Regiment z.b.V. 109* as well as other artillery units or the *Flak Regiment 18*. On 5 December, during the critical phase of operation MARS, the division reported the following additional heavy weapons:

3 heavy batteries (II./AR 43) with 8 guns (15 cm)
10 light batteries (Art. Rgt. z.b.V. 109) with 23 guns (10.5 cm)
4 guns (7.62 cm, Soviet)
3 guns (12.2 cm Soviet)
7 heavy anti-aircraft batteries (Flak Rgt. 18) with 26 guns (8.8 cm Flak)
17 guns (2 cm Flak)
3 light anti-aircraft batteries (Flak Rgt. 18) with 36 guns (2 cm Flak)

These figures show, not surprisingly, that *Flieger Division 7* was considered to be the strongest division of *VI. Armee Korps*, if not of *9. Armee*. *Generalleutnant* Hans Jordan,[25] commanding general of

---

22 Break action, single shot flare guns with rifled barrels, used for signalling, illumination and target marking as well as for camouflaging with smoke grenades.
23 A salvo rocket launcher, nicknamed by the Allies 'Moaning Minnie'. Despite its name the rockets had a calibre of 10.5 cm.
24 *Fallschirm Artillerie Regiment 1* was equipped with 10.5 cm *Leichtgeschütz 40*, a recoilless artillery gun.
25 Hans Jordan (Scheuern bei Rastatt, 27 December 1892–Munich, 20 April 1975), *Generalleutnant* (from 1

VI. Armee Korps, particularly emphasised the 'energetic leadership' of the 'excellent division', which had 'the best human material' and 'excellent equipment'. In this assessment, *197.* and *205. Infanterie Divisions* are referred to as 'moderate' and the *330. Infanterie Division* as 'poor' divisions. [26]

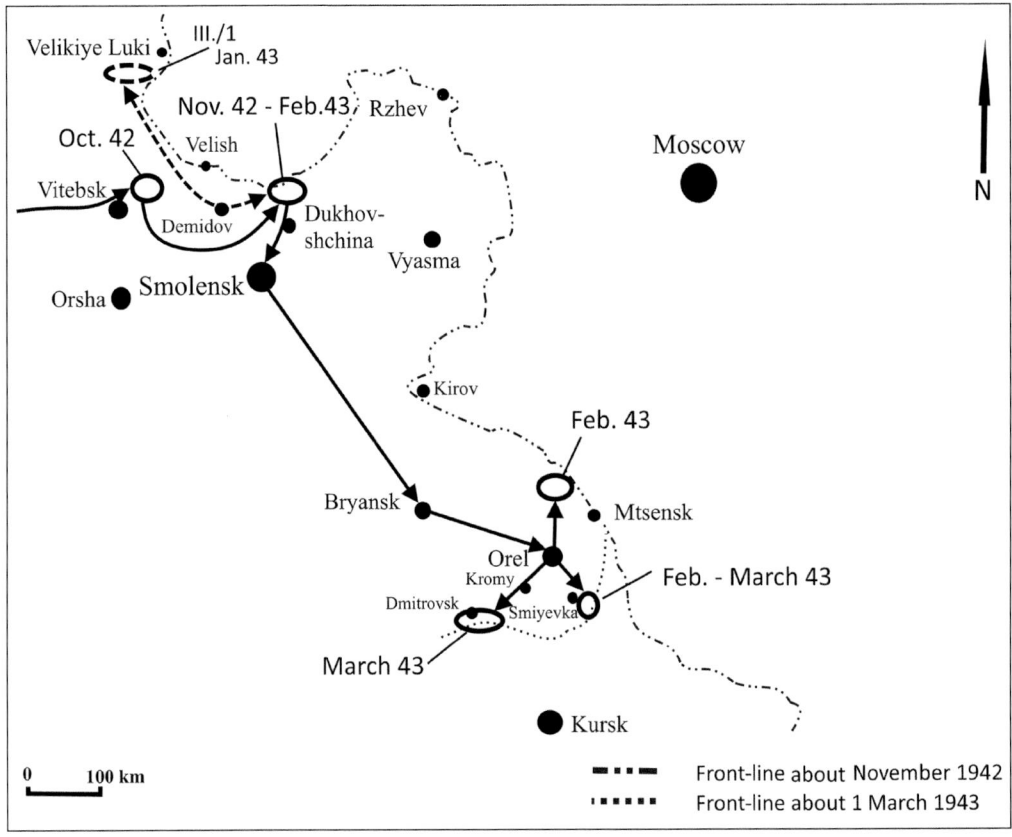

Fallschirmjäger Regiment 1's areas of operation during the winter of 1942–1943 near Smolensk and Orel.

January 1943 *General der Infanterie*); RK (5 June 1940), Oak Leaves (16 January 1942) Swords (20 April 1944), DKiG (23 December 1943); Commissioned with the leadership of the VI. AK 1 November 1942–31 December 1942, as *Kommandierender General* 1 January 1943–20 April 1944; Led *9. Armee* in 1944 when it was wiped out near Bobruisk.

26 BA-MA BW 57-38: Telex VI. AK to AOK 9 dated 3 December 1942 at 8:15 p.m.

4

Operation MARS

Soviet Plans[1]

In the summer of 1942, the German *Wehrmacht* launched an offensive in the south of the Eastern Front (*Fall Blau*) with the aim of attacking Stalingrad on the one hand and the Caucasus on the other, trying to reach the oil fields around Baku. The Soviets were taken completely by surprise as they had been expecting an offensive towards Moscow. The German armies were able to make significant advances, extending and at the same time overstretching their front line, making it difficult to secure. To fill the gaps, troops from allied countries with little combat experience and inadequate equipment were deployed, such as Hungarians and Romanians, to protect the flanks of *6. Armee* at Stalingrad.

By the end of the summer much territory had been conquered, but the German strategic position on the Eastern Front proved weak. Since the end of 1941, Stalin had been receiving massive supplies of weapons, tanks, fuel, food, raw materials (aluminium, steel, etc.) and much more from the US and Britain under the lend-lease programme, which the Germans had been unable to predict and consider in their planning. This made possible an effective Soviet counter-offensive, on a scale that the *Wehrmacht* had not anticipated. The supreme command of the armed forces of the Soviet Union (Stavka) planned to counter the German advances by launching several offensives simultaneously, all named after planets. A breakthrough was to be achieved, followed by a roll-up of the German front in the south and in the central sectors. The first phase, operation URANUS, was to encircle Stalingrad and destroy *6. Armee*. In the second phase, operation MARS was supposed to crush *9. Armee* in the Rzhev salient. The outcome of URANUS is well known, but MARS, which is of greater importance to the *Fallschirmjäger Regiment 1*, is less well known, making it necessary to go into more detail on this point.

The two operations must be seen as closely linked. MARS was originally intended to be the first and URANUS, a few days later, only the second strike to break the German front from the Sea of Azov to the north. The aim was not only to recapture Stalingrad and defeat *Heeresgruppe Süd* (or *Heeresgruppe A* and *B*) but also *Heeresgruppe Mitte* with Smolensk as its centre. The first orders were issued from Stavka on 1 October – MARS was to begin on 12 October.[2] However, both operations were postponed several times due to unsuitable autumn weather conditions, which made it difficult to move troops on the already deteriorated roads.[3]

---

1 This chapter is based on David Glantz, *Zhukov's Greatest Defeat – The Red Army's Epic Disaster in Operation Mars, 1942* (Lawrence: University Press of Kansas, 1999) and Svetlana Gerasimova, *The Rzhev Slaughterhouse: The Red Army's Forgotten 15-Month Campaign Against Army Group Center, 1942–1943* (Solihull: Helion, 2013).
2 David M. Glantz, *After Stalingrad – The Red Army's Winter Offensive 1942–1943* (Solihull: Helion, 2009), p.43.
3 Pritt Buttar, *Meat Grinder – The Battles for the Rzhev Salient 1942–43* (Oxford: Osprey, 2022), p.251.

The primary target of operation MARS was Rzhev. It was an important railway link from Velikiye Luki to Moscow and had to be secured. In addition, *Generaloberst* Walter Model's *9. Armee*,[4] which defended this area, was to be destroyed by attacks from several sides. Stavka's planning for MARS and URANUS began in mid-September while *Flieger Division 7* was still in France and Germany. Stalin approved Deputy Commander-in-Chief Georgy Zhukov's plan on 26 September 1942.[5] There were to be three main lines of attack: The Western Front – a Front was the equivalent of a German *Heeresgruppe* (army group) – under the command of Colonel General Konev,[6] was to attack north-east of Sychevka in a westward direction, while in the opposite direction, from east to west, the Kalinin Front (General Purkayev)[7] was to attack near Bely and along the Luchesa valley, pushing into the salient. To this end, further attacks by the two fronts were to be carried out from north to south, for example at Molodoi Tud. Only after the successful completion of this operation was it planned – albeit only very superficially – that in a second phase, operation JUPITER,[8] these forces would continue their offensive in the direction of Vyazma and Smolensk. At the same time, the 43rd Army and the 4th Shock Army were to advance towards Smolensk via Dukhovshchina.

Zhukov, who was fully committed to MARS, ordered General Purkayev not only to break into the Rzhev salient with his Kalinin Front with three spearheads, but also to prepare a fourth thrust with the 3rd Shock Army (Major General Galitzky)[9] much further to the west towards Velikiye Luki. This was intended to divide and tie up as many German forces as possible. For this purpose, the Kalinin Front was reinforced with three mechanized corps. The problem was that the thrust of the Kalinin Front was fragmented and severely weakened by the several different focal points of the attack. This proved to be one of the main reasons for the failure of MARS.

Zhukov's plan to involve Velikiye Luki more extensively in the operation grew, and in mid-November he ordered Purkayev to additionally weaken the 41st Army (Major General Tarasov),[10] which was to attack Bely, in favour of the 3rd Shock Army. Korchagin's 2nd Mechanized Corps was therefore detached and sent to the east of Velikiye Luki to reinforce the latter.[11] Why such strong forces

---

4   Otto Moritz Walter Model (Genthin, 24 January 1891–suicide, Duisburg, 21 April 1945), *Generalfeldmarschall*; RK (9 July 1941), Oak Leaves (17 February 1942), Swords (2 April 1943), Diamonds (17 August 1944).
5   Georgy Konstantinovich Zhukov (Strelovka, 1 December 1896–Moscow, 18 June 1974); Deputy Commander in Chief of the Soviet Armed Forces, Chief of Staff, Marshal of the Soviet Union (18 January 1943). 1955–57 Soviet Defence Minister. He accepted the surrender of the German *Wehrmacht* on 9 May 1945 in Berlin; Glantz, *After Stalingrad*, p.41.
6   Ivan Stepanovich Konev (Lodeino, 28 December 1897–Moscow, 21 May 1973) was commander of the Western Front from September 1942 to the end of March 1943. From August 1943 Army General, from February 1944 Marshal of the Soviet Union. He is considered the liberator of the Auschwitz concentration camp and of Prague.
7   Maksim Alexeyevich Purkayev (Nalitovo, 26 August 1894–Moscow, 1 January 1953); Army General. Due to his lack of success in the context of operation MARS, he was relieved from his command of the Kalinin Front in April 1943 and sent to command the Far Eastern Front.
8   See Glantz, Zhukov's Greatest Defeat, p.24.
9   Kuzma Nikitovich Galitsky (Taganrog, 24 October 1897–Moscow, 14 March 1973). As Major General he commanded the 3rd Shock Army from August 1942 to November 1943. For his successful capture of the city of Velikiye Luki he was promoted to Lieutenant General. Later he became commander of the 11th Guards Army and rose to Colonel General. After the war he was promoted to Army General.
10 German Fyodorovich Tarasov (29 March 1906–KIA near Debrecen, 19 October 1944), Major General.
11 Ivan Petrovich Korchagin (Byltsino, 24 August 1898–Moscow, 24 July 1951). He took command over the 2nd Mechanized Corps as Major General in September 1942, which he led under changing names until the end of World War II. In January 1943, he was promoted to Lieutenant General.

were committed for the attack on this town is not clear, as there were no significant German forces in the area and the aim of the thrust was limited to the capture of Velikiye Luki, an important railway junction which was helpful for Soviet logistics, and Novosokolniky, which would have severed the railway connection between *Heeresgruppe Nord* and *Mitte*.[12]

Tarasov was certainly a successful division commander, but he was simply overwhelmed by the task of leading 41st Army. During Hitler's operation BARBAROSSA, he had led the Soviet 249th Rifle Division with great success. In May 1942 he was given command of the 41st Army, which was located opposite the German 9. *Armee* at Bely. The failure of MARS led to his removal as commander of this army. He was then given command of an NKVD reserve army which was reorganised into the 70th Army within the Central Front in February 1943. When the offensive south of Orel (described in this book) failed, he was again relieved of his command. Tarasov was later killed in action at the Battle of Debrecen in Hungary in 1944.

On 17 November 1942, Stalin gave his approval for the launch of two operations, URANUS on 19 November and MARS on 25 November.

In order to disguise the actual objective, Bely, the Soviet 41st and 43rd Armies feigned concentrations of troops further southwest to give the impression of intending to break through on the road to Dukhovshchina towards Smolensk. This was intended to draw troops away from the Bely sector and thus weakening the defence of the real objective. *Fallschirmjäger Regiment 1* of *Flieger Division 7*, which would have been attacked only in the second phase called JUPITER, was positioned exactly in this simulated attack direction.

German Expectations for Autumn 1942

After the successful operations of the summer of 1942 (*Fall Blau*), it was now up to the *Wehrmacht* to consolidate and hold the conquered areas. No offensive operation of its own by *Heeresgruppe Mitte* was planned for this winter; it was limited to defending the line that had been reached. The fundamental error in the German assessment of the situation was a misjudgement of the Red Army's human and material resources, which had been significantly increased by the US lend-lease programme, and of its offensive capacities and leadership, which had since been improved by accumulated experience.

Hitler on the other hand was convinced that the Red Army was basically defeated, although German intelligence reports suggested otherwise, concluding 'that the Red army retained considerable reserves capable of major offensive operations.'[13] Hitler's staff assumed that the Red Army's main thrust would be directed against *Heeresgruppe Mitte* because of its proximity to Moscow. The Red Army was not thought capable of carrying out two major offensives at the same time. Above all, the assessment of *Fremde Heere Ost*, the military intelligence organisation of the *Oberkommando des Heeres* (OKH), initially pointed in this direction. It was not until October 1942 that the possibility of an offensive in the south was added to the assessment.[14] This misconception may have been reinforced by information given from a Soviet double agent.[15]

---

12   Buttar, *Meat Grinder*, p.252.
13   Buttar, *Meat Grinder*, p.245.
14   Gregory Liedtke, *Enduring the Whirlwind – The German Army and the Russo-German War 1941–1943* (Solihull: Helion, 2016), p.278.
15   Geoffrey Jukes, *Stalingrad to Kursk – Triumph of the Red Army* (Barnsley: Pen & Sword, 2011), pp.107–109.

Based on observed and assumed troop concentrations in the Toropets area, north of Smolensk, on 5 October 1942, Hitler and his staff, on whose influence and assessment of the situation his decisions were based, expected a Soviet offensive in the autumn, either from the north towards Smolensk or from the east towards Velikiye Luki. *Heeresgruppe Mitte* urgently needed reinforcements for its divisions which had been battered by the enemy's summer offensives.

To this end, the area around Velikiye Luki in particular was to be reinforced by newly formed *Luftwaffen Felddivisionen* and kept ready for a counterattack on Toropets. The first of these divisions had been hastily formed in the autumn of 1942 at Goering's instigation. The *Luftwaffe* personnel were poorly trained and therefore, as reality soon showed, of very little combat value. South of Velikiye Luki, *II. Luftwaffen Feldkorps* with *3.*, *4.* and *6. Luftwaffen Felddivision* was deployed, with the first units arriving at Nevel around mid-October 1942. The attack on Toropets should have been carried out by *11. Armee* under Manstein's command with *12. Panzer Division, 3. Gebirgs Division, 83.* and *291. Infanterie Division*. This plan was still in force on 16 November 1942. When the Soviet offensive around Stalingrad proved successful, the attack group of *11. Armee* was dissolved on 20 November and Manstein with his staff of AOK 11, was ordered south.[16]

In return, the *Oberkommando der Wehrmacht* (OKW) considered a two-pronged offensive against Model's *9. Armee* possible, an assessment that was increasingly confirmed by Red Army defectors.[17] That a Soviet offensive in the area of *9. Armee* was imminent, had been recognised by AOK 9 as well as by *Heeresgruppe Mitte* and *Fremde Heere Ost*.[18] This assessment now also prevailed at OKW.[19] Even the targets and objectives were correctly assessed by the staff of *9. Armee* at the beginning of November, with the exception of the westward thrust towards Velikiye Luki and Demyansk,[20] although the target Velikiye Luki had already been identified by Hitler a month earlier and prisoners' statements had pointed this out several times. It is not clear why the AOK 9 came to a different assessment of the situation. On 2 November 1942, the Chief of the General Staff of the German Army (part of OKH), *Generaloberst* Zeitzler,[21] presented Hitler with a map showing the distribution of the Soviet armoured forces, although contrary to the reality on the ground, relatively few of these had been identified in the Toropets area. It is possible that based on this information, the threat to Velikiye Luki was assessed as low.[22]

On 9 October, OKW decided to transfer *Flieger Division 7* from Germany to Smolensk.[23] On Hitler's express orders, the division was to be deployed as a coherent formation, undivided. The *Oberbefehlshaber der Luftwaffe, Reichsmarschall* Göring, had requested this in view of the negative

---

16   Percy E. Schramm (ed.), *Kriegstagebuch des Oberkommandos der Wehrmacht* (Augsburg: Weltbild, 2005) vol.2, 1942, part 2, pp.793, 967, 993.
17   Schramm (ed.), *Kriegstagebuch des OKW 1942/2*, pp.801, 868.
18   Central Archives of the Ministry of Defence of the Russian Federation (CAMO), Stock 500, finding aid 12451, file 335, image 17.
19   Schramm (ed.), Kriegstagebuch des OKW 1942/2, p.825.
20   The report by *Oberst* Georg Buntrock, Ic of AOK 9, dated 29 October 1942, is mentioned in Glantz, *Zhukov's Greatest Defeat*, p.33. *Fremde Heere Ost* in its assessment dated 6 November 1942 does foresee an attack 'with weaker forces' on Velikiye Luki. (CAMO, stock 500, finding aid 12451, file 335, image 26.
21   Kurt Zeitzler (Goßmar near Luckau, 9 June 1895–Hohenaschau, 25 September 1963), *Generaloberst*; Chief of General Staff of the *Heer* as successor of *Generalfeldmarschall* Halder.
22   Schramm (ed.), *Kriegstagebuch des OKW 1942/2*, p.889.
23   Schramm (ed.), *Kriegstagebuch des OKW 1942/2*, p.811.

experience of the winter of 1941–1942 near Leningrad. The division had been dispersed and not deployed as one unit, and suffered heavy losses as a result.

Now, in its second deployment on the Eastern Front, the division's assigned sector, with a front length of about 54 kilometres, lay north of the Demidov-Dukhovshchina-Yartsevo line. As the sector was later extended, the front line may have been as long as 74 kilometres, a figure found in various sources.[24] This line covered the approach to Smolensk, the centre of *Heeresgruppe Mitte* from the north. The division was placed under the command of *VI. Armee Korps* (VI. AK), which was part of *9. Armee* and managed to defend this sector of the front for almost half a year.

Surprised by the magnitude of the offensive at Stalingrad, OKH was forced into a state of constant crisis management. Now the signs of an imminent further offensive against *Heeresgruppe Mitte* were becoming more pronounced.

However, the exact timing of the Soviet offensive against the central part of the Eastern Front remained largely unknown to the Germans. In particular, the many shifts on the part of the Red Army, mostly due to weather conditions, caused a certain easing of tensions in the German front-line troops, but not in the command posts, where the pressure of uncertainty built up. A particular date the offensive was expected for was 7 November 1942, the anniversary of the October revolution, but it passed uneventfully. As a precaution, Hitler had given explicit orders to hold the positions.[25]

From 22 November on, AOK 9 knew from prisoner statements and other indicators that the attack would take place on 25 or 26 November. All forces were therefore put on alert on 24 November and selective artillery bombardments of suspected Soviet movement routes and possible assembly areas began.[26]

MARS

The main Soviet axis of attack lay to the north and north-east of the operational area of *Flieger Division 7*, which was not directly involved in these major battles, but felt their effects. The Germans were constantly expecting an attack on the division's sector and the Red Army did everything possible to maintain this impression. When the offensive finally began on 25 November, the Soviet forces broke deep into the front of *9. Armee* near Bely and further north-east into the Luchesa Valley. The Germans, however, were able to stop and contain the initial breakthrough, counter-attacked, and subsequently cleared the area. Further attacks on the Rzhev salient from the north and west (Sychevka) were also stopped.

On 28 November 1942, the Demyansk salient, held by *Heeresgruppe Nord*, was attacked by the Soviet Northwestern Front. Three major encirclements of German forces were now possible, not only at Stalingrad, but also in the central and northern sectors.

In contrast to URANUS, operation MARS was ultimately a failure, resulting in a staggering 200,000 to 300,000 Soviet casualties, not counting the losses at Velikiye Luki, which amounted

---

24 BA-MA: BW 57-39: a sketch mentions 54 kilometres. Other sources give a front length of 74 kilometres or even 90 kilometres. See Stimpel, *Fallschirmtruppe – Osten und Westen*, p.70; Klaus J. Peters, *Fallschirmjägerregiment 3 – A pictorial History: Vol.2 – The War Missions* (San José: Bender, 1995), p.321.
25 Schramm (ed.), *Kriegstagebuch des OKW 1942/2*, p.800. *Führerbefehl Nr. 2* dated 5 November 1942.
26 Buttar, *Meat Grinder*, p.273.

Operation MARS; Situation 30 November 1942.

to a further 104,000.[27] According to Russian sources, MARS cost the Red Army 215,674 casualties (70,373 dead and missing, 145,301 wounded and sick). Glantz, on the other hand, puts the figure at around 335,000 casualties (100,000 dead and missing, 235,000 wounded and sick).[28] Liedtke estimates total Soviet losses in the operations around Rzhev, Velikiye Luki and Demyansk at around 500,000 men and 2,000 tanks destroyed, compared to the German losses of between 60,000 and 90,000 men. These German losses, however, could hardly be compensated for afterwards.[29]

In favour of the much more successful operations URANUS and LITTLE SATURN in the south, the failed operation MARS was long ignored or played down by the Soviet side. One success, however, was the immobilisation – and at the same time considerable weakening – of the German forces in the centre, so that sufficient reinforcements could not be transferred to relieve Stalingrad. To what extent

---

27 Buttar, *Meat Grinder*, p.374.
28 Glantz, *Zhukov's Greatest Defeat*, pp.304, 379; Glantz, *After Stalingrad*, p.89; Gregory Liedtke, *Enduring the Whirlwind – The German Army and the Russo-German War 1941-1943* (Solihull: Helion, 2016), p.286 fn.39; Buttar, *Meat Grinder*, pp.421–433.
29 Liedtke, *Whirlwind*, p.287.

this was planned and intended, or simply a welcome side-effect of the spectacular failure of operation MARS remains a matter of debate among historians.[30]

Only at Velikiye Luki did the Kalinin Front achieve limited success in capturing the town and tying down German forces, which was the original intention.[31] *III. Bataillon/Fallschirmjäger Regiment 1* was deployed here in January 1943. Both the Demyansk corridor and the Rzhev salient were withdrawn in an orderly fashion in January and February 1943, ultimately due to the successful operations URANUS and LITTLE SATURN and the need to free up troops to avert the crisis in the south.

The fact that the MARS offensive did not directly target the section of *Flieger Division 7* gave many paratroopers and military historians the impression that the Soviet side had realised that this was not exactly the weakest spot of the defensive line and that a breakthrough would therefore have been a much more costly affair.[32] However, the impression that the presence of the paratroopers would have been enough to divert attacks elsewhere is false: Stavka's plans were already fixed before *Flieger Division 7* was even in position. The paratroopers would only have been in the path of the 43rd Army's attack in the planned second phase JUPITER, after the successful conclusion of MARS.

For the paratroopers at the front, it was a period of waiting, which the command tried to fill actively to avoid carelessness and inattention. The division commander, *Generalmajor* Heidrich, who had been an infantry-school instructor before the war, felt that his paratroopers lacked proper infantry training. As a result, positions were constantly repaired and expanded, training was carried out and, above all, many aggressive raiding patrols were sent out to disturb and demonstrate to the enemy: 'The no-man's land in front of us is ours.' This was also an attempt to maintain the offensive character of the paratrooper force.[33]

As already mentioned, *Flieger Division 7* was to be deployed undivided by direct order of the *Führer*, but soon contingents were sent to other front sections of *Heeresgruppe Mitte* due to imminent danger.

---

30 Glantz, *Zhukov's Greatest Defeat*; Glantz, *After Stalingrad*, p.443; Gerasimova, *Rzhev Slaughterhouse*, pp.104, 121; Jukes, *Stalingrad to Kursk*, pp.104–115.
31 Jukes, *Stalingrad to Kursk*, p.109.
32 Stimpel, *Fallschirmtruppe – Osten und Westen*. pp.71, 73. He shares the opinion of *Oberst* Heilmann, commander of FJR 3; Götzel, *Student*, p.386; Erich Busch, *Die Fallschirmjäger Chronik 1935–1945* (Friedberg: Podzun-Pallas, 1983), p.41.
33 Ben Christensen, *1st Fallschirmjäger Division in World War II – Vol.1, Years of Attack* (Atglen: Schiffer, 2007), p. 84.

5

Transfer of the Paratroopers to Smolensk

After a relatively quiet summer in France, the paratroopers of *Fallschirmjäger Regiment 1* were in for an exciting few days. The division moved to Germany in September 1942. Initially, the division was to be transferred to the Caucasus to carry out a parachute mission. Planning for this operation began in mid-September 1942. The air transport would have been to the Kerch Peninsula, in the east of the Crimea. From there the airborne operation intended to support *Heeresgruppe A* in the region of the north and south Caucasus, either around the river Terek or to take Tuapse. After a meeting of the regimental commanders with *Generalleutnant* Petersen in Berlin on 3 October 1942, the first orders were issued by the regiments on 4 October to be ready on the 6th.[1] The necessary equipment had been distributed and some units were already sitting in their Junkers Ju 52 transport aircraft with their parachute equipment in place when the operation was suddenly cancelled. Since insufficient air-transport capacity was available, the transfer of the division would have taken too long. As the operation could only have taken place before the onset of the autumn mud season, its cancellation became inevitable.[2]

The equipment had to be returned and the soldiers went back to their barracks, but soon another transfer order came. The destination remained unknown to the ordinary soldiers. Only gradually did they find out: They were to return to the Eastern Front 'into their old foxholes'.[3] The chronological sequence is not clear, as Hitler's decision to transfer *Flieger Division 7* to Smolensk, as mentioned above, had been taken on 9 October. There is no further reference to be found about the planned parachute operation except in the memoirs of Kurt Student and other paratroopers.[4] The division continued to prepare for an airborne operation until 14 October when the new order arrived.

The soldiers received winter clothing, as *Hauptfeldwebel* Willi Wagner of *I. Bataillon* recalls in a letter to his wife dated 15 October 1942: 'Today I received a beautiful fur jacket and enough warm underwear. Also, a face protection.'[5] He obviously appreciated this for he had learned his lesson the

---

1 Special order issued by FJR 3 on 4 October 1942, cited in Gerhard Jacob, *Der letzte Befehl ist heilig!* (self-published), pp.138–139.
2 Hermann Götzel, Kurt Student, *Generaloberst Kurt Student und seine Fallschirmjäger* (Friedberg: Podzun-Pallas, 1980), p.369.
3 BA-MA, BW 57-81: Diary of Ernst Germer.
4 Götzel/Student, *Generaloberst Kurt Student*, p.369. See also, for example, Zimburg, *Kriegserlebnisse*, p.47; BA-MA, BW 57-81: Diary of Ernst Germer; Hoover Institution Library & Archives (HILA): Memoires of Ludwig Heilmann, 2004C60 Box 1.
5 Archive Franz: Wagner, letter dated 15 October 1942.

previous winter. Rüdiger von Zimburg recalls an incident with him as an instructor in Stendal in the Winter 1941–1942:

> Our first march was ten kilometres, and we were allowed to put on our coats and not carry weapons. Because it was so cold that morning, we didn't need have to wear steel helmets, just our flying caps and earmuffs … Our platoon leaders *Feldwebel* Koch and *Hauptfeldwebel* Willi Wagner … wanted to show us recruits that a little bit of cold shouldn't bother you, so they walked with bare ears. When he announced the parole in the afternoon, he had a completely bandaged head with two huge cotton ears. He had frozen his ears so badly that he was still wearing his bandage after 1½ months.[6]

No wonder his nickname was 'Stubborn Willi'. He was '*Spieß*' (German military slang for the company sergeant major) of 3. *Kompanie*, and as such responsible for all non-combat matters and had to relieve the company commander of all bureaucratic duties. He was married with one child. Wagner was later killed in action at Laterza in Italy on 16 September 1943 in a fight with British paratroopers.

The transport of *I. Bataillon* began on 19 October 1942 in Braunschweig (not Stendal, where the battalion was garrisoned), where they had been waiting for the airborne mission.

The exact actual strength of the battalion on that day is not known, but on 7 October it consisted of 25 officers, 194 NCOs, and 632 men.[7]

The train station was a hive of activity as final preparations were made for the transport. Wagons were loaded, wood burning stoves for the cattle wagons in which the troops were to be transported had to be organised, and the floors had to be covered with straw. The doors of the wagons were also nailed shut so that only one side could be used for entry and exit. About 23–25 men were assigned to each wagon. After a long wait, the train carrying *I. Bataillon* left at around 10:00 p.m. that night. The soldiers slept on their luggage or on straw laid out in the wagons. Some of the more resourceful paratroopers even brought along a hammock.

II. Battalion moved east from Tangermünde on 20 October, leaving at 7:00 a.m. The battalion had an actual strength of 22 officers and officials, 782 NCOs and men, and was equipped with 19 trucks,

Paratroopers of *Fallschirmjäger Regiment 1* during their transport to the East. (Private collection)

---

6   Zimburg, *Kriegserlebnisse*, p.24
7   BA-MA, RL 20/83 in BW 57-84: KTB Nr. 2 Kdo. Flughafenbereich 16/XI, Stendal.

Vitebsk at the arrival of the division. (Private Collection)

6. Kompanie in Vitebsk on 25 October 1942. (Private Collection)

eight cars and 21 motorcycles.[8] *III. Bataillon* left its garrison at Gardelegen during the night of 20 to 21 October with 25 officers, 178 NCOs and 942 men as well as 12 trucks, three cars and eight motorcycles. The regimental staff left Stendal on 21 October with two officers, 150 NCOs, 594 men and 157 trucks and cars.[9]

The train journey took about four days and went via Berlin, Poznan and Warsaw to Vitebsk. The battalions arrived at intervals between 24 and 25 October. The journey was cold and there were several long stops along the way, some because of partisan activity.

At 9:00 a.m. on 25 October, the battalions marched on foot to their assigned areas around Yanovichy, where the regimental command post was located. This was an area ruled by partisans, where several villages were to be fortified for protection against them. *I. Bataillon* marched through Yanovichy, north to Glazomichy, where the battalion established its command post. The companies were stationed in the area, with *2. Kompanie* in Pukchyna.

A distance of about 50 kilometres was marched in 24 hours with full packs in cloudy weather and occasional showers. For the paratroopers, this march took place 'under "difficult conditions", as everyone had to wear two pairs of socks, one pair of foot wraps and two more pairs of newspaper foot wraps.'[10] *II. Bataillon* was stationed east of Yanovichy in Saitseva (staff and *8. Kompanie*), in Lepina (*5. and 6. Kompanie*) and Obrok-Nish (*7. Kompanie*). The exact locations of *III. Bataillon* are unknown apart from *11. Kompanie* under command of *Oberleutnant* Jegella, which was to the southwest of Yanovichy at Pivovari. Therefore, the rest of *III. Bataillon* was most probably in the area south of the town.

Hauptfeldwebel Willi Wagner, of *3. Kompanie*, wrote to his wife on 27 October:

> The conditions here are exactly the same as last winter at Leningrad. The weather was still fine during the journey, but the further east we went, the worse it got and the colder it got … We are now about 30 kilometres behind the front, southwest of Rzhev. We've built bunkers for half of the company because there weren't enough shelters. The bunkers are better, too, and above all there are no bugs, which you can find in every house. I live in the same room as the boss. There

---

8 BA-MA: BW 57-84: War Diary of 7.Kp./II./FJR 1.
9 BA-MA, RL 20/83 in BW 57-84: KTB Nr. 2 Kdo. Flughafenbereich 16/XI, Stendal.
10 Alfons Wanderwitz, *Kompaniegeschichte 11./FJR 1* (Manuscript, self-published, 1978), p.8.

During the long march a *Hauptmann* or *Stabsarzt* treats a blister of one of the paratroopers of the *III. Bataillon*. (Private Collection)

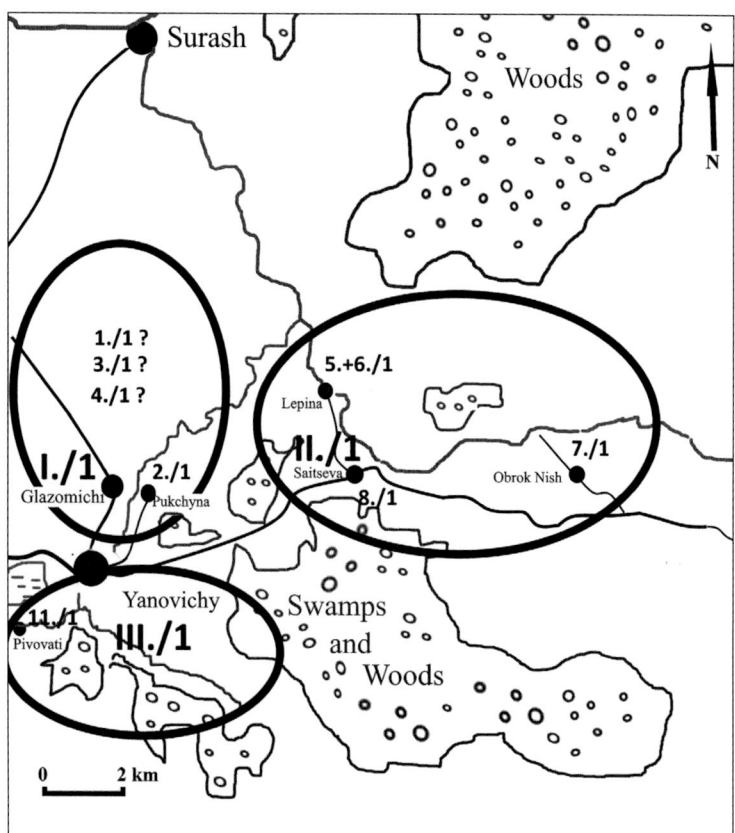

Accommodation and operational areas of the regiment near Yanovichi, north-east of Vitebsk at the end of October.

Fallschirmjäger with locals near Yanovichi, at the end of October or the beginning of November 1942. (Private Collection)

are still a lot of 'bandits', which used to be called partisans, hanging around in this area, so there is shooting all night. Of course, we protect ourselves accordingly. Otherwise, I'm fine. You don't need to worry.[11]

Feldwebel Germer of *3. Kompanie* – equipped with an artist's eye – was more impressed by the beauty of the landscape:[12]

It was a beautiful day, the colours are very different from ours, so pure and delicate. The land is in shades of grey, brown, and green tones, delicately tinged with purple in the sun. The nearby forest shines in lush green and behind it the pigeon-blue shadow of a distant forest greets you from afar. Above it all a sky that shines in wonderful pastel shades.[13]

He regretted that he did not have time to paint but had to devote himself to such mundane tasks as building a bunker. Germer, a trained painter, began his compulsory military service on 18 April 1939 and joined *Fallschirmjäger Regiment 1* as a volunteer on 13 July 1939, where he served for almost the entire duration of the war. A brave soldier who was awarded the Knight's Cross and the German Cross in Gold, he was wounded six times and by the end of the war had the rank of *Oberleutnant*. After the war, he worked as a professional photographer.

Ernst Germer as *Fahnenjunker-Oberfeldwebel* in 1944 after being awarded the Knight's Cross for his action at Pesaro, Italy. (Private Collection)

---

11 Archive Franz: Wagner, letter dated 27 October 1942.
12 Ernst Germer (Nienburg, 15 December 1917–Braunschweig-Stöckheim, 13 October 1990); DKiG 24 June 1943; RK 29 October 1944.
13 BA-MA, BW 57-81: entry 26 October 1942.

For other units elsewhere, moving into position was not quite so idyllic. When *6.* and *7. Kompanie* advanced towards Lepina on 27 October, they were ambushed by a group of about 10 partisans and came under rifle and machine gun fire as well as shellfire from mortars from a neighbouring village. They retreated after a brief exchange of fire. Walter Heinkelein of *5. Kompanie* recalls that partisans attacked their camp which 'went up in flames' immediately upon their arrival at night, 'ammunition exploded, mines went off, a mess, hardly anyone was able to save some of his luggage and weapons, everything was burned'.[14]

Heinkelein, a trained barber from Crailsheim, joined as a volunteer – first in the *SA Standarte Feldherrnhalle* and later in *Fallschirmjäger Regiment 1* in 1939. To commence jump training he needed – because he was so young – his parents' consent.[15] He took part in all the campaigns of the regiment until March 1944, was wounded several times and was awarded the Iron Cross 2nd and 1st Class, *Erdkampfabzeichen* (Ground Combat Badge) and the Wound Badge in Gold. He even was nominated for the German Cross in Gold and for promotion to *Oberfeldwebel* at the end of the war but did not receive either. He received his final wound in Berlin on 24 April 1945, when he escaped from a hospital to avoid Soviet captivity only to fall into British hands. Heinkelein had a hairdressing salon in Crailsheim after the war.[16]

Walter Heinkelein as *Oberjäger*. (Estate of Walter Heinkelein, Archive Crailsheim)

The following days the paratroopers were mainly busy digging trenches and positions, and fighting the bugs and lice that the soldiers had picked up in their civilian quarters and could not get rid of for a long time. On 28 October there was a heavy bombing raid on Vitebsk. On the next day they witnessed an air battle above Saitseva, in which three Soviet fighter planes were shot down, and also on 30 October over Glazomichy, in which a German Me 109 and two Soviet Ratas went down. These days were a time to get used to the conditions at the front, especially for the newcomers.

Feldwebel Germer went into the forest to fell birch trees for the construction of the bunker: 'In the forest you feel good when you no longer have to see the Russian huts. The forest brings you closer to home, you no longer feel so far away from it.'[17]

---

14 Walter Heinkelein (Crailsheim 19 January 1920– ibid., 5 December 2000), *Feldwebel*; Walter Heinkelein, *Recollections* (Manuscript, Stadtarchiv Crailsheim)
15 Stephan Janzyk, *Deckname Fall Weiß – Deutsche Fallschirmjäger im Polenfeldzug 1939* (Herne: VS-Books, 2015), pp.90–91.
16 For his biography see Gerhard Herm, *Hitler, Göring und ich – Ein Fallschirmjäger im Dritten Reich* (Crailsheim: Baier Verlag, 2005).
17 BA-MA, BW 57-81: entry 30 October 1942.

German signpost near Yanovichy. (Private Collection)

Like *Fallschirmjäger Regiment 1*, *Fallschirmjäger Regiment 4* arrived in full on 26 October and was stationed a few kilometres east of Vitebsk in the area of Vorony – left and right of the road to Smolensk – where they had no known encounters with partisans.[18]

Most of *Fallschirmjäger Regiment 3* had arrived on 28 October and took up positions on the road Vitebsk-Smolensk at Lyosno, around Velyashkovichy and Kolishky to protect towns in the vicinity. Here, too, a partisan attack had to be repelled.[19] The rest of the division had not yet fully arrived in Vitebsk at this time – the last of a total of 60 trains were expected on 30 October 1942.[20]

---

18 Donth, *Fallschirmjäger Regiment 4*, pp.16–17. BA-MA, RL 33/69, KTB 1 of FJR 4, entry on 27 October 1942.
19 BA-MA, RL 33/56; HILA: Memoires of Ludwig Heilmann, 2004C60 Box 1, p.111.
20 CAMO: 500_12454, file 637, p.247.

6

To the Frontline

The regiment's otherwise uneventful stay at Yanovichy came to an end on 30 October, when a new order to deploy arrived. Adolf Hitler's direct order (Individual Order No. 47) to *Heeresgruppe Mitte* stated:

> *7. Fliegerdivision* [sic] is with immediate effect tactically subordinated to *Heeresgruppe Mitte*. The division is to be deployed immediately on the left wing of *9. Armee* at the probable focal points of the defence, namely along the Dukhovshchina–Starina road and the railway line in the front.
> The division may only be deployed as a formation.
> The removal of individual units is forbidden.
> Army units and formations deployed in the future section of *7. Flieger Div.* will be subordinated to the division.
> The integration of *7. Flieger Div.* into the front is intended to shorten the front for *197. [Infanterie] Div.* and to free up the *Jäger* battalions as an intervention reserve. It is important that *7. Flieger Div.* be deployed as soon as possible.
> The intended deployment and the probable time of taking over the defence section and relieving are to be reported by 11 a.m. on 31 October for consultation with the *Führer*.[1]

The background to this order – that the division can only be deployed as a formation – probably had its origins in the events of the winter of 1941–1942, when *Flieger Division 7* was deployed in fragmented form and suffered high losses. Again and again, smaller units subordinated to other formations in trouble were 'burned' by them to protect their own troops. Also, these subordinate units often received fewer supplies than their own troops. These facts are repeatedly described in field reports from that winter.[2]

On 30 October the *Oberkommando* of *9. Armee* (AOK 9) – the army high command – under *Generaloberst* Model learned of the arrival of *Flieger Division 7* and was both pleased and relieved to welcome a division with the 'best, well-trained personnel and good weaponry.'[3] The part of the front where the division was to operate was considered to be particularly vulnerable, and the defences had

---

1 Archive Paul Bernhard: Copy made from files at BA-MA.
2 See also BA-MA, RH 26-197/21 in BW 57-82: Basic Order No. 6 of the Operations Department of the OKH, *General der Infanterie* Zeitzler of 7 November 1942, which devotes an entire chapter to the treatment of so-called '*verpumpte Truppen*' (slang for lend out units), and BA-MA, RH 20-9/118 in BW 57-82: Letter of *Generaloberst* Model, commander of *9. Armee*, dated 22 January 1943, to his commanding generals and division commanders.
3 NARA, T 312-R 310: KTB AOK 9, Nr. 6, Ia *Führungsabteilung*, vol.3, entry 30 October 1942.

now been greatly improved as a result. However, Model's joy was tempered by the division's serious weakness: 'The *7. Flieger Division* did not have any heavy anti-tank guns.'[4]

Model himself had great military skills, especially in defence, and was particularly loyal to Hitler, who often used him as a 'fire brigade' in trouble spots. For his subordinates he was a difficult commander with a particularly hot temper.

From 1 November 1942 *Flieger Division 7* was under the command of *VI. Armee Korps*, commanded by *Generalleutnant* Jordan. In his divisional order of 1 November, the division commander *Generalleutnant* Petersen, specified the deployment. The division was to be positioned between *330. Infanterie Division* (to the left) and *197. Infanterie Division* (to the right). *Kampfgruppe Walther (Fallschirmjäger Regiment 4)*[5] replaced *Sicherungsbataillon 642* and *Jägerbataillon 6* on the left side of the divisional sector – and *Kampfgruppe Heidrich (Fallschirmjäger Regiment 3)*[6] replaced *Jägerbataillon 13* and *Grenadier Regiment 347* on the right side of the sector. *Fallschirmjäger Regiment 1* was to be deployed in the Tegerino-Volkova-Uchakova area as an intervention reserve. The command posts of the regiments were in Ribshevo for *Fallschirmjäger Regiment 3* (later also the divisional command post) and in Tverdy for *Fallschirmjäger Regiment 4*.[7] The task of the division was not only to defend its section of the front, but also to conduct active and aggressive combat missions and constantly reconnoitre enemy activities in order to be able to prepare countermeasures at an early stage.[8]

Generaloberst Walter Model. (Szukaj w archiwach, 3/2/0/-/12726)

Transport to the new areas of operation was unproblematic since the roads were passable and enemy aerial reconnaissance was hampered by low cloud cover. In the days before the ground froze it was a different experience as *Oberstleutnant* Heilmann, commander of *III. Bataillon/Fallschirmjäger Regiment 3*, recalls the difficulties: 'Here the motor vehicles ploughed through the softened ground, slid off the road, sank and got stuck. Sometimes we tried to get them across the open field only to be dragged out again by tracked vehicles.'[9]

Beginning with the night of 2 to 3 November, the division moved into positions north of Smolensk with *Kampfgruppen Heidrich* and *Walther*, taking command of the sector at 12 noon on 4 November. *Fallschirmjäger Regiment 1* left its positions around Yanovichy and first moved as a reserve on 31 October to Rudnya, which was on the Vitebsk-Smolensk road, where *3. Kompanie* arrived at 11:00 a.m. Parts could also have been located around Tveritino at the junction of the Vitebsk-Smolensk and Orsha-Rzhev roads.[10]

---

4   NARA, T 312-R 310: KTB AOK 9, Nr. 6, Ia *Führungsabteilung*, vol.3, entry 2 November 1942.
5   The battlegroup consisted of FJR 4; *3.* and *4. Kompanie/Fsch.Pz.Jg. Abt. 7*; staff, *2.* and *3. Kompanie/Fsch. MG.Bat.*; Pi.Btl. 665; *3. Kompanie/Fsch.San.Abt.*
6   The battlegroup consisted of FJR 3, *Fsch.Pi.Btl.* minus 1 company; staff, *1.* and *2. Kompanie/Fsch.Pz.Jg. Abt.; 1. Kompanie/Fsch.MG.Bat.*; *2. Kompanie/Fsch.San.Abt.*
7   BA-MA, RH 26 -197/21 in BW 57-38: divisional order n. 2, 1 November 1942.
8   BA-MA, BW 57-38: order of VI. AK to *Flieger Division 7*, 2 November 1942.
9   HILA: Memoires of Ludwig Heilmann, 2004C60 Box 1, p.112.
10 Zimburg (2./FJR 1) states that his company was at Tveritino, west of Smolensk, while Germer (3./FJR 1) places

A radio vehicle KFZ 17 of the signal platoon (*Nachrichtenzug*) of *Fallschirmjäger Regiment 1* trying to get out of the mud. (Private Collection)

In a Russian village. (Private Collection)

6. *Kompanie* on the road Rudnya-Smolensk-Moscow, already at colder temperatures. (Private Collection)

Trucks of the *Fallschirmjäger* on a corduroy road during the Rasputitsa. (Private Collection)

There the regiment was supplied with much appreciated goods: 34 cigarettes per man, skin cream, eggs and chocolate. There were also changes of command, for example, the commander of *3. Kompanie*, *Hauptmann* Gessner,[11] was transferred to the regiment's command reserve and was replaced by the very popular *Oberleutnant* Otto.[12] The weather became very wintry, with blizzards and cold prevailing. In addition, the clocks were changed to wintertime on 3 November. As *Feldwebel* Germer noted: 'Dawn is at 4:30 a.m. and nightfall at 4 p.m.'[13] In winter, Moscow time deviated from Berlin by two hours, 4:00 p.m. for the Germans was 6:00 p.m. for the Soviets.

On that day, 3 November, *Generaloberst* Model received an order directly from Hitler (Individual Order No. 54) prohibiting the holding of a regiment of *Flieger Division 7* in reserve. '[T]he Div. should be used as a formation in the main line of defence, because its equipment and training it is more suitable for a tough defensive fight than for flexible counter-attacks'.[14] Hitler probably still had in mind the perceived lack of infantry training of the paratroopers deployed in Crete – which was certainly no longer the case – and thus completely ignored the aggressive nature of airborne troops.[15]

The front line of *Flieger Division 7* was extended eastwards and now included the Starina sector in its entirety.[16] This was where the long-awaited Soviet offensive was expected to hit.

Generalmajor Heidrich signed his last order to his regiment on 7 November and took command of a brigade, while *Oberstleutnant* Heilmann led this regiment from that moment on. Heidrich recalled being flown in a Fieseler Storch to take command of a brigade when he was still commander of *Fallschirmjäger Regiment 3*. He was assigned as a divisional commander and the regulations required that he had previously commanded a brigade. *Brigade Heidrich* included, among other units, the reinforced *Fallschirmjäger Regiment 4* as well as *Pionier Bataillon 655* and a light battery of guns. The brigade was located on the left front section of *Flieger Division 7*. The following morning, he is said to have been recalled because *Generalleutnant* Petersen had gone to Berlin, and he was supposed to take over command of the division immediately. About a week later, on 16 November, he was officially appointed divisional commander with effect from 1 November 1942. There is confusion about the exact dates of the actual handovers, the 7th is the most likely date, as it is from the war diary of *Fallschirmjäger Regiment 3*. The war diary of *Fallschirmjäger Regiment 4* mentions being under command of *Brigade Heidrich* at noon on the 4th[17] while the morning report of *Flieger Division 7* mentions a *Kampfgruppe Heilmann* on 5 November. To add to the confusion the war diary of *Fallschirmjäger Regiment 3* states on a different page that Heidrich was transferred away from the regiment on 10 November.[18] Heidrich himself confirmed that he had taken actual command of

---

his company in Rudnya. Dr Müller mentions for 31 October *1. Kompanie* at Savyenki, 1.5 km east of the road crossing Smolensk. *II. Bataillon* was definitely in Rudnya as VI. AK notes in its war diary on 31 October 1942. See Zimburg, *Kriegserlebnisse*, p.54; Dr Ludwig Müller, *Damals* (Würzburg: self-published, 1981), p.44; NARA, T-314 R-310, KTB VI. AK, Abt. Qu.. No. 3, Vol.24, 1–31 October 1942; BA-MA, BW 57-81.

11 Otto Gessner (1 April 1915–?), *Hauptmann*. Went into allied captivity on 17 May 1944 (missing?).
12 Johann Otto (1 March 1909–KIA, Castiglione, 20 June 1944), *Hauptmann;* DKiG 24 June 1943. He commanded *I. Bataillon* in February 1944 at Monte Cassino.
13 BA-MA, BW 57-81.
14 NARA, T-312 R-310: KTB AOK 9, Nr. 6, Ia *Führungsabteilung*, vol.3, entry 3 November 1942. BA-MA, BW 57-38.
15 See also Magnus Pahl, 'Kreta 1941 – Die "schwarze Madonna" der deutschen Fallschirmtruppe', in Pahl & Wagner (eds), *Hitlers Elitetruppe? – Mythos Fallschirmjäger* (Dresden: be.bra, 2021), p.15.
16 CAMO: 500_12454, file 637, pp.230–231; BA-MA: RH 24-5/117.
17 BA-MA, RL 33/69.
18 BA-MA, RL 33/54.

Generalmajor Heidrich in a Fieseler Storch ready for take-off. (BDF Archive)

the division earlier, recalling that a week had elapsed between his assumption of command and being appointed commander.[19] The daily reports of the VI. AK mention *Brigadestab* Heidrich from 5 November until 11 November. *Brigade* Heidrich is still mentioned in a status report of *Flieger Division 7* dated 14 November 1942.[20]

Heidrich handed over the brigade to *Oberstleutnant i.G.* Häring, who led it until 20 February 1943 as *Brigade Häring* (thereafter it was again called *Kampfgruppe Walther*).

This change of command was to determine the future of the division as the new commander, Heidrich, entirely the former infantry school instructor, turned the already well-trained division into a formation of high combat value. His division was later regarded as one of the best in the *Wehrmacht* during the Italian campaign. Heidrich later wrote:

> From that day on, I thoroughly organised the division's defence and, above all, constantly promoted an understanding of defence. I had secretly observed that the idea of defence was completely neglected throughout the *Wehrmacht*. Since I had thoroughly studied defence in depth during my time in the *Reichswehr*, I was able to make valuable suggestions to the troops. In particular, I encouraged active reconnaissance activities by the troops. While the infantry divisions hardly advanced beyond the main line of defence, my division competed with the Russians in daily reconnaissance operations. The division carried out more than 800 reconnaissance patrols, most of them successful, within a quarter of a year.[21]

---

19 Richard Heidrich, 'Mein Soldatenleben', *Der Grüne Teufel – Mitteilungsblatt der deutschen Fallschirmjäger* (1951), December, p.3.
20 BA-MA, BW 57-39.
21 Heidrich, 'Mein Soldatenleben', p.3.

Hauptmann Kratzert, who led *III. Bataillon/Fallschirmjäger Regiment 3* also noted in his memoirs: 'Since *General* Heidrich had taken over *7. Fliegerdivision*, there had been plenty of war games and visits.'[22]

In order to emphasise his wish, on 17 November 1942, he issued 18 pages of 'Guidelines for the establishment of defence and the conduct of defensive combat',[23] an expression of his meticulousness, but also of his pedantry. Heidrich was also dissatisfied with the existing system of strongpoint defence. His successor as commander of *Fallschirmjäger Regiment 3*, Ludwig Heilmann, described the situation as follows:

> The main line of defence consisted only of individual strongpoints, as had become common practice on the Russian front, due to the lack of soldiers. A temporary adjustment of the last winter had become permanent. The troops had already come to terms with the partisan nests in the rear of the front. Those who had only learned their trade during the war didn't know any better. The general wasn't opposed to modern methods at all, but he didn't want a strong point system. He believed the infantry's combat principles, which were still valid, to be correct, that any enemy attack would collapse in front of the main line of defence when fully equipped with all weapons. But he also compared the main line of defence to a rubber band that snaps back into place as soon as the pressure is released. But in Russia there were special conditions and the war consisted of nothing but stop-gap solutions.[24]

Fallschirmjäger Regiment 1 remained in the area west of Smolensk until 6 November, when first *I. Bataillon* was transferred to Verdino where the regimental command post was located and where the night was also spent. The journey, which lasted all day, took place in heavy snowfall and bitter cold. *Feldwebel* Germer, riding on a solo motorbike with *Obergefreiter* Peter as a pillion passenger, despite being properly dressed stated the obvious: 'I'm terribly cold, especially my feet and hands.'[25] The next day, the companies marched to their assigned areas near Starina, where many young soldiers received their baptism of fire by Soviet artillery.

The men of signals platoon (*Nachrichtenzug*) of *Fallschirmjäger Regiment 1* setting up communication lines between the units.
(Private Collection)

Men of the signals platoon of the regiment taking a break.
(Private Collection)

22 Kratzert, *Vom k.u.k. Offizier zum Ritterkreuzträger*, p.87.
23 BA-MA, RL 22/123: Richtlinien für das Einrichten zur Verteidigung und die Führung des Abwehrkampfes.
24 HILA: Memoires of Ludwig Heilmann, 2004C60 Box 1, p.113.
25 BA-MA, BW 57-81: entry 6 November 1942.

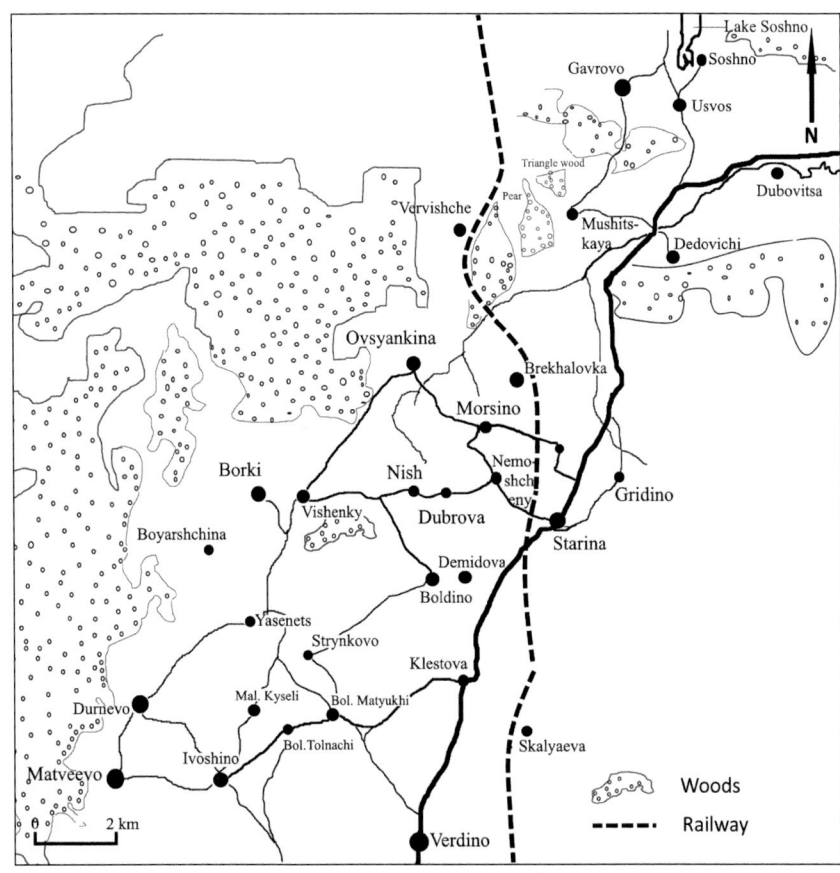

The area of operation of *Fallschirmjäger Regiment 1* around Starina.

As always when soldiers move into a new place, they start digging trenches and constructing bunkers, in this case *Oberleutnant* Mössinger of *1. Kompanie*. (Private Collection)

For the construction all advantages of the terrain are exploited. (Private Collection)

The result: a well camouflaged bunker of which only the entrance can be seen. (Private Collection)

Major von der Schulenburg set up his battalion's command post at Starina, while *Oberleutnant* Vogler's *1. Kompanie* took up position at Dubrova,[26] *Oberleutnant* Kissling's *2. Kompanie* moved into Morsino to the right,[27] and *Oberleutnant* Otto's *3. Kompanie* moved to Brekhalovka. The latter position lay across a railway line and a road and was therefore reinforced with one platoon each of *4.*, *13.* and *14. Kompanie*, as well as several 8.8 cm anti-aircraft guns and 'a lot of artillery'.[28] All in all, the company including the subordinated units had now a serious strength of 291 men.

The 8.8 cm anti-aircraft gun was commonly known as the *Acht-acht* ('eight-eight') by the Germans and as the 'eighty-eight' by the Allies. This gun was very effective against tanks especially against the Soviet T-34, KV-1 and KV-2 heavy tanks.

The battalion's defensive line was six and half kilometres long. Here the Soviet main thrust towards Smolensk was expected. On the right was *197. Infanterie Division*, commanded by *Generalmajor* Ehrenfried-Oskar Boege.[29] On the left *III. Bataillon* had to defend a stretch of six kilometres. By this time, it began to get colder and colder, with temperatures dropping to -15°C on 7 November. The autumn mud season, which prevented any movement or offensive action, was finally over.

In this 12.5-kilometre-wide section – out of the 54 kilometres the division had to defend – the regiment had to protect part of the main road link and an important supply line between Dukhovshchina, Starina, and north-east to Bely, along which the front from Starina to Bely was built. A Soviet breakthrough to the south along this road would have been dangerous for Smolensk and would have seriously affected the supply of the troops deployed around Bely. It is therefore understandable that a possible Soviet focus of attack was expected in this area.

AOK 9 – as well as *Heeresgruppe Mitte* – anticipated this attack on 7 November: 'The signs of an imminent enemy offensive are becoming more and more intense. The army has prepared for 7 November. At 8.50 a.m. Chief of Staff 9 [*Generalmajor* Krebs of AOK 9][30] reports to Chief of Staff H[eeres] Gr[uppe] Mitte Oberst Wöhler][31] their assessment of the enemy: the enemy is about to attack at the focal points.'[32]

Generaloberst Model personally assured himself at *VI. Armee Korps* of its preparedness. It was a dangerous time for the regiment as Schulenburg's *I. Bataillon* moved into its new positions that day, while Becker's *III. Bataillon* did not do so until the following day. But contrary to further reports from defectors that the attack would begin at 12 noon, all was quiet on 7 November. Zhukov had postponed the start of the offensive to 25 November, as the attack formations had not yet reached their starting positions due to weather-related delays.

While *III. Bataillon* was moving into position west of Verdino – replacing *Hauptmann* Kratzert and his *III. Bataillon/Fallschirmjäger Regiment 3* during the night of 8 to 9 November – it suffered its first

---

26 Josef Vogler (Mainz, 20 May 1915–?); *Hauptmann* from 1 April 1943.
27 Werner Kissling (or Kießling) (Schloss Bistritz, 8 September 1908–KIA at Kriuki, 3 March 1943), *Oberleutnant*.
28 BA-MA, BW 57-81: entry 8 November 1942.
29 Ehrenfried Oskar Boege (Ostrowo, 11 November 1889 – Hildesheim, 31 December 1965), *General der Infanterie*; RK 22 December 1941, Oak Leaves 21 September 1944, DKiG 13 January 1943. At the end of the war he commanded *18. Armee* in the Kurland battles and went into Soviet captivity. He was released in 1955.
30 Hans Krebs (Helmstedt, 4 March 1898–Berlin [suicide], 2 May 1945), *General der Infanterie* and last Chief of the General Staff of the German Army High Command (OKH).
31 Otto Wöhler (Großburgwedel, 12 July 1894–ibid., 5 February 1987); *General der Infanterie*. He commanded the relief operation Velikiye Luki this winter. After the war he was convicted of war crimes at the Nürnberg tribunals.
32 NARA, T-312 R-310: KTB AOK 9, Nr. 6, Ia *Führungsabteilung*, vol.3, entry 7 November 1942.

casualty. *Gefreiter* Josef Graczyk of *14. Kompanie/Fallschirmjäger Regiment 5* was seriously wounded and died three days later in hospital.

As already pointed out, the main line of defence was not a continuous manned line, but a system of mutually supporting strong points, as described by *Gefreiter* Walter Fricke of *10. Kompanie*:

> No trenches, no closed line. Just a strongpoint system. A few Russian houses with defences all around them. Like a little fortress. Standing guard, building a bunker, eating, and sleeping. Under each house there was a cellar full of potatoes … Only then did we go to our guard posts. During the day there was only one man watching. The Russian was a thousand meters away and we rarely saw one. Nevertheless, we were always vigilant.[33]

Walter Fricke,[34] originally a farm worker, joined the paratroopers as a volunteer in 1941 and saw action that autumn at Leningrad with *10. Kompanie*. Wounded at Gribushino in January 1943 he remained with his battalion during the Italian campaign until March 1944 when it was transferred to France as *III. Bataillon* of the new *Fallschirmjäger Regiment 5*.

On Monday 9 November it was sunny and -18°C. Gröschke's *II. Bataillon* moved into the area around Bol as a reactive reserve behind *I.* and *III. Bataillon* in Matyukhi, northwest of Verdino. The regiment was now fully deployed and in position.

If the section had been sparsely manned before, it was now particularly strong, not only in terms of combat value but also in numbers. This led to conflicts over accommodation with other units in the area. The staff of *VI. Armee Korps* was busy throughout 9 November sorting out accommodation issues, mediating, and intervening.[35] Heilmann also described these conditions in his memoirs:

> Behind the sparsely manned sections of the front there were still empty spaces. In the vast forests there were isolated villages, probably marked on the map, but never entered by a German soldier. All traffic to the front was along the main road, from which the supply routes branched off to the individual divisions. All the houses and huts along the supply routes and in the nearby villages were densely manned with staffs and rear detachments. Those who just had arrived found no accommodation at first.[36]

The other units of *Flieger Division 7* were to the west (left) of *Fallschirmjäger Regiment 1*, first *Fallschirmjäger Regiment 3*, then *Fallschirmjäger Regiment 4* (*Brigade Häring*). To the west of the road from Starina to Dukhovshchina lay extensive marshes, lakes and forests – an area which is now a national park. The division's defensive positions were partly on the southern border of this area, partly in the centre of it, based on various lakes and villages which were developed into fortresses.

In general, the hilly and undulating terrain was favourable to defence. The main fighting area was on higher ground than the enemy positions. In the sector of *Fallschirmjäger Regiment 1* there was little ground cover, good vantage points and firing positions, in some places up to a range of five kilometres. All light and heavy infantry weapons could be used.

---

33 BA-MA, BW 57-89: Walter Fricke, *An die Gewehre! An die Gewehre!* manuscript.
34 Walter Fricke, (1921–1995); *Oberfeldwebel*.
35 BA-MA: RH 24-5/117, VI.A.K. KTB 3, vol.51, p.15.
36 HILA: Memoires of Ludwig Heilmann, 2004C60 Box 1, p.115.

This picture taken by *Gefreiter* Fritz Lorenz of *6. Kompanie* shows landscape in front of the main line of defence. The enemy was behind the tree line in the background. While taking this picture Lorenz seemed to feel quite safe but nevertheless carefully stays not too far off the ground. (Private Collection)

A paratrooper of *Fallschirmjäger Regiment 1* in a well build bunker with his MG 34. (BArch, Bild 101I-553-0836-02A/Dahm)

Group picture of the NCOs of 9. Kompanie (left to right): Unknown, *Oberjäger* Hermann Homberg, *Feldwebel* Werner Fleischhauer, *Feldwebel* Oskar Schrack, unknown. (Private Collection)

On the left, in the area of *Fallschirmjäger Regiment 3*, was a wooded area with poor observation possibilities, sometimes only up to 50 metres, only a small field of fire and good opportunities for the enemy to approach the positions undetected. Apart from the wooded area, the section was not safe from armoured attacks. Behind the main line of defence were large, more or less impenetrable woods, a refuge for partisans. In the area of *Fallschirmjäger Regiment 4* the terrain was more open again.

The existing field fortifications were still sparse and laid out in a strong point system. There were no wire obstacles, and small depressions were only occasionally mined. Mines laid haphazardly in earlier battles were a particular danger in some places. There were no anti-tank obstacles. The shelters and bunkers were only shrapnel proof and the whole position was not camouflaged. At the beginning there were also no connecting trenches or fake positions. The paratroopers had to work hard during the coming weeks to properly fortify their positions and area of defence. They reinforced their positions with barricades and obstacles, making a Soviet attack, already a logistical challenge, even more difficult.

Wherever necessary and possible, the fields of fire in front of the positions were cleared and trees left and right along the supply routes were cut, to make them safer from partisan attacks.

To the right of Schulz's regiment was *197. Infanterie Division* along the road to Bely, the neighbour to the left of the division was *330. Infanterie Division*.

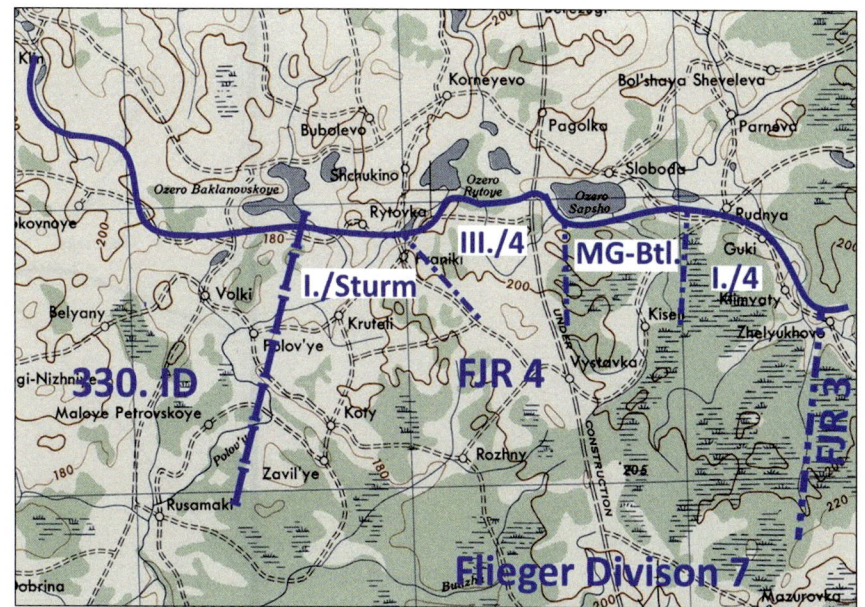

Deployment area of *Flieger Division 7* – left wing.

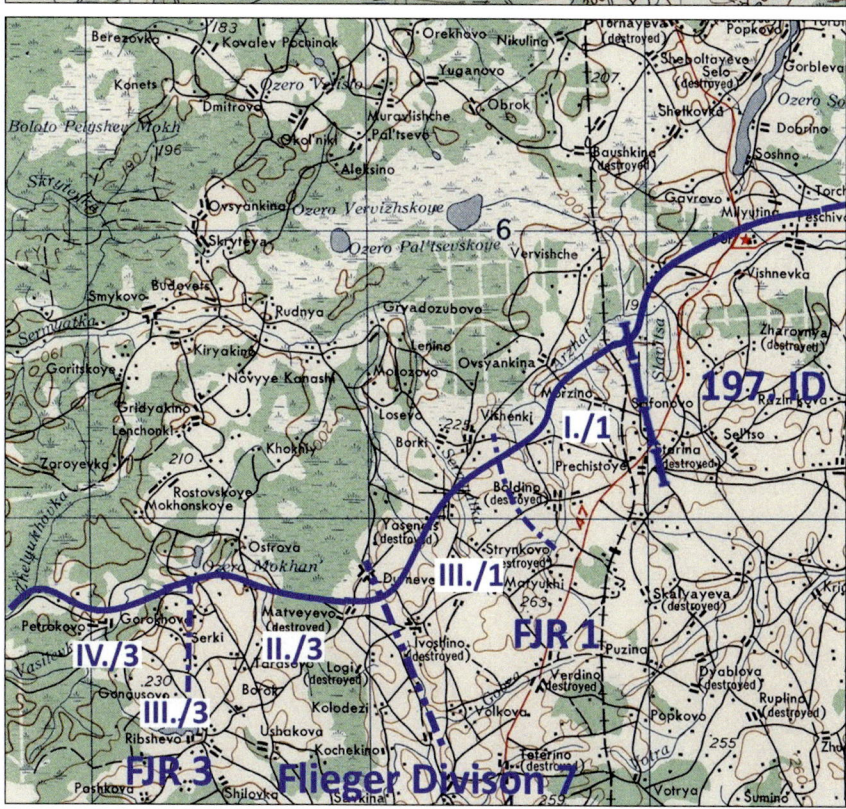

Deployment area of *Flieger Division 7* – right wing.

7

Partisans

Some of the forests in the hinterland of the section of *Flieger Division 7* were controlled by partisan units.[1] The division was therefore ordered to fight them. The partisans were a problem, especially in the section of *Fallschirmjäger Regiment 3*, were they threatened its supply routes through the extensive forests. The threat was also psychological. Especially in the dark, the soldiers had to expect a partisan behind each tree.

Due to the perforated front line, there was a lively exchange between the Soviet units in the front and the rear, which *Generalmajor* Heidrich had to prevent.[2] For this task Heidrich initially had the support of *Polizeiregiment 13* and *Jägerbataillon 4* and *8*. The latter was soon transferred to *20. Panzer Division* which was also tasked with fighting partisans. Ludwig Heilmann recalled:

> The partisans controlled the hinterland. They also hung about in the regimental sector and could not be caught. Our raiding parties followed the footprints like Indians, were usually ambushed and were the only ones to suffer losses. The *Jäger* had to cut their way through the thicket with their knives. It was like being in the jungle and a permanent failure. The partisans moved with the instinct of a wild animal in the jungle. Even the smartest paratrooper was no match for these rangers.[3]

As the paratroopers were unable to intervene successfully, one of the first measures taken by *Generalmajor* Heidrich on 11 November 1942 was to set up a *Fallschirmjäger Schi-Bataillon* (paratrooper ski battalion). It was a highly mobile reserve of *Flieger Division 7* and was also used to fight partisans. For this purpose, each regiment had to surrender one company – that of *Fallschirmjäger Regiment 1* formed *1. Kompanie* of the battalion.[4] This levy did not cause any noticeable reduction in the regiment's combatant strength, but it did show up in the actual strength reports – between 8 November and 5 December there was a visible reduction of 254 men. Considering that the regiment had suffered some 73 casualties during this period, as well as a number of cases of typhoid fever, it is reasonable to estimate that at least 100 to 150 men were transferred.[5]

Accordingly, *Fallschirmjäger Regiment 3* provided soldiers for *2.* and *Fallschirmjäger Regiment 4* for *3. Kompanie*. The division's *Kradschützenkompanie* (motorcycle company) was intended to be *4. Kompanie*,

---

1 For this chapter see Stimpel, *Fallschirmtruppe – Osten und Westen*, pp.79–87.
2 BA-MA: BW 57-38, Telex of VI. AK dt. 6 November 1942.
3 HILA: Memoires of Ludwig Heilmann, 2004C60 Box 1, p.116.
4 BA-MA, BW 57-41: Rudolf Donth, *Chronik der 2. Kompanie des Fallschirmjäger Ski-Bataillons*, typescript.
5 BA-MA, RH 24-6/287.

Gefreiter Hans König of the *Schi-Bataillon* putting on his skis just before doing a messenger run. (BDF Archiv)

but was detached from the battalion on 19 December 1942 and assigned to *Fallschirmjäger Regiment 1*. The ski battalion commander was *Hauptmann* Heinz Näser (of *Fallschirmjäger Regiment 3*) until 30 December, then *Hauptmann* Kanthak of the *Kradschützenkompanie*, and from 16 January 1943 on *Hauptmann* Voßhage.[6]

The companies were formed and trained for the purpose of fighting partisans which included moving on skis, as very few of the paratroopers could ski. The *Schi-Bataillon* was rarely used for its intended purpose. After intensive training, the three companies were initially used for ski liaison runs and long-distance reconnaissance patrols in the rear of the division. These various individual actions and strenuous patrols were moderately successful. Partisan's tracks were found, but they were misleading. The paratroopers, inexperienced in forest warfare, were happy about this, because 'they could have killed us with their caps,'[7] so exhausting were these reconnaissance patrols for them. Otherwise, the 'ski-paratroopers' were mainly used for supply and messenger runs.

On 21 December 1942, a blocking position was taken to catch infiltrated partisans. An unsuccessful operation at best,[8] after which, from mid-January on, the battalion took over a defensive strip on the left wing of the division, where it relieved *II. Bataillon/Fallschirmjäger Regiment 1* on 19 January 1943. The battalion became later *II. Bataillon* of *Fallschirmjäger Regiment 4*.

---

6   Karl Voßhage (Voshage), (21 May 1908-car accident near Andernach, 1973). He survived the war and became an *Oberstleutnant* of the Bundeswehr. After he took his leave he became a priest, his original profession.
7   BA-MA, BW 57-41: Donth, *Chronik*, p.10.
8   BA-MA, BW 57-41: Donth, *Chronik*, p.22.

A platoon of ski paratroopers lined up for the roll call. (Private Collection)

More successful was a company of local Russians (company 'Ivan') under the command of a Russian lieutenant (or captain) Meyer. They operated largely independently and without control by the division, using equally cruel methods as the partisans they were fighting. The paratroopers perceived these Russian anti-partisan fighters as 'unsettling' (*'unheimlich'*) because of their brutality.⁹

Major Mors, as the first General Staff Officer (Ia) of the division, sent a message to *VI. Armee Korps* remarking that company 'Ivan' 'compares less to a German company than to the partisans it is fighting.' He also pointed out the brutality of this counter-partisan group: The 'company is kept tightly together by its leader and is frequently used. Excesses against the Russian civilian population do not always seem to be avoided.'¹⁰

In one of the few joint operations, Rudolf Donth of *2. Kompanie/Fallschimjäger Schi-Bataillon*,¹¹ reported that the 'cooperation [was] not good because the Russians fought too brutally and without orders. Captured Russians, including civilians, were shot immediately.' He also recalled another mission with this company, which he described as successful, but was still glad when the cooperation ended.¹²

A veteran of the Crete and the Leningrad campaigns, Donth rose from ordinary soldier to *Oberleutnant* and was awarded the German Cross in Gold and, at the end of the war, the Knight's Cross. He joined the German *Bundeswehr* in 1956 and rose to the rank of *Oberstleutnant*. On 19 June 2001 he passed away.

---

9   BA-MA, BW 57-41: Donth, *Chronik*, p.18.
10 BA-MA, BW 57-39: Telex of *Flieger Divison 7* to VI. A.K. dated 27 January 1943.
11 Rudolf Donth (Schreiberau-Hirschberg, 16 Februray 1920–Hahnenklee, 19 June 2001), *Oberleutnant*; RK 14 January 1945, DKiG 14 June 1944.
12 BA-MA, BW 57-41: Donth, *Chronik*, p.18.

Despite these measures, partisans remained a constant threat until the end of the deployment. According to a report of *Flieger Division 7* for the period from 27 January to 27 February 1943, numerous operations were carried out, most of which – apart from operations of the 'Ivan' company – were unsuccessful reconnaissance patrols of *Fallschirmjäger Regiment 3*.[13] Many patrols were carried out by the regiment's *Radfahrzug* – the bicycle platoon. During this period 59 partisans were killed and 25 were captured. However, the small number of German casualties, one dead and three wounded as well as five wounded 'Ivan soldiers' suggest that quite a significant number of the 'fallen partisans' may have been victims of executions rather than combat. The war diary of the regiment speaks of Soviet combatants from a larger partisan group which had infiltrated from another area. Since weapons were captured (nine Soviet light machine guns, seven automatic rifles, 11 rifles, six sub-machine guns, one radio), it can be assumed that at least most of them were indeed partisans, while a part was most likely civilians.[14]

Oberjäger Rudolf Donth in March 1943. (BDF Archive)

Fallschirmjäger Regiment 1 did not see action against partisans, because there were hardly any in the rear of its section. There remained, however, a threat of partisan and small regular Red Army units, infiltrating through the front line of into the rear of the neighbouring *197. Infanterie Division*.

---

13 BA-MA, BW 57-39.
14 BA-MA, BW 57-39.

8

Aggressive Reconnaissance

In general, the soldiers perceived this period as uneventful, which in truth it was not. For the paratroopers themselves, the time on this front was characterised by reconnaissance patrols into enemy territory, small attacks on enemy positions, repelling the same from the Soviet side, small skirmishes, artillery fire, etc. Almost every day each company sent out reconnaissance patrols, and there was always some form of Soviet disruptive and diversionary action. It is therefore impossible to examine each and every one of these in this context, but rather to concentrate on the larger actions and missions, that were recorded in the war journals of higher formations or others that were mentioned in the diaries and memoirs of participants.

There were casualties – wounded and dead – almost every day. Soviet snipers, mortar fire, artillery barrages and occasional friendly fire took their toll. *Feldwebel* Germer noted in his diary: 'Platoon leader meeting with *Oberleutnant* Otto (*3. Kompanie*). At the same time, the command post came under well-aimed artillery fire. A bunker window is shattered.'[1] Others were not so lucky. On 12 November, *Oberarzt* Ludwig Müller of *4. San-Kompanie*,[2] which ran the dressing station at Starina, noted in his diary that seven wounded from *III. Bataillon* had been treated that day and one of them had died. He mistakenly mentioned that the soldiers were from *II. Bataillon* but there is nothing in the casualty lists to confirm this. He seems to have summated the casualties of 11 and 12 November. In the casualty list of *III. Bataillon* only five entries can be found on that day, all of them *11. Kompanie* at

Debriefing of a reconnaissance patrol of III platoon of *6. Kompanie* (from left to right): Unknown, unknown, Harrer, Lehman, unknown, *Oberfeldwebel* Richard Schneider (KIA Alekseyevka, 15 February 1943), *Oberjäger* Leo Kromp (WIA Alekseyevka 15 February 1943), *Gefreiter* Langhans, unknown. (Private Collection)

---

1 BA-MA, BW 57-81: entry 11 November.
2 Ludwig Franz Müller (Würzburg, 19 August 1913–17 January 2001), *Oberstarzt*.

Demidovo. The fallen soldier was 18-year-old *Jäger* Erwin Sobetzek, who had been killed in action the day before. The others mentioned by Müller apparently were not seriously wounded and remained with their unit.

Dr Ludwig Müller, originally a dentist, joined the Luftwaffe in 1940 and received training as a *Kriegs Sanitäts Offizier* – a medical officer – and as a paratrooper. He rose through the ranks from *Gefreiter* to *Oberstabsarzt* and took part in the campaigns on the Eastern Front 1942–1943, Sicily and Italy until the end of the war. His *4. San-Kompanie* at Starina was commanded by *Stabsarzt* Dr Frido Hachmeister and belonged to *Fallschirm-Sanitätsabteilung* of *XI. Flieger Korps* attached to *Flieger Division 7*.

On 13 November a group of about 60 Soviet soldiers attacked the position of *3. Kompanie* at Brekhalovka:

> Alarm! Flares light up the area. Battle noise on the right at *III. Zug*. I [*Feldwebel* Germer] ran back again (running off in a fur vest and trainers) and report to the boss, who called for barrage of his own artillery by firing a red flare. The company command post is then taken under mortar fire. The Russians who cut through the barbed wire on the seam between *I.* and *III. Zug* (platoon) were immediately recognised and repulsed. They lost three prisoners and one man killed. Own booty: one MG, rifles and hand grenades.[3]

Herbert Karl Abratis as *Hauptmann* in 1944. (BArch, Bild 146-2006-0070/CC-BY-SA 3.0)

On 14 November, a group of *III. Bataillon* attacked and took a commanding height south-west of Durnevo, which they then were able to hold against a Soviet counterattack. The booty was considerable: 45 prisoners, four machine guns, two anti-tank rifles and 40 rifles.

On 15 November the first heavy snow of this winter fell at -5°C. It snowed again and again until 19 November, with temperatures rising to 0°C. During the night of 18 to 19 November, *Oberleutnant* Abratis,[4] *7. Kompanie*, which was kept in reserve, relieved *1. Kompanie* at Vishenki.

A very ambitious officer, Abratis joined the *Wehrmacht* in 1936 and was transferred to *Flieger Division 7* in April 1940. He took command of *7. Kompanie* in February 1942 and was appointed full commander during the campaign on 23 December 1942. He was awarded the Knight's Cross for his temporary command of *II. Battalion* during the First Battle of Monte Cassino on 24 October 1944. In the final battles against the Soviets, he was killed, south of Stettin, while commanding *Fallschirmjäger Regiment 27*.

---

3   BA-MA, BW 57-81.
4   Herbert Karl Abratis (Babenten, 21 March 1918–KIA Rosengarten south of Altdamm, 15 March 1945); *Major*; RK 24 October 1944, DKiG 15 March 1943.

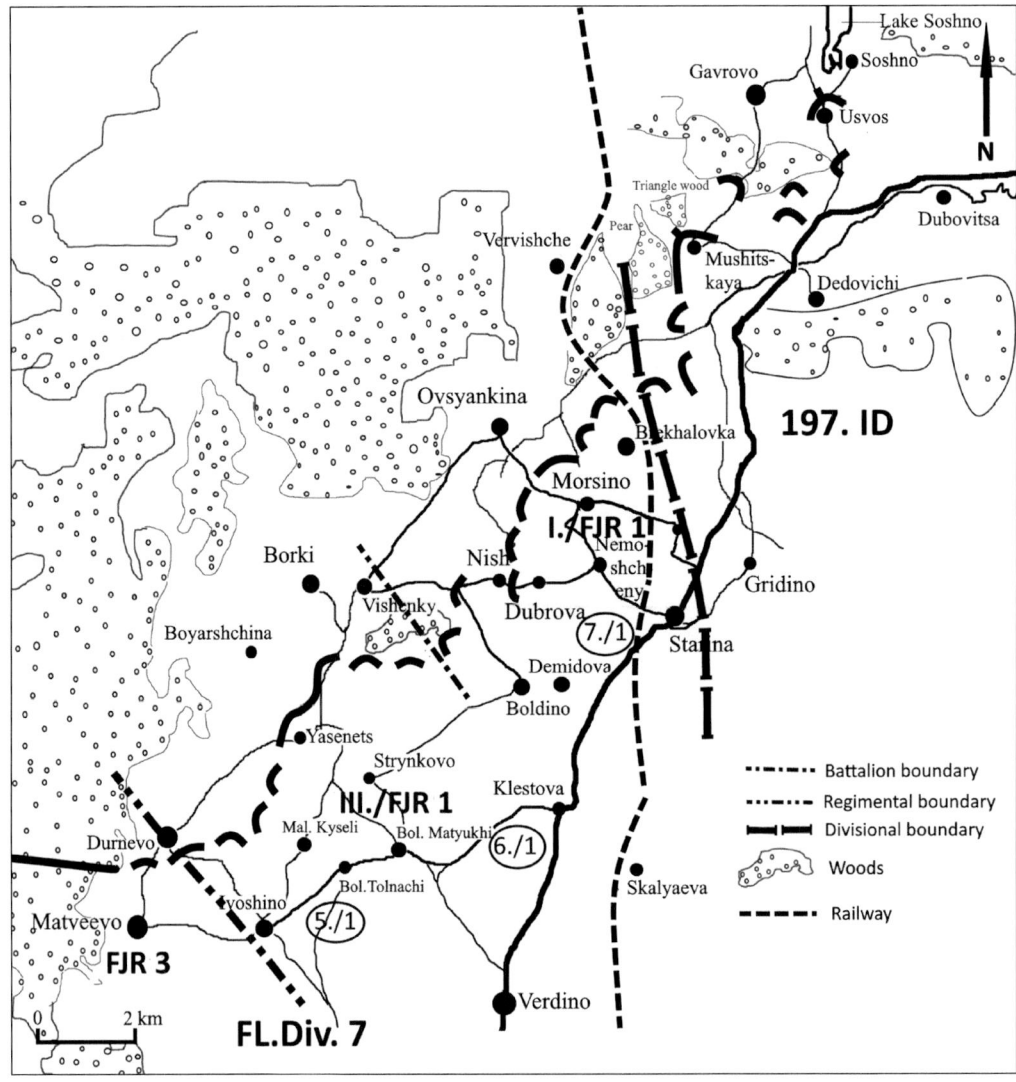

Positions of *Fallschirmjäger Regiment 1* on 17 November 1942.

9

The Raid at Durnevo

Another attack by *III. Bataillon* took place in the early hours on 21 November near Durnevo. Two platoons of *9. Kompanie* (or rather a reinforced platoon) led by the inexperienced *Leutnant* Paul Singer,[1] supported by a backup of two groups of *11. Kompanie* led by *Feldwebel* Karl Hans Wittig were to attack Soviet positions in front of *9. Kompanie*.[2]

Wittig joined *Regiment General Göring* in 1937 and volunteered as a paratrooper. He took part in the campaigns in Austria, Poland, Netherlands, Crete and Russia as a member of *11. Kompanie*. During the assault on Crete he was seriously wounded three times, but survived and returned to duty. During his second Eastern Front deployment, covered in this book, he was awarded the German Cross in Gold for his conduct at Durnevo, Velikiye Luki and Gribushino on 20 March 1943. Later in the campaign he successfully led *11. Kompanie* during the attack on Nagorniy, for which he was awarded the Knights Cross on 5 February 1944, the second soldier in the division to receive this high decoration for his conduct in this campaign (of only two awarded – Schulenburg being the first). This was a big achievement as NCOs rarely received this award. After seeing action in Italy at Salerno, Ortona and Anzio in 1943–1944 he went with his battalion to France where he was promoted to *Leutnant* and platoon commander in *10. Kompanie/ Fallschirmjäger Regiment 5*. He was taken prisoner by the British in Belgium on 3 September 1944.

Wittig described the 21 November action in an article published after the war, so it is presented here in more detail.[3] In the early hours, with temperatures below -5°C and a 'strong easterly wind',[4] *Feldwebel* Wittig's half-platoon set off on a two-hour march to the command post of *9. Kompanie*, which he reached around 4:00 a.m.

Karl-Hans Wittig as *Feldwebel* in February 1944 with his newly awarded Knight's Cross. (Archive BDF)

---

1 Paul Singer (1919–?), from 1 March 1943 *Oberleutnant*.
2 Karl-Hans Wittig (Seegläsgen, 27 July 1918–Nürnberg, 29 December 1984), *Leutnant*.
3 Karl-Hans Wittig, 'Der rettende Stoßtrupp von Durnewo – Ein Glück, daß die Elfte im Zuschauerraum saß', DDF (1968), vol.1, pp.7–10.
4 Wittig remembers -22°C, but the war diary of the other regiments suggest higher temperatures between 0 and -5°. BA-MA, RL 33/54 and 69.

Behind the main line of defence, the connecting routes are marked every 50 metres by a pole driven into the ground. And that's a good thing, because the wind drives the snow crystals in front of it and blows over the smallest depression in this flat area. Even on this so-called supply route, we sometimes sink up to our knees in the loose snow.

Oberleutnant Merkordt was commander of *9. Kompanie* since April 1942 and was a veteran of Crete.[5] Before the Orel mission he took command of *12. Kompanie* at the beginning of February. Later in this campaign he got wounded at Stolbetskoye on 17 February 1943. After his recovery he returned to the regiment and commanded *14. Kompanie* until the end of December. From May 1944 on, he was commander of *I. Bataillon* and went into Polish captivity on 2 September 1944 near Pesaro where he was most probably executed together with other officers of his battalion two days later.[6] For his conduct during this winter campaign he was awarded the German Cross in Gold on 20 March 1943.

Merkordt now instructed *Leutnant* Singer who had little to no combat experience and *Feldwebel* Wittig on the planned attack. The task of Singer's group was to break into the enemy trench system and eliminate a Soviet artillery observer who was harassing the company with very accurate artillery fire on their positions. The latter was sitting 'in the turret of a disabled German tank that has been buried into the ground.' Wittig's half-platoon of *11. Kompanie* was held in reserve.

After a short break in a barn, the platoon was sent to its starting position. 'The guides lead us away from the road down on beaten tracks into the gorges that cut deep into the plateau here. We walk along the bottom. In doing so, we bypass the heights where the trench system of *9. Kompanie* is located.' Wittig's group spread out, took cover, and lay in wait. They were experienced soldiers. His group 'works like clockwork. I have trained my men to the best of their ability and my squad leaders are old hands. We don't shout a lot; the men respond to signs.'

Half an hour later a field-telephone line was set up to Wittig, connecting him directly with the command post of *9. Kompanie* and to the battalion commander, *Major* Rolschewski. In the meantime, *Leutnant* Singer's raiding party had penetrated the enemy trench and was involved in heavy fighting. *Feldwebel* Wittig, realising that Singer must be in trouble, reacted quickly and moved forward with his tactical reserve.

Oberleutnant Fritz Merkordt during the winter campaign December 1941. (Private Collection)

> Heavy Russian rifle and machine-gun fire is hitting us. In between, hand grenades explode with a short and sharp bang. *Leutnant* Singer is involved in a violent trench fight. With my runner I rush

---

5 Fritz Merkordt (Holzwickede, 8 September 1910–presumably executed by Polish troops near Pesaro, about 4 September 1944), DKiG 20 March 1943.
6 Account Grünes (archive of the author) and account of *Oberfeldwebel* Dallinger in 'Suchliste 9' in DDF (1953). Volksbund dated his death 4 September 1944.

to the mouth of the gorge. The Russian trench system, which I only know from above, from our trench, stretches out in front of us not three hundred metres on the flat plain. The raiding party blew up paths through the barbed wire entanglement. Fountains of snow and dirt whirl through the air. Ivan shoots a barrage and is already firing on the trench we have taken. The German fire is slowly dying. I hear more and more the rolling detonations of Russian hand grenades and the high-pitched creaking of Maxim machine guns.

Singer's assault party was cut off and clearly could neither advance nor retreat on its own. Escaping the heavy enemy artillery fire by running fast towards it, Wittig's platoon entered the Soviet trench system without any casualties. He immediately sent *Oberjäger* Karmin with his group to deal with the artillery observer, and with the rest he joined Singer's troops stuck in the enemy trench. The *Leutnant* was seriously wounded, and his soldiers were not doing well either, they were 'leaning against the trench wall with pale faces.'

Wittig grasped the situation and took the initiative. A confusing trench fight developed. 'I took command. The trampled snow in the trench is disgusting, you slip and slide more than you run.' He made his way to *Leutnant* Singer, who was lying unconscious with a wound in his hip and being bandaged by a medic. Wittig organised his evacuation and that of the other wounded, as well as repelling a Soviet counterattack that was forming. The bitter fight was fought with hand grenades and machine gun fire at close range to give Karmin time to approach and eliminate the artillery observer.

Paratroopers of *Fallschirmjäger Regiment 1* fighting in a trench. The camouflage clothing they wore made the paratroopers indistinguishable from Soviet soldiers. (BArch, Bild 183-J21578/Freyer)

Wittig's men fought their way forward through the trench by throwing hand grenades and jumping from corner to corner, firing with their submachine guns, giving the enemy no chance to regain control. They came under heavy artillery fire.

> The artillery hits in our sector are devastating, some on the Russians, some on us. There is a howl and a roar in the air, the frozen earth twitches as if it were doing the dance of St. Vitus. Ivan has grasped what is happening in his trench. Regardless of his own people, he pounded the position with heavy artillery fire.

Karmin's group had not yet eliminated the observer.

> The thunder of the detonations takes our breath away. Howling shrapnel tore through the air, swirling snow and dust. Frozen earth rains down on us. Impact follows impact. It's like a miracle; we [Wittig's platoon] haven't had a single casualty yet. … I take the rest of the platoon and keep running forward in the trench while under artillery fire. There is only one hope for us now: we have to run faster than the enemy's annihilating fire can adjust. Thank God it worked! The artillery fire hits the trenches behind us, throwing wooden beams and people into the air. Horrible, the Russians who had just surrendered to us are now being killed by their own countrymen.

While Wittig held off another Soviet counterattack, *Oberjäger* Karmin managed to blow up the tank with the observer inside, preventing a renewed artillery attack on the paratroopers in the Soviet positions. With the objective of the attack now achieved, the attack group slowly withdrew. Squad after squad disengaged and rushed backwards, blowing up shelters, bunkers and even foxholes as they went.

As his adrenaline level dropped, Wittig was able to grasp the horror of the battle around him:

> While moving back we see how hard the fight was in the trench. You didn't notice it in the excitement of the battle, but dead Russians lie in heaps at every corner, at every dugout. Our new hand grenades have reaped a terrible harvest. It's not the first time I've seen images like this, but it's always a choking feeling when I see those cramped, bloody, tattered corpses and having to think that just a few minutes ago those corpses were living soldiers, with the same hopes and with the same fears as us. I don't think I'll ever get used to such images.

At 10:00 a.m. the paratroopers arrived back at the positions of *9. Kompanie*.

The assault group had successfully destroyed 1,300 metres of enemy trenches and blown up or smoked out 20 bunkers with flamethrowers. According to German reports, the Soviets lost 300 soldiers killed and wounded, and 18 prisoners. The German losses were comparatively light with three dead and 10 wounded including *Leutnant* Singer and *Oberjäger* Karmin. The battalion suffered a further nine casualties that day at Ivoshino, probably from artillery fire. Dr Müller treated 18 wounded at the medical station from midnight to 2:00 a.m.[7]

On the same day *Major* Rolschewski handed over command of *III. Bataillon* to *Hauptmann* Becker. He had taken over command of the battalion from his predecessor *Oberstleutnant* Schulz in July 1942 and was now transferred to division headquarters where he became special envoy of the division for gas defence.[8] Later he was transferred to Germany where he was appointed Ib (Second Staff Officer) of *2. Fallschirmjäger Division*. His commander *General der Fallschirmtruppe* Ramcke described him as

---

7   Müller, *Damals*, p.56.
8   BA-MA, RL 33/54; Rolschewski is mentioned in this function on 18 December 1942 but does not appear in the personnel list of the division end of March 1943.

Several participants of the raid at Durnevo were awarded the Iron Cross 2nd Class (left to right): *Gefreiter* Friedrich Westphal (signals platoon), unknown, *Gefreiter* Heinz Duggen (11. Kp.), unknown, Alpers (?). (Private Collection)

an 'always cheerful brave man.'[9] In 1944 he defended the fortress Saint-Malo in Brittany with a combat group *Fallschirmjäger Regiment z.b.V.* (consisting of parts of the divisional staff of *2. Fallschirmjäger Division, III. Bataillon/ Fallschirmjäger Regiment 7* and various parts of the army) and went into Allied captivity on 17 August 1944.[10]

On 23 November, only two days later, another raid of *III. Bataillon* took place. It was again successful. The result: 11 enemy dead and three prisoners. On the 24th, beginning from about 2:00 to 3:00 a.m., a raiding party of *2. Kompanie* destroyed a 250-metre-long trench near Ovsyankina and blew up five bunkers; 29 Soviet dead were reported. Dr Müller had to take care of two wounded who were evacuated by Fieseler Storch.[11] One of them, 28-year-old *Oberfeldwebel* Willi Mayer from Berlin and a member of the staff of *I. Bataillon/Fallschirmjäger Regiment 1*, died on

The cemetery for the fallen paratroopers of the regiment at Verdino with its first graves. The paras went there on skis. (Private Collection)

---

9 Hermann Bernhard Ramcke (Schleswig, 24 January 1889–Kappeln, 4 July 1968), *General der Fallschirmtruppe*; RK 21 August 1941, Oak Leaves (145) 13 November 1942, Swords (99) and Diamonds (20) 19 September 1944. He was commander of *2. Fallschirmjäger Division* in Brittany in 1944 and a vocal supporter of the Nazi Party. After the war he was convicted of war crimes. Hermann Bernhard Ramcke, *Fallschirmjäger – Damals und danach* (Oldendorf: Schütz, 1973), p.33.
10 Willi Kammann, *Der Weg der 2. Fallschirmjäger Division* (Munich: Schild Verlag, 1998), 3rd edition, p.92, and the organisational chart in its appendix.
11 Müller, *Damals*, p.62; Ancestry/WASt, G-A 605/0060.

18 December 1942 in the Dukhovshchina field hospital from leg wounds caused by a mortar round. The other wounded man was *Oberjäger* Ernst Schlimme, who recovered, only to be killed in action a year later near Ortona on 3 January 1944.

During this time the paratroopers improved their bunkers, built decoy positions and improved their own positions. The command bunker of *3. Kompanie* for example was made of sturdy logs, covered with three layers of logs, with earth and straw in between, and half a meter of earth on top. Inside there were shelves, tables, and benches and at the entrance even a small anteroom with a small storage room lined with boards. They found some potatoes from a farmer's storage. 'Will they last for the duration of our stay?' wondered *Feldwebel* Germer.[12]

The graves of *Jäger* Hermann Seyen (KIA Morsino 20 November 1942), *Obergefreiter* Erich Schilk (KIA Dubrova, 13 January 1943) both from *2. Kompanie* at Verdino. (Private Collection)

Paratroopers of *6. Kompanie* while improving their trenches, left to right: *Oberjäger* Leo Kromp, Arlautski, MG 34 gunner Lehman, unknown, *Obergefreiter* Sengenberger of the kitchen squad. (Private Collection)

---

12 BA-MA, BW 57-81: Entry of 22 November 1942.

10

The Offensive Hits Others

From 16 November on, tensions rose, as all commanders expected that a Red Army offensive was imminent. *Generaloberst* Model expected an attack on his army's northern front, on Sychevka from the east, and on Bely from the west. The indicators of an attack date of 25 November increased. *Generalleutnant* Jordan's *VI. Armee Korps* expected the main thrust against the section of *Flieger Division 7* and especially the sector of *Fallschirmjäger Regiment 1*: '… the target of enemy attacks [will] initially be the area around Starina, the dominant high ground north-west of Verdino, at Hill 221 (north-west of Tverdy) and west of it. The focus of the defence has to be in these areas.'[1]

Eventually, on 25 November, MARS began, attempting to eliminate the Rzhev salient by attacking at several points, although not at all the expected ones: Sychevka had been guessed correctly by the Germans, at Bely the thrust came further south than predicted, and *9. Armee* was surprised by attacks on the northern side of the salient.[2] The lack of attacks on the Starina area,[3] also completely unexpected, followed the original Stavka plans to attack there later, after the successful completion of MARS.

The weather was not favourable. Blizzards, driving snow and poor visibility prevented both Soviet and German air support from being effective. At Bely and in the Luchesa valley area, north-east of the positions of the paratroopers, the German front was breached in multiple places.

The paratroopers could hear the sounds of battle but were not directly affected by the fighting but security had to be established on their right flank, since the Soviet forces which had penetrated the front at Bely posed a threat. However, in this phase the direction of attack of 41st Army was still to the east and not to the south.

The only unit of paratroopers which was directly confronted with MARS was *Oberleutnant* Herbert Lehmann's *4. Kompanie/Fallschirm Pionier Bataillon 7* (reduced by a platoon), which was subordinated to *2. Luftwaffen Felddivision*, the right neighbour of *197. Infanterie Division*, beginning on 7 November. This company saw heavy action until it returned to its division on 5 December 1942.[4]

---

1   BA-MA, RH 24-6/120 in BW 57-38: VI. AK corps order dated 22 November 1942.
2   NARA, T-312 R-310: AOK 9 KTB 6, *Führungsabteilung*, vol.3: 24 October–31 December 1942: entry of 25 November 1942.
3   NARA, T-312 R-308: AOK 9, KTB 7, *Führungsabteilung, Anlagen* IV,1. January–12 February 1943. *Erfahrungen während des russischen Großangriffes gegen den Block der 9. Armee in der Zeit vom 25.11.–16.12.1942*, dated 4 January 1943.
4   Heinz Austermann, *Von Eben Emael bis Edewechter Damm – Fallschirmjäger, Fallschirmpioniere* (Holzminden: Fallschirmpionier-Gemeinschaft, 1971), pp.112–113.

Feldwebel Germer was not alone in wondering why the front line in the area of *Fallschirmjäger Regiment 1* was so heavily manned, while the positions of the right neighbour, *197. Infanterie Division* were clearly inadequate, especially because of the difficult and unclear terrain. The soldiers were eager to do something and felt like they were being misused, as Germer noted in his diary: 'In today's *Wehrmacht* report: Russian breakthrough into the large Don salient and south-west of Stalingrad. Not good news. And we're sitting in this boring section. … Now we know that the Russians have taken the road about 30 kilometres to our right. You can hear strong detonations. Everything is quiet here.'[5]

On 28 November the war diary of *9. Armee* again recorded two reconnaissance patrols of *Fallschirmjäger Regiment 1.*[6] *Oberleutnant* Nagel,[7] a platoon leader of *3. Kompanie,* was with a group in no-man's-land from 7:30 a.m. to 10:30 a.m. They found the area north of the river Arshat up to 1,500 metres to be free of enemies. Northwest of Strynkovo along the road to Durnevo, a reconnaissance patrol of *III. Bataillon* was also on the move from 3:00 a.m. to 6:00 a.m. Two enemy bunkers were blown up and one prisoner was taken during this raid. All of these were signs that the Red Army had shifted its centre of gravity elsewhere and that attacks were unlikely. As before, *I.* and *III. Bataillon* were directly on the main defensive line, while *II. Bataillon* was dispersed in companies as a reserve behind the two others. The regimental bicycle platoon under command of *Oberleutnant* Dennerlein and the engineer platoon under command of *Leutnant* Weser were available as further regimental reserves at Verdino.[8]

A highly welcome reinforcement were the newly introduced self-propelled guns (SFL) of the *Fallschirm Panzerjäger Abteilung.*[9] During the period from 10 to 21 November, some of the anti-tank crews of *Flieger Division 7* were trained on these new devices near Divassy, between Ribshevo and Smolensk. Three platoons of three 'tractors' each were combined into the so called *SFL Kompanie* (later *6. Kompanie*) under the command of *Oberleutnant* Urban, who additionally received his own 'tractor' as command vehicle. These *Panzerjäger* Marder II (Sd.Kfz.131) were 7.5 cm anti-tank guns (Pak 40/2) mounted on a Panzer II chassis. Protected with 30 mm steel plates, the combat compartment was open at the top and rear, which exposed the crew to shrapnel.

Initially, *Leutnant* Brammer's and *Leutnant* Stain's platoons were stationed at Starina in support of *Fallschirmjäger Regiment 1.*[10] Later in February 1943, Brammer's platoon and *Oberfeldwebel* Pusch's third platoon followed the regiment to Orel.

---

5   BA-MA, BW 57-81: Entry of 25 and 26 November 1942.
6   NARA, T-312 R-307: AOK 9, KTB 6, *Anlagen III*/daily reports 11 November–31 December 1942: AOK 9 to HrGM *Zwischenmeldung*, 28 November 1942, 7:45 p.m.
7   *Oberleutnant* Karl Heinz Nagel (Bitterfeld, 16 January 1917–KIA Aleschenka, 5 March 1943).
8   Friedrich Dennerlein (Fürth, 17 July 1912–KIA Nagorniy, 19 February 1943) *Oberleutnant*. Otto Weser (Leipzig, 13 September 1914–KIA Muravchik, 20 March 1943), *Leutnant.*
9   This anti-tank unit was originally formed in 1939 as *Pak-Kompanie 7* for *Flieger-Division 7*, and later renamed in *Fallschirm Panzerjäger Abteilung* in 1940. In May 1943 the renamed *Fallschirm Panzerjäger Abteilung 1* with six companies became part of the new *1. Fallschirmjäger Division* (Information kindly provided by Ingo Apel, 16 March 2024).
10 Bruno Brammer (1918–bef.1983), *Leutnant*. In Italy he was no longer with the *Fallschirm Panzerjäger* but with *7. Kompanie/FJR 1*. Walter Stain (Prague, 27 December 1916–Mainstockheim, 3 February 2001) *Oberleutnant*. After the war he became a politician and 1954–1962 Bavarian Minister of State for Work and Social Affairs.

The platoon of *Leutnant* Stain of *6. Kompanie/ Fallschirm Panzerjäger Abteilung* receives its new Marder II self-propelled anti-tank guns. (Private Collection)

Heavy snowstorms again made it difficult for both sides to carry out their tasks ('the sentries cannot see 20 metres away'),[11] so that apart from occasional artillery fire, not much happened from 29 to the morning of 30 November. Everyone was busy shovelling snow because the trenches and foxholes were constantly being filled up with blowing snow. In the evening, the paratroopers had time to light the first candle on the Advent wreath and tell each other stories.

A little further north-east near Bely, 29 November was the most critical day on

Shovelling snow became a daily necessity for the paratroopers. (Private Collection)

---

11   BA-MA, BW 57-81: Entry 29 November 1942.

this sector of the front. Forces of the Soviet 41st Army had broken deep into the German front to the east and the reinforcements requested by Model had not yet arrived. On 30 November Germer observed that he had 'counted 120 tanks' of *19. Panzer Division* passing Starina along the road from Dukhovshchina towards Bely. He must have counted all vehicles, as the panzer regiments of *19.* and *20. Panzer Division* combined fielded about 70 tanks for the coming attack.[12]

Increased enemy activity was again observed in front of the positions of *3. Kompanie* on that same day. Terrain within sight of the paratroopers was suddenly occupied by enemy soldiers. Red Army construction crews built an improvised road through the forest north of their positions. The Soviet side probably wanted to tie up the paratroopers here as much as possible so that they could not be withdrawn to fight the incursion at Bely, or else preparations were already being made for JUPITER. Starting on 1 December, *9. Armee* was gaining the upper hand, and the Soviet 41st Army was slowly losing ground. On the 4th, Tarasov ordered his troops to go on the defensive. Locally, however, numerous tactical attacks continued.

For the paratroopers it was a time of uncertainty. The Soviet side sent more and more reconnaissance patrols, and the paratroopers were also moving around in no-man's land. A group of *Hauptmann* Zuber's *6. Kompanie* went to the area south of Vishenki on the evening of 1 December for an aggressive reconnaissance patrol.[13] The enemy must have been taken completely by surprise, because the group managed to break into the trench system without casualties, destroying two bunkers and taking four prisoners. Thirteen fallen Red Army soldiers remained behind.

Hans-Georg 'Bubi' Zuber as *Leutnant* during the first years of the war. He was promoted to *Hauptmann* on 1 August 1942 and was commander of *6. Kompanie* during the winter of 1942–1943. (Private Collection)

Hauptmann Zuber – it is not confirmed at what period exactly during this campaign he led his company – 'graduated from high school and completed classical training in the *Luftwaffe*. Trained as an observer, he becomes a *Leutnant* and volunteers for the paratroopers. We call him *"Bubi"* [boy]. He is sporty, natural, reserved. He settles difficult and unpleasant situations calmly, helped by his humour and boyish smile. In doing so, he can always act as a personal role model. He does not like Gröschke.'[14] Zuber later led *I. Bataillon/Fallschirmjäger Lehr-Regiment 21* and fought in France. After the war he joined the German *Bundeswehr* became *Generalmajor* and was from 1975–1976 *Gruppenleiter* at the *Bundeskanzleramt* under Chancellor Helmut Schmidt. He was also elected by the Military Committee of NATO as Deputy Director at the International Military Staff, Brussels.

On 2 December a particularly heavy snowstorm raged, during which a reconnaissance patrol of *7. Kompanie* as well as several of *III. Bataillon* reconnoitred east of Durnevo. Beautiful weather with sunshine followed on the 3rd. The good visibility made further reconnaissance patrols during daylight hours impossible.

---

12   Buttar, *Meat Grinder*, p.336.
13   Hans-Georg Zuber (1 November 1916–2 May 1995), *Hauptmann*; DKiG 26 October 1944.
14   Bernhard & Broder, *Guerre Mondiale*, p.24.

During the night of 4 to 5 December, another attack by *II. Bataillon* took place in dense fog at -3°C. *Leutnant* Vornberger with a platoon (28 men) of *7. Kompanie* attacked enemy positions at Hill 224.5 north of Vishenki. Vornberger had previously reconnoitred the area on 2 and 3 December. The advancing group was first spotted by a listening post 10 metres in front of the Soviet positions. As the Russian tried to run away, he was shot. The trench system was rolled up and the attackers suffered five wounded, including *Leutnant* Vornberger. One of the wounded, *Oberjäger* Mull,[15] later died in hospital.

On the same day, an aggressive reconnaissance patrol from *3. Kompanie* set out to lay an ambush on a road, which had been identified as being under construction in order to disrupt the work. However, the Soviets spotted the approaching troops and laid an ambush of their own. Neither side fell into the other's trap. So, they watched and waited for the other to move for several hours. Finally, the paratroopers returned to their positions without having achieved anything.

For *VI. Armee Korps*, *Flieger Division 7* was the best division of the corps, and also the division commander *Generalmajor* Heidrich – not surprisingly – rated his division very highly at the beginning of December, but criticized its logistical aspects:

> The already high level of training of the troops has continued to improve over the past four weeks. Morale of the soldiers is good. Particular difficulties are caused by insufficient fuel and winter equipment supplies to the division. The division is completely immobile off the main roads. Regular supply is not guaranteed everywhere when there is heavy snowfall. When providing additional winter clothing, the significant shortage of felt boots, winter hats and mittens with cuffs pose a threat to the troops' performance. The troops are undiminished in their fighting power and can be used for any task.[16]

While in reserve behind *III. Bataillon*, paratroopers of III platoon, *6. Kompanie*, set up road marker posts for the snow plough near Boldino at the end of November 1942. The platoon leader was *Oberfeldwebel* Schneider and the leader of 2nd group was *Oberjäger* Nollen. (Private Collection)

---

15 Gerhard Mull (Wilhelmsburg, 13 October 1920–Starina, 6 December 1942), *Oberjäger*.
16 BA-MA, RH 24-6/124 in BW 57-38: Situation report of *Flieger Division 7* to VI. AK.

Civilians, who as always are the hardest hit in wars, leaving their homes around Verdino, trying to get to safety. (Private Collection)

The paratroopers take a break while chatting with a driver of a much needed supply transport. (Private Collection)

11

Rearrangements

The situation at Bely had been by and large defused, the 41st Army had lost its offensive power and went over to the defensive.

But now *9. Armee*, for its part, concentrated forces around the penetrated area. *XXX. Armee Korps* planned an attack from the south towards Bely with the newly brought up *19. Panzer Division*, *20. Panzer Division* and *1. SS Kavallerie Division* to encircle the Soviet forces. On 4 December, *VI. Armee Korps* received the order that a parachute regiment should be removed from its front sector and transferred, together with an anti-aircraft and anti-tank unit, to its neighbour on the right (*XXX. Armee Korps*). This was obviously Model's idea, who at first tried to officially release a regiment 'as a reserve' in order to then deploy it to another location as quickly as possible. Heidrich wanted to keep his division together, fought back, and informed the *Luftwaffe* high command directly. In the war diary of *VI. Armee Korps* it is stated with foresight: 'According to the regulations for the deployment of the *7. Flieger Division* it can already be predicted with some probability that the AOK will not succeed with its intention.'[1] Before 4 December, *Generalleutnant* Jordan had ordered the division to transfer an anti-aircraft battery to the right section boundary of the corps to *197. Infanterie Division*.

Heidrich refused as he first had to obtain approval from the Commander-in-Chief of the *Luftwaffe* (Göring) which was not given. Jordan complained about this to *Generaloberst* Model in a letter dated 7 December 1942.[2]

As was to be expected, the plan was not approved by Hitler either, so Model had to revoke the order given on 5 December. His new plan was to instead transfer *Grenadier Regiment 347* – consisting of two battalions and belonging to *197. Infanterie Division* – to *XXX. Armee Korps*. This regiment would then be replaced by two battalions of *Fallschirmjäger Regiment 1* by moving the division boundary to the right. Despite being tactically subordinated to *Generalmajor* Boege's *197. Infanterie Division*, the two battalions were still within the section of Heidrich's division. 'This step is all the more justifiable as *7. Flieger Division* has a particularly high fighting power and on the other hand no signs of an expansion of the enemy offensive against VI. AK are to be seen.' Thus, Model issued the necessary orders at 12:45 a.m. on 5 December. The move was to take effect during the night of 6 to 7 December.[3]

Accordingly, during the night of 5 to 6 December, the individual companies of *II.* and *III. Bataillon* withdrew from the front to act as a reserve at Starina. The process was delayed, so that the withdrawal had to take place in broad daylight, albeit during a snowstorm, and was therefore noticed by a Soviet

---

1 BA-MA, RH 24-6/123: VI.A.K. KTB 3, vol.54, p. 4, entry 5 December 1942.
2 BA-MA, RH 20-9/96 in BW 57-38.
3 NARA, T-312 R-310: AOK 9 KTB 6, *Führungsabteilung*, vol.3: 24 October–31 December 1942: entry 5 December 1942, 6:10 p.m.

Generalmajor Heidrich inspects the positions at the front, December 1942. (BArch, Bild 101I-553-0836-24A/Dahm)

artillery observer. A direct artillery hit on a sledge caused the withdrawing *II. Bataillon* three seriously and three lightly wounded men. One of the former – *Jäger* Bukowitz – succumbed to the wounds in his lower leg a couple of days later.[4]

Snow drifts delayed the rapid transfer to the new areas of deployment. By the evening of 6 December, it was clear that the exchange could not take place before the night of 7 to 8 December. Model – feared for his outbursts – was visibly enraged because of this. The war diary of *VI. Armee Korps* notes diplomatically: '[Model] insists emphatically that this particularly urgent and important replacement be carried out by all means as soon as possible under the personal responsibility of the commanding general' of *VI. Armee Korps*, *Generalleutnant* Hans Jordan.[5]

Despite the snowstorm, in the early hours of 7 December Gröschke's *II. Bataillon* managed to move into its new positions at Mushitskaya and Suya thereby replacing *I. Bataillon/Grenadier Regiment 347*. Its combat train was stationed at Gridino, not far from Starina, *5. Kompanie* was now to the right of *3. Kompanie*, to the north facing west was *6. Kompanie* in two strong points, *7. Kompanie* was at Mushitskaya facing west and north. Battalion headquarters with *8. Kompanie* as reserve was in a wood to the east of *6. Kompanie* across the road to Bely. If the strongpoints were not in a village,

---

4 *Jäger* Joseph Bukowitz, born in Güssing/Austria on 25 January 1923 died at the main dressing station at Starina on 8 December 1942.
5 NARA, T-312 R-310: AOK 9 KTB 6, *Führungsabteilung*, vol.3: 24 October–31 December 1942: entry 6 December 1942, 7:20 p.m.

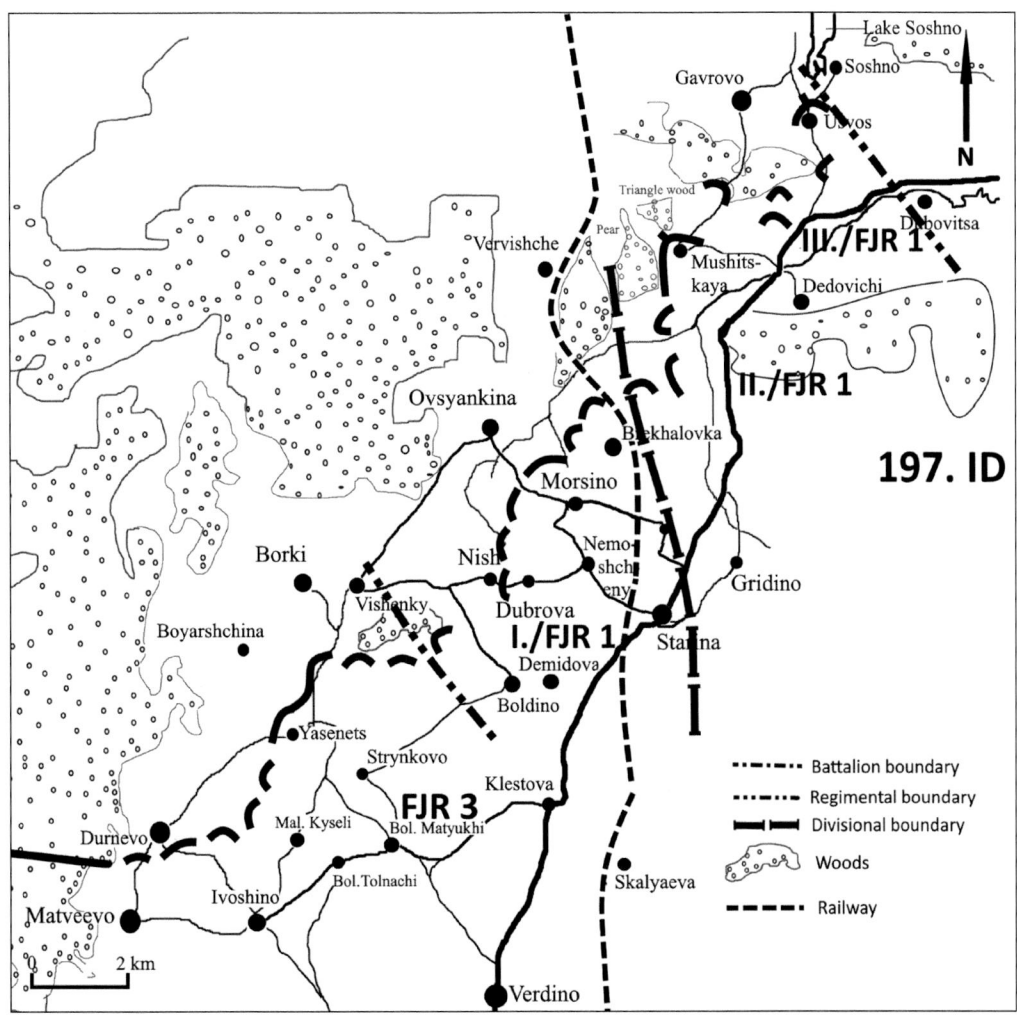

Positions of *Fallschirmjäger Regiment 1* on 8 December 1942 – *II.* and *III. Bataillon* are subordinated to *197. Infanterie Division*.

they were given names such as *Mampe* (after a liquor brand), *Wiesengrund* (meadow ground) – both 6. *Kompanie*'s – or Barok, Orchid and Tabor.

The landscape in front of the slightly elevated positions of *II. Bataillon* was rather flat, in summer it would have been swamps and wetlands, with forests to the east, called the small and large 'Pear Forest' because of their shape. The Russian positions were behind the forest at Vervishche, about two kilometres away. The forest to the north of Mushitskaya was named 'Peter's Forest'. In between was a small patch of wood called 'Triangle Forest'. These forests were the target of many reconnaissance patrols.

The self-propelled anti-tank gun platoon of *Feldwebel* (from 14 December 1942 *Leutnant*) Stain was also relocated with the battalion. On 10 December, Stain reconnoitred his new position. Doing that, he experienced first-hand just how dangerous it was behind the main line of defence:

A paratrooper in front of the position *Wiesengrund* (meadow ground) of *6. Kompanie*. In the background the treeline of the 'Pear Forest' can be seen. (Private Collection)

In the rear of *Wiesengrund* the paratroopers were living in small and well camouflaged earth bunkers. (Private Collection)

Gefreite Sierl and Lorenz of *6. Kompanie* arrive at their new position at *197. Infanterie Division,* named 'Mampe' after a famous brand of liquor, on 6 December 1942. (Private Collection)

In a large forest regiment command post. Discussed my transfer here. Continued on the road again. Strange circumstances. No continuous front line. A few more positions along the road itself. Swamp. No man's land. Strange conditions in the village further north. In the village a battalion command post, north of it a large hollow. On the other side of it the Russians. Supply traffic uninterrupted, despite in full view of the enemy. One wonders: what is actually going on with the Russians? – Back again via Selye, where we are supposed to move in … Here the commander

The transport of the few and necessary belongings of the paratroopers was mostly done with the help of sledges. (Private Collection)

did not show up, apparently, he hadn't found us. Set off on foot as darkness falls; we still had about 15 km ahead of us … Suddenly there was gunfire all around us. Muzzle flashes were clearly visible. Partisans. I fire cautiously with my MPi [submachine gun] as I only had 25 rounds and my pistol. Brammer just his pistol. Luckily a column of trucks arrived that we stopped.[6]

A gun crew of platoon Brammer setting up a false position near Verdino. (Private Collection)

---

6   Walter Stain, 'Kriegstagebuch', *Traditionsgemeinschaft Fallschirmpanzerjäger Abteilung 1*, Jahresbrief 16 (1983), pp. 93–94.

A Marder II self-propelled anti-tank gun being repaired after it slid off the road and broke its track. (Private Collection)

This group of *6. Kompanie* has built its bunker under the hut in the background. (Private Collection)

Oberleutnant Mössinger at the entrance of the command bunker of *1. Kompanie*. (Private Collection)

Becker's *III. Bataillon* was also moved to the right and relieved *II. Bataillon/Grenadier Regiment 347* during the morning of 8 December, although this process took until 5:50 p.m. Heavy snowdrifts further delayed the transport of the relieved grenadiers. The previous section of *III. Bataillon* was taken over by *Hauptmann* Kratzert's *III. Bataillon/Fallschirmjäger Regiment 3*.

The two battalions of *Grenadier Regiment 347* which had thus been released were transferred to *XXX. Armee Korps* on 9 December and were to fight the Soviet incursion at Bely. The push north of *19. Panzer Division*'s had already begun on 7 December and the pocket was closed by noon on 8 December, trapping a considerable part of 41st Army inside.[7]

Kampfgruppe Schulz – which now consisted of Gröschke's and Becker's battalions as well as the regimental staff – was tactically subordinated to *197. Infantry Division*, with Heidrich immediately trying to get his troops back under his own command. *General* Jordan however, rejected this request and left the divisional boundaries as they were.[8]

Over the next few days, the Soviet Air Force carried out bombing raids on the paratroopers' positions. The hospital bunker at Starina was hit on the 9th, killing four men, none of them from *Fallschirmjäger Regiment 1*.[9] The bunker at the command post of *3. Kompanie* also received a direct hit – luckily without further casualties. Some planes were shot down by the Germans.

The change in the sector of the *197. Infanterie Division* was observed by the Soviets, who obviously wanted to know who had now taken up these positions and sent reconnaissance patrols towards *II. Bataillon*'s section. Otherwise, the next few days were quiet in *Fallschirmjäger Regiment 1*'s sector, apart from reconnaissance patrols that continued to be carried out almost daily, some of them with surprising results. For example, a patrol of *6. Kompanie* found only abandoned positions in the 'Big Pear Forest' (*Großer Birnenwald*).[10]

---

7   Glantz, *Zhukov*, p.241.
8   BA-MA, RH 24-6/123: VI. AK, KTB 3, vol.54, p.8.
9   Müller, *Damals*, p.65.
10 BA-MA, RH 26-197/22: KTB 197. ID, Dez. 1942 (Anlagen).

12

Skirmishes before Christmas

A Soviet platoon of 45 men attacked the positions of *3. Kompanie* which also constituted the boundary between *Flieger Division 7* and *197. Infanterie Division* at 1:15 a.m. on 14 December. The raiding party attacked:

> …coming from the bottom of the stream one kilometre north-west of Brekhalovka, swinging from there to the east near the southern exit of the village, attacking the left wing of our positions. The attack was supported by artillery fire, heavy [mortar fire] and light mortars carried by the raiding party. The raiding party was repulsed by immediate countermeasures. It was destroyed in a counterattack and four prisoners were taken. Enemy casualties: 16 killed and four captured.[1] Loot: three machine guns, ten rifles, three MPi [submachine guns], one flare gun, two stretchers, hand grenades and infantry ammunition. Own casualties: three killed, two seriously and six slightly wounded. The following paratroopers distinguished themselves in fending off the attack: *Feldwebel* Timmann, *Oberjäger* Grund, *Obergefreiter* Finker and [*Oberjäger*] Wendt,[2] *Gefreite* Krahmer and Gerhardt (*3. Kompanie*) and *Obergefreite* Haug and Brendel (*14. Kompanie*).[3]

The three fallen of *3. Kompanie* were *Oberjäger* Jochade,[4] *Gefreiter* Golletz,[5] and *Gefreiter* Wolff.[6] The latter two had stepped on a mine while searching the terrain.[7]

This raiding party must also have entered Starina as Dr Müller recalls that a Soviet shock troop managed to penetrate the town after brief mortar fire. This was repulsed by the reserve of the medical company. Of these 15 men, six were wounded.[8] Two of the attackers were also wounded and taken prisoner by the Germans.

Hauptfeldwebel Willi Wagner's responsibility was to bury the fallen.

---

1 The daily report of 14 December 1942 of AOK 9 mentions 15 Soviet dead and five prisoners (NARA, T-312 R-307: AOK 9 KTB 6, *Anlagen II*. Daily reports 11 November–31 December 1942).
2 Lothar Wendt (Bitterfeld, 1 January 1917-KIA Aleshenka, 5 March 1943), *Oberjäger*.
3 BA-MA, BW 57-81: Entry 14 December 1942.
4 Gustav Jochade (Waldmühl, 14 October 1914–KIA Brekhalovka, 14 December 1942), *Oberjäger*.
5 Erwin Golletz (Schönwald, 14 April 1923–KIA Brekhalovka, 14 December 1942), *Gefreiter*.
6 Herbert Wolff (Petersdorf, 16 February 1921–KIA Brekhalovka, 14 December 1942), *Gefreiter*
7 Archive Franz: Wagner, letter dated 16 December 1942. Ancestry/WASt.
8 Müller, *Damals*, p.67. Dr Müller puts these events mistakenly on the 13th at 3:00 a.m. It must have been the same Soviet raiding party as all reports only mention an attack during the night 13 to 14 December (see NARA, T-312 R-307: AOK 9 KTB 6, *Anlagen II*. Daily reports 11 November–31 December 1942).

Village in the rear area of *Flieger Division 7*. (BDF Archive)

Today I had the sad task of burying our dead comrades. We decorated the graves with fresh pine branches. They rest here next to other comrades in a heroes' cemetery. By the way, I have seen beautiful heroes' cemeteries laid out here by the *Wehrmacht*. In the middle of the war, everything possible is done for our dead comrades. Hopefully we won't have to make a cross every day like we did on the Neva last winter. It will be a sad Christmas for their families.[9]

A reconnaissance patrol of *7. Kompanie*, sent to investigate the cause of the engine noises heard at night in the so-called 'Pear Forest' (*Birnenwald*) and 'Triangle Wood' (*Dreieckswald*), came under heavy fire on 15 December. The group of 20 men attacked enemy positions about a kilometre away from their own lines. The Soviet soldiers must have been taken completely by surprise, as only two of the paratroopers were wounded, while nine enemy dead were reported. The favourable outcome of this skirmish was due to German artillery support, which allowed the attackers to break away from the enemy. On the same day, the sentries of *3. Kompanie* could hear 'singing, commanding, celebrating Russians and the noise of tracked vehicles' coming from the direction of Ovsyankina and 'Pear Forest'.[10] The soldiers took this as an unmistakable sign that something was about to happen. Accordingly, these reconnaissance observations led the AOK 9 to the following assessment of the situation, which was relevant to the paratroopers: '…opposite VI. AK the enemy has become more restless. The 43rd Soviet Army has expanded its sector to the east. It is believed to have a total of eight large formations, of

---

9   Archive Franz: Wagner, letter dated 16 December 1942.
10 BA-MA, BW 57-81: Entry 15 December 1942.

Briefing by *Hauptmann* Zuber, commander of *6. Kompanie*, before a reconnaissance patrol. (BArch, Bild 101I-553-0838-20A/Ottmar Haas)

A MG gunner of *Fallschirmjäger Regiment 1* showing a smile for the photographer of a propaganda company. (BArch, Bild 101I-553-0831-31/Ottmar Haas)

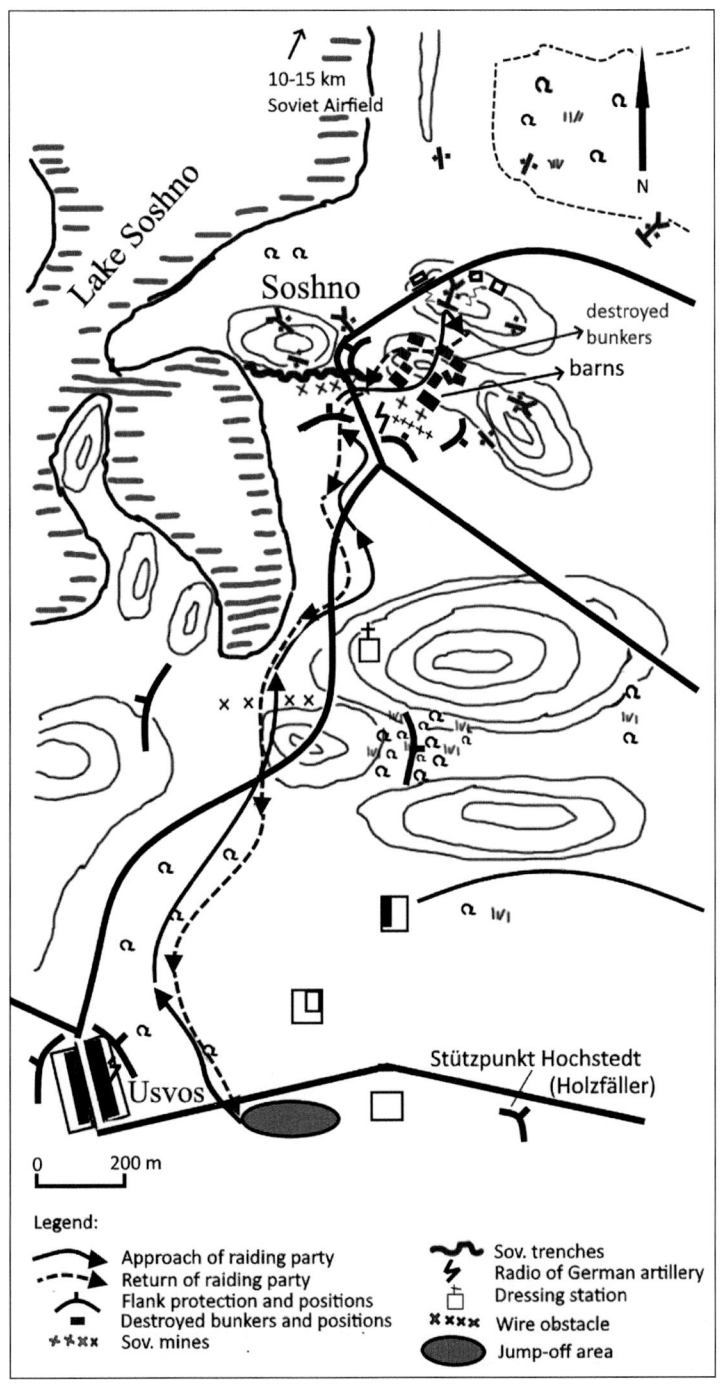

The Raid on Soshno, 15 December 1942.

which five or six are known. The possibility of stronger enemy attacks on Starina and in the direction of Demidov must be expected.'¹¹

On the same day, the last encircled and severely decimated remnants of the 41st Army managed to break out of the Bely cauldron towards their own lines, leaving behind their heavy weapons and equipment.

During the night of 15 to 16 December, a strong raiding party of *III. Bataillon* led by the commander of *12. Kompanie*, *Oberleutnant* Krause,¹² set out to attack an enemy position on the southern edge of Lake Soshno. The operation was carried out by 36 men of *12. Kompanie*, a group of regimental engineers, and 15 men from a minesweeper and flamethrower demolition squad. The task of flank protection was assigned to four groups of *10. Kompanie* (*Oberleutnant* Voges,¹³ total strength one officer and 48 men).

The Soviet positions on the southern outskirts of the village of Soshno were about one and half kilometres north of the German ones and were manned by elements of the 2nd Battalion/Rifle Regiment 1347. It took the attacking force about three hours to make the approach, wading through deep snow, negotiating a wire barrier, and crossing minefields. A group of engineers and two shock groups were able to get into the enemy trench system quietly and unnoticed by the Russians. They took out four residential bunkers and two machine gun emplacements by using flamethrowers and concentrated charges. One prisoner was brought in.

Alerted by the noise of the explosions the Russians opened fire on the intruders from the east and west with six to eight machine guns. Also, an anti-tank gun opened fire from the opposite hillside, which was 200 metres north of the point of penetration. Mortar fire from the Tymosheva area was inaccurate and landed in a hollow between the anti-tank position and the point of penetration. German artillery fire was now requested and provided. About 100 shells were fired at these positions near Tymosheva. The shells were on target after three minutes which stopped the enemy from firing. The shock groups and the engineer group continued the attack and took another three machine gun bunkers, then stormed through the hollow, took the anti-tank gun position and blew up the gun as well as another residential bunker on the northern elevation. The attack group then came under fire from a 2cm gun and mortars. A counterattack by a Soviet platoon of about 30 men towards the flank in the eastern direction was repelled. German artillery fired a barrage which enabled the group to disengage and slowly move back to their starting position where they arrived after 45 minutes, at 3:45 a.m. The attack group had destroyed 12 bunkers, one 4.7cm anti-tank gun and took two prisoners. The raiders claimed 96 enemy casualties.¹⁴ The paratroopers lost one man killed and two wounded, all from the regimental engineer platoon.¹⁵

---

11   NARA, T-312 R-307: AOK 9, KTB 6, *Anlage IV* – Army orders and instructions, vol.9, 26 November–31 December 1942: Assessment of the situation of *9. Armee* on 15 December 1942 at 10:00 p.m. (dated 17. December 1942).
12   *Oberleutnant* Alfred Oswald Krause (Klein Tuchen, 6 December 1907–KIA Gribushino, 16 January 1943), posthumously promoted to *Hauptmann*.
13   *Oberleutnant* Heinrich Voges (Hannover, 22 April 1914–Hospital Orscha, 7 February 1943). He died of his wounds received at Gribushino on 16 January 1943.
14   NARA, T-312 R-307: AOK 9 KTB 6, *Anlagen II*, daily reports 11 November–31 December 1942. BA-MA, RH 26-197/22: 197. ID, KTB Dez. 1942 (*Anlagen*), *Anlage 57*: after action report of *Kampfgruppe Schulz*, dated 17 December 1942.
15   Among them Hermann Ettl (Ramming, 18 June 1918–KIA Soshno, 16 December 1942), *Obergefreiter*; Albert Ecklhammer (Herneck, 7 November 1922–KIA Italy, 4 September 1944) *Obergefreiter*.

On that same day *Obergefreiter* Friedrich Schumacher of *3. Kompanie* was killed by friendly artillery fire while on a reconnaissance patrol.[16]

Two days later, in the early morning hours of 18 December, it was *11. Kompanie*'s turn to carry out an aggressive reconnaissance patrol. The target was the village of Gavrovo, north-east of Mushitskaya. *Gefreiter* Fricke of *10. Kompanie* also took part in this mission which led into a trap:

> An enemy outpost position was to be terminated. Our group with *Oberjäger* Schober was a tactical reserve. Was lucky again. Although the 'newcomers', like us back then, wanted to prove themselves. The opportunity should come soon. Group 8 and 9 march. First the engineers with flamethrowers and concentrated charges. We waited. Then from afar there was cracking of gunshots, detonations and then silence. From somewhere someone is yelling 'Forward shock reserve!' That's for us. *Oberjäger* Schober ahead. Then me with the MG. What's going on over there? Nothing moves, not a soul to be seen. In a row, 10 metres apart from man to man, we crept almost silently through the nearly meter-deep snow through the forest, weapons ready to fire. Then suddenly the forest seemed to breathe fire. *Oberjäger* Schober was hit. Good that the snow is so deep and gives us cover. The fir branches that have been shot down fall on us like ripe apples. I try to figure out where the fire is coming from and then my eyes get bigger and bigger. Ten steps in front of me a long ladder – no – two together. At least 25 rungs per ladder and a real big nest at the top. From up there the *Oberjäger* had been shot. Lying on my back with my MG … I shoot at the Russian sitting there. I raise my head cautiously. I can clearly see the muzzle flash from the slit of an earthen bunker 30 metres away. Then comes the command: Disengage! Now I must provide covering fire. I'm firing wildly at the earth bunker. The others can gain land [run away]. Now me, let's go. Two sets of three, left hook, right hook, hit it. Bullets rustle menacingly over my head. Everywhere they leap and jump backwards. Finally, we were out of range. Apart from our *Oberjäger*, nobody got hurt … In front of the bunker there was still the radio of the shock group. My two machine gunners volunteer to retrieve it. Of course, Fricke has to give covering fire. I wished the radio to hell. So, get back to the main line of defence. Just the three of us. Always elbowing through the deep snow, using it for cover. Now it counts. All that my '*Spritze*' [syringe] can shoot flies against the Russian bunker. The two make it. Pull the heavy equipment with them, crawling on the ground. Then my ammunition belt was empty. We rush back in big leaps. The radio operator is dead, Sepp calls out to me. We can make it. A sad bunch is going home.[17]

The patrol reported an unlikely 10–15 enemy dead, but also their own casualties of two dead, three missing and 15 wounded.[18] Among the fallen was *Oberleutnant* Jegella, the company commander of *11. Kompanie*. The operation had clearly failed, even if the reports upstairs were supposed to convey a different picture. The sober reports of *197. Infanterie Division* that day were stylised in the daily reports of the AOK 9 to 'successful reconnaissance troop operations', the enemy deaths were rounded

---

16 BA-MA, BW 57-81: Entry 16 December 1942; casualty list.
17 BA-MA, BW 57-89: Fricke, *An die Gewehre!*
18 *11. Kompanie*: *Oberleutnant* Gerhard Jegella (Wernigerode, 5 August 1914), *Oberfeldwebel* Alfred Schlimper (Oberreichenbach, 26 March 1900), *San.-Obergefreiter* Rudolf Liebelt (Siegersdorf, 3 August 1920), *Gefreiter* Hans Schäfer (Dresden, 22 April 1922); *10. Kompanie*: *Oberjäger* Valentin Schober (Üngershausen, 22 March 1919).

Reconnaissance patrol in the woods in front of the main line of defence. (BDF Archive/Dahm)

up to 100 to be on the safe side.[19] *Oberstleutnant* Schulz later visited the wounded at the dressing station. Because of the meter-deep frozen ground the graves for the dead had to be excavated with hand grenades.[20]

At the same time, a more successful operation of *1. Kompanie* was conducted towards a forest corner north of Vishenky, in which an anti-tank position with guns and a bunker were destroyed. The immediate Soviet counterattack was repulsed, with an estimated 50 to 60 enemy casualties. The paratroopers' own losses of three wounded were again extremely low in comparison.

Oberleutnant Jegella in his *11. Kompanie* command bunker with *Feldwebel* Schneider. (Private Collection)

---

19   NARA, T-312 R-307: AOK 9 KTB 6, *Anlagen II*, daily reports 11 November–31 December 1942.
20   Müller, *Damals*, p.68.

Early the next day, a reconnaissance patrol of *2. Kompanie* led by *Feldwebel* Elsner, attacked a Soviet position on the opposite side. An anti-tank gun was destroyed, and prisoners were brought in, and around 30 Soviet soldiers paid with their lives. Here, too, there were German losses: two dead,[21] two seriously and seven lightly wounded. Bad luck would have it that at the time of the attack on the Soviet side an exchange of troops was taking place, temporarily doubling the soldiers in the trench. *Feldwebel* Elsner himself received a serious wound. *Hauptfeldwebel* Willi Wagner visited him at the field hospital and was shocked.

> He always was full of life before. I would not have recognized him laying wounded in the dressing station if he hadn't called out. Then he said, 'Now I know what health is worth, you can't pay for it with millions.' He may now get the German Cross in Gold, but what's the use of that if he remains a cripple all his life?[22]

An additional paratrooper, *Gefreiter* Zehenter, who was missing and believed dead, was able to return to his own lines the next day with a prisoner and told his story to *Gefreiter* Rüdiger von Zimburg:

> When the patrol had to withdraw, Zehenter had just jumped into the Russian trench while the Russian sentry ran away in the direction of our minefields. He ran after him but thought it was one of his comrades who mistook him for a Russian. Outwardly we were indistinguishable from the Russians because we wore the same fur hats and camouflage clothes. When he reached him, he was startled to find out that it was an Asian. Since the Russian had a fairly large wound on his head, Zehenter took a bandage and dressed the wound. As a result, the Russian was so grateful that he wanted to give him a large wallet full of money. Since they were in a ditch which had not been under fire, Zehenter figured that they would wait here until evening and began negotiating with the Russian. The Russian tried to persuade him to come with him, claiming that he would be fine with them. Zehenter told him that he would be taken to a nice military hospital where he would be properly cared for. During the day the Russian fell asleep. So, he took his weapons, buried them in the snow, and then brought him back to us in the evening. He also managed to get the Russian taken to the hospital in Dukhovshchina as promised.[23]

Based on the reconnaissance results of this patrol as well as statements by prisoners and defectors, *Generalmajor* Heidrich expected 'in the Brekhalovka-Morsino-Dubrova area, perhaps also across the boundary line with the section of *197. Infanterie Division*, an enemy attack within the next few days.'[24] As a preventive measure, the *Kradschützenkompanie* of the division was moved to Starina and more alarm units with heavy weapons were sent to Boldino. *Generalmajor* Heidrich also suggested a strong attack with two battalions to the west from the Mushitskaya area and asked that 'air reconnaissance

---

21 *Obergefreiter* Heinz Hase (Berlin, 28 May [or December] 1920), *Obergefreiter* Horst Joel (Berlin-Tempelhof, 10 September 1921).
22 Archive Franz: Wagner, letter dated 30 December 1942.
23 Zimburg, *Kriegserlebnisse*, p.65.
24 BA-MA, RH 24-6/126 in BW 57-38: Telex of *Flieger Division 7* to chief of staff of VI. AK dated 19 December 1942, 2:40 p.m. BA-MA, RH 26-197/22 197. ID, KTB Dez. 1942, (*Anlagen*), no.70: statements of prisoners suggesting an attack.

be increased and to attack artillery and staging areas north of Ovsyankina'.²⁵ The attack plan was rejected as not feasible due to lack of sufficient forces and ammunition but increased aerial reconnaissance and the use of combat aircraft forces were promised by *VI. Armee Korps*.²⁶ The medical company complained 'we have no more fuel to transport the wounded.'²⁷

On 20 December there was another small-scale attack by *III. Bataillon*, this time carried out by *9. Kompanie*, on a Soviet base in a forest southwest of Usvos and south of Lake Soshno. Three bunkers were destroyed, 37 enemy dead were counted. The raiding party itself had three wounded.

On 21 December, a patrol of *6. Kompanie* unexpectedly came across a group of Red Army soldiers and got into a firefight generating 20 enemy casualties. A few days later, on 29 December 1942, *Obergefreiter* Martin Apitz was awarded the Iron Cross 2nd Class for his bravery during this skirmish.²⁸

Apitz joined the Luftwaffe in 1939 and was transferred to *Fallschirmjäger Regiment 1* in 1942 where he joined *6. Kompanie*. After the winter campaign 1942–1943, which he survived unscathed, he participated with his battalion in the Italian campaign and fought at Ortona and Cassino, where he was wounded on 13 February 1944. Having returned to his unit in June – now decorated with the Iron Cross 1st Class – he fought in September 1944 at the Gothic Line where he was wounded again on 3 September 1944. He entered British captivity in Schleswig on 14 May 1945.

Martin Apitz as *Oberjäger*. (BDF Archive)

Two proud recipients, *Gefreiter* Langhans, and *Gefreiter* Apitz of *6. Kompanie*, showing off their first award, the Iron Cross 2nd Class on 29 December 1942. (Private Collection)

---

25 BA-MA, RH 24-6/126 in BW 57-38: Telex of *Flieger Division 7* to chief of staff of VI. AK dated 19 December 1942, 2:40 p.m.
26 BA-MA, RH 24-6/126 in BW 57-38: telex of Ia of VI.AK to *Flieger Division 7* dated 19 December 1942, 9:15 p.m.
27 Müller, *Damals*, p.68.
28 BA-MA, BW 57-84: Awarded on 29 December 1942 (Award certificate).

13

Christmas and New Year

General Jordan of *VI. Armee Korps* still expected 'an attack on the corps' front unconcerned considering the strength of its own defence.'[1] But nothing happened. The divisional commander, *Generalmajor* Heidrich, was aware of the relative peace and gave his paratroopers the opportunity to go on leave. As *Hauptfeldwebel* Wagner noted: 'Each month eight men of our company get 20 days of leave counting from reaching the border of the *Reich*. In France it was only four men.'[2] For Wagner it was not possible to go home and visit his wife and new-born son. 'I cannot leave. Who else would be doing all the work here?'

The next few days passed largely peacefully, allowing the soldiers to celebrate Christmas in their bunkers. Heidrich, as well as *Oberstleutnant* Schulz and the battalion and company commanders, used the somewhat quieter time to visit the forward positions. The soldiers had decorated their bunkers for Christmas. Recognitions for bravery such as the Iron Cross 2nd Class were awarded on this occasion (for example to *Feldwebel* Voigt of *7. Kompanie*) but also Christmas presents were handed out by the company '*Spieß*'.

Hauptfeldwebel Wagner wrote to his wife about his Christmas duties: '

> Some comrades in my company didn't receive a package for Christmas from home because they are without parents. Making them happy was the most beautiful and greatest joy of Christmas for me. Some comrades received a parcel from the *Führer* as a Christmas present. But it wasn't enough for everyone. So, I made some Christmas parcels for those on behalf of the company. Lots of good stuff, cigarettes and a big sausage were in the packages. Then I put a pine branch and a warm Christmas greeting from Santa Claus of the Eastern Front on top. It was a greeting from home. I then put these parcels in the large mailbag that came late with the field post on Christmas Eve. With that we drove on Christmas Eve by sledge through the beautiful Christmas landscape to the positions. Almost everyone got a parcel, and we were very happy that we came with this mail on Christmas Eve. For many it was the long-awaited Christmas parcel that was only to be opened on Christmas Eve. I distributed all the presents myself, went from bunker to bunker and wished everyone a Merry Christmas. Then I went to the foremost posts, where they keep watch for Germany close to the enemy. Again, I shook hands with everyone and wished them a Merry Christmas … This walk through the positions and bunkers lasted until 4:00 a.m … Yes, honey, that was the best Christmas I've ever had.[3]

---

1 BA-MA, RH 24-6/125: VI. A.K. KTB 3, vol.55, p.5, entry 22 December 1942.
2 Archive Franz: Wagner, letter dated 28 December 1942.
3 Archive Franz: Wagner, letter dated 25 December 1942.

Oberstleutnant Schulz decorates several paratroopers with the Iron Cross 2nd Class around Christmas 1942. (BArch, Bild 101I-552-802-39/Dahm and Bild 101I-552-0802-34/Dahm)

The crew of the self-propelled anti-tank guns were able to celebrate Christmas in proper bunkers, while other paratroopers closer to the frontline had to make do with smaller earthen shelters. From left to right: *Obergefreiter* Ott, *Gefreiter* Weigt, *Gefreiter* (?) Meiser, *Obergefreiter* Uhlworm, *Oberjäger* Haller, all of *Oberleutnant* Hofmann's platoon. (Private Collection)

The memories of this Christmas are important to many. For Walter Fricke of *10. Kompanie* it was also 'one of the most beautiful war Christmases.'

> Willi Burian, an officer cadet, had already prepared for this feast in Germany with tremendous foresight and made it quite an experience for me [Fricke]. His mother was his ally. Starting with a white tablecloth on our bulky bunker table, to fresh coffee, to our own verses and gifts. Our 'old man' *Oberleutnant* Brügel was so impressed that he stayed in our bunker for almost two hours.[4]

Gefreiter von Zimburg of *2. Kompanie* could

> … hardly imagine a more spiritual Christmas … Later, lying on my bunk, I started to open my presents and then found all the good things. One of these parcels also contained wonderful, lined leather mittens that my father had brought home from Russia during World War I … Then I did my sentry duty and inaugurated the mittens. The night was so bright and the mittens so warm and everything was so peaceful that it was hard to believe there was a war going on.[5]

Preparations were also going on at *3. Kompanie* and *Feldwebel* Germer recalls:

> We decorated the tree with eleven candles and tinsel, and we attached pinecones with wire on the branches. In every bunker the people were devoutly trying to take care of the Christmas tree. One built candle holders, another decorated the tree, and yet another arranged the plates. Everyone was a big kid again and put their heart and soul into it. Just like at home … Afterwards there was mulled wine with a dash of rum and spiced with cloves. The table was suddenly full of cakes and pastries. Everyone had saved something … Lots of cookies and candies, biscuits and a pair of suspenders [had arrived from home]. I had one package from my parents and G. The joy was great!

---

4   BA-MA, BW 57-89: Fricke, *An die Gewehre!*
5   Zimburg, *Erinnerungen*, p.66.

But everywhere the same questions were asked: '*Oberjäger*, will he [the enemy] attack today? If he just leaves us alone today. Otherwise, he will be in a lot of trouble!'[6]

The fact that the two battalions of Schulz' regiment were not within the full command of *Flieger Division 7* but 'on loan' elsewhere was not appreciated at the highest levels of command and pressure was exerted on *Heeresgruppe Mitte*, which in turn was forwarded to AOK 9. Without a doubt this was a result of Heidrich's complaints to his superior *Luftwaffe* commands as he wanted the whole division under his command. The subject was discussed in a meeting between Model and Jordan in the presence of Heidrich and Boege on 23 December. The units intended to replace them, *Grenadier Regiment 347* and *I. Bataillon/Grenadier Regiment 321*, were not yet strong enough. On 20 December *I.* and *II. Bataillon/Grenadier Regiment 321* had a total combatant strength of 486 men, while *I.* and *II. Bataillon/Grenadier Regiment 347* could muster only 146 men. For comparison, the average battalion size of the paratroopers was about 600 men.[7] The relief of the paratroopers was therefore made dependent on the arrival of sufficient replacements.[8]

Seven days later Becker's battalion (combatant strength 562 men) was finally replaced by *I. Bataillon/Grenadier Regiment 321* (combatant strength 289 men) without disruption and was transferred back to the division. Gröschke's *II. Bataillon* had to remain in the sector of *197. Infanterie Division* for the time being.

On New Year's Eve a wounded paratrooper of *5. Kompanie* suddenly appeared in front of the positions of *3. Kompanie* at Brekhalovka. He reported that seven men from a reconnaissance patrol had been surrounded by a Soviet scouting party near the destroyed railway bridge north of their positions. *Oberleutnant* Nagel immediately advanced with two groups but was only able to rescue three survivors. The area was searched until evening for the four missing and severely wounded men by a platoon of *5. Kompanie*. During this process a firefight ensued with a Russian reconnaissance patrol of 30 men. The fallen or seriously wounded paratroopers were obviously extracted by the enemy. At least three of them died shortly afterwards.

On New Year's Day at midnight, the artillery, mortars and machine guns as well as other infantry weapons fired a five-minute long surprise fire towards the enemy positions and into the air. This received a similar response from the opposite side and there were casualties. Dr Müller, newly promoted to *Oberarzt*,[9] noted: 'We have three wounded to take care of. A gut shot dies. A bad start into the New Year.'[10]

This 'New Year's Eve Fireworks' was quite a sight as *Hauptfeldwebel* Wagner wrote to his wife that he had never seen anything like it before: 'All weapons that were at hand fired tracer ammunition from all barrels, so that the projectiles were flying towards the Russians like glowing threads. In between, white flares went up all along the front so that it was as bright as daylight. It was a terrific picture like I have never seen or experienced before.'[11]

Heidrich summed up the status of his division at the turn to the New Year:

---

6   BA-MA, BW 57-81: Entry 24 December 1942.
7   NARA, T-312 R-307: AOK 9, KTB 6, *Anlage IV* – Army orders and instructions, vol.9, 26 November–31 December 1942, combatant strengths on 20 December; dated 21 December 1942.
8   BA-MA, RH 20-9/106 in BW 57-38.
9   Müller learned of his promotion per 1 November on 17 December 1942. Müller, *Damals*, p.68.
10   Müller, *Damals*, p.71.
11   Archive Franz: Wagner, letter dated 1 January 1943.

Meeting at the headquarter of *9. Armee* on 23 December 1942 (left to right): *Generalmajor* Ehrenfried Oskar Boege (197. ID), *Generaloberst* Walter Model (*9. Armee*), *Generalleutnant* Hans Jordan (VI. AK), *Generalmajor* Richard Heidrich (FlDiv 7). (BDF Archiv)

Remembrance card of *Gefreiter* Hans Edmeier of *4. Kompanie*. Born on 31 May 1921 in Niederalteich, Bavaria, he was seriously wounded in the legs and thighs by shrapnel from an artillery shell on his bunker at Morsino on 28 December 1942. He was taken to the dressing station at Starina, where his death could only be confirmed. (Private Collection)

The commander of *I. Bataillon*, *Major* Graf von der Schulenburg and his regimental commander *Oberstleutnant* Schulz, December 1942. (BArch, Bild 101I-553-0826-10A/Dahm)

The training level of the troops is constantly improving. The replacements, which are weak in terms of numbers and training, is not yet of benefit to the troops because … they must first be made ready for action. As a result, the occupation of the main line of defence is sometimes very thin. With the withdrawal of a heavy anti-aircraft detachment with three heavy and two light batteries, the anti-tank defences, especially on the right wing of the division, have been considerably weakened, and gaps that have arisen have to be gradually closed by increased use of mines … Morale of the troops is high. The deficiencies reported in the previous month regarding supply of winter equipment and additional winter clothing, in particular felt boots, have not yet been remedied … The troops are fully ready for any task that is within their limited mobility.[12]

The division's shock troop experiences were reported by Heidrich to his superiors. The paratroopers had learned to respect the Soviet soldiers: 'Russian defends himself to the last man. Cannot be captured … Russian himself very agile in the terrain and cautious. Never uses the same tracks, dumps, observation posts, etc. Uses mines a lot. Difficult to surprise lately, because extremely attentive.'[13] Particular attention should be paid to the detailed preparation and the correct composition of the shock groups, he suggested, and during implementation, care should be taken to strictly stick to the plan and to break off operations immediately when it becomes obvious that surprise is no longer possible.

The new year began as the old one had ended – with reconnaissance patrols from both sides and occasional artillery fire. On 2 January, a reconnaissance patrol of *3. Kompanie* was able to determine

---

12 BA-MA, RH 24-6/128, p.206 in BW 57-39.
13 BA-MA, RH 24-6/128 in BW 57-39: Telex of *Flieger Division 7*, Ia, to VI. AK dated 2 January 1943.

that the Soviet side was preparing for defence, so no further attacks from that side were to be expected in the near future. One reason was the fighting at Velikiye Luki, which was under attack by the Soviet 3rd Shock Army. There, the German side also threw the last reserves into battle to relieve those trapped within the city.[14]

Thus AOK 9 received orders from *Heeresgruppe Mitte* to release forces from its area of command so that they could be sent to the Velikiye Luki area. At the same time, Model wanted to intervene again in *Flieger Division 7*'s area of command, which provoked reactions from *Oberkommando des Heeres*: On 8 January, it was 'again pointed out with particular emphasis that subordinating any parts of *7. Flieger Division* among army formations remains strictly forbidden.'[15] But only two days later the situation had changed:

> The conspicuous enemy movements of the last days in front of VI. AK do not appear to be confirmed as preparations for an attack because, according to the latest documents, the enemy deployed the 32nd Rifle Division and 78th Tank Brigade to 3rd Shock Army at Velikiye Luki … On the orders of *Heeresgruppe Mitte*, prepare one battalion of *7. Flieger Division* for immediate use at Vel. Luki.[16]

The next day, 11 January 1943, *III. Bataillon* was transported to Velikiye Luki.

Cold days were to come, it had already reached -15°C.

---

14 BA-MH, RH 26-197/25: 197. ID, KTB, *Anlagen* January 1943, no.12.
15 CAMO, 500_12454, file 632: Telex of Ia of *Heeresgruppe Mitte* to AOK 9.
16 NARA, T-312 R-317: AOK 9, KTB 7, Ia, 1 January–25 March 1943, entry 10 January 1943.

14

III. Bataillon at Velikiye Luki

The Development of the Situation Around Velikiye Luki

As already mentioned, the Kalinin Front had to perform two thrusts within the framework of operation MARS. One – the main thrust – was aimed against the northern and eastern flanks of the Rzhev salient held by *9. Armee*, while a second of the Soviet 3rd Shock Army – reinforced by parts of the 41st and 43rd Army – was directed at Velikiye Luki. The city was an important railway crossing near the boundary between *Heeresgruppe Nord* and *Mitte*. Defending was *LIX. Armee Korps* or *Gruppe von der Chevallerie*,[1] which stood under direct command of *Heeresgruppe Mitte*. The offensive in that sector had more the character of a supporting measure with the limited aim of taking Velikiye Luki and Novosokolniky, as did the concurrent offensive of the North-Western Front against Demyansk.[2] *Heeresgruppe Mitte* had not expected such a strong push in a remote region, which consequently was occupied only by weak German forces. The situation did not change even as the assessment of the intelligence branch *Fremde Heere Ost* of 6 November 1942 became known, which stated that a Soviet thrust 'most probably with weak forces toward Velikiye Luki' was assumed.[3] The Soviet offensive began here on 24 November 1942 and by the 26th Velikiye Luki was surrounded. As in the case of Stalingrad, Hitler forbade a timely withdrawal or breakout of forces against the advice of all responsible military commanders.[4]

From then on, *Heeresgruppe Mitte* tried to relieve the trapped parts of *83. Infanterie Division*. This surrounded battle group consisted of *Grenadier Regiment 277* under *Oberstleutnant* von Sass,[5] as well as various supply troops normally active in the rear of the front – a total of around 7,000 men. The relief effort was assigned to *Gruppe von der Chevallerie*. Desperately needed and promised reinforcements like *12. Panzer Division* were directed away at the last moment to fight the incursion at Bely. *General* von der Chevallerie thus did not have sufficient resources, and it was not surprising that he was not able to achieve anything by mid-December. As *9. Armee* had been able to fend off MARS in

---

1 Kurt von der Chevallerie (Berlin, 23 December 1891–KIA Kolberg, 18 April 1945), *General der Infanterie*; RK 23 October 1941, Oak Leaves 19 December 1943 (357). He commanded LIX. AK from 28 December 1941 until 5 February 1944. Formally being retired on 31 January 1945 he went missing at Kolberg and was presumably killed. See Mark C. Yerger, Leslie Fiorenza, *Honoring those they led – Decorated Field Commanders of the Third Reich: Command Authorities, Award Parameters, and Ranks* (Solihull: Helion, 2016), p.93.
2 Robert Forczyk, *Velikiye Luki – The Doomed Fortress 1942–43* (Oxford: Osprey 2020), p.12.
3 CAMO, 500_12451, file 335.
4 Schramm (ed.), *Kriegstagebuch 1942*, part 2, p.793.
5 Eduard Freiherr (Baron) von Sass (Berlin, 11 September 1900–executed Velikiye Luki, 16 January 1946) *Oberst*; RK 19 December 1942.

the meantime, further reinforcements could now be brought forward for a renewed relief attempt. *Generalfeldmarschall* von Kluge, the commander of *Heeresgruppe Mitte*, sent his Chief of Staff, *Generalleutnant* Otto Wöhler,[6] on 13 December to lead a combined assault group consisting of *83. Infanterie Division, 291. Infanterie Division* and parts of *20. Infanterie Division (mot.)*. He was assigned to *Gruppe von der Chevallerie* and arrived at his command post in Lobno on 15 December to organise the relief attack on Velikiye Luki.

While Wöhler's relief attempt made no progress either, the situation in Velikiye Luki became more and more precarious. The number of casualties increased, and the ammunition situation became more and more desperate. Due to the heavy use of air transport capacity for the supply of Stalingrad and the bad weather, the trapped units were inadequately supplied from the air. From 27 December 1942, '*Luftwaffe Gefechtsverband Wilke*' was formed under *Oberst* Wilke, commander of *Kampfgeschwader 53*. The group consisted of the cargo glider squadron DFS-VK(S) V with six Heinkel He 111 bomber aircraft and 15 Gotha Go 242 gliders, as well as *Kampfgeschwader 4* and *53*.[7]

Generalleutnant Wöhler at a meeting in Romania April 1944. (BArch, Bild 183-2007-0313-500/Mittelstaedt, Heinz/CC-BY-SA 3.0)

This is where the idea of using paratroopers came up for the first time. On 16 December, at the instigation of the *Luftwaffenkommando Ost*, *Unteroffizier* Lorenz from a Go 242 glider squadron was parachuted out of an He 111 over Velikiye Luki, to prepare a landing strip for the gliders. One glider was able to land the next day. Lorenz remained the only soldier who parachuted into Velikiye Luki. *Heeresgruppe Mitte*'s request for the deployment of paratroopers was denied by *Luftwaffenkommando Ost* on 18 December 1942:

> 7. Flieger Division not equipped for parachuting. Until arrival of one full battalion from home, about 6–8 days needed. One battalion needs 53 special [Junkers] Ju [52] with bottom hatch. Only one available here. If deployment is necessary, it is most expedient to request a ready formation from home via OKH. Implementation very difficult due to enemy defence and narrowness of landing area.[8]

On 18 December, with 5,707 men still fighting in Velikiye Luki, the trapped group had already suffered casualties of 19 officers and 1,279 NCOs and men since 25 November. The relief operation of the 9,000 men strong *Gruppe Wöhler* was not advancing fast enough,[9] and a breakout of the encircled

---

6   Otto Wöhler (Großburgwedel, 12 July 1894–ibid., 5 February 1987), *General der Infanterie*; RK 14 August 1943, Oak Leaves 28 November 1944 (671), DKiG 26 January 1942. He was convicted of war crimes at the Nürnberg tribunals and released 1951.
7   For details see Georg Schlaug, *Die Deutschen Lastenseglerverbände 1937–1945 – Eine Chronik aus Berichten und Tagebüchern* (Stuttgart: MotorBuch, 1985), pp.90–99, 271.
8   CAMO, 500_12454, file 653: Heeresgruppe Mitte (ed.), *Der Kampf um Welikije Luki vom 24 November 1942–16 January 1943* (Heeresgruppe Mitte, 1943), p.27.
9   On 19 December 1943 *Gruppe Wöhler* was composed among others of the following formations: 291. ID (GrenRgt 506, 505, 504), 20. ID (mot.) (GrenRgt 76, 90), 83. ID (GJRgt. 138, G.Rgt. 251), parts of *3. Gebirgs*

group and thus the abandonment of the city – which was certainly still possible at that time – was again expressly forbidden by Hitler on the 19th. On the same day he made the same fateful decision for Stalingrad. In both cases, he would have allowed it only if the city could stay in German hands. On the next day, 20 December, von Sass considered such a partial breakout to be impossible:

> I respectfully request that the order given yesterday for a breakout be rescinded. After a thorough examination of the overall situation, the execution of the order is impossible because of the large number of casualties, the loss of heavy weapons and lack of ammunition. The order to defend the city could no longer be carried out because the Russians are attacking non-stop.[10]

The situation for the trapped *Gruppe von Sass* became more difficult by the day. Repeated pleas from *Heeresgruppe Mitte* to Hitler for freedom of action or permission to break out fell on deaf ears. Thus, rescue was becoming increasingly unlikely. *Oberstleutnant* von Sass repeatedly requested reinforcement by paratroopers, as on 30 December: 'If two paratrooper companies with all their weapons and flamethrowers [could be dropped] tonight, then further holding possible.'[11] An impractical idea, born out of desperation. The necessary equipment was not available because it was in Germany. Even if it had been, it would not have been of much help in this situation and would hardly have contributed to changing the situation.

Air supply was only possible to a limited extent; many of the supplies dropped by He 111 bombers of the *Gefechtsverband Wilke* were destroyed on impact or landed on enemy positions. Infrequent supply by cargo gliders was still possible. These were used to transport supplies of ammunition, food, etc., but also occasionally soldiers. After the first glider landed on 17 December, a total of nine gliders were able to land on 29 and 30 December, and another three on 6 January; later attempts were mostly unsuccessful. On 4 January an attempt failed, and on 6 January three gliders attempted to land of which one crashed. On the 7th another attempt failed, and one glider was shot down. All in all, 25 cargo gliders were deployed of which six abandoned their attempt during approach and two were shot down. The 17 which did land brought much needed supplies and ammunition, as well as 74 soldiers and 30 glider crew.[12] Most of them perished.

The fighting strength and number of soldiers who could still be deployed in the garrison of Velikiye Luki began to dwindle. On 30 December, the garrison still had a combatant strength of 2,098 men. From that day on, the majority of von Sass's group lay trapped in the eastern part of the city separated from about 500 men who were still in the citadel on the western edge of the city.

Generalleutnant Wöhler prepared another relief attack, operation TOTILA, which was launched on 4 January 1943. However, the arrival of the necessary reinforcements was delayed. Only a third of *205.* and *331. Infanterie Division* were at his disposal on that day, but due to the urgency of the situation the attack was launched despite the most adverse circumstances. Wöhler could only advance slowly, pushing forward a narrow thumb-shaped 'tube' towards Velikiye Luki. On 6 January,

---

Division, *Jäger-Bataillone 1* and *3*, *Sicherungs-Bataillon 343* and *Pionier-Bataillon 743* a.o.. The total strength on 18 December was 9,042 men. CAMO, 500_12454, file 653: Heeresgruppe Mitte (ed.), *Welikije Luki*, p.28.
10   CAMO, 500_12454, file 653: Heeresgruppe Mitte (ed.), *Welikije Luki*, p.31–32.
11   CAMO, 500_12454, file 653: Heeresgruppe Mitte (ed.), *Welikije Luki*, p.47: Radio message 30 December 1942 at 8.34 a.m.
12   Schlaug, *Lastenseglerverbände*, pp.99, 271; CAMO, 500_12454, file 653: Heeresgruppe Mitte (ed.), *Welikije Luki*, appendix 4; BA-MA, BW 57-82: Order of the day, *Luftwaffenkommando Ost*, dated 22 January 1943.

Generalfeldmarschall von Kluge ordered two more battalions, one from *205. Infanterie Division* and *8. Jägerbataillon*, to reinforce *Gruppe Wöhler*. Meanwhile the combatant strength of individual battalions had already dropped dramatically to between 60 and 100 men in this short time![13]

On 8 January, *Generalfeldmarschall* von Kluge again applied to the *Oberkommando des Heeres* for the deployment of a paratrooper battalion.

The next day, 9 January, von Kluge personally visited Wöhler and von der Chevallerie, which shows the importance of this attempt to relieve the garrison and also how bad the reserve situation of the *Heeresgruppe* was. A combat group of 83 men from *Jägerbataillon 5*, supported by nine tanks under the command of *Major* Tribukait,[14] reached the isolated citadel in a surprise attack, which was defended by the smaller part of the encircled forces. However, Tribukait's initial success was short-lived; the open corridor could not be held because there were not enough troops available to secure it. Tribukait, himself short of fuel for his vehicles to break out and return, was now trapped in the citadel as well. His tanks and armoured vehicles were quickly rendered useless by Soviet artillery fire. Tribukait's mission was highly risky and ill-conceived – a failure that cost precious resources, but earned him the Knight's Cross. After all, he acted on the direct orders from von Kluge.

On 10 January, Hitler finally, and far too late, gave permission to withdraw the remnants of the besieged city, thus abandoning it. At 4:50 a.m. on the 11th, *Heeresgruppe Mitte* finally received permission to send a battalion of *Flieger Division 7* to Velikiye Luki.[15] By this time, operation TOTILA, the relief of Velikiye Luki by *Gruppe Wöhler*, had already failed and the deployment of the battalion was pointless.[16]

Becker's Men Arrive

III. Bataillon, which was at rest in the area of Boldino, southwest of Starina, was alerted at 1:15 a.m. on 11 January.[17] This happened several hours before the authorisation was received by *Heeresgruppe Mitte* at 4:50 a.m.,[18] which suggests that the *Oberkommando der Luftwaffe* had informed the paratroopers faster than was the case via the army communication channels. The general command of *VI. Armee Korps* was only informed of the battalion's departure.[19] The commander of *III. Bataillon*, *Hauptmann* Karl-Heinz Becker, was flown in advance by a Fieseler Storch at 11:30 a.m. from Starina to his divisional commander *Generalmajor* Heidrich in Ribshevo, who, together with his First General Staff Officer (Ia), *Oberstleutnant* Trettner,[20] briefed Becker on the mission at Velikiye

---

13 CAMO, 500_12454, file 653: Heeresgruppe Mitte (ed.), *Welikije Luki*, p.57: Combatant strength of individual battalions of *Gruppe Wöhler* on the eve of 6 January after deploying all reserves available: 331. ID: I./GrRgt 559 (abt. 60 men); I./GrRgt 558 (abt. 120 men); II./GrRgt 558 (abt. 100 men); 291. ID: I./GrRgt 505 (abt. 60 men).
14 Günther Tribukait (Greifswald, 29 May 1909–executed Yugoslavia, 26 February 1947), *Oberst;* RK 8 February 1943. He was convicted of war crimes in Yugoslavia and received the death penalty.
15 CAMO, 500_12454, file 633.
16 Forczyk, *Velikiye Luki*, p.81.
17 BA-MA, RH 24-59/53 in BW 57-82: After-action report Becker.
18 CAMO, 500_12454, file 633.
19 BA-MA, RH 24-6/128, war diary of VI. Armee Korps, entry 11 January 1943.
20 Heinrich Trettner (Minden, 19 September 1907–Mönchengladbach, 18 September 2006), *Generalleutnant;* RK 24 May 1940, Oak Leaves 17 September 1944. In 1943 commander of the *4. Fallschirmjäger Division* in Italy, 1964–1966 *Generalinspekteur* of the German *Bundeswehr*.

Luki and the subordination of his battalion to *Gruppe Wöhler*. Shortly afterwards, Becker flew on to Opuchliki, where he arrived at around 2:30 p.m. and was briefed by *General* von der Chevallerie. On the one hand, the battalion was to be deployed for the relief of Velikiye Luki, on the other hand for screening the Lobno–Belodedovo area of the 'tube', the now finger shaped front line towards the encircled city.

The battalion, which had a strength of 516 men on 10 January, had in the meantime been reinforced by a group or even half a platoon of the regiment's engineer platoon,[21] one platoon of *14. Kompanie/ Fallschirmjäger Regiment 5*, but – according to the casualty lists – also an unspecified number of individual paratroopers of *6., 8., 14., 16.* and *17. Kompanie* of *Fallschirmjäger Regiment 3* were present.[22] It also seems that volunteers from the divisional staff troops came along as at least one of them got wounded. The departure was delayed due to bad weather conditions, which slowed down the arrival of the transport vehicles. The battalion was ready to depart at 7:30 a.m., the first vehicles arrived as early as 8:30 a.m., but the last ones not until 2:00 p.m., so the whole column could not start to move until 3:00 p.m.[23] The column travelled through the night starting from Starina via Yartsevo-Smolensk-Rudnya-Vitebsk-Nevel to Opuchliki, where the men arrived in groups from 11:15 a.m. onwards, 'frozen to ice lumps'.[24] The companies took up quarters in the vicinity: Staff and signal platoon in Smyki, *11. Kompanie* in Urybkova, *10.* and *12. Kompanie in* Shutova, *9.* and the platoon of *14. Kompanie* in Spasbalasdyn.

III. Bataillon on the way to Velikiye Luki, in the centre is *Oberleutnant* Horbach, the commander of *11. Kompanie*. (Private Collection)

---

21 The casualty lists show four fallen engineers and three wounded paratroopers of the regimental staff, who were most probably also members of the engineer platoon.
22 The casualty lists prove that members of FJR 3 as well as *14. Kompanie*/FJR 5 were present at Velikiye Luki.
23 *Flieger Division 7* reported obviously falsely on 11 January that the battalion had left at 11:00 a.m. BA-MA, RH 24-6/128, p.92 in BW 57-39.
24 BA-MA, BW 57-89: Fricke, *An die Gewehre!*

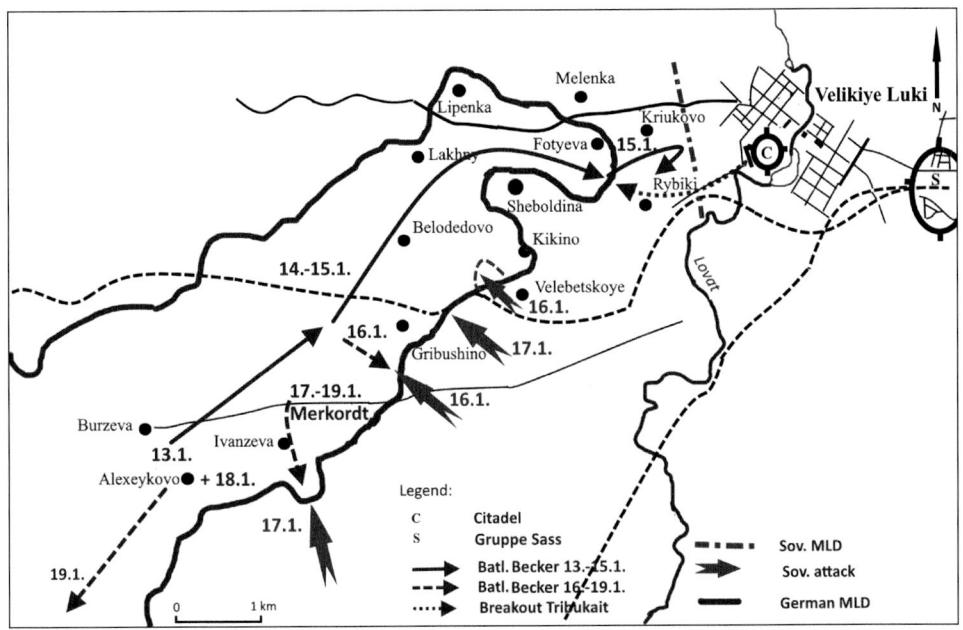

III. Bataillon at Velikiye Luki, 13–19 January 1943.

On the morning of the next day, 13 January, the battalion was transferred to Alexeykovo (arrival 1:50 p.m.) and subordinated under *205. Infanterie Division* under *Generalmajor* Seyffardt.[25] Becker had previously travelled ahead with his company commanders to *Generalleutnant* Wöhler in Lobno, but he referred them to this division. At 12 noon, the officers reported to Seyffardt, who first briefed them and later informed them at about 5:30 p.m. that it would not be possible to deploy on the same day. Becker's battalion remained in the bivouac near Alexeykovo, where it came under Soviet artillery fire and suffered its first casualties (five men wounded). The soldiers were miserably cold:

> No foxholes, no bunkers, we tried to warm ourselves up. We had a stove on our truck, but no wood. So we had to get wood. But all around us there was only snow and more snow. But back there, there are *Nebelwerfer* cannons, and next to them wooden boxes, ammunition boxes. Are they empty? We are lucky and the stealing is successful. We were now sitting tightly packed on the truck and everyone was trying to catch some warmth.[26]

In the meantime, *Gruppe Wöhler* had pushed the 'tube' relatively close to the city, as far as Fotyeva,[27] and – as wrongly assumed by Wöhler – Rybiki, to within a kilometre of the citadel. This was a thin

---

25 Paul Seyffardt (Weilburg/Lahn, 4 March 1894–unknown, 20 September 1979) *Generalleutnant*, RK 10 January 1942, DKiG 18 October 1941. He commanded *205. Infanterie Division* from 1 March 1942 until 5 November 1943 and went into Allied captivity as commander of *348. Infanterie Division* in Belgium in 1944.
26 BA-MA, BW 57-89: Fricke, *An die Gewehre!*
27 In German maps and sources, the village is also called 'Fotnewa' or 'Fotijewa.'

A paratrooper in the coverless terrain around Velikiye Luki. (BArch, Bild 183-J21628/Ottmar Haas)

finger trying to touch the city with its tip, a much too narrow tube in which the soldiers were defenceless against enemy artillery. The Soviet heavy artillery could fire into the uncovered area, ranging from one to three kilometres wide, without having to fear any significant return fire. The attack wedge was simply too narrow, as *General* Seyffart later correctly noted in a field report.[28]

For the night of the 14th to the 15th, a relief attack on the citadel and on the eastern part of the city was initially planned, which *III. Bataillon* was intended to carry out. At 10:45 a.m. the battalion received orders to advance to the railway line south of Belodedovo, where it arrived at 5:30 p.m. and bivouacked there. After the officers had been briefed on the planned attack by *Oberstleutnant* Schönberger, commander of *Grenadier Regiment 353* (205. ID), and after the paratroopers prepared to depart at 10:00 p.m., the attack was called off at 10:15 p.m., as it had not been approved from 'above'. So, the battalion remained on the spot, entirely out in the open in significant sub-zero temperatures.

At a meeting at 4:00 p.m. on 14 January between the generals von Kluge, Wöhler and von der Chevallerie, the latter assessed the situation to the effect that an advance along the road, as demonstrated by *Major* Tribukait, and a clearing and shielding of a pathway which could be used by motor vehicles was no longer possible because of the strong Soviet defence.

> According to the unanimous opinion of GFM v. Kluge, *General* von der Chevallerie and *General* Wöhler, a continuation of the attack in the direction of the citadel during the night of 15 January does not promise success since the troops at the head of the attack are almost completely exhausted. The enemy has concentrated a semicircle around the top of the attack wedge and is

---

28   CAMO, 500_12454, file 663: report of *205. Infanterie Division* about the fighting south-west of Velikiye Luki, dated 24 January 1943.

providing cover to his own troops by heavy fire. The space is too large to be able to effectively engage the enemy by artillery.[29]

In the conversation, von der Chevallerie suggested what he considered the last option to free the trapped:

> With the forces available, including the paratrooper battalion, we can at best achieve a surprise push to the citadel, taking advantage of the night, and still bring back the citadel crew, including their wounded, during the same night. This operation requires preparation, for which we must take our time until tomorrow [15 January]. If the paratrooper battalion does not return with the entire citadel garrison to our current lines by daybreak on the 16th, but must remain in and near the citadel, it is certain that the Russians will push such strong forces between our line and the citadel in the course of the 16th that the citadel will be once again enclosed. In this case we lack the forces to rescue these enclosed troops.[30]

It is obvious that the generals expected or accepted the failure of the mission.[31]

The generals' assessment of the situation mentioned the heavy artillery fire, from which the deployed paratrooper battalion also suffered. *Hauptmann* Becker, whose battalion lost more and more casualties in the uncovered terrain, but also through increasing frostbite (six men on the 14th alone), asked to be transferred back to their previous quarters at Alexeykovo, which was refused by *Generalmajor* Seyffardt. The men remained in their bivouac area southwest of Belodedovo at -20 to -25°C in the snow and in uncovered terrain. It was the third night that the paratroopers had to spend unprotected in the open in this way. They could not dig in because of the thin snow cover and the frozen solid ground, nor could they make any kind of fire to keep warm because of enemy observation. They could only press themselves flat on the ground, in hollows, in the face of artillery fire and hope not to be hit by shrapnel. Otherwise, the soldiers could only spend the time 'leaning against a truck and, because of the frozen ground, standing alternately on their left and right legs.'[32] All the other *Wehrmacht* soldiers in the 'tube' were exposed to these harsh conditions as well.

The Relief Attempt by the Paratroopers

Shortly before noon on 15 January Becker received word, after another freezing night, that he was now to attack the following evening. His battalion was placed under the direct command of *Generalleutnant* Wöhler.

At the same time, the situation in the city deteriorated dramatically: contact with *Oberstleutnant* von Sass in the east of the city was lost in the morning and the last radio message, received at 10:35 a.m., was incomprehensible. To von der Chevallerie it was now very likely that the eastern part had fallen into the hands of the Soviets. At best, individual pockets of resistance could remain.[33]

---

29 CAMO, 500_12454, file 653: Heeresgruppe Mitte (ed.), *Welikije Luki*, p.69.
30 BA-MA, RH 24-59/52 in BW 57-82: Minutes of the presentation of the *General* von der Chevallerie to the commander-in-chief of the *Heeresgruppe Mitte* von Kluge on 14 January 1943, 4:00 p.m., transcribed on the same day.
31 Heinz Kretschmar, 'III./Fallschirmjäger-Regiment 1 – Blitz-Einsatz Welikije Luki Januar 1943', DDF (1991) vol.1, p.11.
32 BA-MA, BW 57-89: protocol by Günther Behrmann.
33 In fact, *Oberstleutnant* von Sass surrendered the next day, 16 January 1943 at 4:00 p.m. after the soldiers of the 917th (Estonian) Rifle Regiment threatened to blow up his bunker. (Forczyk, *Velikiye Luki*, p.85).

At 1:10 p.m. *Major* Tribukait was informed of the impending attack towards the citadel:

> Assault group reinforced paratrooper battalion will attack in the direction of the citadel at 7 p.m. today in order to relieve the garrison and clear the citadel this night. An advance via Lovat towards the eastern part can only be carried out with light assault troops along the railway. The garrison of the eastern part must make their way tonight in groups along the railway to Rybiki (1 km southwest of the citadel). Melenka, Kryukovo, Sheboldina, Kikino, Velebetskoye occupied by enemy. Rybiki, Fotyeva, Lachny, Belodedovo in own hands. ... Wöhler.[34]

This was a gross error, because the belief that Rybiki was in German hands was a misconception which existed beginning 12 January and all planning and situation assessments were based on it. *Gruppe Hauptmann Borho* had lost its bearings in the night of 12 January and sent this false report, which was not corrected later. The group was actually in Kopshino, west of Velebetskoye.

This was discovered too late and is one of the main causes of the delays that followed and of the ultimate failure of the mission. A short, quick advance along the Rybiki road to the southwest corner of the citadel was therefore not possible and the attack had to be made over more difficult terrain. In addition, the attack distance increased to almost one and half kilometres as the crow flies. This fact had only become apparent shortly before the subsequent meeting with Becker. According to the after-action report of *Gruppe von der Chevallerie* this fact became known around noon. But Wöhler still believed Rybiki was in German hands at 1:10 p.m.[35]

Hauptmann Becker received his order directly from *Generalleutnant* Wöhler in a briefing at 3:30 p.m. Becker was assigned an engineer company under command of *Major* Renner with flame throwers and explosives, a horse-drawn sledge column of 40 vehicles under the command of *Rittmeister* Rautschuss and the medical group of *Stabsarzt* Dr von Bülow. In addition, he was given a radio vehicle without snow chains – not suitable for off-road use – and an armoured reconnaissance vehicle with a radio. Becker was to attack the Soviet positions with heavy assault groups and then push through to the southwest side of the citadel with his entire force. Some quickly assembled army units under *Oberstleutnant* Schönberger were to shield the flanks of the attackers to the north and south with the 'forces placed at his disposal for this purpose, which were made up of unfit army units, some without winter and camouflage clothing and without any operational experience'[36] Becker with his battalion was to rescue the garrison and the wounded from the citadel. Given enough time, another push was to be made into the city to free the units trapped within. Becker claims that he received an important instruction from Wöhler: 'In case of failure of means of communication, an independent withdrawal is to be carried out by the commander *Hauptmann* Becker.'[37] Also if the mission could not be completed by daybreak, he could abort the mission at his own discretion. Apparently Wöhler also realised that Becker's chances were slim, and he probably wanted to give him an opportunity to break off the operation and thus prevent the battalion from being wiped out. This explicit addition that the operation could be aborted cannot be found in the war diary of *LIX. Armee Korps*. There it is merely stated that the 'mission must be completed by first light of 16 January', which, however, implies an abort if the mission is not feasible.[38]

---

34   CAMO, 500_12454, file 653: Heeresgruppe Mitte (ed.), *Welikije Luki*, p.71; 500_12474, file 736.
35   See above and CAMO, 500_12474, file 734, p.32.
36   BA-MA, RH 24-59/53: After action report of *Hauptmann* Becker.
37   BA-MA, RH 24-59/53.
38   BA-MA, RH 24-59/32: entry 15 January 1943.

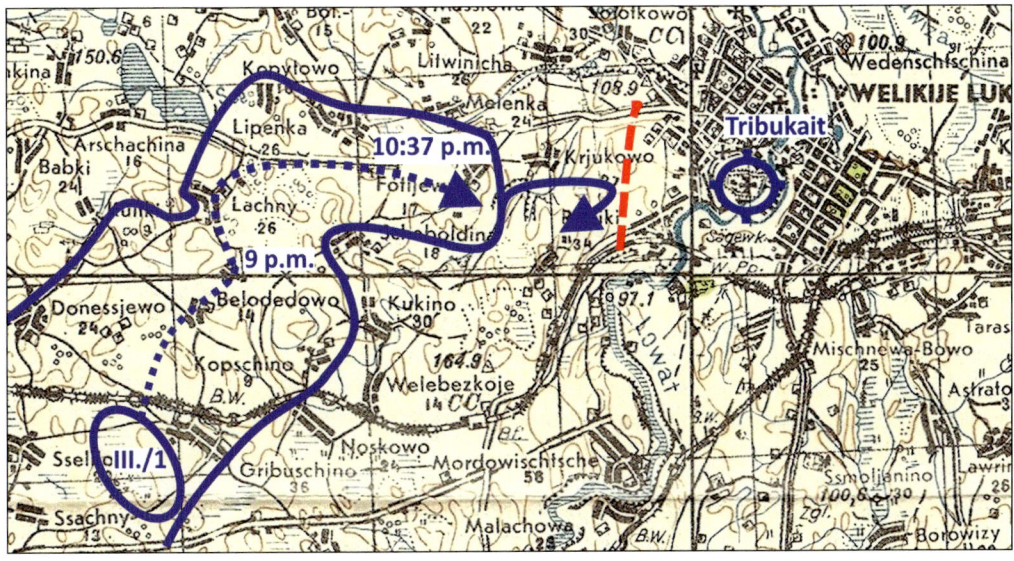

The relief attempt of *III. Bataillon* on 15 January 1943.

The start of the attack was delayed once again, as the new situation meant that approval of the operation by *Heeresgruppe Mitte* was needed. This meeting was not over until 5:30 p.m. and Becker's company commanders were briefed immediately afterwards. At the same time, Becker received the order to proceed to *Oberstleutnant* Schönberger's command post in Belodedovo. Ten minutes later, Becker was at his own command post and briefed the engineer company under his command and the commander of the sledge unit.

11. Kompanie under *Oberleutnant* Horbach formed the attacking section with a heavy machine gun group,[39] *12. Kompanie* and three engineer demolition and flamethrower squads were to push north of Rybiki to the southwest entrance of the citadel, thereby shielding the group to the south and north. Behind *11. Kompanie*, *10. Kompanie* was to reinforce the shielding to the north and east according to its own situation assessment. The battalion staff, two engineer demolition groups, parts of *12. Kompanie* and a mixed anti-tank platoon of *14. Kompanie* were to form the assault reserve. *9. Kompanie* with a subordinate heavy machine gun group of *12. Kompanie*, and two engineer demolition and flamethrower squads were intended as reinforcements for *11. Kompanie* and for a possible push into the eastern part of the city.

Oberleutnant Karl Horbach, who commanded *11. Kompanie* probably between 18 December 1942 and 16 January 1943, when he was wounded at Gribushino. (Private Collection)

---

39 Karl Horbach (Bingen, 5 December 1915– Bingen, 16 January 2006), *Major*.

The battalion left the area south of the Belodedovo railway line around 7:00 p.m. – the originally intended start time of the attack – and reached Schönberger's command post at 7:30 p.m. However, Becker found no one to brief him. This was belatedly done personally by *Oberstleutnant* Schönberger, his adjutant, and *Leutnant* Brink, a staff officer of *Artillerie Regiment 183*, accompanied Becker on his mission as liaison to the artillery. He later reported to *Generalmajor* Seyffart that when he arrived at *Oberstleutnant* Schönberger's command post at 8:15 p.m., he also found Becker there.[40] Becker reported that his battalion did not set off until 8:45 p.m., apparently omitting a stopover in his report, for *Leutnant* Brink states that the battalion did not arrive until about 9:00 p.m. at a command post 'Simons' located 400 metres northeast of Belodedovo. From there, *Oberstleutnant* Schönberger led the battalion via Lachny to Hill 147, from where the attack was to start. Becker judged that this was a one and a half kilometre diversion and that Schönberger mistakenly had led them to a hill 400 metres northeast of Hill 147. On the part of the paratroopers, there was also the assertion that Schönberger had gotten lost because he had been 'supplied with other fuels'[41] – meaning he was probably drunk – which significantly delayed the approach. *Leutnant* Brink did not want to recognise Schönberger's intoxicated status and therefore refused to confirm this in writing to *Hauptmann* Becker. *Leutnant* Brink gave his report orally to Seyffart in the presence of *Oberstleutnant* Schärpler, commander of *Artillerie Regiment 183*, and *Oberleutnant* Domay, first orderly of *205. Infanterie Division* on 22 January 1943 at 10:30 p.m. This protocol has been signed only by the general and not by *Leutnant* Brink. Seyffart obviously did not want to tarnish his regimental commander, which would have reflected badly on himself as well. *Oberstleutnant* Schönberger could not be questioned as he was wounded severely on 16 January. It seems that this case had been silently covered up.[42] 'Becker's battalion was divided into a lead company, a company as flank security and a company as advance group. *Leutnant* Brink went with the leading group. *Leutnant* Brink then saw *Oberstleutnant* Schönberger for the last time at [Hill] 147.'[43]

The delays caused Becker to ask Wöhler around 10:00 p.m. whether the mission, which according to the original plan should have started at 7:00 p.m., should be continued at all. He did not get an answer. Unsurprisingly, the radio car, which was not suitable for off-road use, had gotten stuck and was not available; the radio of the armoured reconnaissance vehicle had malfunctioned. Why he could not use *Leutnant* Brink's means of communication is not mentioned further. Becker started his attack of his own accord from Hill 147.0 at 10.37 p.m. and was able to advance about one kilometre to the east by 11:40 p.m. Here Becker paused; *11. Kompanie*, as the attacking unit, was about 150 metres in front of a trench system running north-south with 11 identified bunkers and wire obstacles. It was a defensive system previously established by the German defenders of Velikiye Luki, now occupied by Soviet soldiers. The paratroopers took fire from several bunkers.

Walter Fricke of *10. Kompanie* experienced enemy contact from the second row:

> The leading group is already in contact with the enemy. The bullets whiz back and forth like fireflies. Signal rockets can be seen. Over there you can hear the 'plub' when mortars fire. If they hit this column, this sledge caravan, then good night at six. Then they do fire, we can hear them coming without pause. Luckily too inaccurate. Nevertheless, we claw ourselves firmly into the snow in this area with little cover.[44]

---

40   BA-MA, RH 24-205/34 in BW 57-82: Protocol 'Rybiki' dated 23 January 1943 signed by *Generalmajor* Seyffart.
41   BA-MA, BW 57-89: protocol by Günther Behrmann.
42   BA-MA, RH 24-205/34 in BW 57-82: Protocol 'Rybiki'.
43   BA-MA, RH 24-205/34 in BW 57-82: Protocol 'Rybiki'.
44   BA-MA, BW 57-89: Fricke, *An die Gewehre!*

From the account of *Leutnant* Brink we know more details of what followed:

> The battalion had been marching towards Rybiki for about 45 minutes when *Leutnant* Brink wanted to get an orientation from *Hauptmann* Becker and was told by an officer of the battalion that *Hauptmann* Becker was at the end of the column. Russian flares were being fired at the time and there was some infantry fire. The leading company stopped, and a heavy machine gun fired a few short bursts. After a few minutes the battalion marched on. *Leutnant* Brink stayed with his radio operators to await *Hauptmann* Becker, who came along with the mid-section of the battalion and took cover 50 metres to the side behind a small mound of earth. *Leutnant* Brink lay down next to him and questioned him about his intentions. *Leutnant* Brink got no answer, but *Hauptmann* Becker gave the order: 'Battalion halt! Battalion – About turn march!' – *Leutnant* Brink was surprised and inquired why he would turn back [he did not know of Wöhler's order to Becker] … *Hauptmann* Becker grumbled that he refused to proceed further with the attack after this sour briefing by a drunken *Oberstleutnant*. He would rather repeat the attack.[45]

Becker thought that if he continued with the attack he would jeopardise the mission, since the delay and slow progress would inevitably have meant that the operation (the evacuation of the wounded) would have taken until well into the morning and the battalion would not have been able to repel the strong Soviet forces in daylight. After his communications also failed, he broke off the operation of his own accord – which his order also expressly demanded – in order to postpone it for 24 hours.

At first, those involved could not understand this termination. 'The companies, since no one knew what was going on, went back completely scattered, no one knew why the attack was broken off.'[46] Fricke was also wondering: 'The whole thing about return march. Why return? That's anyone's guess. But orders are orders, as we all know.'[47] At 12:30 a.m. Becker personally reported to *Generalleutnant* Wöhler, while the battalion arrived back in its initial position south of Belodedovo by around 3:00 a.m.

Fricke observed soberly:

> For hours, taking detours in the hills and valleys that always look the same, we arrive dead tired in the morning at the compound where our trucks are parked. Death-like we sleep on the wagon. Crowded together, half sitting, half lying, warming each other, we doze. The paddock is opened to have a little relief. We have already checked off Velikiye Luki. There probably wasn't much left to save and it wouldn't have paid to sacrifice another battalion.[48]

Between 3:00 p.m. on the 15th until they returned to the trucks, the battalion suffered 25 wounded and two missing, although there was little fighting. The wounds were mainly inflicted by artillery fire.

There was to be a rude awakening for the exhausted paratroopers.

---

45 BA-MA, RH 24-205/34 in BW 57-82.
46 BA-MA, RH 24-205/34 in BW 57-82.
47 BA-MA, BW 57-89: Fricke, *An die Gewehre!*
48 BA-MA, BW 57-89: Fricke, *An die Gewehre!*

The Escape of the Citadel's Garrison

Earlier, at 11.55 p.m., *Heeresgruppe Mitte* overheard a radio message from *Generalleutnant* Wöhler to *Major* Tribukait: 'Separate assault group under the leadership of *Hauptmann* Becker is coming from artillery target point 361 via 374–373. Watch out and counterattack. Password Rome.'[49]

After Wöhler had received word from Becker that he had broken off the attack and wanted to continue the next evening, he notified the citadel at about 1:15 a.m. This radio message did not reach *Major* Tribukait, as the radio station had been destroyed in the meantime.

Tribukait himself was clearly under no illusions. In his after-action report, he stated that at around 4:00 p.m. he had received the order from *Gruppe Wöhler* to clear the citadel.

> It is impossible to consider evacuating the citadel with the help of the paratroopers, by transporting the 200 wounded! How are vehicles supposed to get in and out of here through the enemy's main line of defence? Even if paratroopers get through against all expectations, the enemy will use everything, especially tanks, to prevent their withdrawal. What to do if paratroopers don't come?[50]

Tribukait had therefore decided to prepare everything for evacuation, leaving behind the 200 wounded. When at 11:00 p.m. there was still no sign of the paratroopers – although the gunfire which hit the approaching paratroopers must have been heard – the group consisting of the men who were still able to do so, got ready and broke out of the citadel at 2:00 a.m. At 5:30 a.m. this group reached their own lines – only 102 men strong. On the way, the group had suffered further losses of 10 men.

In the course of the day, more dispersed troops arrived from the citadel, which meant that in the end 186 men managed to escape. Only four men arrived from the eastern part of the city, who were able to report on the last hours of the *Gruppe von Sass*. All this happened in freezing cold temperatures; -32°C was measured on 16 January.

The survivors offered a devastating sight, *Oberst* Karl Wilke recalled: 'I will never forget what these exhausted people looked like after weeks of holding out in the city and citadel of Velikiye Luki. They were unresponsive. We had to spoon horse meat broth into them, they couldn't eat anything else for the time being. Sleeping, sleeping and drinking broth was the only thing we could offer them.'[51]

In his after-action report *Hauptmann* Becker referred to a written statement of *Generalleutnant* Wöhler, underlining that this breakout had only been made possible by the attempted attack of the paratroopers.[52] However, this narrative is not supported by the reports of Tribukait, *205. Infanterie Division* and *Gruppe von der Chevallerie*. Rather, one generally can feel the disappointment about Becker's decision to call off the operation, even if it was objectively judged to be correct and the operation to be not very promising. Becker simply did not want to waste his men senselessly; it was a decision of a responsible troop leader based on a recognised change of the situation on the ground and which moreover was within the framework of his orders received from Wöhler. The subject of the possibly drunken *Oberstleutnant* Schönberger was left out of the official reports, and Becker did

---

49 CAMO, 500_12454, file 659; see also BA-MA, RH 24-59/52 in BW 57-82.
50 CAMO, 500_12474, file 736: After-action report of *Major* Tribukait.
51 BA-MA, BW 57-92: Letter of Karl Eduard Wilke dated 20 March 1979, at the time *Oberst* and commander of *Luftwaffe Gefechtsverband Wilke*.
52 BA-MA, RH 24-59/53 in BW 57-82: After-action report Becker.

not say a word about it in his after-action report either. Certainly, Becker would have made a corresponding verbal statement to Wöhler, but Seyffart protected *Oberstleutnant* Schönberger and rejected the accusation. The accused was severely wounded the next day and so could not comment on the matter. In addition, Becker and his battalion had by then literally saved *205. Infanterie Division*, its staff, and *Generalleutnant* Seyffart personally, through their courageous action. This is probably why the narrative reported upwards, which was also used for propaganda purposes, was framed in such a way that in the end all those involved stood in a positive light.[53]

Since a further attempt to relieve Velikiye Luki had now become pointless, the attack was halted. The situation of *Gruppe Wöhler* now became increasingly dangerous, as the troops in the exposed and narrow attack 'tube' were also in danger of being cut off and encircled. Only a short time after Tribukait's group arrived, heavy artillery fire and attacks with tank support began. The paratroopers who were resting in the Belodedovo area also were hit by artillery fire. After this very exhausting and not exactly successful night, the soldiers now had to endure further particularly demanding and dangerous days.

Gribushino

In the morning hours of 16 January, the paratroopers were sitting in their transport vehicles catching a couple hours of sleep. South of Gribushino and east of the location of *III. Bataillon*, the *Alarm-Bataillon Witebsk* lay in their positions facing to the east. Due to a Soviet attack, which began at 7:30 a.m. with artillery fire, this rather weak battalion of hastily assembled soldiers 'of all trades' abandoned its positions at 8:40 a.m.[54]

For the exhausted sleeping paratroopers, events came thick and fast, for at 8:30 a.m. they found themselves in the midst of an enemy attack of 450 men (four battalions according to a prisoner testimony, which would be four times that amount), supported by nine tanks in the front line and four more at a distance of 200 metres.

Gefreiter Fricke of *10. Kompanie* woke up from his sleep and found himself in an inferno:

> Out of the blue, a storm roars over us. It seems to be raining shells from thousands of guns. Me, all of us jumped from the truck fast as lightning seeking cover somewhere. Others came too late. Direct hits in the truck. Dead, wounded, chaos. Medics have their hands full. Without rest at 40 degrees below zero, mostly without gloves, they put on their bandages. Fighter planes roar overhead, firing with all guns and dropping small bombs. They turn back, fly in again to bring death and destruction. Bombers too, dropping their loads. Everywhere you look, black clouds of smoke above the white snow. Is this the end? Karl Egger is with me. We are without weapons. They're lying in the truck. The first T-34s rattle by. Karl and I find good cover under the nearby railway line. We must watch idly. We can't tear tanks apart with our bare hands. Shooting wildly, the tanks curved around, ran over soldiers, crushed the trucks. But then assault guns roll up on

---

53 Ottmar Haas, 'Fallschirmjäger in siegreichem Kampf mit Sowjetpanzern' (Paratroopers in victorious battle with Soviet tanks), *Wiener Kronen Zeitung*, 10 February 1943, p.2 and 'Fallschirmjäger sicherten Heimkehr der Luki-Kämpfer' (Paratroopers secured the Luki fighters' return home), *Badener Zeitung*, 13 February 1943, pp.1–2, and others.
54 BA-MA, RH 24-59/53 in BW 57-82: After-action report Becker.

The Soviet attack on Gribushino on 16 January 1943.

the opposite hill. Bang-boom and the first Russian tank is on fire. They clean up. Paratroopers also hang on to the Russian tanks like burrs to attach their sticky charges. Everyone wants to crack one. *Oberleutnant* [Krause] from *12. Kompanie* successfully cracked one but was killed by the explosion. Finally, there is peace, the tanks are left smoking and burning. Come on, let's go, we must get weapons. Ours were crushed by a tank. But everywhere there are the weapons of the wounded and dead lying around. Then the familiar 'Hurrah' sounds from the hill. They come towards us like ants, waving their rifles. Next to me an assault gun rolls up, fires at the Russians, further to the right the *Nebelwerfer* howl. They fire their rockets directly into the Russian masses. The company gathers for the counterattack. An impact directly in front of me knocks me out. Blood runs down my face and a fountain of blood shoots out of my felt boot. I wave to Karl and shout that I'm going to the dressing station.[55]

Becker then took command over this section of the front on his own initiative, first sealing off the breach at Hill 168.5 and clearing it in a counterattack, which must have been carried out by Horbach's *11. Kompanie* and here most probably by *Feldwebel* Wittig's platoon, as he received the German Cross in Gold for an action like this.[56] *10.* and *12. Kompanie* repulsed the main attack, moved into the posi-

---

55 BA-MA, BW 57-89: Fricke, *An die Gewehre!*
56 See the English translation of the recommendation for the Knights cross given at his entry in <www.tracesofwar.

Paratroopers of Fallschirmjäger *Regiment 1* after a mission carrying an MG 34. (BArch, Bild 101 I/553/838/37A/ Ottmar Haas)

tions abandoned by the *Alarm-Bataillon* and screened off to the east. They could see that the fighting there had been brutal. 'Our soldiers [of the *Alarm-Bataillon*] were being beaten to death with rifle butts, even though they had their hands up.'[57] *11. Kompanie* was then at heights 300 metres north of Hill 168.5, while *9. Kompanie* and an anti-tank platoon of *14. Kompanie/Fallschirmjäger Regiment 5* took up positions along the railway embankment to the north. At 9:10 a.m., *10.* and *12. Kompanie* had to repel three waves of attacks, each of about 250 men with two tanks. In the midst of these battles, 14 Soviet fighter planes attacked the battalion's positions at 9:30 a.m., six bombers at 10:05 a.m. and again six bombers at 10:30 a.m. Several tanks were able to break through the main line of defence. Of these tanks, three were destroyed by paratroopers in close combat, one by an anti-tank gun from *Panzerjäger Abteilung 205* and another five by an assault gun from *Sturmgeschütz Abteilung 185* (*Leutnant* Briel).

At 10:45 a.m., the battalion was again placed under command of Seyffart's *205. Infanterie Division* and again repelled an attack of 150 men at about 12:20 p.m. Afterwards – at about 2:00 p.m. – Becker sent first a group under *Feldwebel* Jaschke, then a platoon with 22 soldiers of *9.* and *11. Kompanie* under command of *Feldwebel* Fleischhauer to support groups of *II. Bataillon/Grenadier Regiment 335* of *Hauptmann* Gruber on the right, adjacent to the road, and *Hauptmann* Fischer at Hill 172. North

---

com>.
57 BA-MA, BW 57-89: Fricke, *An die Gewehre!*

of Gribushino, a Soviet breakthrough with tank support was successful at Kopshino, which resulted in the loss of the village.

Only a 10-minute Stuka attack provided the battalion with short-term relief at 1:25 p.m. The rest of the afternoon included additional Soviet artillery fire and air raids as well as local attacks on the positions of the paratroopers.

Becker's battalion suffered heavy losses on this day: initially Becker reported 24 dead, 130 wounded, and 16 missing, which was subsequently updated based on the casualty list to 29 dead, 120 wounded, of whom at least nine subsequently died of their wounds, and nine missing. The total number of dead and missing is thus 45. The discrepancy between the 130 wounded initially reported and the traceable 120 is probably due to slightly wounded who remained with the troops.[58] After *Oberleutnant* Krause had fallen *12. Kompanie* was taken over by *Leutnant* Söhnke.[59]

During the night of the 16th to the 17th, the German positions continued to be under Soviet artillery and mortar fire.

Feldwebel Fleischhauer was wounded in the morning at around 10:30 a.m. together with two other soldiers from his platoon, so *Feldwebel* Jaschke took command of the platoon. Jaschke had to fight off several attacks in the further course of the day. At 3:00 p.m., 200 men attacked in four waves on a front of 100 metres, and at 4:25 p.m. a new attack briefly succeeded in breaking into the platoon's positions, which were held through close combat. Having barely survived this, the left wing of the platoon was attacked at 5:30 p.m. Here too, the positions were held through close combat. Another attack on the right section of the platoon took place at 8:00 p.m. Again, a break-in succeeded, which was finally repelled by counter-attacking reserves. During this day, the platoon suffered one dead and 11 wounded, including the previously mentioned *Feldwebel* Fleischhauer and his two soldiers.

On the 17th, a Soviet attack took place early in the morning between Gribushino and Ivantseva, during which a break-in into the German main line of defence was achieved at Hill 172.[60] In order to seal this breach, *9. Kompanie* under command of *Oberleutnant* Merkordt, to whom *11. Kompanie* was also subordinated, was alerted at 6:00 a.m. and subordinated to *Grenadier Regiment 76 (mot.)*. In addition to Merkordt, this group had a strength of only 72 NCOs and men. Together with *Kradschützenbataillon 30*, they succeeded in retaking the lost positions on the so-called *Panzerhöhe* ('Tank Hill') at 11:30 a.m. Merkordt's weak force suffered casualties of one killed and five wounded, the beaten back enemy lost 35 killed and 28 captured. Merkordt's battle group was now incorporated into the main line of defence of the *Kradschützenbataillon* between *3.* and *2. Kradschützenkompanie* on said *Panzerhöhe*. Merkordt had to hand over one group of eight men to *4. Kradschützenkompanie* and form a reserve of 13 men.

After Merkordt had marched off at 8:00 a.m., the positions of the remnants of *III. Bataillon* were under constant fire from heavy Soviet artillery, 'Stalin organs' (Katyusha rocket launchers) and anti-tank guns. Then, at 8:25 a.m., the first Soviet attack of the day on the battalion's positions was initiated by 50–100 men and three tanks, the latter providing covering fire for the advance. At 8:40 a.m. *12. Kompanie* was attacked by about 40 men, followed by another attack at 9:00 a.m. This time the

---

58   Casualty list, Volksbund, Ancestry/WASt.
59   Gerhard Söhnke (1916–?), *Leutnant*.
60   In the history of *11. Kompanie* a Hill 147 is mistakenly mentioned. In contemporary maps east of Ivanzeva only a Hill 172 can be found. Most probably a confusion with Hill 147 from which the attack on Velikiye Luki should have started on 15 January. Alfons Wanderwitz: *11. Kompanie/Fallschirm-Jäger-Regiment 1* (privately printed, 1978).

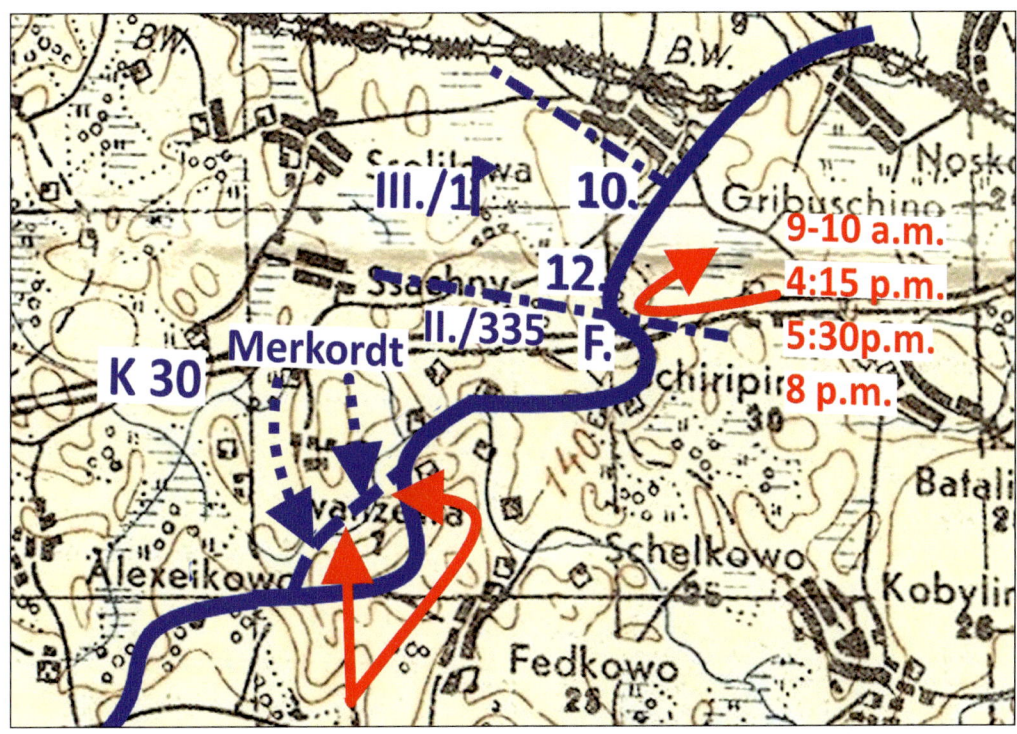

The situation at Gribushino on 17 January 1943.

section of *III. Bataillon* was attacked by 240 men and two tanks. In the sector of *12. Kompanie* tanks managed to breach the line of defence, the situation was saved by a counterattack led by *Leutnant* Söhnke (10:00 a.m.). Soviet fighter planes and bombers dropped their loads over the German positions, Soviet infantry attacked again and again until late at night (last at 11:10 p.m.), while three German He 111s, 10 Ju 87s and four fighter planes were able to intervene on the side of the Germans.

On 17 January, the battalion reported 16 dead, 47 wounded and two missing. A number that was subsequently increased by additional reports and by the wounded who died of their wounds. In the end, there were 25 dead and missing, and 51 wounded.[61] The paratroopers remained in their positions until 4:45 a.m. on the 18th. Then they were finally relieved, pulled out, and transferred to Alexeykovo as an operational reserve of *205. Infanterie Division*.

Jaschke's platoon was also relieved in the morning hours of the 18th and arrived at the battalion at around 7:00 a.m. In total, the platoon suffered three dead and 13 wounded within 41 hours.

Merkordt's combat group remained in its positions on the 18th and had to endure a Soviet artillery barrage until 8:00 a.m., which was followed by an infantry attack on the *Panzerhöhe*, that was beaten off. Merkordt, in association with *Kradschützenbataillon 30*, had to cover the retreat of *205. Infanterie*

---

61 Casualty lists, Volksbund, WAST/Ancestry. In the casualty lists members of 16. and 17. Kp./FJR 3 and 14.Kp./FJR 5 are mentioned.

Division.⁶² In the process, this group was able to repel another Soviet attack at about 5:00 p.m., again after lengthy artillery preparations. Merkordt lost another two killed and four wounded. In front of his positions 250 dead and wounded Soviet soldiers were counted.

On 18 January, the embattled Gribushino and Hill 174.2 were finally lost. The breach was sealed off. Becker's battalion, now numbering only 159 men, intended to make another counterattack on Gribushino, but this did not take place. In preparation, Becker formed a weak company 'Söhnke' from his remaining battalion and a combat group '*Stab*' (staff) under command of *Oberleutnant* Schulze.⁶³ In the afternoon, the battalion's billet near Alexeykovo was hit by artillery fire, resulting in one dead and 15 wounded. The counterattack was called off at 3:00 p.m., the battalion remaining in Alexeykovo until the 19th. The 'tube' began to collapse, but the Germans were able to withdraw in an orderly fashion. On the evening of the 19th, the battalion, or what was left of it, was moved to Lobno.

Also on 19 January, *Kampfgruppe Merkordt* endured heavy artillery fire and repelled an enemy reconnaissance patrol of 15 men in the evening at around 7:00 p.m. Merkordt lost another man, *Obergefreiter* Hacker, and one wounded. During the night of 20 January, Merkordt's group was finally pulled out (with the loss of another dead and one wounded) and was transferred to the battalion which was already in Lobno.

 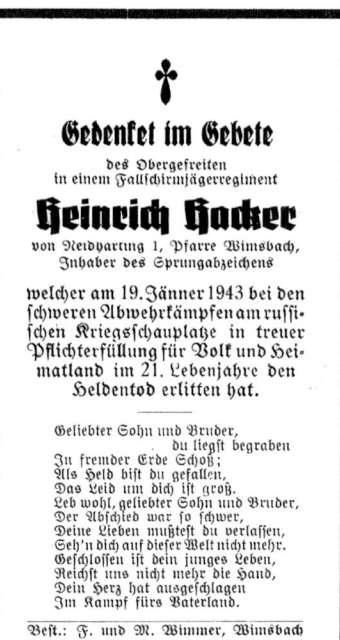

Remembrance card of *Obergefreiter* Heinrich Hacker (pictured as *Gefreiter*) of *9. Kompanie*. He was killed by a bullet to the head near Ivantseva. (Private Collection)

---

62 Wanderwitz mentions mistakenly 17. I.D., a formation which lay in France at the time (*XXV. AK, 7. Armee, Heeresgruppe West (D)*). Alfons Wanderwitz: *11. Kompanie/Fallschirm-Jäger-Regiment 1* (privately printed, 1978).
63 Georg Schulze (1912–?), *Oberleutnant;* DKiG 24 June 1943.

On 10 January 1943, the battalion had a strength of 516 men without the additional subordinate units. On 23 January, Becker's reinforced battalion had a total combatant strength of 162 men (six officers, including two doctors, 54 NCOs and 102 enlisted men) with a supply strength (*Verpflegsstärke*) of 287 men. This number also includes those men who could not fight, but needed to be fed. That shows that a considerable number of slightly wounded, or sick remained with the unit.

Becker reported that his reinforced battalion suffered 47 killed, 25 missing and 244 wounded during the Velikiye Luki operation.[64] The casualty lists drawn up later correct the figures to 51 dead and 12 missing, as well as 255 wounded, 26 of whom died of their wounds.[65] This corresponds to a casualty rate of 63 percent of the battalion's combatant strength. The company commander of *12. Kompanie*, *Oberleutnant* Krause, was killed in action and *Oberleutnant* Voges, platoon commander of *10. Kompanie*, succumbed to his wounds a short time later at a hospital in Orsha. Becker himself was wounded (but remained with the troops), as were his company commanders *Oberleutnant* Brügel (10. Kp.), *Oberleutnant* Horbach (11. Kp.), as well as the platoon leaders *Oberleutnant* Neukum (9. Kp.), *Leutnant* Kühnast (11. Kp.) and *Leutnant* Petersen (signals platoon leader). Horbach lost his leg but returned later to active duty without seeing any action anymore and was promoted to *Major*. After the war he became a communal politician for the FDP in Bingen (Rhineland). Kühnast died as a *Hauptmann* on 15 February 1944 in the Bad Nauheim military hospital of a brain abscess, which suggests that he never recovered from his wound which he received at Gribushino (shrapnel to the head).[66]

There were also many cases of frostbite and other illnesses that were not recorded as battle injuries. In the Orel campaign, which followed shortly afterwards, the battalion was clearly weakened – despite the addition of replacements and the return of slightly wounded men.

In a letter dated 18 January, *Generalleutnant* Seyffart thanked *Generalmajor* Heidrich with the words '[Your men] have helped me a lot, without Becker I would be over there now [in Soviet captivity] with my command staff.'[67] Heidrich then suggested that *Hauptmann* Becker should be awarded the Oak Leaves to the Knight's Cross for his defensive performance at Gribushino, but this was rejected by Hitler as Becker had previously broken off the attack on Velikiye Luki.[68]

The Velikiye Luki relief operation was a bitter defeat for the *Wehrmacht*, and one that could have been avoided. A war correspondent, Ottmar Haas, who had accompanied Becker's battalion, propagandised the events at Gribushino in an article that appeared in several newspapers, whereby the loss of Velikiye Luki receded into the background. The paratroopers were stylised as tank-busting heroes who had enabled the garrison of the city to break out of it. The latter, however, is only mentioned in a subordinate sentence at the end, as this was, after all, a reference to the defeat that was to be concealed.[69]

---

64 Ben Christensen, The 1st Fallschirmjäger Division in World War II – Volume One: Years of Attack (Atglen: Schiffer, 2007), pp.286–287.
65 This is the total number including the other troops of the *Flieger Division 7* who came along (staff of FJR 1, 14./5, FJR 3); Verlustliste, Volksbund, Ancestry/WASt.
66 In his WAST file card, *11. Kompanie*/FJR 1 is still listed as his unit. He does not appear in later casualty lists or otherwise in Italy. (WAST/Ancestry: G-A 813/0452).
67 BA-MA, BW 57-89.
68 Kretschmar, 'Einsatz Welikije Luki', p.11.
69 Ottmar Haas, 'Fallschirmjäger in siegreichem Kampf mit Sowjetpanzern', *Wiener Kronen Zeitung*, 10 February 1943, p.2 and 'Fallschirmjäger sicherten Heimkehr der Luki-Kämpfer', *Badener Zeitung*, 13 February 1943, pp.1–2, and others.

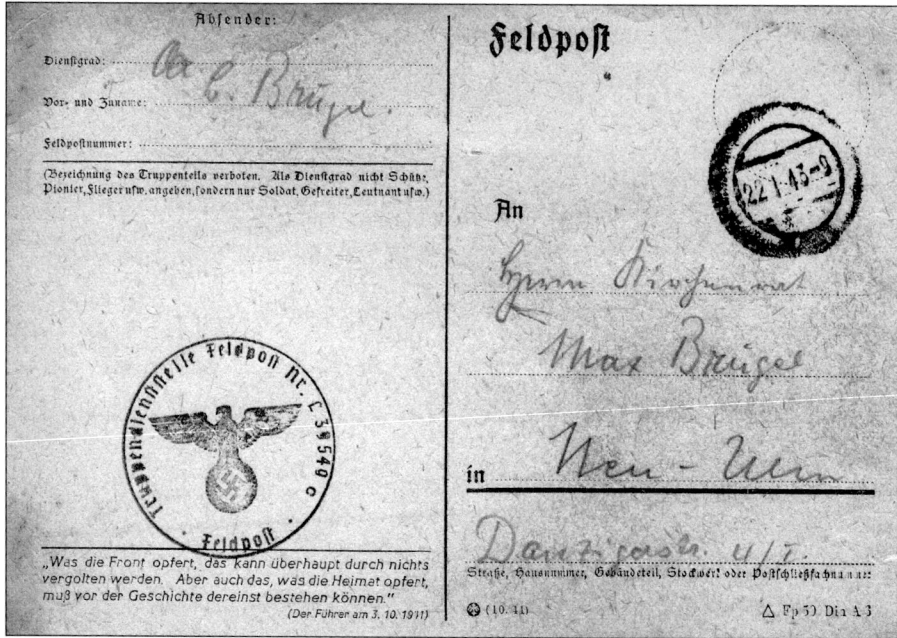

Field postcard of *Oberleutnant* Brügel to his father in Neu-Ulm (Bavaria), informing him that he has been wounded, dated Warsaw, 21 January 1943: 'Dear Papa, In the fighting around Vel.L. into which we were thrown, I was slightly wounded in the right shoulder by a shell splinter and am in a transport towards the *Reich*. It's not bad at all. I was very lucky again because the splinter got stuck in my shoulder blade. I don't know where I am going, hopefully to South-Germany. Best wishes from your grateful Bernhard'. (Collection Stephan Janzyk)

For the Red Army, it was a dearly bought victory, the only apparent success of operation MARS, but it could not be exploited further. Hitler's nonsensical halting order caused the same fate for those trapped in Velikiye Luki as it did in a completely different dimension two weeks later in Stalingrad. According to their own figures, the Soviets took 3,944 German prisoners (including 54 officers) at Velikiye Luki, captured 113 guns, 97 mortars, and 20 tanks and assault guns. The captured commander of the city's defenders, von Sass, was executed as a war criminal in Velikiye Luki along with seven others in 1946 after a short show trial.[70] Only 11 of the German soldiers taken prisoner in Velikiye Luki returned after the war. The author Robert Forczyk describes the treatment of these prisoners of war by the Red Army as a war crime. Immediately after the surrender, the wounded and other prisoners are said to have been shot indiscriminately or left outside to freeze to death. Of the prisoners, only a very few survived the first days of captivity, only to die later. All this and the trials, including the death sentences, are seen by Forczyk as revenge for the dogged defence of the city.[71]

The Soviet 3rd Shock Army is said to have lost 104,000 men, of which 31,700 were dead and missing in action (irrevocable losses).[72] Most likely, the Soviet losses were higher. The Soviet side usually understated its losses in official accounts, while on the German side the figures of own losses are relatively accurate.

According to German figures, about 5,000 men were killed in Velikiye Luki itself whereas *Gruppe Wöhler* suffered 12,000 total casualties in its attempt to relieve the city. The combatant strength of *205. Infanterie Division* alone was reduced from 3,475 men on 1 January 1943 to 584 men on 19 January 1943.[73] Elsewhere, 3,220 casualties are reported for the division.[74] On 20 January, the Ia of *Gruppe von der Chevallerie*, *Oberstleutnant* Braune-Krikau, even speaks of 13% remaining strength of this division and 17 percent of *331. Infanterie Division*.[75] The Luftwaffe also suffered losses: *Gefechtsverband Wilke* lost 28 aircraft as well as 11 Go 242 (of 15) and six DFS 230 cargo gliders in the relief attempt.[76] These frightening figures can – with all caution and the danger of abstraction – give a sense of the scale of these battles.

Generaloberst Model recognised – probably also under the impression of the heavy losses of *III. Bataillon* at Velikiye Luki – that there was a need for improvement in the deployment of subordinate troop units. In a letter dated 22 January 1943, he announced to his commanding generals and division commanders that he would closely examine the treatment of troop units 'on loan', whose deployment was necessary in the defensive battles in all places and had led to heavy intermixing of formations. Battalions were correctly brought in quickly but were immediately used for counterattacks without knowledge of the terrain or the situation: 'Revelatory documents will emerge after the return of "borrowed" troop units through reports of the leaders of these units, which should be encouraged. A thorough evaluation of these documents must conclusively lead to the end of abusive diminution of

---

70 *Generalleutnant* Fritz Georg von Rappart (was taken prisoner in 1945, commanded Grenadier Regiment 227 in 1943), *Major* Wilhelm Sonnewald (local commander of Velikiye Luki), *Hauptmann* Walter Knauf and four other non-commissioned officers and enlisted men. See also Forczyk, *Velikiye Luki*, pp.88–89.
71 Forczyk, *Velikiye Luki*, p.85.
72 <Soldat.ru/doc/book/chapter5_10_1.htmls> in Internet Archive (archive.org) (accessed 25 November 2017).
73 CAMO, 500_12474, file 633: After-action report of *Generalleutnant* Wöhler, attachment f.
74 CAMO, 500_12474, file 732: 4–18 January; CAMO, 500_12454, file 653: Heeresgruppe Mitte (ed.), *Welikije Luki*, 4–22 January and appendix 7.
75 CAMO, 500_12474, file 732, telex to HGrM 10 January 1943, 3 a.m.
76 BA-MA, BW 57-82: Order of the day by the commanding general of *Luftwaffenkommando Ost*, *General der Flieger* Robert Ritter von Greim, dated 22 January 1943.

Paratroopers pulling a sledge. (BDF Archive/Helmut Pirath)

other troop units and putting them in a worse position in every respect (supply, awards, etc.) than one's own troops.'[77] *Generalmajor* Heidrich thus had every reason to resist the attempts to tear his division apart with all his might.

On 24 January, the order was received by *LIX. Armee Korps* that Becker's battalion was to be transferred back to *Flieger Division 7* by rail transport. This was not possible until 30 January.[78] The battalion finally arrived at *Flieger Division 7* in the Gorodets area on 2 February. Due to casualties and men on sick leave, the battalion's combatant strength had dropped to 144 men, reflecting the urgent need for rest and refreshment. It therefore remained in reserve behind the left wing of the division.[79]

---

77 BA-MA, RH 20-9/118 in BW 57-82: letter dated 22 January 1943 (Ia, Nr. 526/43).
78 BA-MA, RH 24-59/54.
79 BA-MA, RH 24-6/129 VI.A.K. KTB 3, vol.57.

15

I. Bataillon 11 January–8 February 1943

While *III. Bataillon* fought at Velikiye Luki, Schulenburg's *I. Bataillon* remained in its section north of Starina on the extreme right wing of *Flieger Division 7*. The first half of January 1943 passed quietly; the whole attention of the Kalinin Front was directed towards Velikiye Luki. Occasional artillery fire from both sides interrupted the monotony of waiting, mutual stalking and observation. On 18 January, a Soviet reconnaissance party of 15 to 20 men was repelled in front of the positions of *3. Kompanie*. The next day a raiding party of *2. Kompanie*, led by *Leutnant* Thede,[1] attacked positions south and southeast of Ovsyankina and brought in a prisoner who testified that a Soviet attack was planned within the next few nights. As a result, reserves were positioned behind *3. Kompanie*, where the main thrust was expected: two groups of *3. Kompanie*, one group of the regimental bicycle platoon, and one self-propelled anti-tank gun. In the end, the expected attack did not take place.

On the same day, 19 January 1943, the battalion, which now lay alone in front of Starina – *II.* and *III. Bataillon* had been withdrawn – was placed under the direct command of *Flieger Division 7* and shortly afterwards, that same evening, *VI. Armee Korps* was informed by AOK 9 that the battalion was to be relieved by a unit of *197. Infanterie Division* and then moved behind the left wing of *Flieger Division 7*.

After an enquiry on 21 January about how many vehicles the battalion would need for a transfer, rumours began to circulate among the soldiers about an imminent relocation. On 23 January, the news came in that the transfer would take place in six days. No background information was communicated to the soldiers. They were therefore wondering where they were going. Stalingrad? Back to Germany?

A zither player visited *3. Kompanie* and his songs made the soldiers forget the front for a few hours, among them *Hauptfeldwebel* Wagner:

> The gentleman was 63 years old but still very spry. He played such beautiful songs and sang along with them so that it made me homesick. Well, what can the *Landser* [ordinary soldier] dream of? … Yes, darling, that was an hour of home melodies. How I'd love to listen to beautiful music with you on our radio again. Here at the exchange, we often hear such beautiful music through the telephone. Then the whole bunker crew wants to put the receiver to their ear.[2]

---

1   Hans-Heinrich Thede (Kiel, 11 March 1917–KIA Kriuki 3 March 1943), *Leutnant*.
2   Archive Franz: Wagner, letter dated 29 January 1943.

A machine gun position of the paratroopers. (BDF Archive)

Additionally, patrols were sent into the no-mans land on 24 and 25 January under *Oberfeldwebel* Hoffmeister of IV platoon of *2. Kompanie*. Officer candidate *Gefreiter* von Zimburg gained his first patrol experiences:

> In the early hours of 25 January, I went on my second patrol, again with Hoffmeister and *Oberjäger* Schneider. We wanted to find out how near the Russians had approached with their skis. We found circles with directional arrows in the snow about 150 metres in front of our most forward posts, but they only pointed to our false positions. We had built these mock positions out of snow 100 metres behind our real positions and had scattered ash on their rear side to simulate positions in aerial photographs. During the night we lit matches, we also made small fires or shot disturbing fire from the false position, so that the Russians assumed that the false position was the real one and the real one was the false position. Apart from these signs, we found nothing; since there was already too much daylight, we had to get back to Dubrova.[3]

Rüdiger von Zimburg joined the parachute force as a volunteer in 1941 and took part in the campaigns in Russia during the winter of 1942–1943, Italy 1943–1945 and Austria 1945.[4] Wounded several times, he became an officer and led *11. Kompanie* in Italy at the Gothic Line and was awarded the German Cross in Gold. At the end of the war, he was an *Oberleutnant* and led a battalion of *Fallschirmjäger Regiment 30* in Austria. He avoided captivity, studied law and later became a director in an Austrian industrial company. Also, he became a reserve officer in the Austrian army and finally held the rank of *Oberst*.

On 25 January, several Soviet attack groups of 50 to 100 men were also repulsed, by *197. Infanterie Division* on the

Rüdiger von Zimburg at the end of the war as *Oberleutnant* with German Cross in Gold, Iron Cross 1st and 2nd class, Ground Assault Badge, Paratrooper Jump Badge and Wound Badge in Silver. (Private Collection)

---

3 Zimburg, *Kriegserlebnisse*, p.72.
4 Rüdiger von Zimburg (Zell am See, 29 June 1923–Bad Gastein (mountain accident), 20 June 1993), *Oberleutnant*.

right of the battalion, and by the battalion itself. The fighting could be heard by *Feldwebel* Germer of *3. Kompanie*:

> During the night the Russian was very restless; in general, they seem to fear an attack at night much more than we do! ... There was a lot of noise from our neighbours to the right (hurrah-cries of the Russians). Enemy attacked our section with strong assault troops (50–100, so over company strength) which were repulsed everywhere. Increased alert, but everything remains quiet.[5]

Also, an enemy scouting party on skis was observed in front of the battalion's positions, which were new and reinforced the impression that the enemy's reconnaissance was scanning the front for weak points.[6]

On the same day, *Hauptfeldwebel* Willi Wagner wrote to his wife about daily life in the positions:

> The day of our transfer is coming closer and closer. This will mean some sleepless and probably cold nights. It seems as if winter is just beginning. At the moment it is quite cold. The temperature may be around -30° [he exaggerates only a little: on the 24th it was -21, on the 25th -5°C].[7] But I will dress warmly. I have a thick pilot's fur combination, and some felt boots, so the cold can't do me much harm. But it's still uncomfortable on the lorry when you're driving for a long time. Hopefully we will at least find some bunkers and enough wood in our corner. Our current location used to be a small town. We have demolished over three quarters of it so far for bunker construction and firewood. They were all wooden houses. Our bunkers were also winterized and built safely. It took a lot of work, but we felt quite comfortable, and, above all, we had no bugs, which usually live in every bunker. Tomorrow we'll have a quick bath and put on some fresh clothes.[8]

But he also got lucky, which he mentions to his wife: 'However, the Russian has become very cheeky in the last few days and wanted to disturb us while we were bathing. Just when we were in the sauna, he shot at us with his artillery. The hits were all in the immediate vicinity of the sauna. But miraculously no one was wounded.'[9]

On the 26th, the men of the battalion were informed that they would be relieved by *II. Bataillon/ Grenadier Regiment 347* during the night of 29 to 30 January. They immediately began preparations and built sledges for the transport. On 28 January, 'a preliminary detachment arrived from the infantry that is to take over our section ... Ordinary ammunition remains in the positions, special ammunition remains with the units. *3. Kompanie* comes to Klestova [a hamlet] into the section *III. Bataillon/Fallschirmjäger Regiment 3. 3. Kompanie* received over 60 pairs of felt boots, so that now every man has one pair of guard boots.'[10]

Initially, the battalion was to be transferred to *II. Bataillon* on the left wing, but this plan was abandoned as there was no fuel available. The battalion remained behind the right wing of the division.

---

5   BA-MA, BW 57-81: Entry 25 January 1943.
6   BA-MA, RH 24-6/130 in BW 57-39: telex of Fl.Div.7 to VI. AK., 25 January 1943, 9:00 p.m.
7   BA-MA, RL 33/54.
8   Archive Franz: Wagner, letter dated 25 January 1943.
9   Archive Franz: Wagner, letter dated 25 January 1943.
10 BA-MA, BW 57-81: entry 28 January 1943.

The paratroopers of *Flieger Division 7* procured wood everywhere and demolished the wooden houses of Starina and the vicinity. (Private Collection)

For the next few days, the battalion lay in peace in the Klestova-Skalyaeva area and reinforced the so-called second position on both sides of the Dukhovshchina-Starina road. *Hauptfeldwebel* Wagner wrote knowingly to his wife: 'But there will certainly and probably come a time when I may not be able to write for weeks. At present we are waiting for our transfer and with it begins a new phase of our deployment here.'[11]

---

11 Archive Franz: Wagner, letter dated 4 February 1943.

16

II. Bataillon 11 January–8 February 1943

At the time *III. Bataillon* was transferred to Velikiye Luki, *II. Bataillon* was still preparing an attack in its section at *197. Infanterie Division*. Daily patrols by *6.* and *7. Kompanie* scouted the Soviet positions (base '*Russenpfad*' – Russian trail) for more than a week. On 14 January the attack (codenamed operation 'Pommery') took place in -25°C and clear weather. The attack group of 220 men consisted of *7. Kompanie* (one officer, 90 men), a group of *8. Kompanie*, and a platoon of *6. Kompanie* (one officer and 29 men). To the west, in the direction of Vervishche, *Hauptmann* Zuber, the commander of *6. Kompanie*, took over flank security with 30 men and the bicycle platoon (one officer and 30 men). To the northeast, the battalion reserve under *Oberleutnant* Kröhnke (one officer and 31 men) provided covering fire.

The attack is described in the war diary of *7. Kompanie*:

> After *6. Kompanie* (4:50 a.m.) and *7. Kompanie* (5:10 a.m.) reached the ordered assembly area, *Oberleutnant* Abratis pushed forward an advance guard, which was quickly targeted by very alert Russians at 5:15 a.m. *Oberleutnant* Abratis decided to attack immediately, at the same time the Russian telephone lines were cut. The approach was made more difficult, but not slowed down, by darkness, very cold weather (-25 degrees) and above all by the pine thicket and the countless hand grenades. Numerous casualties were inflicted by explosive charges triggered by trip wires. Under domes of fire and quick movement, the shock groups broke into the positions with splendid bravery. The Russians fought back to the utmost; ten bunkers were blown up. 40 Russians were killed, eight prisoners including one lieutenant, four machine guns, one mortar, 33 rifles and equipment captured.[1]

That the attacking group ran into problems was observed by *Feldwebel* Germer of *3. Kompanie*:

> Tight fire control could be observed from the abrupt fire of our own weapons hitting the targets. After my quick report to the chief, I assigned the mortars of *4.* and *13. Kompanie* as well as the batteries of the assigned artillery to join the defensive fire, with fire on the southern part of the 'Pear', in the bushy area between Ovsyankina and 'Pear' and on the bunker height between

---

1   BA-MA: BW 57-84: War Diary of 7.Kp./II./FJR 1.

Paratroopers of the 6. *Kompanie* on patrol in the 'Little Pear Forest'. The lack of visibility in the forest and the resulting difficulties are clearly evident. (Private Collection)

A heavy mortar position of the paratroopers. (BDF Archive)

Ovsyankina and Vervishche. The Russian responded with fire on [our positions] (they were searching for the firing positions of our heavy mortars).[2]

The war diary of *7. Kompanie* mentions 'own losses: four killed, nine seriously wounded, 32 slightly wounded.'[3] In its first interim report on 14 January 1943 *197. Infanterie Division* erroneously reported casualties of three killed, 15 seriously wounded and 10 slightly wounded. Dr Müller correctly gave a total of 41 wounded,[4] which is confirmed by the casualty lists. One of the seriously wounded later died in hospital, bringing the total to five killed: *Obergefreite* Glenewinkel (6. Kp.),[5] Oberlehberg,[6] Helten,[7] Bormann (all 8. Kp.),[8] and Kläner (7. Kp.)[9] who died of his wounds on 16 March 1943 at field hospital 2/551, Smolensk.[10] The war diary of *9. Armee* mentions this action but inflates the number of destroyed bunkers from 10 to 28.[11]

---

2 BA-MA, BW 57-81: Entry 14 January 1943.
3 BA-MA: BW 57-84: War Diary of 7.Kp./II./FJR 1.
4 Müller, *Damals*, p.72.
5 Wilhelm Glenewinkel (Hannover, 8 December 1919), *Obergefreiter*.
6 Wilhelm Friedrich Oberlehberg (Essen, 4 December 1921), *Obergefreiter*.
7 Josef Helten (Hülschrath/Neuss, 10 October 1917), *Obergefreiter*.
8 Wilhelm Bormann (Hannover, 14 March 1922), *Obergefreiter*.
9 Helmut Kläner (Bremen, 2 May 1922), *Obergefreiter*.
10 Volksbund, casualty lists, Ancestry/WASt.
11 NARA, T-312 T-317, KTB Nr.7 AOK 9, Führungs-Abteilung, 1 January–25 March 1943.

Major Kurt Gröschke, commander of *II. Bataillon* in December 1942. (BArch, Bild 101 I/552/802/18/Dahm [cut out])

On the same day, *197. Infanterie Division* was informed that *II. Bataillon* would soon be relieved and would have to be replaced by the division's own forces.[12] On 16 January, *Heeresgruppe Mitte* sent a telex to AOK 9 with the order that the battalion finally was to be relieved and was to be put at the disposal of *Flieger Division 7*. With this reserve, the division was responsible for protecting both boundaries – on the right to *197.* and on the left to *330. Infanterie Division*. AOK 9 decided that the battalion, together with the staff of *Fallschirmjäger Regiment 1*, should be transferred as a reserve to the area behind the left boundary.[13] This measure became necessary because at Velish, which lay in the section of *330. Infanterie Division* and *86. Infanterie Division*, attacking Soviet units had succeeded in breaking into the town. German forces had to be called in to help and secure the area.

> It is necessary to rectify the situation at Velish as soon and strongly as possible. To accomplish this at least one battalion west of the Dyna is to be freed by immediate deployment of *Marsch Bataillon 257* to be transferred to Velish. Also, the general command [of *VI. Armee Korps*] is to move *II. Bataillon/Fallschirmjäger Regiment 1* in a way that if need arises *Grenadier Regiment 556* of *330. Infanterie Division* can be released for deployment at Velish.[14]

On the part of the Soviets, attempts were made, with little success, to influence the morale of the Germans through propaganda: 'The Russians provided some variety. A loudspeaker was set up and we heard this: "Well, there you are from the 5. and 6. *Kompanie*. Did you have a good Christmas? We are on our last day today. There is still time to come to us. There are beautiful women waiting for you. But then will come the great offensive."'[15] Needless to say, there was no offensive.

During the night of 17 to 18 January, *II. Bataillon* was relieved by *299. Pionier Bataillon*. At 9:30 a.m. on the 18th this process was completed, and the battalion waited in Gridino for onward transport, which took place on the 19th. Only *I. Bataillon* remained behind at Starina and was now directly under command of the division. Likewise, the self-propelled gun platoons of *Leutnant* Stain and *Leutnant* Brammer remained with this battalion.

---

12 BA-MA, RH 26-197/24: 197. ID, KTB, 1 January–30 June 1943, p.15.
13 BA-MA, RH 24-6/128, f 146 in BW 57-39.
14 BA-MA, RH 24-6/128 in BW 57-39: telex AOK 9 to VI. AK. of 17 January 1943, 10:00 p.m.:
15 Stain, 'Kriegstagebuch', p.96.

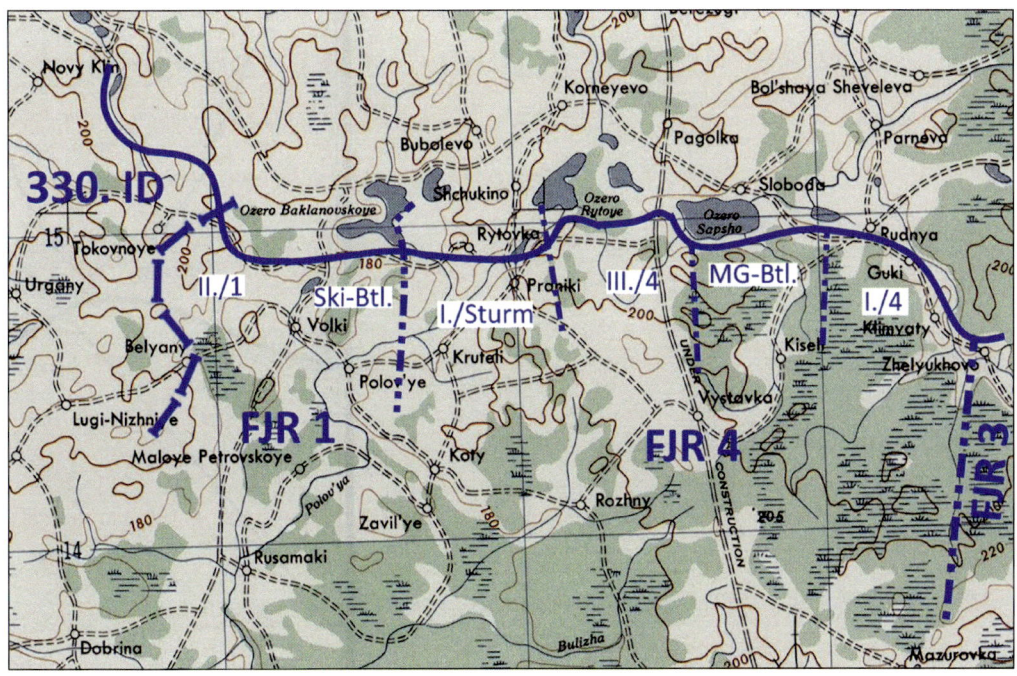

The section of *Fallschirmjäger Regiment 1* on the left wing of *Flieger Division 7* on 21 January 1943.

The departure was delayed because the ski battalion of *Flieger Division 7* was also called up and was to be deployed together with *II. Bataillon* on the far-left side of the division' section as part of the newly formed *Kampfgruppe Schulz*. A fuel truck's accident was the cause for the delay.[16] The ski battalion began to move into its new positions during the night of 18 to 19 January.

Gröschke's battalion was finally transported by motor vehicles on the 20th via Dukhovshchina-Demidov-Saborye to the left divisional boundary to Volki and relieved *Grenadier Regiment 556*, which was transported to Velish. *7. Kompanie* remained behind in Volki as the battalion's intervention reserve, while the other three companies took up positions about three kilometres to the north. On the night of 21 to 22 January, a tragic incident occurred there:

> At 9.45 p.m., the patrol which was on trench duty in the section of *5. Kompanie* noticed two people in a position unoccupied by the company, who retreated backwards as they approached. The patrol pursued them, called out to the men, who were wearing snow-white camouflage suits, 'Halt! Who goes there?' When the men did not answer, the patrol opened fire. One of them, they were Russians, was wounded and carried away by the second man. At the same time, a neighbouring machine-gun position spotted 35 to 40 Russians who were approaching the position one by one. Under fire from the MG, the Russians retreated leaving two dead …[17]

---

16 BA-MA, RH 24-6/128 in BW 57-39.
17 BA-MA: BW 57-84: War Diary of 7.Kp./II./FJR 1.

Landscape in front of the positions of *6. Kompanie* ('*Hein Höhe*', '*Stützpunkt Geyer*'. *Hauptmann* Kerfin was killed by friendly fire in front of similar positions on an elevation to the right. (Private Collection)

At 1:00 a.m. *Hauptmann* Kerfin,[18] the company commander, called *Feldwebel* Wolf. He asked him if he would be willing to retrieve the two dead Russians lying in front of the barbed wire, so that their units could be identified, as had been requested by the division. *Feldwebel* Wolf volunteered and went in front of the trench.

> He moved forward to the wire obstacle, but when it became clear that he alone could not get the Russians back who were frozen to the ground, *Hauptmann* Kerfin got out of the trench and moved forward as well. After a short time, several bursts of machine gun fire were fired at *Hauptmann* Kerfin from own positions. He was hit in the knee and head and died instantly.[19]

The machine gun platoon of *13. Kompanie/Fallschirmjäger Regiment 1* was supposed to cover the area in front of the trenches from the side. Unfortunately, Kerfin forgot to inform them to hold their fire.

The very respected *Hauptmann* Kerfin, a veteran of the campaigns in Poland, Rotterdam (where he was awarded with the Knight's Cross), Crete and Leningrad, was buried at the Saborye cemetery on 25 January 1943 in the presence of the divisional commander, *Generalmajor* Heidrich.

It became also known at *II. Bataillon* on 26 January that it would be relieved during the night of 29 to 30 January. *Oberleutnant* Abratis handed over the command of his *7. Kompanie* to *Oberleutnant* Jaenicke on 27 January, as he had to go to the field hospital at Saki due to a wound or illness.[20]

On 2 February, an internal reorganisation took place: *7. Kompanie* relieved one platoon each of the *5.* and *6. Kompanie* (*Oberfeldwebel* Stöppler and *Oberfeldwebel* Schneider) at Bolshoye Shugailovo in -12°C and overcast skies.

---

18 Horst Ludwig Walter Kerfin, (Insterburg, Ostpreußen, 21 March 1913–KIA Volki, 22 January 1943), *Hauptmann*. He received the Knight's Cross on 24 May 1940 as *Oberleutnant* and platoon leader of *11. Kompanie*/FJR 1 for his conduct at Rotterdam.
19 BA-MA: BW 57-84: War Diary of 7.Kp./II./FJR 1.
20 BA-MA: BW 57-84: War Diary of 7.Kp./II./FJR 1: two dates are mentioned: 27 as well as 31 January 1943.

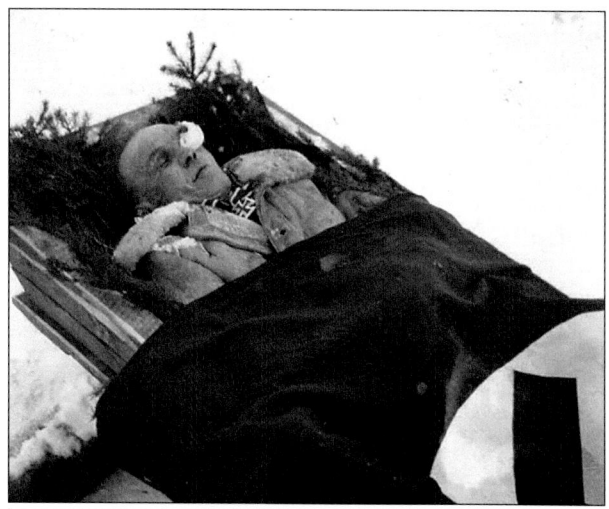

Death is a daily reality of the soldier at the front line: The body of *Hauptman* Kerfin is laid to rest in a simple coffin. As bearer of the Knight's Cross he was buried with military honours in presence of the divisional commander *Generalmajor* Heidrich. (Estate of Walter Heinkelein, Archive Crailsheim)

Lodgings of *6. Kompanie* well protected from enemy view at Strongpoint 'Geyer'. (Private Collection)

Oberjäger Anton Rieken (KIA Alekseyevka, 15 February 1943) in discussion with *Feldwebel* Willi Nollen from *6. Kompanie* at strongpoint 'Geyer'. (Private Collection)

After uneventful days, the transfer order to Orel arrived on 7 February. The transfer of the battalion took place during the night of 9 to 10 February, after its section had been handed over to *Jägerbataillon 4*.

The ski battalion remained in its positions but was now under command of *Kampfgruppe Walther*. Also, *14. Kompanie/Fallschirmjäger Regiment 5* commanded by *Oberleutnant* Höhn,[21] which had also been attached to *Kampfgruppe Schulz*, stayed behind.[22]

A snowstorm rages in January at Kholm in the rear area of *Fallschirmjäger Regiment 1*, making the supply runs difficult. (BDF Archive)

---

21   Max Höhn (Coburg, 12 May 1919-KIA, Garborov, 7 December 1943), *Oberleutnant*. After the winter deployment he was transferred to the staff of *Fallschirm Panzerjäger Abteilung 2* of *2. Fallschirmjäger Division*.
22   BA-MA, RL 33/69, pp.159–162.

17

The Crisis in the South

Soviet Intentions on the Southern Flank of *Heeresgruppe Mitte*

After the fall of Stalingrad on 2 February 1943, considerable forces of the Red Army had been freed for further offensives. According to Glantz's explanations,[1] it is clear that the Stavka planned to crush *Heeresgruppe Mitte* through multiple offensives. On 29 January successful offensives of the Bryansk and the Voronesh Fronts started towards Kharkov and Kursk, which also hit the southern flank of *Heeresgruppe Mitte*, in particular *LV. Armee Korps*. The strategic plans of the Stavka involved the formation of a new front, the Central Front, using the most recently freed armies of the Don Front around Stalingrad and others that were available as reserves.[2] This Central Front was to be established behind the Bryansk Front, which faced the German *2. Panzer Armee* under the command of *Generaloberst* Schmidt.[3]

Schmidt, commander of *2. Panzerarmee* from December 1941, was one of the few who protested the 'Commissar's Order' that required the summary execution of Soviet commissars and even openly opposed it. He also vehemently opposed any treatment of prisoners that violated international law. This attitude, the arrest of his younger brother for espionage, and the discovery of letters critical of the regime led to his dismissal on 14 April 1943.

Generaloberst Rudolf Schmidt, the commander of *2. Panzer Armee*. (BArch, Bild 183-2005-1017-520/Moosdorf [Mossdorf]/CC-BY-SA 3.0)

---

1   Glantz, *After Stalingrad*, pp.228–320.
2   Glantz, *After Stalingrad*, pp.258–259:The Central Front consisted of: 21st, 65th and 70th Army (6 divisions); 16th Air Army; 2nd Tank Army; 2nd Guards Cavalry Corps; 37th 51st, 52nd 67th Guards Rifle Division; 23rd, 69th, 112th, 149th, 193rd, 194th, 264th, 325th, 354th and 375th Rifle Divisions; 10th Anti-aircraft Artillery Division; 502nd, 1180th and 1188th Anti-Tank Artillery Regiment; 114th, 136th and 143rd RGK (Stavka Reserve) Mortar Regiments; 56th and 92nd Guards-mortar Regiments; 12th Anti-aircraft Artillery Battalion; 4th RGK Artillery Division; 6 Tank Regiments – all these troops were consolidated on 23 February 1943.
3   Rudolf Schmidt (Berlin, 12 May 1886–Krefeld, 7 April 1957), *Generaloberst*. See Johannes Hürter, *Hitlers Heerführer – Die deutschen Oberbefehlshaber im Krieg gegen die Sowjetunion 1941/42* (Munich: Oldenbourg, 2007), p.602; Chris Helmcke, 'Generaloberst Schmidt – Denken und Handeln im Vernichtungskrieg', *Militärgeschichte* (2017), issue 1, pp.14–17.

On 4 February 1943, Colonel General K.K. Rokossovsky was ordered to Moscow to see Stalin.[4] He was the previous commander of the Don Front, who was mainly responsible for the liberation of Stalingrad, where he interrogated *Generalfeldmarschall* Paulus as recently as 2 February 1943. During their conversation that same night, Stalin congratulated him and gave him his new assignment. Rokossovsky was to take over command of this new Soviet front.

According to the order of the Stavka, the creation of the Central Front would begin on 6 February 1943 and would be completed within six days. Rokossovsky, planned to start operations on 15 February. He identified the greatest challenge as the obvious, the timely arrival of the troops, which were still at Stalingrad.[5] It is understandable that this more than ambitious time schedule was bound to cause problems. Logistics, arrival times of the formations, as well as weather conditions were not properly estimated. The idea was that the Bryansk Front under Lieutenant General M.A. Reyter should advance on Bryansk by attacking from the north towards Belev with 61st Army,[6] from the east on Mtsensk with 3rd Army, from the south with 13th Army and via Maloarkhangelsk with 48th Army on Orel. The Central Front was to insert itself a little further south between the Bryansk Front and the Voronezh Front pushing first westwards with parts turning north via Karachev towards Bryansk. The purpose of this operation was primarily to encircle *2. Panzer Armee* in Orel. This was accompanied by a push of the Western Front from Kirov southwards towards Bryansk. The Western Front stood under the command of Lieutenant General Ivan Stepanovich Konev (see chapter 'Operation MARS') until 27 February 1943, followed by Lieutenant General Vasily Danilovich Sokolovsky.[7]

The second objective of the Central Front was to advance with the other parts, the 2nd Tank Army, further westward and then turn north towards Smolensk and Orsha, while in return the Kalinin Front near Velish was to push south towards these two cities. The Western Front was also to join this offensive with a thrust from Kirov towards Smolensk. If everything had gone according to these plans *Heeresgruppe Mitte* would have been crushed.[8]

While the Central Front was forming, Kursk fell into the hands of 60th Army (Voronezh Front) on 8 February, north of which the 48th Army under Major General G.A. Khalyuzin,[9] from 12 February Lieutenant General Romanenko,[10] and 13th Army under Major General (from 14 February Lieutenant General) Pukhov gained ground.[11] The latter two armies were part of General Reyter's

---

4 Konstantin Konstantinovich Rokossovsky (21 December 1896–3 August 1968), Marshal of the Soviet Union, Marshal of Poland, Polish Minister of Defence 1949–1956.
5 Boris Sokolov, *Marshall K.K. Rokossovsky* (Solihul: Helion, 2015), pp.235–236.
6 Max Andrejevich Reyter (Ventspils (Latvia), 24 April 1886–Moscow, 6 April 1950), Colonel General. From September 1942, he was commander of the Bryansk Front. He was relieved of command at the end of March 1943 and finally relieved of all active command in September 1943, when he was appointed commander of the Southern Urals Military District. His failure in the battles for Orel clearly led to this demotion.
7 Vasily Danilovich Sokolovsky (Bialystok, 21 July 1897–Moscow, 10 May 1968), Marshal of the Soviet Union. After the war Commander-in-Chief of the Group of Soviet Occupation Forces in Germany and Supreme Chief of the Soviet Military Administration.
8 Glantz, *After Stalingrad*, pp.252–259.
9 Grigory Alexeyevich Khalyuzin (Verkhneuralsk, 10 February 1897–Moscow, 27 September 1975) General Lieutenant. He was afterwards appointed deputy commander of 61st Army.
10 Prokofi Logvinovich Romanenko (25 February 1897–10 March 1949), Colonel General. He commanded 48th Army from 12 February 1943 until the end of 1944, when he had to resign for health reasons.
11 Nikolai Pavlovich Pukhov (Grishovo, 25 January1895–Moscow, 28 March 1958) Colonel General. He commanded the 13th Army until after the end of the war in 1946.

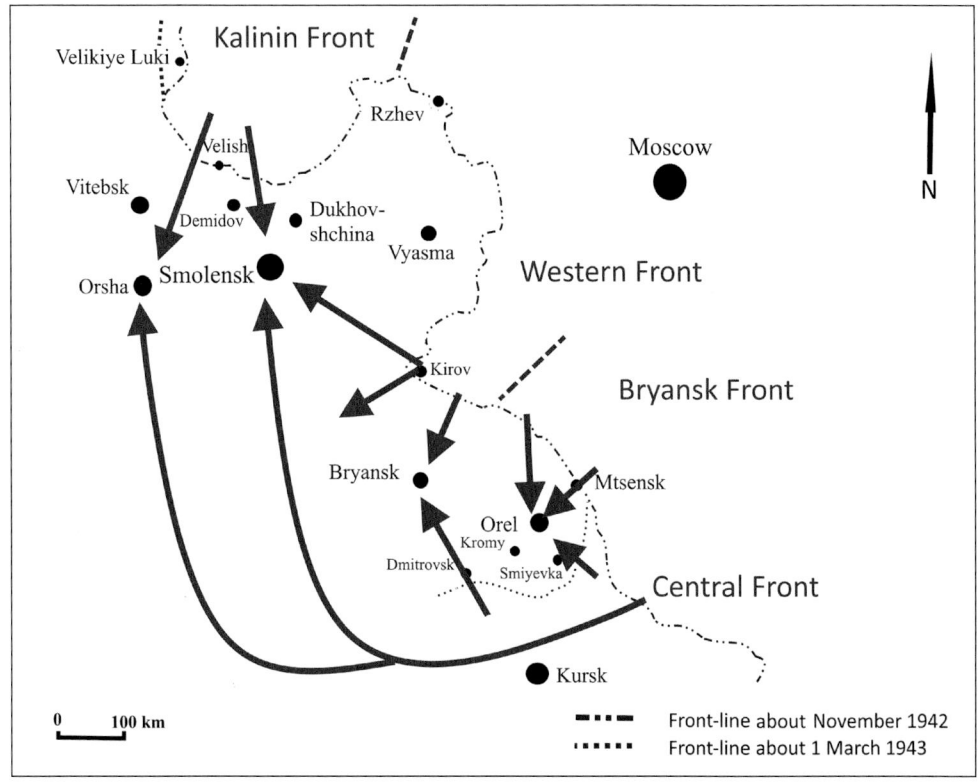

The Soviet strategic plan for the annihilation of *Heeresgruppe Mitte* of 6 February 1943.

Bryansk Front. One objective of Pukhov was to crush the German forces around Maloarkhangelsk, which General Reyter reconfirmed on 9 February, both armies were then to advance north towards Bryansk and Orel respectively. The offensive of these two armies began to lose momentum on 12 February when the availability of ammunition, rations and supplies became very critical.[12] The attack objective of the Bryansk Front, Orel, was supposed to fall as early as 17 February according to the Stavka's extremely ambitious planning, but this did not succeed. The success of the operation now depended on Rokossovsky's Central Front.

The Central Front – which was still in the process of being formed and at that time (9 February) only existed on paper – was to support the left flank of the Bryansk Front.[13] Rokossovsky's planed start of operations on 15 February proved impossible because the Central Front could only assemble most of its troops on 23 February and was in fact only ready by 25 February, as the transport of troops took more time than planned. Due to these delays and difficulties, the plans had to be changed. The Central Front was subsequently given Bryansk and Orel as new objectives. The push towards Smolensk had to be postponed.

---

12   Glantz, *After Stalingrad*, p.250.
13   Gerasimova, *Rzhev Slaughterhouse*, pp.127–129.

German Plans and Situation Assessments

The massing of forces in front of the German lines was detected and the staff of *2. Panzer Armee* and *Heeresgruppe Mitte* were largely able to predict the centre of gravity of the attacks, or at least to work out what the other side was planning. However, only the effects in the immediate vicinity were considered, while the ambitious overall concept of the advance on Smolensk from the south was probably not grasped to its full extent. It became clear to the German troops at the front through prisoner interrogations on 10 March 1943 that the main thrust of the 70th Army (Central Front) was directed towards Bryansk to encircle *2. Panzer Armee* in Orel.[14] However, German intelligence reports from *Fremde Heere Ost* asserted this in its situation assessments of 7 and 22 February 1943, where it already understood that the main thrust of the 13th Army on Orel, the attempt to envelop *LV. Armee Korps* and thereby roll up the whole of the southern front of *Heeresgruppe Mitte*.[15]

The great good fortune of *Heeresgruppe Mitte* was that, as early as mid-January, planning had begun for operation BÜFFELBEWEGUNG (BUFFALO MOVEMENT), a controlled withdrawal of Model's *9. Armee* from the Rzhev salient to shorten the front and free up substantial forces to be thrown against Soviet attacks from the south. Even before BUFFALO MOVEMENT was launched on 1 March – Hitler had approved the operation on 6 February, the same day the Stavka made their plans for the annihilation of *Heeresgruppe Mitte* – units and formations were being withdrawn from *9. Armee* to be transferred to the trouble spots on the southern front of *Heeresgruppe Mitte*, leading to repeated complaints from Model. It should be noted that *Heeresgruppe Mitte* largely succeeded in spoiling the Stavka's plans. Manstein's successful counter-offensive in the south around Kharkov, which tied up troops intended for the Central Front, also helped.

It is evident from *Generaloberst* Schmidt's assessment of the situation on 10 February that he was already attempting to protect himself in the event of defeat and to shift the blame to other factors.[16] He argued that *2. Panzer Armee* had had to surrender eight divisions since September 1942, so that at this point the 308-kilometre-long frontline was already insufficiently manned, and no reserves were available.

Schmidt's request for reinforcements of 23 January 1943, because of the sparsely occupied front line in general and also because of the lack of automatic weapons, was rejected by the OKH Chief of Staff, *Generaloberst* Zeitzler. Since it might have been necessary to withdraw additional forces from this relatively quiet section of the front due to the development of situation in the south (Stalingrad) no reserves could be spared for Schmidt. However, the situation changed with dramatic speed and only a short time later the right wing was the most endangered section of the army group.

Luftwaffenkommando Ost, commanded by *General* Ritter von Greim was able to bring most of its planes to the airfields around Orel, mainly *Jagdgeschwader 51* 'Mölders', which was equipped with new Fokke-Wulf Fw 190 fighter planes as well as He 111 and Ju 88 bombers. On the Soviet side only a long-range bomber force was able to hit the German rear with success – mainly railway stations. During the day the German fighters enjoyed almost complete air superiority. Bryansk Front's 48th Army had to endure He 111 bombing raids.[17] The Luftwaffe units could not be deployed on all focus

---

14   NARA, T-315 R-634: *12. Panzer Division*, KTB, Anlagenheft 1 zum Tätigkeitsbericht Nr.4, Abteilung Ic 1.1.1943–28.2.1943, Anlagen 1-120; Prisoner interrogation No. 22, 10 March 1943.
15   CAMO, 500_12451, file 335.
16   NARA, T-313 R-153: PzAOK 2, KTB 3, vol.1., entry 10 February 1943: Assessment of the situation.
17   Christer Bergström, *Black Cross – Red Star, Air War over the Eastern Front, Volume 4 – Stalingrad to Kuban* (Eskilstuna: Vaktel, 2019), pp.208–209.

points at the same time, which gave 15th Air Army, which was to support Bryansk and Central Front, in between the opportunity to fly attacks on railway stations and artillery positions around Orel at the end of February.[18] At the beginning of March intensified activity by *Luftwaffenkommando Ost* in support of *2. Panzer Armee* hampered the Bryansk and Central Front's movements.[19]

LV. Armee Korps under *General der Infanterie* Erwin von Vierow was under heavy pressure from constant attacks after 29 January and had to fall back.[20] The combatant strengths of *45. Infanterie Division* and *383. Infanterie Division* dwindled rapidly. On 10 February the main line of defence held despite losing extensive terrain in the days before. Continued attrition of the already battered German divisions was expected, as were the main thrusts first from Pnyri to the north, second from the south on Glubki in the right section of *383. Infanterie Division* and third against the left section of *45. Infanterie Division*. As von Vierow was obviously not able to handle the subsequent crisis, OKH decided that he was to switch command with *General der Artillerie* Freiherr (Baron) von Roman,[21] the commander of *XX. Armee Korps* on 14 February. Von Roman took back command of his corps on 10 March after saving the situation for *LV. Armee Korps*.

In addition, Soviet movements indicated possible enemy attack intentions in the area north of Mtsensk.

> In front of the right section of the *112. Infanterie Division* [on the northern wing of the army] systematic advancing of [Soviet] forces are also observed. This is the location of *Grenadier Regiment 350* of the *221. Sicherungs Division* which is not fully suited for large-scale fighting. Opposite of the northern front of the *112. Infanterie Division* the enemy has also brought in reinforcements in motorised transport in the strength of about one regiment. It is not yet clear whether this is a diversionary manoeuvre or preparation for an advance to the south-west. The apparently completed enemy deployments in front on this section of the front suggest the latter.[22]

To counter the imminent danger, on 10 February, as one of the reinforcements intended for the southern wing of *Heeresgruppe Mitte*, *Fallschirmjäger Regiment 1*, was detached from the northern part of the front and transferred 400 kilometres to the south to *2. Panzer Armee* in the Orel salient. The regiment was to be transferred to the army as a reserve under the – once again – strict instruction that it was to be deployed only as a whole unit.[23] This point subsequently had to be largely ignored due to the dramatic development of the situation.

In accordance with the Soviet planning described above, the Soviet attacks and penetrations of the German front took place at many different points without a discernible centre of gravity, so that the arriving paratroopers were immediately thrown into different defensive positions to stop the enemy who

---

18   Bergström, *Black Cross – Red Star, Volume 4*, p.213.
19   Bergström, *Black Cross – Red Star, Volume 4*, p.216.
20   Erwin von Vierow (Berlin, 15 May 1890–Tecklenburg, 1 February 1982), *General der Infanterie*, RK 15 November 1941. He was afterwards sent to France as military commander of North-West France and was taken prisoner of war by the British as commanding general of the *Generalkommando Somme* on 1 September 1944.
21   Rudolf Freiherr von Roman (Bayreuth, 19 November 1893–Schernau, 18 February 1970), *General der Artillerie*. RK (19 February 1942) Oak Leaves (28 October 1943). He successfully led different army corps as commanding general until the end of the war and fell into American captivity in May 1945.
22   NARA, T-313 R-153: PzAOK2, KTB 3, vol.1., entry 10 February 1943: Assessment of the situation.
23   NARA, T-315 R-153: PzAOK 2, KTB, 10 February 1943, p.4: Conversation between *Generaloberst* Schmidt and *Generalfeldmarschall* von Kluge at 8:00 p.m.

might break through or who had already broken through. In addition, the already confusing situation changed hourly, with reserves being moved from one location to another. This was done partly by lorry or horse-drawn sledges, but often also on foot. These movements were hampered by heavy snowstorms, which repeatedly made the transport routes impassable, and by extremely low temperatures.

Weather conditions were generally changeable. During February and March, it became increasingly warmer, and thaws alternated with snowstorms, frost and generally cold weather. It was these changing conditions, as well as the lack of prepared shelters and emplacements that made it very difficult for all units thrown into this battle to maintain their fighting strength. There were high casualties from frostbite and exhaustion. The attackers of the Central Front did not fare much better, as the Soviet soldiers were rushed from Stalingrad with no time to rest due to the ambitious time schedule, and thrown into battle as they arrived. Moreover, as prisoner testimonies confirm, soldiers were forcibly recruited from the newly liberated villages and thrown into battle poorly equipped and without any further training. The *Luftwaffe* succeeded in attacking the transport lines of the Central Front as it had only one railway line available to transport its forces from Stalingrad to Yelets. This line was an obvious target for German bombers who were able to successfully disrupt these transports. In addition, the transport columns moving towards the front along the only access road via Livny were under constant air attack.[24]

One gets the impression of a breathless, uncoordinated race, in constantly evolving circumstances, coupled with wishful thinking, which literally bled both sides dry. The Winter Battle of Orel was significant; it was not an 'unimportant' sideshow, or merely a struggle for the existence of the *2. Panzer Armee*, but of the entire *Heeresgruppe Mitte*.

Attempts to Relieve *Flieger Division 7*

On 9 January Hitler decided to withdraw *Flieger Division 7* from the front north of Smolensk and to assign it to *Heeresgruppe Don* or *Heeresgruppe B*. It would be replaced by a division brought in from the west.[25] Thus, on 12 January 1943, the *Führer*'s corresponding order reached *Heeresgruppe Mitte*, according to which *Flieger Division 7* was to be relieved and transferred at the beginning of February. A general staff officer of *9. Armee* noted this in its war diary with regret and spontaneously – and most unusually – paid tribute to this division:

> Even if the necessity of this measure [the replacement of the *Flieger Division 7* with a division brought in from the west] must be seen in the context of the wider situation, the army is extremely reluctant to lose this outstanding formation, which represents the mainstay of the entire western front [of *9. Armee*], and the western division promised in its place can replace it neither in numbers nor in fighting strength.[26]

---

24 Bergström, *Black Cross – Red Star, Volume 4*, p.214.
25 Percy E. Schramm (ed.), *Kriegstagebuch des Oberkommandos der Wehrmacht* (Augsburg: Weltbild, 2005) vol.3, 1943, part 1, p.29.
26 NARA, T-312 R-317; AOK 9, KTB Nr. 7, *Führungsabteilung*, 1 January–25 March 1943, entry 12 January 1943. Several battalions had already been detached for the relief of Velikiye Luki or to *Heeresgruppe Mitte*, which thinned out the front very much without fighting and was constantly deplored in the war diary of *9. Armee* (3 January: One battalion of IR 353 and PiBtl of 205 ID; 6. and 7. January: II./GR 353 and JägerBtl 8, 10 January: III./Lw.F.Rgt. *Moskau* and III./FJR 1).

THE CRISIS IN THE SOUTH   141

The very next day, 13 January, the OKH sent a telex to *Heeresgruppe Mitte* confirming this plan, stating that *327. Infanterie Division* would replace the division in mid-February. However, it remained uncertain what would happen to the division afterwards.²⁷ The planned replacement was repeatedly cited with concern in the war diary of AOK 9:

> Finally, after the planned exchange of the 7. Fl.Div. for the 327. ID, the front of VI. AK will also be seriously weakened … Due to the withdrawal of significant forces, the fronts are now so thinly manned everywhere that a large proportion of enemy attacks and advances inevitably lead to incursions into the front, with only a small number of forces available to seal them off.²⁸

As late as 27 January, OKH insisted on an accelerated replacement of the *Flieger Division 7* by *327. Infanterie Division*. The former was to gather as an OKH reserve north of Smolensk.²⁹ On 2 February – after Stalingrad had finally fallen – AOK 9 learned that *327. Infanterie Division* which was brought up from Italy could not join this army, since it was urgently needed on the southern wing of *Heeresgruppe Mitte* and was redirected to *2. Armee* near Kursk. This development was not viewed with displeasure, as was noted in the war diary, as *Flieger Division 7* thus remained with *9. Armee*.³⁰

Nevertheless, on 3 February, Göring ordered the *Fallschirmjäger-Ausbildungsregiment 1* to be transferred to France to establish a new formation. This regiment was in the Gomel area and was engaged in both training new recruits and fighting partisans.³¹ Exactly when this order was executed is not certain. As late as 8 February, *4. Kompanie* of this regiment suffered losses of at least nine dead, missing and wounded in an engagement with partisans near Babichy, 50 kilometres north of Gomel.³²

On 5 February, an order was received to send a regiment of paratroopers by air to Dnepropetrovsk.³³ The news was received at 7:30 p.m. by *9. Armee*, which was concerned: 'A drastic measure!' The same evening *Heeresgruppe Mitte* was informed 'that a strong [I.] and a weak [III.] battalion of *Fallschirmjäger Regiment 1* (currently in reserve) were ready to leave immediately, the III./1 [meant to be II./1] could only be detached after other forces had been brought in.'³⁴ This could happen in two to three days. The war diary of *VI. Armee Korps* smugly noted: 'According to earlier experience it is also by no means certain that the regiment will be transferred, since the *Reichsmarschall* [Göring] himself decides on the deployment of the units of *7. Flieger Division*.'³⁵

It turned out exactly as expected. The following day, the regiment remained in position. The *Oberkommando der Luftwaffe* (OKL) reversed this order – after all, the division was to be deployed as a whole formation and not to be divided. A back and forth between the parties involved ensued, which ultimately led to a day being lost and the regiment not being released from the front until 7 February.

On 7 February at 1:00 a.m., the order of the army command of *9. Armee* was received by *VI. Armee Korps* that in the morning of the same day *Fallschirmjäger Regiment 1* (regimental staff, *I.* and *III. Bataillon*) were to be brought to Smolensk to be transported to Orel to *2. Panzer Armee*, while *II.*

---

27   CAMO, 500_12454, file 633.
28   NARA, T-312 R-317; AOK 9, KTB Nr. 7, entry 13 January 1943 and nearly identical on 24 January.
29   CAMO, 500_12454, file 633.
30   NARA, T-312 R-317; AOK 9, KTB Nr. 7, entry 2 February 1943.
31   CAMO, 500_12454, file 633.
32   Casualty list.
33   CAMO, 500_12454, file 633.
34   NARA, T-312 R-317; AOK 9, KTB Nr. 7, entry 5 February 1943.
35   BA-MA, RH 24-6/129; VI. AK, KTB 3, vol.57, entry 5 February 1943.

Bataillon was to be relieved by *Jägerbataillon 4* as soon as possible and was also to be sent on its way. By 10:30 a.m. *III. Bataillon* had begun to depart, but heavy snowdrifts hindered the transport. The last parts of *I. Bataillon* moved on 8 February at 8:00 a.m. The relief of *II. Bataillon* was delayed because snowstorms prevented *Jägerbataillon 4* from moving in. The relief could only be carried out during the night of 9 to 10 February.

At 1:55 p.m. on 8 February, *Flieger Division 7* received a preliminary notice from the *Oberkommando der Luftwaffe* that one more regiment was to be released and taken by air transport to Kharkov. This information prompted the author of the war diary of *9. Armee* to remark: 'How this detachment is to be carried out in practice remains a mystery for the time being.'[36]

Fallschirmjäger Regiment 1 would be provided with particularly strong anti-tank defences, since the second regiment which was to be transported by air could not carry them. *Heeresgruppe Mitte* only received written notification of this from OKH at 8:40 p.m. The order clearly stated that the army group was to 'detach another regiment of *7. Flieger Division* from the front as soon as possible and make it available for air transport in the Smolensk area.'[37] The plan was never carried out, however, and the other regiments of the division remained in their positions.

The negotiated solution to this apparently prolonged conflict with the OKL was probably to leave *Flieger Division 7* where it was for the time being and, as a concession to *Heeresgruppe Mitte*, to allow the regiment to be used as a reserve in the army group's own area.

Thus, on 10 February at 8:00 p.m. *Generalfeldmarschall* von Kluge instructed *Generaloberst* Schmidt about the deployment of the paratroopers: 'A parachute regiment of *7. Flieger Division* is to be transferred to the army, which is to be placed under command of the army as a reserve after its arrival in Orel. The high commander of the *Heeresgruppe Mitte* emphasizes that the regiment is to be deployed as a unit if possible.'[38]

After arriving at Orel, *Fallschirmjäger Regiment 1* was deployed at various focal points of *2. Panzer Armee* and, contrary to the explicit instructions of *Heeresgruppe Mitte*, was completely torn apart in the process. Individual battalions and even companies were subordinated to different units and formations and were only slowly reunited piece by piece over the course of a month, so the path of the individual battalions and sometimes companies has to be considered individually but can often only be pieced together due to a lack of sources.

---

36   NARA, T-312 R-317; AOK 9, KTB Nr. 7, entry 9 February 1943.
37   CAMO, 500_12454, file 633.
38   NARA, T-315 R-153: Pz.AOK 2, KTB, 10 February 1943, p.4

18

The Transfer of *Fallschirmjäger Regiment 1* to Orel (9–14 February 1943)

The regimental staff, *I.* and *III. Bataillon* of *Fallschirmjäger Regiment 1* were resting in Smolensk on 8 February 1943 and awaited their transfer to Orel – *II. Bataillon* still had to be detached from the front and the units reinforcing the regiment were also still on their way to Smolensk.

On the evening of the 8th, *VI. Armee Korps* received the necessary orders from the high command of *9. Armee*:

1) 7. Fl.Div. will provide 168 trucks for the onward transport of FschJgRgt 1 from Smolensk, which, if they are not needed for the transport of II./FschJgRgt 1 to be detached during the night of 9/10 February, are to be immediately deployed to Smolensk.
2) Regimental staff, I., III./FschJgRgt 1 will leave Smolensk on 10 February early in the morning by truck via Roslavl in the direction of Bryansk. Destination still to be decided.
3) If not required by the division, one KrKw [ambulance] platoon is to be transferred to FschJgRgt 1.
4) One *Flak Abteilung* [anti-aircraft-gun battalion] of the division is to be detached during the night of 9/10 February.
5) General command [*VI. Armee Korps*] reports with the daily report on 9 February when II./FschJgRgt 1 and the *Flak Abteilung* can start from Smolensk.[1]

Finally at 7:05 p.m. on 9 February, written authorization from OKH was received by *Heeresgruppe Mitte*, thereby amending the orders already given on 5 and 8 February, to move a parachute regiment to the southern wing as soon as possible.[2] At 9:10 p.m. *Heeresgruppe Mitte* issued an order to *Flieger Division 7*, stating that *Fallschirmjäger Regiment 1*, reinforced by a *Flak Abteilung* (*I./Flak Regiment 501* which was attached to *Flak Regiment 18*, formerly subordinated to *Kampfgruppe Walther*)[3] under the command of *Hauptmann* Buhre, and an ambulance platoon, was to move in an accelerated 'motor vehicle march' through Bryansk to Orel. The regiment was to be deployed by the *Panzer Armee Oberkommando 2* (PzAOK 2) for the *Heeresgruppe* in such a way 'that it could be brought forward

---

1 BA-MA, RH 20-9/118, f 12185 in BW 57-39: telex AOK 9 to VI. AK, 7:00 p.m., 8 February 1943.
2 CAMO, 500_12454, file 633.
3 *Flak Regiment 501* consisted only of this mixed *Abteilung* and had no regimental staff. It was attached to *Flak Regiment 18* which was part of *6. Flak Division* (Information kindly provided by Ingo Apel, 17 March 2024).

both in the direction of Mtsensk and to the south.[4] To fulfil this objective, the regimental staff had to leave as soon as possible on 10 February with all the elements of the regiment that could be loaded onto lorries by noon that day. It was expressly forbidden to wait for the entire regiment to be assembled, as the crisis in the south of the army group was considered to be too serious. The remaining parts were to follow the next day.

The paratroopers of *Fallschirmjäger Regiment 1*, who had been resting in Smolensk since 7 and 8 February, used the very short waiting time to clean themselves and their equipment. *Oberfeldwebel* Wagner, corresponded with his spouse on 10 February:

> For two days I have been stationed in Smolensk waiting here for further transfer. We are going to go south. Today I was here for delousing. But I don't have lice, I just wanted to take a decent bath. You must take every opportunity here to wash properly. Besides, you'll be examined in the facility right away and that can't hurt either, even if you're not ill.[5]

Others, like *Gefreiter* von Zimburg, used the time to do some sightseeing: 'By and large, Smolensk was completely destroyed. However, the cathedral on a hill, which housed the so-called "Godless Museum",[6] was undamaged. Unfortunately, I didn't have time to have a closer look at it. Before the war, Smolensk must have been a very pretty city.'[7]

In Smolensk some organisational reshuffles took place, for example, *Oberleutnant* Otto took over the leadership of *3. Kompanie*.[8]

The exact strength of the regiment before it marched off to Orel can only be determined with limited accuracy. However, the files of *Heeresgruppe Mitte* contain an undated organisational chart of *Fallschirmjäger Regiment 1*, which must have been prepared by the regiment itself or by *Flieger Division 7* for *Heeresgruppe Mitte* around mid-February 1943.[9] It contains the combatant strength of the battalions and heavy weapons but does not include *Flak Abteilung I./501*. Accordingly, at the departure from Smolensk the regiment consisted of the following:

The Uspensky cathedral in Smolensk. (Private Collection)

---

4 BA-MA, RH 24-6/132, f 19, in BW 57-39: Telex of HGr *Mitte* to VI. AK and *Flieger Division 7*, which was sent as well to AOK 9 and PzAOK 2 on 9 February 1943, 9:10 p.m.
5 Archive Franz: Wagner, letter dated 10 February 1943.
6 All religious objects had been removed from the cathedral by the communists and replaced instead 'by an exhibition showing embryos of various ages fixed in jars'. The Germans removed this exhibition after they took Smolensk in 1941. Werner Wachsmuth, *Ein Leben mit dem Jahrhundert* (Berlin: Springer, 1985), pp.95–96.
7 Zimburg, *Kriegserlebnisse*, p.78.
8 BA-MA, BW 57-81.
9 CAMO, 500_12454, file 637.

Regimental staff (*Oberstleutnant* Schulz):
  signals platoon
  bicycle platoon
  engineer platoon
  13. *Kompanie*: combatant strength: three officers, 107 men, with three platoons of 10 cm *Nebelwerfer*.
  14. *Kompanie*: combatant strength: one officer, 87 men, with two platoons of 4.2 cm Pak (4 guns each), one platoon 5 cm Pak (three guns and one 3.7 cm Pak).
I. Bataillon (*Major* Graf von der Schulenburg): three light and one heavy company; combatant strength: 15 officers, 564 men
II. Bataillon (*Major* Gröschke): combatant strength about the same as *I. Bataillon* [6 February: 446 men]
III. Bataillon (*Hauptmann* Becker) combatant strength: 11 officers, 391 men

Subordinated to the regiment by *Flieger Division 7*:

one platoon 5 cm Pak (3 guns) (*I. Zug, 1. Kompanie, Fallschirm Fla.M.G. Btl.* under command of *Oberleutnant* Wagner)[10]
two platoons 7.5 cm self-propelled anti-tank guns, with three guns each (platoon *Leutnant* Bruno Brammer, platoon *Oberfeldwebel* Pusch of *Fallschirm Panzerjäger Abteilung*) with their own supply train of six trucks.[11]
one group of surgeons
one platoon of ambulances

It is astonishing how quickly *III. Bataillon* was put up to strength after the losses at Velikiye Luki. On 6 February, the battalion still had a strength of 192 men, which means that in the meantime it had been partially replenished from its low of only 144 men. In the short term, 210 men were supplied to the battalion as replacements, although this certainly included a number of those who had recovered from minor wounds and frostbite.

An officer of *I. Bataillon* was sent ahead to the command post of *2. Panzer Armee* (PzAOK 2) to receive the appropriate orders. This battalion was the first to begin its march to Orel; *II.* and *III. Bataillon* were to follow in that order.

The departure of *I. Bataillon*, scheduled for noon, seems to have been delayed, because at least *2. Kompanie* – according to the recollections of a paratrooper of this company – did not leave Smolensk until around 5:30 p.m.[12] while they arrived 'in Bryansk at 8 a.m.[13] on 11 February, completely frozen. It was miserably cold! We again took up quarters in some barracks, where we could sleep until noon. Afterwards we were given something to eat and at 2 p.m. we continued on the road in the direction

---

10 Hans-Theodor Wagner (1918-?), *Oberleutnant*. BA-MA, RH 24-6/288: Officers list *Flieger Division 7* of 15 March 1943.
11 See also: Bruno Brammer, 'Kriegstagebuch', *Traditionsgemeinschaft Fallschirmpanzerjäger Abteilung 1,* Jahresbrief 16 (1983), pp.108–111.
12 This delay is also confirmed by the above-cited letter of Willi Wagner, as he had time to bathe, be medically examined and also write a letter to his wife on this day.
13 *3. Kompanie* arrived at 9:00 a.m. in Bryansk (BA-MA, BW 57-81).

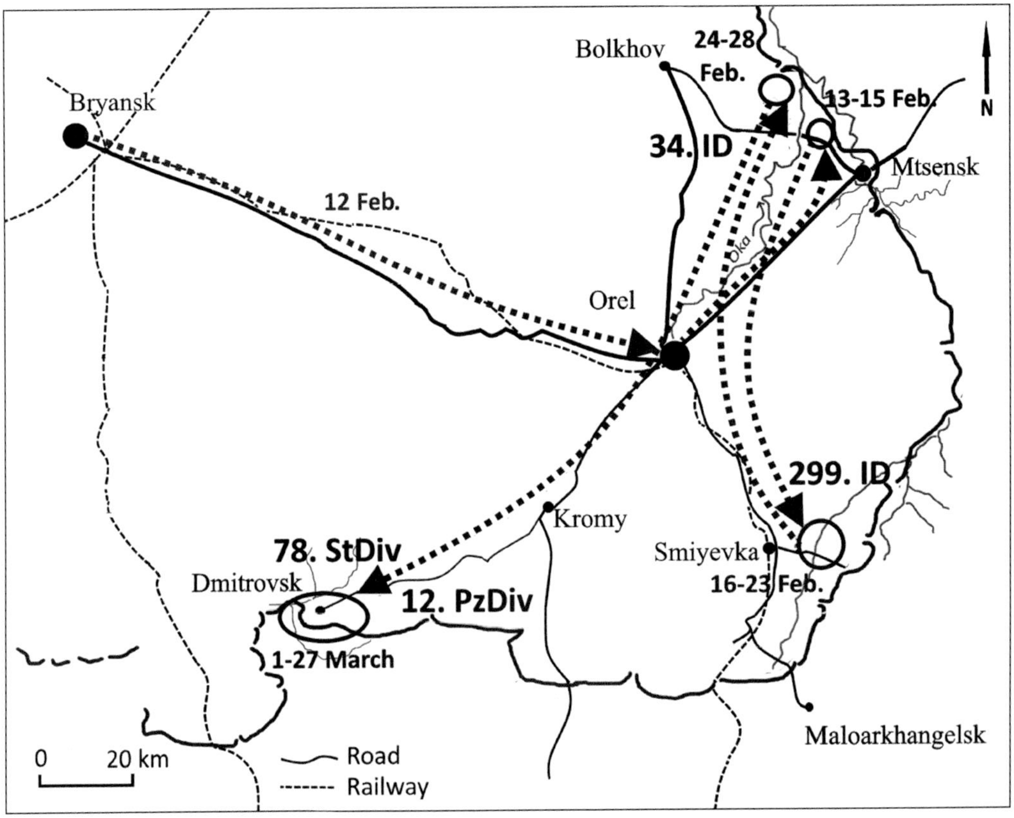

146 SOLID AS A ROCK

Deployment of *I. Bataillon* around Orel, February to March 1943.

of Orel in a snowstorm.'[14] It was indeed bitterly cold at -27°C. On the morning of the 12th, the transport stopped outside Orel to wait for the end of a Soviet high altitude bombing raid that was taking place, which led to 'personnel and material losses' within the city.[15]

While *I. Bataillon* was on its way to Orel, the situation around Mtsensk, which was in the defensive sector of *XXXV. Armee Korps* (*General der Infanterie* Rendulic),[16]

The divisional symbol on the back of the lorry, an arrow pointing down from the right to the left, makes it easy to identify as belonging to *Flieger Division 7*. (Private Collection)

---

14 Zimburg, *Kriegserlebnisse*, p.78.
15 NARA, T-315 R-153: PzAOK 2, KTB 3, vol.1, entry 12 February 1943, p.3.
16 Lothar Rendulic (Wiener Neustadt, 23 October 1887–Eferding, 18 January 1971) *Generaloberst*. As illegal

deteriorated. Also, on its left flank in the sector of *LIII. Armee Korps* and on the corps boundary line between these two, between *296.* and *112. Infanterie Division*, constant feeds of Soviet reinforcements were observed. A major attack was expected here. Therefore, on the 12th, PzAOK 2 immediately sent the battalion on towards Mtsensk, where it was to reinforce the left wing of *34. Infanterie Division*, which had to defend a front section of over 45 kilometres and consisted of *Grenadier Regiment 80, 107* and *253*. To the left was the above mentioned *112. Infanterie Division*. The roads were difficult to pass because of constant snowstorms. No sooner had they been cleared than they were impassable again only two hours later. It took the paratroopers until the next day, 13 February in the morning, to reach Frolovka, northwest of Mtsensk. There the companies were immediately divided up: *1.* and *3. Kompanie* took up positions near Karandakovo; *4. Kompanie* near Vyskrebentsevo; *2. Kompanie* and the battalion staff remained at Frolovka, where they shared quarters with an artillery battalion. Two platoons of *14. Kompanie* were attached to this battalion. Renewed snowfall made roads impassable and 'froze their own movements'.[17]

Gröschke's *II. Bataillon* disengaged from its positions on the left wing of *Flieger Division 7* early in the morning of 10 February at 5:00 a.m., handed over its section to *Jägerbataillon 4* at 7:00 a.m. and marched off to Gorodets. On the same day at 2:00 p.m. the last parts of the battalion left the area of *Flieger Division 7* for Smolensk, and at 2:45 p.m. the last parts of the likewise detached *Flak Abteilung* I./501.[18] In Smolensk the soldiers spent the night in a barracks. It was clear weather at -9°C. The next day they were transported to Bryansk, where they spent the night at an air base.

Paratroopers of *6. Kompanie* on their way to Orel in bitter cold temperatures between 12 and 13 February 1943. (Private Collection)

---

member of the NSDAP since 1932, a veteran of World War I and of the Austrian Imperial Army, he was transferred to the *Wehrmacht* in 1938 and rose from *Oberst* in the general staff to *Generaloberst* and commanded an army group (*Heeresgruppe Ostmark*) at the end of the war. He was found guilty of war crimes in Yugoslavia and Lappland and sentenced to 20 years in prison. On 1 February 1951 he was released.
17 NARA, T-315 R-153: PzAOK 2, KTB 3, vol.1, entry 13 February 1943.
18 BA-MA, RH 24-6/131 VI.A.K. KTB 3, vol.58.

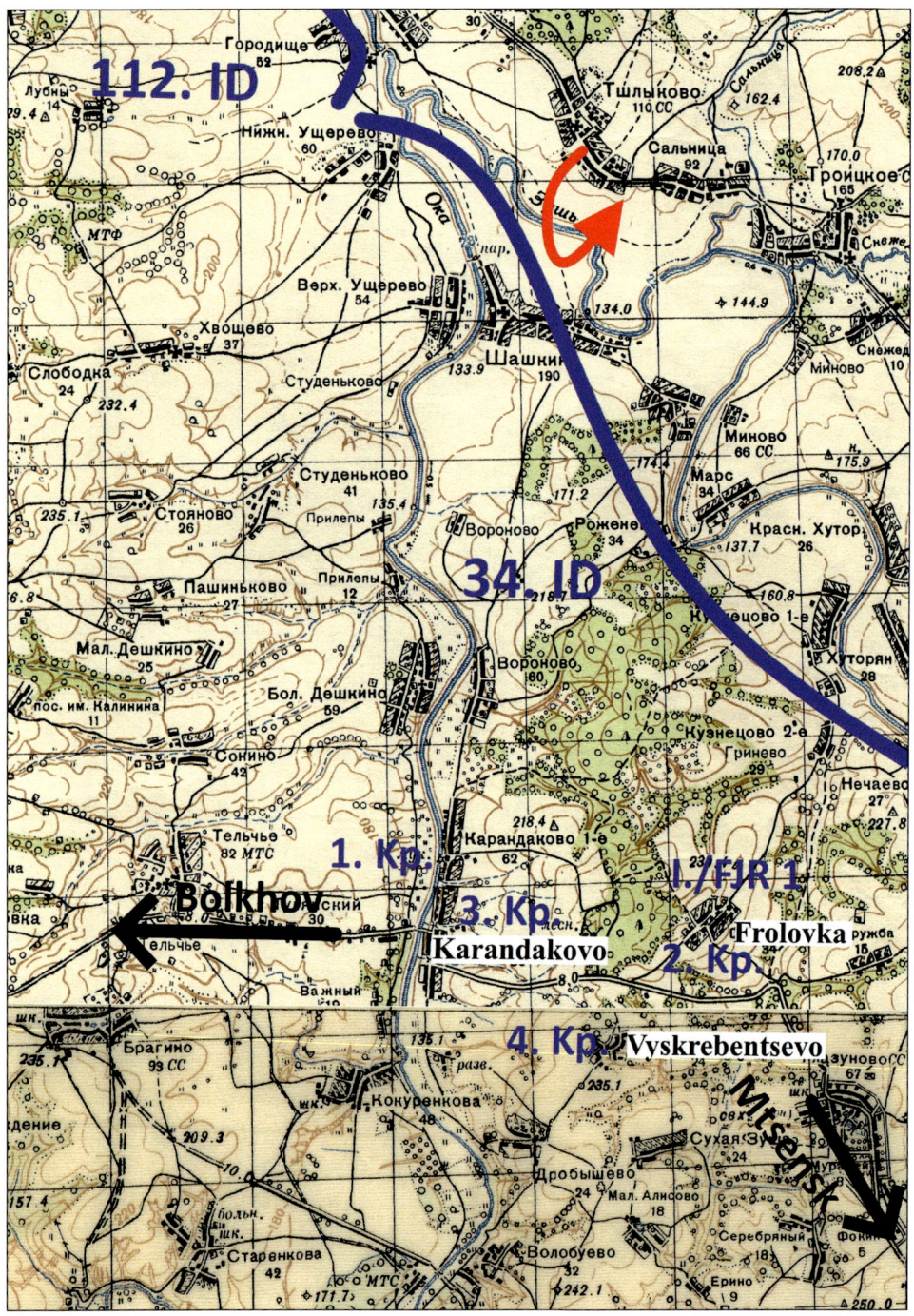

Deployment of *I. Bataillon* in the sector of *34. Infanterie Division* on 13 February 1943.

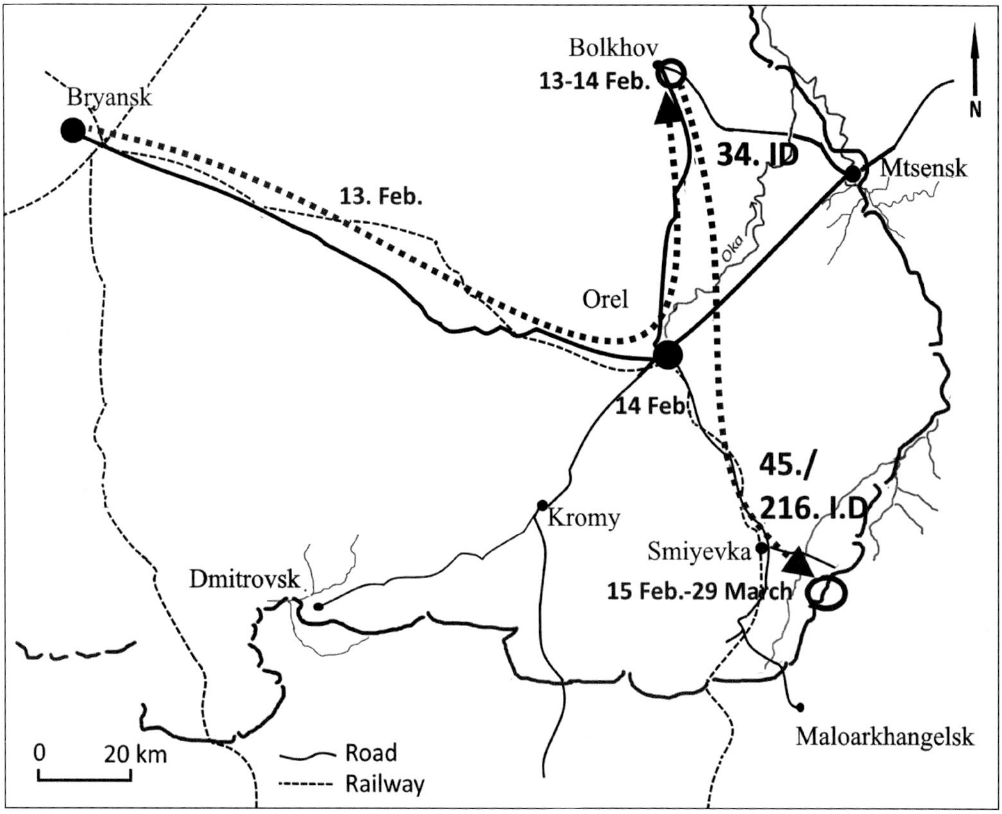

THE TRANSFER OF *FALLSCHIRMJÄGER REGIMENT 1* TO OREL

Deployment of *II. Bataillon* around Orel, February to March 1943.

For the truck drivers, this transport was accompanied by great hardship. Accidents and breakdowns were not uncommon. Here a truck left the road and overturned. (Private Collection)

The convoy of *II. Bataillon* during a refuelling stop near Orel on 13 or 14 February 1943. (Private Collection)

On 12 February, Gröschke's journey continued from Bryansk via Karachev and Orel to Komary, where the battalion spent the night. The weather became worse and worse with a stormy south wind and -31°C. They were transported the next day to Bolkhov, where it was billeted in Vasskova, on the south-eastern outskirts of the city on the Orel road. It thus lay to the west of *I. Bataillon* as a reserve in case of a breakthrough, but only stayed there overnight.

On 13 February at 11:00 a.m. the regimental staff was in Bolkhov, and Schulenburg's *I. Bataillon* had arrived northwest of Mtsensk. At this time Gröschke was enroute between Orel and Bolkhov, parts of *I./Flak Regiment 501* had left Bryansk with one light battery and one Flak 8.8 cm, while Becker's battalion was still advancing towards Orel.[19] It is not known exactly when the latter arrived and where. Was it still sent to the Bolkhov area, like the *II. Bataillon*, or did it leave Smolensk so late that it only passed through Orel on the night of 14 to 15 February on its way to Smiyevka? Presumably the latter, because the roads between Bryansk and Orel were badly covered by snowstorms, making movements very difficult.[20]

In general, the landscape around Orel was different from that around Smolensk, which had become familiar to the paratroopers. 'The landscape was wide-open and interspersed with deep ravines. Endless villages lay in these. Since there was also little forest, the houses were mostly built of stone or mud, not wood like those in the area where we were [with *9. Armee*]. The soil was in many cases already the famous black earth.'[21]

19　CAMO, 500_12454, file 637; Transport movements of *2. Panzer Armee*, 13 February 1943, 11:00 a.m.
20　CAMO, 500_12454, file 637.
21　Ludwig Merker, *Das Buch der 78. Sturm-Division* (Tübingen: Kameradenhilfswerk d. 78. Sturm-Division e. V., abt.1955), p.210.

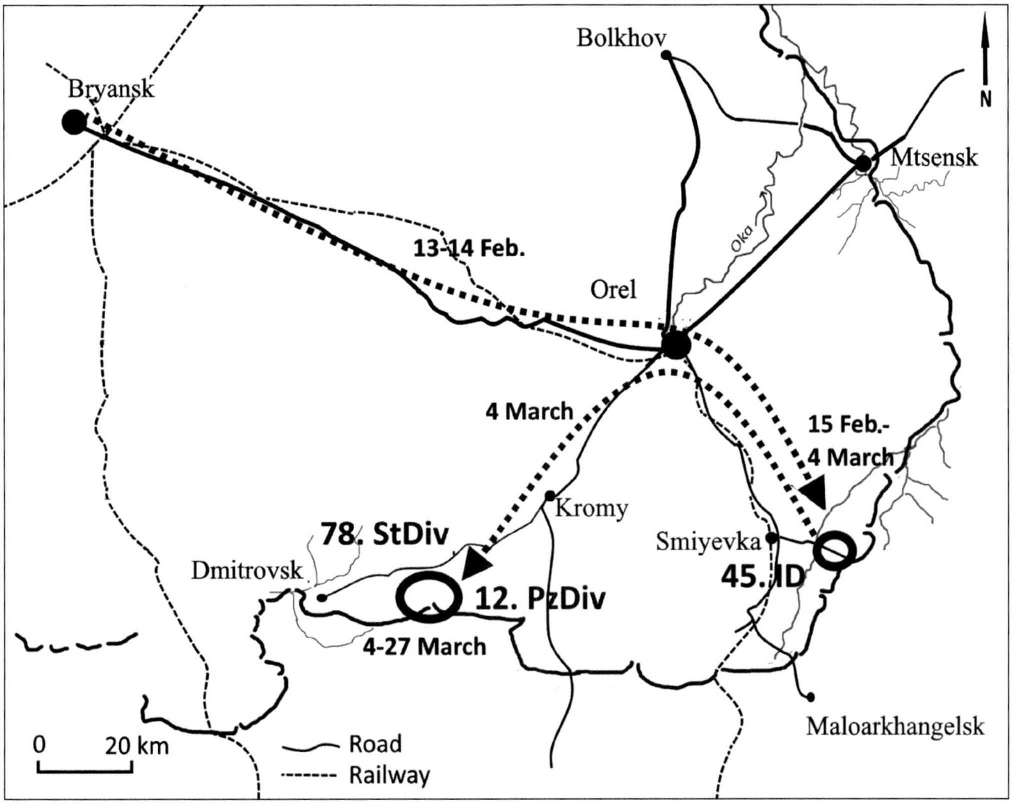

Deployment of *III. Bataillon* around Orel, February to March 1943.

III. Bataillon on the move near Orel with trucks provided by *Flieger Division 7*. (Private Collection)

19

Fallschirmjäger Regiment 1 (without I. Bataillon) 14 February–4 March 1943

The Attack on Alekseyevka

Since the situation around Bolkhov had eased, PzAOK 2, to which the regiment was now subordinated as a reserve, wanted to concentrate it around Orel. The first to leave the area around Bolkhov was *II. Bataillon*. On 14 February at 8:15 a.m. *Major* Gröschke received a call from his regimental commander, *Oberstleutnant* Schulz: the battalion was to march immediately (at 10:00 a.m.) to an area south of Orel where he was to arrive at 2:00 p.m. It was to be accommodated in Lushki on the southern outskirts of Orel, east of the airfield, and in Kukeshev.

No sooner had they arrived, they were given a new marching order. The development of the situation for *45. Infanterie Division* around Smiyevka led *Generaloberst* Schmidt to immediately send the newly freed reserve to counter this developing crisis. At 11:00 a.m. on 14 February, *Major* Karl-Heinz Wirsing,[1] Ia of this division, learned from *Oberst* Wagner,[2] Chief of Staff of *LV. Armee Korps*, that a paratrooper regiment of two battalions as well as four tanks, to be used as mobile anti-tank guns, and one *Flak Abteilung* were to be added to the division. On that day the division command post was still in Alekseyevka.[3] The division had to fall back so rapidly that when the command post moved north to Stolbetskoye, the place was still crammed with retreating train vehicles and could only be defended by a quickly assembled alarm group of 200 men.[4]

Forces of the Soviet 48th Army were able to break into the German front from 14 to 18 February, pushing towards Vasilyevka and Smiyevka at the seam between the *LV.* and *XXXV. Armee Korps* – between *45.* and *299. Infanterie Division*. Connected to these battles on the Soviet side were the 9th Ski Brigade as the spearhead, supported by three tank regiments, followed by the 6th Guards Rifle

---

1 Karl-Heinz Wirsing (Würzburg, 5 April 1907– Würzburg, 29 July 1999), DKiG, later *Generalmajor* and commander of the 1st Mountain Division in the *Bundeswehr* (1962–1965).
2 Werner Wagner (Arnsberg, 30 April 1898–?) *Oberst i.G.*; DKiG 11 February 1942; Chief of Staff of LV. AK until February 1944, from 23 December 1944 until 10 January 1945 leader of 245. ID, from 21 January 1945 leader of *276. Volksgrenadier Division*; went into British captivity on 4 April 1945 near Bad Nauheim.
3 BA-MA, RH 26-45/59: 45. ID KTB, 1 January–15 July 1943, p.146.
4 BA-MA, RH 26-45/59: 45. ID KTB, 1 January–15 July 1943, pp.149–150.

Orel in the Winter of 1941–1942. (Private Collection)

Division and later the 399th Rifle Division.[5] The situation was more than unclear for the Germans; the attacking Soviet 9th Ski Brigade was able to advance almost to the important supply railway station Smiyevka. *LV. Armee Korps* – *General* von Roman has just taken over command – received the order 'to try by all means to establish the connection at the corps boundary to *XXXV. Armee Korps* via Kuban–Andriyanovka and to monitor the penetrated area and the directions of movement of the

---

5 Glantz, *After Stalingrad*, p.274: Glantz could not find any Soviet sources on these events, as Soviet historiography was silent on these unsuccessful battles.

Local villagers near Orel, March 1943. (Private Collection)

enemy by reconnaissance'.[6] For this purpose the corps was reinforced by the only available reserve, *Fallschirmjäger Regiment 1*, which was supposed to restore the situation by counterattack.

The regiment received by telephone the instruction to move to Smiyevka – about 50 kilometres southeast of Orel – and was placed under command of *LV. Armee Korps* (the corresponding telex reached the corps only at 12:30 a.m. on 15 February). Gröschke left with his *II. Bataillon* to go to Orel at 6:00 p.m. on the 14th.[7] Schulenburg's *I. Bataillon* was to remain behind with *34. Infanterie Division*.

In the meantime, Gröschke had to report to the command post of *LV. Armee Korps* in Slobodka, 12 kilometres west of Smiyevka.[8] The battalion arrived there on the evening of 14 February and *Major* Gröschke was ordered to march immediately to Stolbetskoye where he was to report to the commander of *45. Infanterie Division*, *Generalleutnant* Kühlwein. Gröschke left Smiyevka at around 10:30 p.m. with two Kfz 15 four-wheel drive cars,[9] in the direction of Stolbetskoye.

---

6   BA-MA, BW 57-82 and RH 24-35/51: Order of PzAOK 2 to LV. AK of 14 February 1943 10:00 p.m.; NARA, T-315 R-153: PzAOK 2, KTB 3, vol.1: entry 14 February 1943 p.4 and telex in *Anhänge*.

7   BA-MA, RH 26-45/59: 45. ID KTB, 1 January–15 July 1943, p.149: 14 February 1943, 10:00 p.m.: 'Army leader of engineers informs [45. ID] that the I. [recte II.] Btl. of paratroopers left Orel at 6:00 p.m.. The Orel–Smiyevka road is good and without any traffic'.

8   NARA, T-314 R-1376: LV. AK, KTB 3, part IV, p.905. The war journal is contradictory about the location of the command post. From 15 February on the corps command post Slobodka is mentioned, but this was only reported to PzAOK 2 on 17 February: 'Corps command post from 7:00 a.m. Slobodka (12 km west of Smiyevka)'.

9   The *Kraftfahrzeug 15* was the standard medium off-road vehicle of the *Wehrmacht*, based on the Horch 901.

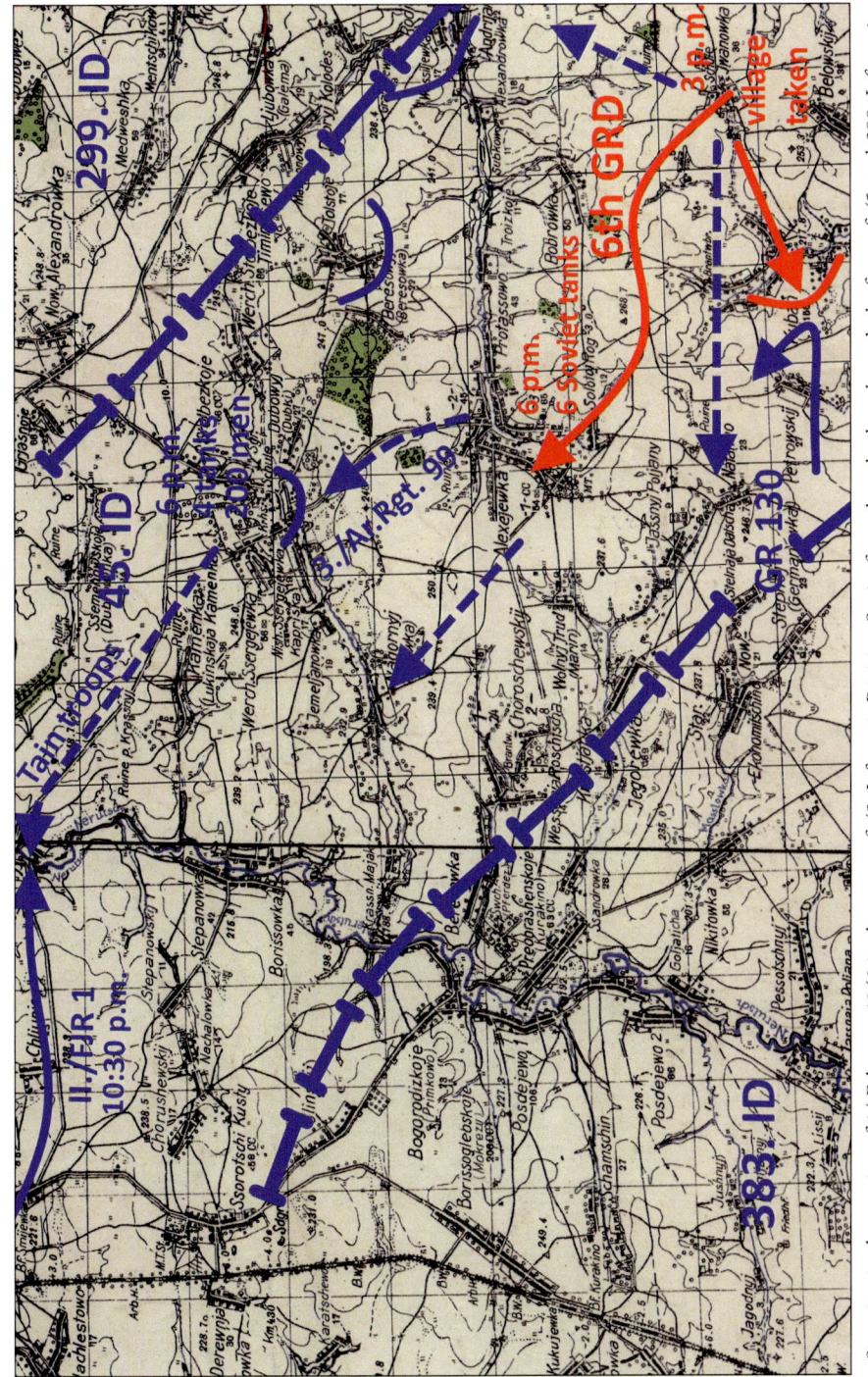

Situation in the evening of 14 February 1943 in the sector of 45. and 299. Infanterie Division. Soviet forces have broken through the front of 45. and 299. Infanterie Division a few kilometres to the south on that day (not visible on the map). The command post of 45. Infanterie Division was in Ivanovka at noon, in Alexeyevka in the afternoon, and Stolbetskoye in the evening. Alexeyevka was defended for a short while by men of an artillery battery who fled after running out of ammunition and destroying their guns.

However, the nightly transport to the area of operations was hindered by the baggage trains of the exhausted *45. Infanterie Division* chaotically flooding back, which considerably impaired the march of the paratroopers of *II. Bataillon* in particular. The road should have been kept clear for them in one-way traffic to the front, but even threats of violence by the field gendarmes regulating the traffic did not help and the area around a bridge near Vasilyevka was 'hopelessly congested.'[10] The road was finally cleared by the paratroopers themselves by overturning the stuck vehicles. The chaos must have been terrifying:

> It took *Major* Gröschke 7.5 hours to drive 17 km [from Smiyevka to the operations area] … The indiscipline of the individual drivers as well as of the columns made progress almost impossible. In their striving to move backwards, neither the columns nor the individual drivers kept to the road, sometimes three vehicles driving side by side, with vehicles getting stuck and blocking all traffic.[11]

The paratroopers themselves were shocked by this chaos and tried in parts successfully to convince some of the fleeing and seemingly terrified soldiers to join them and turn back towards the front.

On 14 February between 10 and 11:00 p.m., Becker passed with his battalion through Orel. The whereabouts of the paratroopers was uncertain at 1:45 a.m. 'where it went, he [*Oberleutnant* Szemmeitat, Schulz's adjutant] cannot say. A search was made in the area, and it was not found.'[12] This cryptic message could, however, also refer to *I. Bataillon*, which was also to march to Orel originally, but was to be recalled and therefore searched for.

In any case, *Hauptmann* Becker arrived in Smiyevka with his *III. Bataillon* at 5:20 a.m. in the morning of 15 February and contacted *Oberst* Wagner (of *LV. Armee Korps*). It was decided to wait first, as *II. Bataillon* had still not arrived in the area of operations of *45. Infanterie Division* due to the congested roads. The wintry conditions – the war diary of the *LV. Armee Korps* notes light snowfall, -9°C and impassable roads – must have been correspondingly harsh.

Finally, at 6:00 a.m., *Oberstleutnant* Schulz and *Major* Gröschke arrived at the command post of *Generalleutnant* Kühlwein in Verkhnyaya (Verkh.) Sergeyevka. The regiment was now under the command of this division. Schulz received the order to attack and take the village of Alekseyevka from Stolbetskoye and passed it on to Gröschke at 9:50 a.m. The attack was originally planned for 11:30 a.m. After the capture of Alekseyevka, the village of Kuban was given as an additional objective, which was also constantly reinforced by the Soviet side.[13]

Throughout this period, constant Soviet reinforcements were observed moving into the break-in area – particularly towards Alekseyevka. The village had only fallen into Soviet hands at around 5:00 p.m. the previous day. Shortly before, *45. Infanterie Division*'s command post was still there. Kühlwein was lucky to get away at the last minute.

As already mentioned, these reinforcements were from the 6th Guards Rifle Division, together with the 9th Ski Brigade and the 28th, 30th Guards Tank Regiments and 43rd Tank Regiment. The attacks of the 6th Guards Rifle Division continued in the area of the *45.* and *299. Infanterie Division* on the morning of 15 February and were all repulsed by the Germans.

---

10 BA-MA, RH 26-45/59: 45. ID KTB, 1 January–15 July 1943, p.151.
11 BA-MA, BW 57-84: Extract of the war journal of II./FJR 1.
12 BA-MA, BW 57-82.
13 BA-MA, RH 26-45/59: 45 ID KTB, 1 January–15 July 1943, p.152.

Paratroopers from *II. Bataillon* with a Marder II self-propelled anti-tank gun moving towards Sergeyevka to prepare for the attack on Alekseyevka, 15 February 1943. (Private Collection)

At 10:00 a.m. *5. Kompanie*, led by *Oberleutnant* Erwin Poppele,[14] who had taken over the company after Kerfin's death, was the first to arrive in Verkh. Sergeyevka and was sent forward to Hill 248.1 to secure the battalion assembly area. At 11:00 a.m. *8. Kompanie*, led by *Oberleutnant* Hans Lucassen,[15] arrived and was also sent forward by the battalion commander to stand by for the attack. *Major* Gröschke went forward with this company. The battalion was supported by six Panzer IVs, anti-aircraft guns from *I./Flak Regiment 501* and *Leutnant* Brammer's platoon of three self-propelled guns or *'Traktoren'* (tractors), which were named by their crews after children's book characters 'Peter', 'Max' and 'Moritz'.

The start of the attack was postponed until 1:00 p.m., as *6.* and *7. Kompanie* had still not arrived due to poor road conditions. Gröschke sensibly objected that without these two companies he was too weak to be able to carry out a successful attack. To enable the attack to start on time, *Major* Gröschke was given the regimental engineer platoon (one officer, 30 men) and the regimental bicycle platoon (one officer, 20 men) as further reinforcements. Schulz ordered the attack despite the fact that a reconnaissance party, which had returned shortly before at 12:30 p.m., had detected strong enemy forces in front of and in Alekseyevka. The patrol, led by a platoon leader of *5. Kompanie*, *Leutnant* Zahn,[16] had clashed with a Soviet patrol in the woods, which was wiped out with the exception of one man who was taken prisoner. *Leutnant* Zahn himself was wounded. Later in Italy, as commander of *5. Kompanie*, Zahn was again severely wounded at Monte Cassino on 21 March 1944. For his actions at Cassino, he was awarded the Knight's Cross on 9 June 1944. Despite the loss of a leg, he returned to active duty in March 1945 to lead his *5. Kompanie* again and was taken prisoner of war on 8 May 1945.

Zahn's men were able to capture a map, whose markings indicated a thrust towards Khoroshevsky and further to the northwest towards Smiyevka.[17] However, the results of the reconnaissance had no further influence on the attack plan, which was to be carried out against all odds. Elements of the *299. Infanterie Division* were to join the attack on the left flank. Combat group 'Fritsche' and parts of *Regiment* 'Bell' as well as *III. Bataillon/Grenadier Regiment 529* attacked Aleksandrovka, Subkovo und Troitskoye, of which the latter could be taken.[18]

---

14 Erwin Poppele (Kissleg, 19 March 1910–KIA S. Angelo, 23 November 1943), *Oberleutnant*; DKiG April 1943.
15 Hans Lucassen (1910–1974), *Hauptmann*; DKiG 1 January 1945.
16 Hilmar Adolf Zahn (Wiesbaden, 6 September 1919– Wiesbaden, 8 March 2008), *Hauptmann*.
17 BA-MA, RH 26-45/59: 45. ID KTB, 1 January–15 July 1943, p.154.
18 BA-MA, RH 26-299/108 in BA-MA BW 57-82 and BA-MA, RH 26-299/103: 299. ID, KTB No. 10, *Anlagenband Nr. 2*.

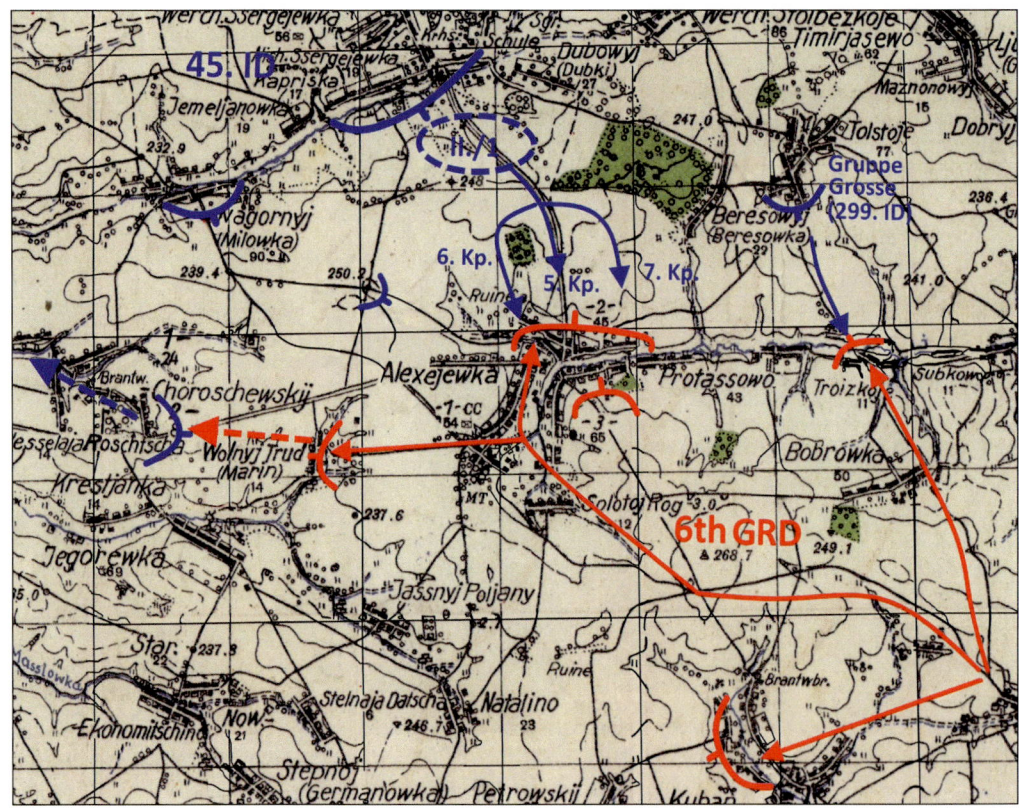

The attack on Alekseyevka by *II. Bataillon* on 15 February 1943.

The war diary of *II. Bataillon* records -9°C and overcast weather.[19] Poppele's *5. Kompanie* formed up behind the tanks and started the attack at 1:00 p.m.,[20] followed by the battalion's engineer and bicycle platoons. The approach on the road to Alekseyevka was made difficult by high and soft snow, in which the soldiers sank up to their knees. About two kilometres north of the attack objective, the attack column was spotted and came under mortar and machine-gun fire, seriously slowing what had initially been a relatively swift advance.

The lack of knowledge of the terrain became apparent when *5. Kompanie* was suddenly faced with a flat slope, more than a kilometre long and completely visible from the enemy side. In these circumstances, even with tank support, it was a challenge to make progress. The company's losses began to mount, the well-placed Soviet mortar and sniper fire were taking their toll.

---

19 Interestingly enough the war diary of *45. Infanterie Division* records for the same day temperatures of -20o C and a clear sky. BA-MA, RH 26-45/59: 45. ID, KTB 1 January–15 July 1943, p.155.
20 The following description of the attack on Alekseyevka is based on an extract of the war journal of II./FJR 1 for 7./FJR 1 (20 October 1942–31 March 1943) in BA-MA, BW 57-84, which is partly reproduced in Bernhard/Broder, *Guerre Mondiale*, pp.329–369.

Oberjäger Heinkelein of *5. Kompanie* was particularly lucky:

> It was a very difficult attack in the freezing cold and deep snow. My group suffered many casualties from head shots, a shot in the stomach, and an arm shot off by a Russian sniper in the run-up to the attack. An explosive projectile hit me in the stomach when I was changing positions, but the projectile only hit my pistol, which I had tucked behind my belt ready to fire, it shredded my pistol and exploded, burning the whole front of my clothing down to the skin. I was so utterly shocked almost out of my mind because I thought my whole insides were hanging out. Even the company commander, *Oberleutnant* Poppele, who was watching from the tank, thought I had fallen too, but to my amazement I didn't think anything had happened to me. That's what they call 'soldier's luck'.[21]

Heinkelein then spotted the sniper who had hit him and managed to take him out.

6. Kompanie on the way to Sergeyevka, just before the attack on Alekseyevka. (Private Collection)

Immediately upon arrival *6. Kompanie* under the command of *Oberleutnant* Fritz Lange was able to join the attack formation.[22] It is not known why the company commander *Hauptmann* Zuber was not present. The reinforcement was more than welcome and *Major* Gröschke immediately deployed the company with two groups of the regimental engineer platoon on the right wing to attack the village.

The tanks had to stop 800 metres short of Alekseyevka because a stream bed prevented them from advancing further. The attackers also came under heavy infantry fire as they approached the village. The paratroopers were now about 700 metres in front of the village, in full view and without proper cover. Two German tanks were hit by anti-tank fire from the village and put out of action. Casualties mounted. The heaviest defensive fire hit the paratroopers from the eastern part of the village.

---

21 Walter Heinkelein, *Recollections*.
22 Fritz Lange (Osterode, 27 July 1911–KIA Alekseyevka, 15 February 1943), *Oberleutnant*.

These rare action-photographs were taken by *Gefreiter* Lorenz of *6. Kompanie* during the attack on Alekseyevka – just before he was wounded. A burning German tank and the village of Alekseyevka can be seen in the hollow in the background. (Private Collection)

In this phase of the battle, the commander of *7. Kompanie, Hauptmann* Abratis, now also reported to Gröschke, who deployed his company on the left wing to attack the eastern part of Alekseyevka.

To support the paratroopers, a Ju 87 dive bomber squadron launched an attack on the village at 1:45 p.m., which the battalion used to advance further towards the village. Unfortunately for the attackers the effect was short-lived, as the bulk of the enemy was positioned south of the village on a forward slope and was not further affected by the bombing. The losses of the paratroopers continued to mount.

In the meantime, parts of *6. Kompanie* managed to enter the western part of the village, fighting their way forward from house to house. The company commanders fell one by one: First *Oberleutnant* Lange, then *Leutnant* Bachinger,[23] *Oberfeldwebel* Schneider and *Fähnrich* Mülders.[24] Communication between *6. Kompanie* and *Major* Gröschke had broken down, so the last man to take command, *Feldwebel* Nollen,[25] sent a messenger with the bad news that there were heavy casualties, no ammunition, and that the attack could not continue unless supplies and reinforcements arrived as soon as possible.

Although Gröschke called for these much-needed supplies several times, his wish could not be fulfilled. The losses also increased in *5.* and *7. Kompanie*, both which also reported a lack of ammunition at 4:00 p.m. The only fire support available were the remaining tanks and Brammer's three self-propelled anti-tank guns, which stood motionless on the slope, and *8. Kompanie*, which followed the attack in a staggered approach. German artillery support was completely lacking. *Leutnant* Brammers 'tractors' which were stuck the same way as the supporting tanks were being used more as assault guns and not as anti-tank guns and were only able to set fire to nine trucks and to shoot at individual houses.[26]

It is not clear if the guns were of Brammer's platoon or Pusch's. Brammer writes about the action as if he was involved, the list of approved close combat actions mentions Pusch's platoon.[27]

---

23 Walter Bachinger (Gaspotshofen, 7 August 1919–KIA Alekseyevka, 15 February 1943), *Leutnant*.
24 Richard Schneider (Kaltenlengsfeld, 2 September 1914–KIA Alekseyevka, 15 February 1943), *Oberfeldwebel*; Karl Mülders (Hau, 20 February 1920–KIA Alekseyevka, 15 February 1943), *Fahnenjunker-Feldwebel* (officer aspirant).
25 Wilhelm Nollen (1918–1999), *Oberfähnrich*. He was awarded the DKiG on 28 April 1943 for this action.
26 Bruno Brammer, 'Kriegstagebuch', p.109.
27 Bruno Brammer, 'Kriegstagebuch', p.109, list of approved close combat actions (BA-MA, BW 57/93).

As no supply of ammunition had arrived by 5:00 p.m., Gröschke decided to draw back *6. Kompanie*, which was heavily pressed in the village, and ordered it to fall back to the line of *5.* and *7. Kompanie*.

Out on the open slope the battalion was still heavily shelled by mortars and could not move. At 7:00 p.m., Gröschke was able to call Schulz via a wire connection that had been established in the meantime and describe the situation. He made it clear that if the attack was to continue, he would absolutely need reinforcements and ammunition because of the already heavy losses. Schulz, for his part, gave a visibly dramatic account of the situation to the command of *45. Infanterie Division*, so that, after a brief consultation between Kühlwein and his commanding general, *General* von Roman,[28] he ordered the battalion to be withdrawn to its initial position at 9:00 p.m. The battalion began to disengage from the enemy at 10:00 p.m. and took up a defensive position at Hill 248 by midnight.

In the daily report of *45. Infanterie Division* the failure of the attack on the heavily occupied Alekseyevka was attributed to the lack of any artillery support; own losses were given as 50 percent, mainly in heavy losses of officers and NCOs.

The battalion's losses were reported immediately after the fighting as follows:

Dead: three officers, 45 NCOs and enlisted men,
Wounded: four officers, 132 NCOs and enlisted men,
Missing: four NCOs and enlisted men.

Feldwebel Otto Büsche of *6. Kompanie* with his wife on their wedding day. He received one of the 11 German Crosses in Gold, which were awarded to members of the *II. Bataillon* for their bravery at Alekseyevka on 28 April 1943. (Collection Stephan Janzyk)

According to the casualty list, the number of these considerable losses must be increased to 139 wounded. The number of dead rose to 63 because another 11 men later succumbed to their wounds and the four missing men mentioned above, were also found to have been killed in action. Added to this are the losses of the regimental staff – the bicycle and engineer platoons – which Gröschke did not mention, with six killed and 14 wounded out of a total of 52 men. The total number of casualties of the regiment on this day thus increased to 222 men: 69 dead, missing or died shortly afterwards of their wounds, as well as 153 wounded who would survive.

Considering the battalion's original combatant strength of just over 500 men when it was transferred to Orel, reports that spoke of 50 percent casualties were hardly exaggerated. Most significantly, a lot of leadership personnel were lost: three officers dead (*Oberleutnant* Lange, *Leutnant* Bachinger, *Leutnant* Vornberger) and five wounded (*Oberleutnant* Lucassen, *Oberleutnant* Abratis, *Leutnant*

---

28 BA-MA, RH 26-45/59: 45. ID, KTB 1 January–15 July 1943, p.155.

Zahn, *Leutnant* Kretzschmar,[29] *Leutnant* Lusche).[30] The highest number of casualties were suffered by *6. Kompanie* with 26 dead or missing and 53 wounded. Whereas *5. Kompanie* suffered 17 dead and 35 wounded, *7. Kompanie* 10 dead and 27 wounded and *8. Kompanie* nine dead and 22 wounded. In addition, there was one dead and two wounded from the battalion's signals platoon. The majority of the fallen could not be recovered and buried, they remained on the battlefield 'in enemy territory'.[31] Of the nine armoured vehicles – six tanks and Brammer's three self-propelled anti-tank guns – three tanks were destroyed while Brammer's 'tractors' did not take a hit.[32]

According to the combat report of *7. Kompanie*, communication was hampered by the absence of the signals platoon. Command and control could only be provided by radio operators, who were also under heavy fire. One man was killed and two wounded when the signals platoon attempted to establish a telephone connection. It could only be established around 7:00 p.m. The location of the fallen, *Jäger* Engelbert Herbst who received a head shot,[33] is given as '700 m north of Alekseyevka on the Stolbetskoye road.' His body could not be recovered.[34]

Remembrance card of *Obergefreiter* Ludwig Schmid, a trained electrician, from *7. Kompanie*. He was one of 69 men of *II. Bataillon* killed in action during the failed attack on Alekseyevka on 15 February 1943.

But it was not only the paratroopers who had problems. In addition to losses due to enemy fire, total exhaustion and frostbite also decimated the paratroopers as well as the deployed forces of the other *Wehrmacht* formations.

The result of this failed attack was devastating. Gröschke's battalion had lost all offensive power and from now on could only be deployed in defence.

That very night of 15 to 16 February, the staffs of the higher commands discussed whether to repeat an attack on Alekseyevka, where more than one regiment and tanks were detected, or to shorten the front because of the steadily strengthening enemy forces. To Schulz's credit he seems to have insisted that his troops had suffered too many losses and were now too weak to attack the village again.

However, the offensive plans for the next day remained in place.

Becker with his battalion had also been brought forward and had moved into its assigned section on the right wing of the regiment.

---

29   Herbert Kretzschmar (1917–?), *Leutnant*.
30   Otto Lusche (1918–?); *Leutnant;* DKiG 19 March 1942. He went into Allied captivity near Cassino on 17 Mai 1944.
31   Ancestry/WASt: Evaluation of the index cards.
32   BA-MA, BW 57-84 Extract of the war journal of II./FJR 1, Bernhard (ed.), *Guerre Mondiale contre moi*, pp.367–368; casualty list of II./FJR 1.
33   Engelbert Herbst (Herten, 27 November 1923–KIA Alekseyevka, 15 February 1943), *Jäger*.
34   Ancestry/WASt, G-B 277/1506.

On the morning of 16 February, there was an argument between Kühlwein and Schulz, which is only documented in the war journal of the division, Schulz's point of view is not preserved, but can be easily guessed. Kühlwein interfered pedantically and started to micromanage details of the regiment's deployment. The self-propelled anti-tank guns should be drawn closer, the battalions did not seem to him to be deployed correctly (*II. Bataillon* should be further forward), then he ordered the deployment of two light guns (probably the 2 cm Flak of the *I./Flak Regiment 501*) north of Hill 248.1, as they had not been deployed at all the previous day (since they could not be brought forward). He also thought that – contrary to Schulz's opinion – there was enough ammunition for heavy weapons. Also, the heavy weapons should be deployed on the right wing and not on the left.³⁵

Schulz reported to Kühlwein that 'reconnaissance had revealed that three Russian 7.62 cm anti-tank guns were in position on both sides of the road at the northern exit of Alekseyevka. There is the impression that the enemy has further strengthened. The heights south of Alekseyevka were heavily occupied.'³⁶ Schulz now wanted to lead the attack east of the village, but he needed time for reconnaissance, so the attack would not take place until the 17th. Kühlwein did not agree to this delay. He ordered the attack to be carried out by a reinforced company and only to defend the section north of Alekseyevka. He also criticized Schulz for not sealing off to the west, despite clear orders to do so. In addition, he also accused Schulz of having made a false report that Hill 252.2 was occupied by the enemy, as one of his own artillery observers had been there during the night.³⁷ Kühlwein's behaviour confirms Hartmann's assessment of him, who described him as a combination of authoritarian and fossilized attitudes, and as a 'difficult, sometimes downright spleenful superior.'³⁸

At 10:15 a.m., Kühlwein had just returned to his command post, when the commanding general of the *LV. Armee Korps*, *General* von Roman called: 'Under all circumstances prevent Russian pushes further west and north. In the event of enemy movements in this direction, counterattacks must be launched immediately. Alekseyevka is no longer to be attacked.'³⁹

A clearly disappointed *Generaloberst* Schmidt phoned *Generalfeldmarschall* von Kluge later on the 16th:

> Schmidt: … Yesterday at 45 as already mentioned, the attack on Alekseyevka failed.
> von Kluge: Which attack?
> Schmidt: The one of the paratroopers, they claim that they can no longer attack because they have such heavy losses.
> von Kluge: But this was our only effort!
> Schmidt: That's quite a bust! They are very brave and well-behaved.⁴⁰

In the aftermath of the fighting for Alexeyevka, *Hauptmann* Zuber, commander of *6. Kompanie*, had to write 26 letters of condolence, like the one pictured to the family of 19-year-old *Gefreiter* Herbert

---

35 Kühlwein had authored several theoretical pamphlets on infantry warfare on individual up to battalion level like *Felddienst-ABC für den Schützen* [Field service ABC for the rifleman] (Berlin, 1932) or *Gefechtstaktik des verstärkten Bataillons* [Battle tactics of the reinforced battalion] (Berlin, 1936). See Christian Hartmann, Wehrmacht im Ostkrieg (Munich: Oldenburg, 2010), 2nd ed., p.148, fn.440.
36 BA-MA, RH 26-45/59: 45. ID, KTB 1 January–15 July 1943, pp.158–159.
37 BA-MA, RH 26-45/59: 45. ID, KTB 1 January–15 July 1943, pp.158–159.
38 Hartmann, *Ostkrieg*, pp.173, 236.
39 BA-MA, RH 26-45/59: 45. ID, KTB 1 January–15 July 1943, p.160.
40 BA-MA, BW 57-82.

```
Dienststelle L 36006 c
Lg. Pa. Posen
                                    Im Osten, den 24. Februar 1943
```

Sehr geehrte Familie K o c h !

Ich habe heute die traurige Pflicht, Ihnen mitteilen zu müssen, dass Ihr Sohn Herbert am 15.2.1943 gegen 15.oo Uhr bei dem Dorf Aleksejewka südostwärts Orel schwer verwundet wurde und am 16.2.1943 auf dem Hauptverbandsplatz verstorben ist.

Die Kompanie hatte den Auftrag, die eingebrochenen Russen im Gegenangriff aufzuhalten und hat ihre Aufgabe mit einem wahrhaft erschütternden Heldenmut durchgeführt. Durch ihren rücksichtslosen Einsatz wurde der Feind aufgehalten und ein allgemeiner Durchbruch verhindert.

Wenn es für Sie einen Trost bedeutet, kann ich Ihnen versichern, dass Ihr Sohn das Bewustsein bis zu seinem Tode nicht wiedererlangte. Er wurde durch eine rus. Kugel in der Brust getroffen.

Am 22.2.1943 wurde er mit 5 anderen Kameraden an der Strasse nach Wasiljewka beigesetzt.

Die Kompanie verliert in Ihrem Sohn einen tapferen Soldaten, der, wohin er gestellt wurde, treu seine Pflicht erfüllte. Er zählt jetzt zu den 9o Fallschirm-Jägern, die in dieser Kompanie bereits ihr Leben für Deutschland gegeben haben. Ihr Leib ist sterblich, aber ihr Geist und Andenken wird, solange es deutsche Soldaten gibt, weiterleben!

Wertsachen und private Gegenstände sind Ihrem Sohn abgenommen und gehen Ihnen in der nächsten Zeit zu.

In sonstigen Fragen wenden Sie sich bitte an das für Ihren Wohnsitz zuständige Wehrmacht- Fürsorge- und Versorgungsamt.

Seien Sie nochmals meines tiefsten Beileids versichert.

                                    Ihr
                                    [signature]
                                    Hauptmann und Kp.-Chef.

Hauptmann Zuber's letter of condolence to the family of 19-year-old *Gefreiter* Herbert Koch.
(Collection Stephan Janzyk)

Koch. In such letters, the true circumstances of the death were often softened in order to spare the relatives the bitter truth. In this case, the paratrooper did not die from a shot in the chest, but to the stomach. In reality, he must have suffered greatly. It reads:

In the East, 24 February 1943

Dear Koch family,
Today I have the sad duty to inform you that your son Herbert was seriously wounded near the village of Alekseyevka, south-east of Orel, on 15 February 1943 at about 15.00 hours and died at the main dressing station on 16 February 1943.

The Company was tasked with holding off the invading Russians as they counter-attacked and they performed with heroism that was staggering. Their ruthless efforts halted the enemy and prevented a general breakthrough.

If it is any consolation, I can assure you that your son did not regain consciousness until he died. He was shot by a Russian bullet in the chest. On 22 February 1943 he was buried with 5 other comrades on the road to Vasilyevka.

The company has lost in your son a brave soldier, who faithfully fulfilled his duty wherever he was sent. He is now one of 90 paratroopers from this company who have already given their lives for Germany. Their bodies are mortal, but their spirit and memory will live on as long as there are German soldiers!

Your son's valuables and personal effects have been secured and will be sent to you in the near future.

If you have any further questions, please contact the *Wehrmacht- Führsorge und Versorgungsamt* responsible for your place of residence.

Please accept once again my sincere condolences.
Yours, Zuber
Hauptmann and *Kp.-Chef*

What was the value of this attack? Alekseyevka was a reasonable target because it was an important road junction. It then became a Soviet assembly area for later attacks. From this village, strong Soviet attacks were launched against Nagorniy and Khoroshevsky until the end of February, in order to push through to Smiyevka and Orel.

It was certainly necessary to act quickly, as the Red Army otherwise would have had the opportunity to reinforce its troops in the village to such numbers that a successful attack would have been impossible. It would not have been the first time that a spirited, determined attack by paratroopers – although outnumbered – was successful. To wait for further reserves was impossible as none were available.

However, the attack slowed down the Soviet advance and gave the withdrawing *45. Infanterie Division* a breathing space so that forces could be reorganised, and supplies and communications could improve.

The delays in getting the battalion to the front caused by the disorderly retreat of *45. Infanterie Division* was probably the main reason for the failure. Had the battalion arrived during the night and been able to attack earlier – while it was still dark – there might still have been a chance of success. It was simply too late. Moreover, due to the high snow, the paratroopers could only approach slowly through terrain completely visible to the enemy. The lack of any artillery support had a particularly aggravating effect – the Stuka attack was far from sufficient. Ultimately, when no ammunition was supplied, Gröschke had no choice but to call off the attack.

When *Leutnant* Zahn's reconnaissance in the morning revealed that the village was heavily manned, it was no longer a very promising idea to launch the attack with newly arrived troops, that were too weak in numbers and unfamiliar with the terrain, especially in broad daylight. Schulz, however, believed the village was only manned by a reinforced company, an opinion not shared by *Generalleutnant* Kühlwein, who believed that the village was manned by an entire regiment, but nevertheless insisted on carrying out this mission.[41] It must have been clear to all those directly involved that the element of surprise could not be achieved in these circumstances, and that an attack would have little chance of success. The attack should have been called off.

Between the lines of *Major* Gröschke's after-action report, one can read that he sought to divert responsibility for the failure onto Schulz, a responsibility which the latter partly accepted in his special order of 17 April 1943, but at the same time he was referring to an order from 'above': 'It was clear to me from the start that this attack had to amount to a sacrifice; this sacrifice was demanded from above and paratroopers must be strong enough to make the necessary sacrifices.'[42]

The pressure exercised on Schulz by his superiors and their expectations were certainly huge, as can be seen from the above-mentioned telephone conversations of Schmidt with von Kluge and the comments in the war journal of *45. Infanterie Division*.

Schmidt stated, very inaccurately, in another conversation with von Kluge, that the paratroopers 'are good, but boringly slow. Getting them moving, that's an enterprise in itself.' The next day he added: 'They are very brave and good. But they can't lead. They have such airs of prima donnas.'[43] From this, the distance of the higher commanders and their staff from reality on the ground and their wishful thinking becomes evident, but the tense situation can also be sensed.

In the veterans' culture of remembrance, the attack on Alekseyevka occupies an ambivalent position. Those who took part in the attack emphasised that they had been there, and the name of the village appears again and again as a keyword. However, if one examines the recollections of Gerhard Broder and Fritz Lorenz from *6. Kompanie*, for example, it becomes clear that they do not say much about it. The former – who did not take part in the operation due to illness – describes it succinctly: 'Our soldiers advance through snowy terrain without cover. Then heavy targeted defensive fire, casualties, shell impacts. Anton Rieken was killed by a direct hit from a mortar round.[44] Only a few reached the houses on the edge of the village. They reported that the Stukas inflicted casualties on the enemy.'[45] And Lorenz: 'At Alekseyevka I had already served my way up and was MG gunner 2, which meant I had to carry the ammunition. In the deep snow, which was well above stomach level, we launched a counterattack, and I was shot in the upper left shoulder.'[46]

Heinkelein only mentioned it because he narrowly escaped injury or death. Above all, it is clear that the NCOs and enlisted men had no idea why this attack was being carried out at all, and had no distinct picture of the enemy situation, due to the short notice and imperfect preparations. This sacrificial failure must therefore have been deeply etched into the psyche of those involved in this attack as a senseless undertaking.

The enterprise had failed fatally and had cost many soldiers their lives.[47]

---

41 BA-MA, RH 26-45/59: 45. ID, KTB 1 January–15 July 1943, pp.158–159.
42 BA-MA, BW 57-84: special order of *Oberstleutnant* Schulz, 17 April 1943.
43 BA-MA; RH 21-2/451 in BW 57-82.
44 Anton Rieken (Wilhelmshaven, 3 January 1920–KIA Alekseyevka, 15 February 1943), *Oberjäger*.
45 Bernhard (ed.), *Guerre Mondiale contre moi*, p.140.
46 Bernhard (ed.), *Guerre Mondiale contre moi*, p.343.
47 BA-MA, RH 21-2/451 in BW 57-82.

The Soviet Attack Towards Smiyevka

The fact that the 6th Guards Rifle Division was able to hold Alekseyevka paid off for the Red Army. The village became the assembly point for the initially successful attack northwest towards the railway station of Smiyevka, which was an important supply hub for all the divisions of *LV. Armee Korps*. The 13th Army, operating to the left (to the west of the 48th Army), was to push west of Maloarkhangelsk towards Trossna into the wide-open flank of *2. Panzer Armee*. For this purpose, Pukhov, recently promoted to Lieutenant General on 14 February, formed Group Novoselsky with the 211th and 280th Rifle Divisions, three ski brigades and the 19th Tank Corps. The prospects for Reyter's Bryansk Front to push successfully towards Orel seemed to be very promising.[48]

The situation on the southern flank of *2. Panzer Armee* was now very critical, since the Soviet forces managed to drive a deep wedge between *45. Infanterie Division* and *299. Infanterie Division* in the area of Alekseyevka and north-west of it.[49] The intention of *Generaloberst* Schmidt was to assemble the last remaining reserves in order to close this gap.

On 16 February, the 48th Army continued to feed reinforcements into Alekseyevka and from there to Volny Trud. The position of Gröschke's battalion on the heights north of the village had now become too dangerous, so on the orders of Schulz he was allowed to withdraw to the already established main line of defence during the night. The withdrawal was covered by Brammer's platoon of self-propelled anti-tank guns.[50] The battalion was now located (from left to right) '1 km south Grasnoye, southwest edge Stolbetskoye – point 248.1 and connection [by *7. Kompanie*] to the right with *III. Bataillon*.'[51] Connection on the left was established by an anti-tank platoon of *14. Kompanie* to *6. Kompanie/Grenadier Regiment 529* (of *299. Infanterie Division*).

Exactly when Becker and his *III. Bataillon* arrived in its area of operations on the right wing of the regiment is not entirely clear. On the 16th at 2:40 p.m., *Generaloberst* Schmidt informed *General* von Roman by phone that the battalion was to be transferred to the corps,[52] although it was already in position that morning. The right wing of the regiment was to be bent strongly to the west in order to protect its right flank.[53] The connection to the neighbour on the right beyond Nagorniy, *383. Infanterie Division*, was still not established. *General* von Roman gave this division the order at 5:30 p.m. to close the gap with parts of *Grenadier Regiment 133*. The remnants of this regiment, under command of *Oberstleutnant* von Elterlein, were originally part of *Generalleutnant* Kühlwein's *45. Infanterie Division*. As the regiment got separated from its division, it was briefly subordinated to the neighbouring *383. Infanterie Division*. The next day, however, the combat group *Stab Elterlein* was back again in the command area of its division, albeit still on the other side of the breach.[54]

On the 16th at 11:00 a.m. Soviet attacks from Alekseyevka on the positions of the paratroopers on Hill 250.2 and Stolbetskoye were repulsed by close combat. This left 50 dead Soviet soldiers and one destroyed KV-1 tank in front of the positions. The defenders were definitely paratroopers of *III. Bataillon* – which is incorrectly said to have arrived only around 2:00 p.m. *9. Kompanie* also sent

---

48   Glantz, *After Stalingrad*, p.267.
49   NARA, T-315 R-153: PzAOK 2, KTB 3, vol.1: Daily report of 16 February 1943.
50   Brammer, 'Kriegstagebuch', p.109.
51   BA-MA, BW 57-84: Extract of the war journal of II./FJR 1.
52   NARA, T-314 R-1376: LV. AK, KTB 3, part IV, p.901.
53   BA-MA, RH 26-45/59: 45. ID KTB 1 January–15 July 1943, pp.162–163.
54   NARA, T-314 R-1376: LV. AK, KTB 3, part IV, p.901.

out a reconnaissance patrol towards Volny Trud and Khoroshevsky where they also endured close combat. Casualties of four killed and 21 wounded paratroopers were suffered that day. Two officers were wounded: *Oberleutnant* Wiener commander of *11. Kompanie* (altogether three wounded) and *Leutnant* Konrad Grau of *12. Kompanie* (altogether one dead, three wounded). *9. Kompanie* lost 10 wounded, *10. Kompanie* one dead and one wounded, while the battalion staff units also lost two dead and two wounded. *II. Bataillon* lost two wounded in Stolbetskoye. The command of *11. Kompanie* was taken over on an interim basis by *Feldwebel* Karl-Hans Wittig, who on that day had distinguished himself once more.

During this time, the regiment was still moving by means of *Flieger Division 7*. These trucks should have been returned immediately by the command of *2. Panzer Armee* (PzAOK 2), which was not immediately possible as the situation changed rapidly. Thus, during the night of 16 to 17 February, the order was issued to *Fallschimjäger Regiment 1* that the necessary means of transport for a battalion were to remain with the regiment 'to be used in future in shuttle traffic to make the whole regiment mobile.'[55] The remainder of the vehicles was sent to Orel and from there returned to the division. The regiment was now largely immobile and depended on transport capacity of other units and formations.

On 17 February, the Soviet 6th Guards Division, together with the II. Battalion/9th Ski Brigade (700 men) and with the support of the 28th and 30th Guards Tank Regiments and the 43rd Tank Regiment,[56] succeeded in breaking through the defensive line of *45. Infanterie Division* at Nagorniy and managed to advance towards the important supply station of Smiyevka, through which all supplies for this part of the front were running, as far as Maloarkhangelsk to the south. The supplies for four divisions of the *LV. Armee Korps* depended on this railway line.[57] To the right of the Soviet attacking force was 143th Rifle Division and on the left flank a regiment of the 399th Rifle Division. Due to the lack of Soviet sources, it is not known who was in charge of this attack.[58]

The arrival of the first units of *216. Infanterie Division* saved the day. They were able to stop the advance and throw the attackers back to the southeast. At the village of Stepanovka on the Neruch River, however, the Soviets formed a new line of defence, where they fought with determination, while being reinforced through the breach constantly. The situation for the Germans was confusing and became ever more critical.

This early morning attack of 6th Guards Division also hit the positions of *9.* and *10. Kompanie* of Becker's battalion, who were located on Hill 250.2 between Alekseyeva and Nagorniy, with full force. The paratroopers were not able to dig in because of the frozen ground and were only able to build small positions out of snow. As these positions were lacking any meaningful cover, several paratroopers got run over by Soviet tanks. The defensive line had to be pulled back onto a line between the northern edge of Stepanovka to the southern edge of Kamenka, leading further to Hill 248, to Kapriska, and the southern edge of Stolbetskoye. Eight tanks (two KV-1 and six T-34) were reported in front of *III. Bataillon*. At 6:55 a.m. *Leutnant* Brammer drove with 'Peter', his Marder II with its mounted 7.5 cm anti-tank gun, through deep snow to help Becker's men. At 7:30 a.m. he managed to score a hit on a T-34 and capture the crew. Around 8:00 a.m. another two guns of Pusch's platoon arrived in support. At a distance of 1,500 metres five Soviet tanks were engaged, one KV-1 and one T-34 were neutralized

---

55 NARA, T-315 R-172: PzAOK 2, KTB 3, *Anlagenband* 50, Telex PzAOK 2 to FJR 1 via 45. ID, dated 16 but sent 17 February 1943 12:20 a.m.
56 Glantz, *After Stalingrad*, p.274.
57 20. PzDiv., 18. PzDiv, 383. ID and 45. ID.
58 Glantz, *After Stalingrad*, p.274.

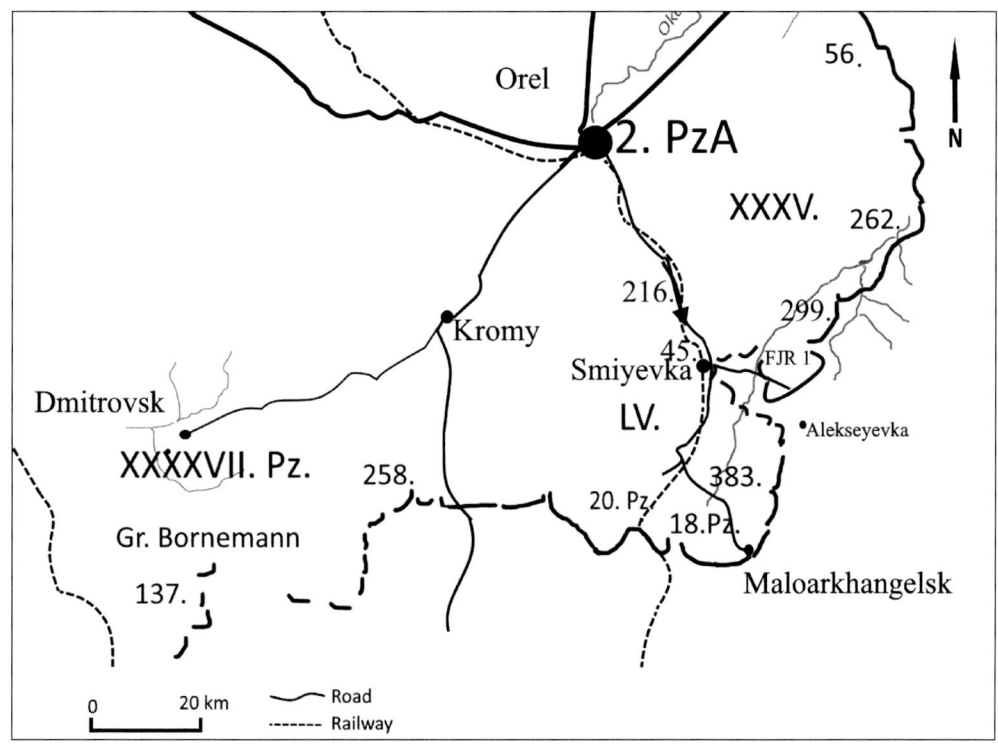

The southern front of *2. Panzer Armee* on 17 February 1943, showing the Soviet breakthrough towards Smiyevka and the positions of *Fallschirmjäger Regiment 1*.

in the process, the other three retreated around 8:30 a.m. While pursuing these tanks, one of the tracks of 'Peter' dislodged from its wheels and had to be repaired out in the open far in front of their own main line of defence, covered only by *Oberjäger* Hässner's gun. The guns later covered the already withdrawn positions of *III. Bataillon* from 10:00 a.m. to 6:00 p.m. from positions on Hill 248. While fending off an infantry attack, the barrel of the self-propelled gun 'Moritz' exploded and was unusable from that moment on. Hässner was able to knock out an American M3 'General Lee' tank with two shots at a distance of 1,600 metres.[59] During these actions Becker's paratroopers also had to defend their positions in close combat.[60]

The gap between Berezovka and Hill 250.2, the right wing of *Fallschirmjäger Regiment 1*, could not be closed while the Soviet advance on Smiyevka was executed unhindered. The rapidly assembled alert units of *45. Infanterie Division* were at first not able to effectively counter this advance and some chaos ensued.[61] Schulz had no connection to Kühlwein's command post, communication had to be relayed through *LV. Armee Korps*. Consequently, messages and orders were delayed for several hours.

---

59 Brammer, 'Kriegstagebuch', p.109.
60 BA-MA, BW 57-93: List of close combat incidents: *III. Bataillon*, parts of *13. Kompanie* and Pusch's platoon of self-propelled anti-tank guns.
61 BA-MA, RH 26-45/59: 45. ID, KTB 1 January–15 July 1943, pp.166–167.

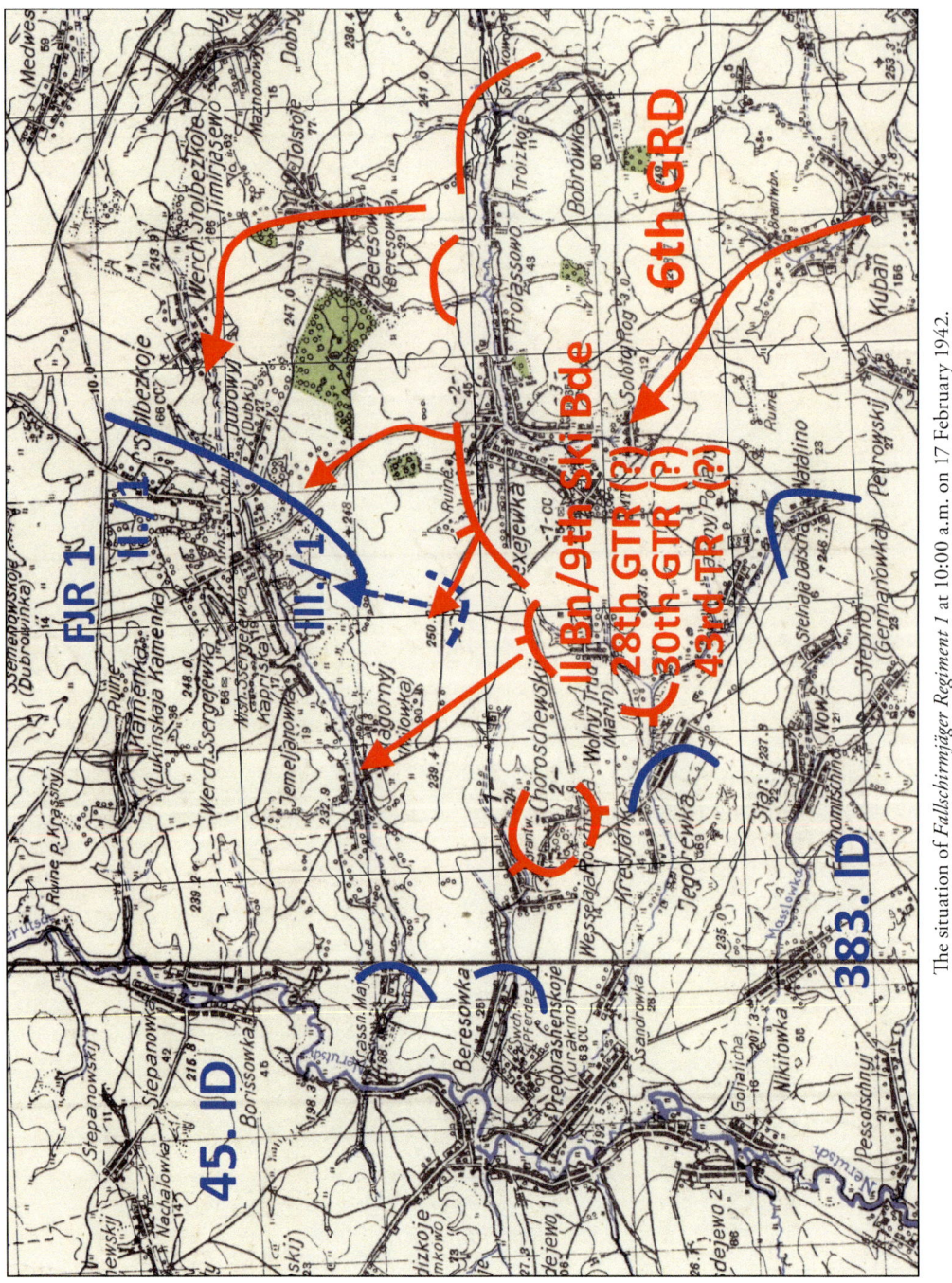

The situation of *Fallschirmjäger Regiment 1* at 10:00 a.m. on 17 February 1942.

Oberstleutnant Schulz interrogates the Soviet prisoners of war.
(Private Collection)

Nine Soviet prisoners of war lined up together with paratroopers for inspection by *Oberstleutnant* Schulz in front of his command post at Kamenka.
(Private Collection)

Repair of the broken track of Brammer's self-propelled anti-tank gun in front of the German positions. (Private Collection)

After pulling back his line of defence, *Oberstleutnant* Schulz needed to cover his right flank. He ordered *Feldwebel* Wittig's *11. Kompanie* to take up positions facing south between the southern edge of Kamenka and the Neruch at 11:30 a.m. Beyond that, Wittig was to conduct reconnaissance patrols against Hill 239.2, Stepanovka and west of the Neruch. This reconnaissance patrol to Stepanovka led to further close combat fighting.[62] To strengthen this flank Schulz deployed two 8.8 cm guns, one near Kamenka and another northeast of this village near the road. Hill 239.2 was of the greatest importance, since it dominated the entrance to the Neruch valley and was indispensable for the planned recapture of Nagorniy. Meanwhile, Hill 248 between Kamenka and Kapriska was occupied by *Oberleutnant* Dennerlein with his regimental bicycle platoon, which later, on the 19th, was replaced by the engineer platoon of *Leutnant* Weser. To protect Vasilyevka, five 2 cm anti-aircraft guns were deployed to provide cover to the south on both sides of the Neruch. The rest of *III. Bataillon* secured the left flank and the connection to *II. Bataillon*. Schulz sent a telex reporting this to Kühlwein at 11:50 a.m. by way of *LV. Armee Kops*, the division received it only at 3:00 p.m.[63]

At 1:10 p.m., *General* von Roman issued a direct order to *Oberstleutnant* Schulz to hold the Kamenka, Kapriska and Stolbetskoye line 'without regard to casualties',[64] which deprived Schulz of the possibility of moving the main line of defence further back, as he had intended in the face of growing enemy pressure.[65] For his part, Kühlwein received orders at 3:10 p.m. to attack and take the village of Khoroshevsky via Berezovka with *Gruppe Elterlein*. Schulz was to join the attack on Nagorniy, which was to be continued afterwards, from Kapriska with as large an assault group as possible. This was the plan, but it could not be executed. Khoroshevsky, which had just been regained, had to be evacuated again during the night.

While the situation on the right flank of the regiment remained more than uncertain, a column of 200 men with horse-drawn sledges approached the positions of *5. Kompanie* on the left wing at about 6:30 p.m. on the road from the direction of Alekseyevka – it was already dark (Moscow time was 8:30 p.m.). At first it was unclear whether they were German or Red Army soldiers. But since they did not react to the password call, the paratroopers opened fire. The column moved off to the south. But now three tanks with about 500 infantry approached the positions of *II. Bataillon* from the direction of Medveshka. Gröschke immediately called for Brammers platoon of self-propelled anti-tank guns which was with *III. Bataillon*. Brammer left immediately but arrived too late to be able to intervene. He later took up position at the eastern exit of Stolbetskoye.[66]

The 4.2 cm anti-tank gun of *14. Kompanie* which was covering the road, immediately opened fire and scored a hit on the first tank, a KV-1, which was knocked out. Shortly afterwards, the gun itself received a direct hit from the second tank. Two of the gunners, *Obergefreite* Hübner and Schröder,[67] were killed, and several others were wounded.[68] However, the tanks could not leave the road because

---

62 BA-MA, BW 57-93: List of close combat incidents: *11. Kompanie* – tactical raid towards Stepanovka with close combat.
63 BA-MA, RH 26-45/62 in BW 57-82.
64 NARA, T-314 R-1376: LV. AK, KTB 3, part IV, p.905.
65 BA-MA, RH 26-45/62 in BW 57-82.
66 Brammer, 'Kriegstagebuch', p.110.
67 Alfred Hübner (Gurkow, 25 August 1921–KIA Stolbetskoye, 17 February 1943); *Obergefreiter*; Heinz Schröder (Berlin, 22 June 1921–KIA Stolbetskoye, 17 February 1943); *Obergefreiter*.
68 Altogether *14. Kompanie* lost four dead and four wounded that day. The two other dead, *Gefreiter* Wilhelm Pershun and *Gefreiter* Hugo Gump, have their place of death noted as 'Alekseyevka' which points to having been with *III. Bataillon*.

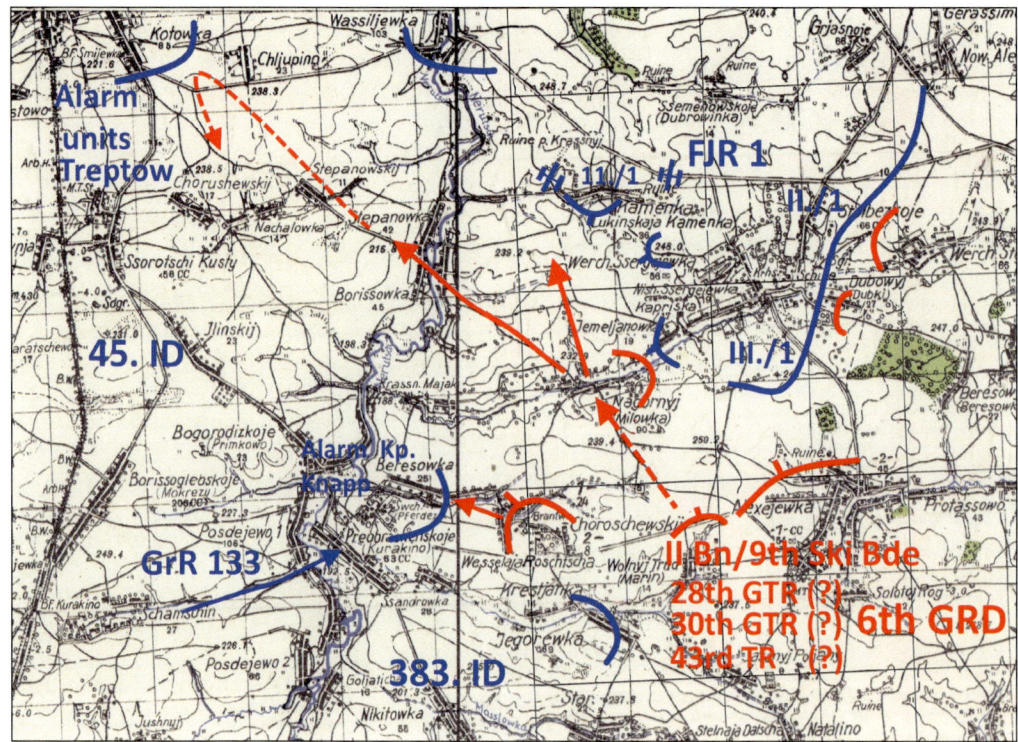

Situation on 17 February 1943, 11:30 a.m.

the snowdrifts on the sides were too high. Paratroopers of *5. Kompanie* succeeded in working their way up to this second tank, a T-34, shot the commander who was looking out of the hatch and destroyed the tank by means of explosive charges. The third tank then retreated. This attack was finally stopped by the combined defensive fire of *5.* and *8. Kompanie*. At the same time, the left wing was attacked by a platoon of Soviet soldiers approaching on skis. However, this platoon was almost entirely wiped out in the process. The fighting came to an end at around 10:00 p.m. A total of three Soviet tanks (two KV-1s and one T-34) were destroyed and 142 enemy dead were counted.[69]

On this day, 17 February, the regiment suffered 35 casualties – 13 killed and missing and 22 wounded – with *III. Bataillon* being the worst hit with nine dead and 17 wounded. Of *9. Kompanie* an *Obergefreiter* was run over by a tank, another one was killed, and two were wounded. *10. Kompanie* lost three dead from artillery fire, five were wounded including its company commander *Leutnant* Söhnke. *12. Kompanie* had three dead that day, all run over by tanks, and five wounded – among them the company commander *Oberleutnant* Merkordt – one soldier of *11. Kompanie* was missing. *14. Kompanie* suffered four dead and four wounded and *13. Kompanie* lost one man wounded. Gröschke's battalion was not so hard hit as Becker's men that day, it lost four men wounded.

---

69 BA-MA, BW 57-93: List of close combat incidents: *II. Bataillon*, III. platoon of *13. Kompanie* and parts of *14. Kompanie*.

The Attack on Nagorniy

During the night of 17 to 18 February, Smiyevka remained heavily threatened, and a breakthrough was imminent, so *Generaloberst* Schmidt ordered *216. Infanterie Division* to Smiyevka to restore the situation and to relieve Kühlwein's depleted and exhausted *45. Infanterie Division*.[70]

Oberst Treptow,[71] the regimental commander of *Panzer Grenadier Regiment 101* of *18. Panzer Division*, happened to be at Smiyevka (probably on his way to take command of the *Panzer Grenadier Brigade z.b.V. 4*, which he commanded February to April 1943). He was commanded to save the railway line and was supposed to attack Stepanovka from Vasilyevka with the help of *III. Bataillon/Infanterie Regiment 386* (216. ID) when he received his orders about 11:00 p.m. This battalion had only just arrived in the late evening hours of the 17th in Smiyevka and was immediately sent by truck to Vasilyevka. Shortly afterwards, however, it came under heavy fire from attacking Soviet tanks near Kotovka, on the outskirts of Smiyevka, at 4:00 a.m. on the 18th. The battalion had to disembark their transport vehicles and immediately went on the defence. The attack on Stepanovka was carried out by weak alert units, quickly assembled at Vasilyevka.

Paratroopers of *III. Bataillon* preparing food, potatoes and millet porridge, near Kamenka in February 1943. (Private Collection)

Oberst Treptow reported at about 6:00 a.m. that the Soviet attack on Kotovka had successfully been repulsed and the battalion was pursuing the retreating enemy. The alert units at the disposal of Treptow at Vasilyevka were at the same time attacking Stepanovka along the river Neruch. At 6:25 a.m Schulz therefore received the order to immediately join the attack of this 'Group Vasilyevka' with his right wing.[72]

In the meantime, Kühlwein did not have the luxury of simply waiting to be relieved. By 2:45 a.m. he gave the order by radio to *Oberstleutnant* Schulz to attack Nagorniy together with *Gruppe Elterlein*

---

70   NARA, T-315 R-153: PzAOK 2, KTB 3, vol.1, 17 February 1943, p.4; NARA, T-314 R-1376: LV. AK, KTB 3, part IV, p.909.
71   Hans Treptow (Zwickau, 30 December 1895–P.O.W. hospital Graudenz, 27 June 1945), *Oberst*; DKiG 19 May 1942.
72   BA-MA, RH 26-45/59 and/62: 45. ID, KTB 1 January–15 July 1943, p.173.

(GrRgt 133). This order had to be transmitted via the radio operator of *LV. Armee Korps* and did not reach Schulz until 4:00 a.m. There was no radio reception due to atmospheric interference. The order to attack was originally given by *General* von Roman, against the advice of Kühlwein, who (properly) considered his existing forces too weak for an attack. Elterlein was ordered to take Khoroshevsky and to continue the attack on Nagorniy. Against all odds, Elterlein succeeded in breaking into in the southern part of the village of Khoroshevsky during the night and continued his attack during the day towards the northern part which was more strongly occupied by Soviet forces.

A considerable problem proved to be the delays and difficulties in radio communication. Schulz reported to Kühlwein as early as 5:00 a.m. that he would support the attack of the alert units from Vasilyevka on Stepanovka with his *Nebelwerfer*, two tanks, two 8.8 and 2 cm guns and would additionally attack with one company if this attack became effective. The message was not received by Kühlwein's command post until 8:50 a.m.[73]

In the morning a self-propelled anti-tank gun and a Panzer IV of the paratroopers succeeded in destroying two Soviet tanks south of Nagorniy, while the Soviet attackers were slowly pushed back from Smiyevka by Treptow. Around noon Elterlein managed to take the northern part of Khoroshevsky, Berezovka fell into German hands as well and at the same time strong retreating Soviet forces from Stepanovsky to Stepanovka were observed.[74]

At 12 noon, the regimental commander of *Infanterie Regiment 386* (of 216. ID), *Oberstleutnant* Gerhard Gnoth,[75] who had just arrived, took over command of his *III. Bataillon*.[76] Contrary to the remarks in the war diary of *45. Infanterie Division*, *II. Bataillon* was not under his command yet. Said battalion did not arrive in the Smiyevka area until the evening of the 18th. The arrival of Gnoth's regiment was delayed – for the same reasons the paratroopers experienced on their arrival on 15 February – due to transports to the rear of the *45. Infanterie Division*.

Elterlein contacted Schulz at 12:20 p.m. to discuss a possible joint attack on Nagorniy. In the afternoon, around 3:40 p.m., *45. Infanterie Division* reported to *LV. Armee Korps* that the attack on Nagorniy by *Grenadier Regiment 133* (Elterlein), *Grenadier Regiment 531* (of 383. ID), *Gruppe Treptow* and *Fallschirmjäger Regiment 1* on Nagorniy had begun. At 4:16 p.m. Schulz was ordered to shorten his right wing and to conduct a combat reconnaissance on Nagorniy. This was intended to support the attack on Stepanovka and Nagorniy. At 6:20 p.m. Schulz sent a reconnaissance patrol to Nagorniy, which was able to establish that the place was 'blocked on all sides for through traffic. The sound of tanks and sledges of withdrawing units' could be heard.[77] A group of *11. Kompanie*, together with support from parts of *14. Kompanie* and of *I./Flak Regiment 501* (probably a 2 cm gun), crossed the river Neruch and reconnoitred aggressively towards Stepanovka, where it encountered close combat with Soviet troops.[78] *14. Kompanie* lost three men killed of whom one was seriously wounded and succumbed to his wounds on the way to the field hospital in Smiyevka,[79] and another four wounded. The men from *11. Kompanie* got away unscathed.

---

73   BA-MA, RH 26-45/62.
74   BA-MA, RH 26-45/59 and/62: 45. ID, KTB 1 January–15 July 1943, p.175.
75   Gerhard Gnoth (Magdeburg, 11 September 1901–Rendsburg, 6 December 1989), *Oberstleutnant*. He was awarded the DKiG on 21 April 1943 for his conduct at these actions at Orel.
76   BA-MA, RH 26-45/59: 45. ID, KTB 1 January–15 July 1943, p.176.
77   BA-MA, RH 26-45/62.
78   BA-MA, BW 57-93: List of close combat incidents: *11. Kompanie*, parts of *14. Kompanie* and 1./501.
79   Helmut Sinka (Neisse, 30 April 1920–KIA Stepanovka, 18 February 1943), *Obergefreiter*, and Walter Rattaj (Münchhausen, 1 August 1919–KIA Stepanovka, 18 February 1943), *Obergefreiter*; Friedrich Weiss (Nürnberg,

Meanwhile the attack by Treptow's men came to a halt near Stepanovsky at about 6:00 p.m., as the Soviets stubbornly defended Stepanovka and the important Hill 239.2.

The German efforts around Smiyevka were also supported by the *Luftwaffe* which put a focus on this area on that day with 125 dive-bomber, 85 fighter-bomber and 35 fighter missions.

On the left wing of the paratroopers, in front of the positions of Gröschke's battalion, the enemy was continuously reinforced with smaller and larger groups near Dubovy, beginning in the early morning hours. The threat grew during the day there as well, so that Schulz expected an attack the next morning.

At 10:50 p.m. the expected large Soviet attack took place under 'uncomfortable'[80] artillery preparation in regimental strength (according to the morning report of *45. Infanterie Division* of 19 February only in company strength), which, however, was fended off. The regiment reported 12 dead Soviet soldiers. Brammer's self-propelled anti-tank gun platoon supported the defence by firing high-explosive shells towards the attackers. He estimated the attacker's strength as one battalion.[81]

Shortly before, in the evening of the 18th, *Oberstleutnant* Schulz received an order by telephone from *Oberstleutnant i.G.* Wirsing, to support the attack on enemy elements which had broken through between Beresovka and Stolbetskoye. This action was to take place on the next day or the same night from 18 to 19 February. The situation was rather confusing. Schulz was to 'establish contact with the parts of GrRgt 531 (383. ID) which had advanced to Hill 239.2 and to join them in the subsequent attack in the direction of Nagorniy' although this regiment never made it to this hill. With 'other parts [of his regiment, Schulz] was to support the taking of Nagorniy by *III. Bataillon/Grenadier Regiment 135* (45. ID), which attacked from the west, by attacking from Kapriska.'[82] In addition, *Oberstleutnant* Gnoth's *Grenadier Regiment 396*, which was still not completely assembled, was deployed. Now Gnoth, by attacking via Stepanovka with his regiment, was supposed to reach at least the important Hill 239.2. To complete this task, his *II. Bataillon* was to carry out the attack on the hill from the direction of Vasilyevka.[83] But the battalion did not arrive there until the evening hours of the 18th. *III. Bataillon* which had been fighting continuously since its arrival the previous evening, was able to take Stepanovsky in the course of the day and waited there for the attack of its sister battalion to happen.

Schulz described the events of that evening in his after-action report:

> On 18 February 1943, 10:35 p.m. the orderly officer of *II. Bataillon/Grenadier Regiment 396* reported to me for liaison. His regiment had orders to attack Nagorniy on 19 February 1943 with two battalions and to take possession of it after Stepanovka had been taken. He inquired how far we could support this attack. He was given the following orientation:
> a) *11. Kompanie* (Kamenka) will advance on [Hill] 239.2 and has orders to join the attack of the grenadier unit. This company will be subordinated to the infantry. The orderly officer received instructions to liaise with it in Kamenka, as the company leader of the *11. Kompanie*, *Feldwebel* Wittig, for his part, had orders to seek liaison.

---

10 October 1921–KIA Stepanovka 18 February 1943), *Obergefreiter*, died on his way to the field hospital at Smiyevka.
80 Brammer, 'Kriegstagebuch', pp.108–110.
81 Brammer, 'Kriegstagebuch', pp.108–110.
82 BA-MA, RH 26-45/62: After-action report of 45. ID about the attack on Nagorniy on 19 and 20 February 1943.
83 NARA, T-314 R-1376: LV. AK, KTB 3, part IV, p.909; see also Martin Jenner, *Die Geschichte der 216./272. Infanterie-Division* (Eggolsheim: Nebel-Dörfler, without year), pp.108–109.

b) The regimental engineer platoon on Hill 248.0 had orders to liaise with *11. Kompanie* and to join the attack on Nagorniy.
c) the regimental bicycle platoon (less one group) and parts of the regimental alarm-units, reinforced by two Panzer IV lg,[84] had orders to stand by on the Western edge of Yemelyanovka to support the attack from the East.

The regiment had deployed the following heavy weapons in immediate support of the attack:

At Yemelyanovka one 8.8 cm anti-aircraft gun, three 2 cm anti-aircraft guns, one 7.5 cm self-propelled anti-tank gun, three 10 cm *Nebelwerfer* and various infantry weapons. From positions east of Hill 248.0, two 8.8 cm anti-aircraft guns were deployed for artillery fire on Nagorniy.[85]

From this point on, radio connection between Schulz and *II. Bataillon/Grenadier Regiment 396* was lost.

Generalleutnant Kühlwein explained the delays in his after-action report stating that the snow conditions had worsened during the night, so that the arrival of the forces planned for the attack had been delayed accordingly.[86] Consequently, the attack could not be carried out as intended. Responsible for the delays was the above-mentioned behaviour of the retreating division's own transport units. No reason is mentioned in the war diary of the *LV. Armee Korps*.[87]

Additional communication problems arose. The telephone connections between the command posts of *45. Infanterie Division* and *Fallschirmjäger Regiment 1* were partly or completely unavailable between 12:30 a.m. and 2:30 a.m. and could not be restored due to a lack of cable layers and construction workers. The regiment could only be reached via the radio of the army corps.

On 19 February at 1:35 a.m. an order was issued by Kühlwein to Schulz stating that, as an infantry battalion had just entered the western part of Nagorniy, the regiment should immediately begin its attack. At 1:50 a.m. Schulz reported to the division that Stepanovka was still in Soviet hands and tanks were positioned in the village.

Further reports also stated that the western part of Nagorniy was supposed to have been taken at 2:15 a.m. by *III. Bataillon/Grenadier Regiment 135*. The approximately 200 soldiers who had managed to enter the village came under heavy fire from six Soviet tanks, so Kühlwein again ordered Schulz at 2:45 a.m. to attack: '*Fallschirmjäger Regiment 1* is informed of this tank action. There is still no sign of help from the paratroopers. [The regiment], to which a telephone connection can be established for a short time, is again ordered to immediately attack enemy on the east and north edge of the village. At the same time, the right wing is to make contact with I./GrRgt 531 at Hill 239.2.'[88]

However, the order to Schulz appears to have been withdrawn, because at 4:10 a.m. he was informed about the postponement of the start of the attack on Nagorniy. The attack on Stepanovka from Vasilyevka by *II. Bataillon* and from Stepanovsky by *III. Bataillon* of *Grenadier Regiment 396*

---

84 This was most probably the *Panzer Kampfwagen IV Version F2* with a long ('lg' for 'lang'/long) very effective 7.5 cm 40/L43 gun barrel. At the beginning the Panzer IV had only a short barrel which proved ineffective against the Soviet heavy tanks.
85 BA-MA, LV. AK, KTB 36358/4 in BW 57-82: Schulz' after-action report on the taking of Nagorniy 19–20 February 1943, dated 22 February 1943.
86 BA-MA, RH 26-45/62: 45. ID, KTB, Attachments vol.2, 1–28 February 1943.
87 NARA, T-314 R-1376: LV. AK, KTB 3, part IV, p.910–912.
88 BA-MA, RH 26-45/59: 45. ID, KTB 1 January–15 July 1943, p.182.

Above: A Marder II self-propelled anti-tank gun in action, March 1943. (BArch, Bild 101I-560-1113-32/Hanns Gross)

Right: An *Obergefreiter* loads his 7.5 cm gun, March 1943. (BArch, Bild 101I-560-1113-20/Hanns Gross/CC-BY-SA 3.0)

did not progress due to adverse snow conditions. The soldiers had to advance in parts through very deep snow at -25°C and with additional snowfalling.[89] From then on, the mission of the paratroopers was 'primarily to support the units holding on 239.2 and III./GrRgt 135 in Nagorniy with armour-piercing weapons.'[90]

Oberstleutnant Schulz's after-action report on the events of that night remains strangely silent about these circumstances. He merely stated, based on his own reconnaissance results, that the reports that

---

89 BA-MA, RH 26-45/59: 45. ID, KTB 1 January–15 July 1943, p.180.
90 BA-MA, RH 26-45/59: 45. ID, KTB 1 January–15 July 1943, pp.182–183.

Nagorniy was in German hands had been false. Patrols of his regiment had reported the village occupied by the enemy. *III. Bataillon/GrRgt 135* had never taken Nagorniy, but rather only fought in its extreme south-western part, was beaten back and had to retreat again in the direction of Khoroshevsky. The Soviet pressure was too great and there were no armour-piercing weapons available, which forced *III. Bataillon/GrRgt 135* to withdraw and disengage from the enemy at about 6:00 a.m. in the morning of the 19th. However, according to a message from *General* Roman to *Generalleutnant* Kühlwein at 8:00 a.m., parts of *Fallschirmjäger Regiment 1* are said to have entered the northern part of Nagorniy.[91]

In any case, Nagorniy could neither be taken, nor could the western part be held that night. The two battalions of Gnoth's *Grenadier Regiment 396* managed to encircle Stepanovka during the night and take it in the early morning hours; the securing of the village was completed at 7:50 a.m. At 9:05 a.m. the good news that 'Stepanovka [was] in our own hands'[92] arrived at Schulz's command post through his neighbour on the left, *Grenadier Regiment 529* (of 299. ID). This regiment had sent out a reconnaissance patrol from Mikhailovka in the morning hours, as the situation on their right flank was unclear. The reconnaissance was carried out by two paratroopers of *2. Kompanie*, which was subordinated to this regiment:

> On 19 February, together with my friend Oskar Schneider,[93] I [*Gefreiter* von Zimburg] was given the task of determining by ski whether the village of Stepanovka, about five kilometres south of Vasilyevka, was still in our hands or already in Russian hands, or where the regimental command post of our right-hand neighbour was located. We moved from Mikhailovka to Hill 248, southeast of Vasilyevka, and from there observed an infantry company attacking Stepanovka. We therefore skied down into the valley and to Stepanovka. The first houses were completely burned down. I can still smell the burnt hay and cattle today. Russians peeked out of some houses as we skied along the road. We weren't really afraid of them. But we soon saw our own soldiers, who directed us to their battalion command post. There we learned that there was a regimental command post about four and a half kilometres to the south. Now we walked to it, made contact and then wanted to get back, cutting across the terrain. It began to snow heavily again and so we almost ran into the Russian positions a few kilometres west of Stolpetskoye. Four kilometres to the west of Stolpetskoye we reached an anti-aircraft battery [the 8.8 cm guns of FJR 1] on the southern edge of Kamenka. From there we reached Mikhailovka via Semenovskoye.[94]

The two paratroopers obviously had no idea that the neighbour to the right was in fact their own regiment.

Gröschke's battalion on the left wing of the regiment was also kept busy. It repelled a Soviet attack near Stolbetskoye at about 8:00 a.m., which cost the lives of eight Red Army soldiers.

After the fall of Stepanovka, an attack on Nagorniy now moved back into the centre of German focus. Kühlwein spoke to Roman at 8:15 a.m. and reaffirmed his intention to take the village, assigning the paratroopers more of a supporting role. At 11:00 a.m. *Oberstleutnant* Wirsing spoke with the Chief

---

91 BA-MA, RH 26-45/59: 45. ID, KTB 1 January–15 July 1943, p.187.
92 BA-MA, RH 26-45/59: 45. ID, KTB 1 January–15 July 1943, p.186; BA-MA, LV. AK, KTB 36358/4 in BW 57-82: After-action report of Schulz.
93 Oskar Schneider (Innsbruck, 30 [20?] April 1922-KIA Germany, 19 February 1945), *Oberjäger*.
94 Zimburg, *Kriegserlebnisse*, pp.79–80. The *I. Bataillon* was subordinated to 299. ID (see below).

of the General Staff of *LV. Armee Korps*, *Oberst* Wagner, asking that the order for the attack initially scheduled for 12 noon, be passed on to *Oberstleutnant* Schulz:

> *Fallschirmjäger Regiment 1* joins the left wing of *Grenadier Regiment 396* attacking from Hill 239.2 against Nagorniy. Attack target north bank of the creek at the southern edge Stolbetskoye. Boundary to *Grenadier Regiment 396*: North edge Stepanovka-Southwest edge Yemelyanovka. The parts of the previous right wing freed up by the severe shortening of the section are to be kept available as a reserve in the Verkh. Sergeyevka area.[95]

Around noon considerable movements of Soviet units towards the rear were be observed. *Luftwaffe* dive bombers (Stukas) flew attacks on the village increasing the pressure. At the same time, however, worrying reports arrived: a column of 1,000 men was approaching through the Lipovets valley towards Alekseyevka. It became critical to begin the attack as soon as possible before these Soviet reinforcements arrived.

A series of misunderstandings arose around this attack, on one hand due to poor communications and on the other due to the conduct of the attacking battalions of Gnoth's *Grenadier Regiment 396*.

The planned start of the attack at 1:00 p.m. was delayed and the battalions of *Grenadier Regiment 396* did not arrive until between 2:30 p.m. and 3:00 p.m. *Oberstleutnant* Gnoth gave two reasons for the delay: Firstly, Hill 239.2 – contrary to information provided by *45. Infanterie Division* – was still occupied by the enemy and could only be taken at 1:15 p.m. 'after laboriously wading through snow 60–80 cm high.' Secondly, poor communications and unfavourable road conditions proved an impediment. Subsequently, the dive-bomber attack, which was supposed to support the attack on the ground, had ended as planned at 1:00 p.m. but could not be exploited.[96]

Schulz went to Yemelyanovka, a village to the east of Nagorniy, at about 3:30 p.m., after it became apparent that the attack had begun. His paratroopers were all in their designated starting positions, *Feldwebel* Wittig with his *11. Kompanie* (together with parts of *6. Kompanie/Grenadier Regiment 396*) was now at Hill 239.2, the regimental engineer platoon at Hill 248 and the rest of the regimental troops lay ready in Yemelyanovka.

At 3:15 p.m. *Grenadier Regiment 531* reported to Kühlwein that its eastward attack towards the western part of Nagorniy had begun. By 4:15 p.m. the forward elements of *III. Bataillon/Grenadier Regiment 396*, which had also to attack the western part of Nagorniy (west of the Borisovka-Nagorniy-Alekseyevka road), reported that it had managed to advance to within one kilometre northwest of the village. Due to heavy enemy fire, they could not continue any further. Meanwhile, more Soviet reinforcements reached the village from the south. Kühlwein reassured this battalion of fire support from *Artillerie Regiment 98*. *Oberstleutnant* Gnoth also received two more assault guns, as the ones assigned to the regiment had either been knocked out or had run out of fuel. Due to the severe cold, the radios of the forward artillery observers failed, so the artillery could only provide limited support to the attack.[97]

---

95 BA-MA, RH 26-45/62: 45. ID, KTB, Attachments vol.2, 1–28 February 1943: After-action report of *45. Infanterie Division* on the taking of Nagorniy on 19 and 20 February 1943, p.2.
96 BA-MA, RH 26-45/62: 45. ID, KTB, Attachments vol.2, 1–28 February 1943: After-action report of Gren.Rgt. 396 on the attack on Nagorniy on 20 February 1943.
97 BA-MA, RH 26-45/62: 45. ID, KTB, Attachments vol.2, 1–28 February 1943: After-action report of *45. Infanterie Division* on the taking of Nagorniy on 19 and 20 February 1943, p.2.

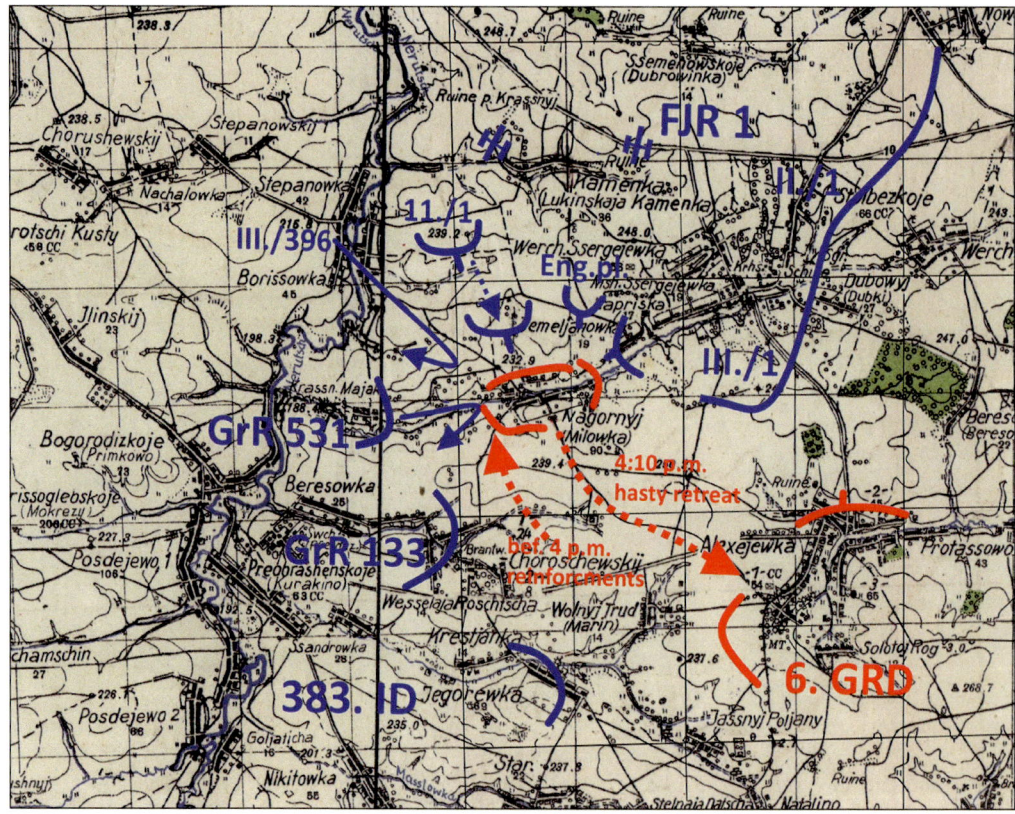

Situation on 19 February 1943 at 4:15 p.m.

As the Red Army's reinforcement of Nagorniy was not unnoticed by the Germans, neither were the intentions of the Germans to the Soviets. Accordingly, the paratroopers came under fire from positions on high ground to the south and the anti-aircraft guns of the paratroopers took up the fight.

> 4:10 p.m. enemy forces in the strength of about one company left the village in a hurry to the southeast. I [Schulz] then gave the order to attack to facilitate the advance of the troops attacking on the right. Under covering-fire the tanks together with the assault troops [of *Fallschirmjäger Regiment 1*] reached the eastern edge of N[agorniy], entered the village about 150 m and occupied it. Erhardt's company [45.ID][98] was brought forward. At the edge of the village 19 prisoners were taken.

---

98 This company is what remained of the *Divisionsbataillon 45*, formed at the beginning of February 1943 from the remnants of the reconnaissance and tank destroyer battalion of *45. Infanterie Division*, under the command of *Rittmeister* Erhardt. See Rudolf Gschöpf, *Mein Weg mit der 45. Infanterie Division* (Linz: Oberösterreichischer Landesverlag, 1955), p.233.

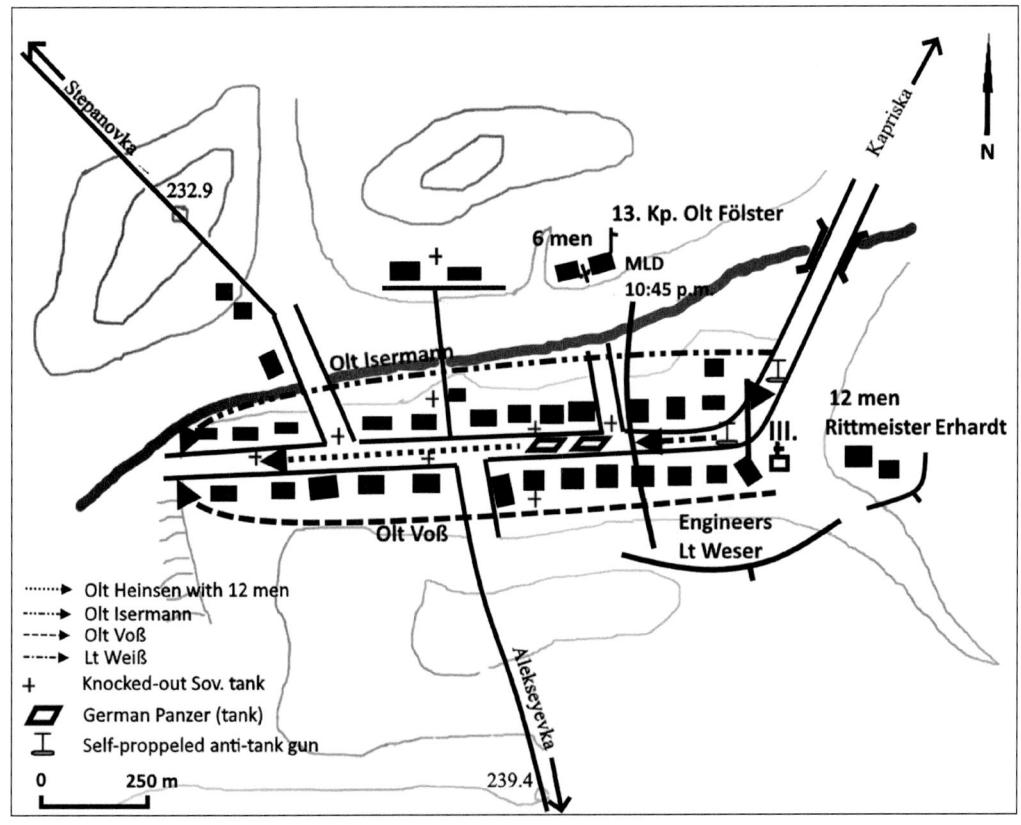

The attack on Nagorniy by *III. Bataillon*.

Stoßgruppe Isermann was ordered to hold the occupied part, with the help of the tanks, to facilitate the advance the engineer platoon of the regiment and *11. Kompanie*.[99]

Meanwhile, *Feldwebel* Wittig with his *11. Kompanie* advanced on Nagorniy from the southern edge of Kamenka in cooperation with parts of *II. Bataillon/Grenadier Regiment 396*.

At 4:50 p.m., the urgent radio message of *Fallschirmjäger Regiment 1*, which was sent at 4:15 p.m., finally arrived at the command post of *45. Infanterie Division* with the following content: 'Please instruct attacking battalions from Stepanovka on Nagorniy to continue attacking even in the dark, as attack group Schulz continues its attack.'[100]

This radio message, which clearly showed Schulz's intention to continue his attack under all circumstances into the clear night, was inexplicably interpreted by *Generalleutnant* Kühlwein merely as a request to the other attacking units, but not as Schulz's own declaration of intent. It must have been dark by 4:30 p.m. or 5:00 p.m. at the latest as sunset was around 4:00 p.m. (Berlin time, which was

---

99   BA-MA, LV. AK, KTB 36358/4 in BW 57-82: After-action report of Schulz, p.3.
100 BA-MA, RH 26-45/62 in BW 57-39.

6:00 p.m. Moscow time). The remaining light was only reflected by snow. Night attacks were generally the exception by the German side as it was common practice to stop an attack at nightfall. However, such attacks were regularly carried out by the Red Army. Consequently, this particular action counts as a remarkable peculiarity.

Schulz's next message was sent at 6:00 p.m. and was received at about 7:00 p.m.: 'Attack on Nagorniy in brisk progress. 5.45 p.m. eastern part in our hands and sealed off to the west. Attack on western part initiated.'[101] Kühlwein again mistook the content of this message as just an observation, he believed the attacking battalion of *Grenadier Regiment 396* to be at that place. Unfortunately, Kühlwein understood all these messages within the rigid framework of his attack order and was unable to grasp what was really happening and that the situation on the ground had changed. Schulz also reported in that same message that in the eastern section of his area of defence three of his 10 cm *Nebelwerfer* were destroyed by direct hits of a Soviet anti-tank gun while changing positions. Schulz reported further:

> Returning to the command post at 6:10 p.m., I discovered that there was no connection with the grenadier battalion attacking on the right and that it had not followed the attack. I ordered *Hauptmann* Becker, who had been sent to N[agorniy], to reorganise our forces, to continue the attack and take N[agorniy] with his own forces. [I r]einforced this battle group with all the soldiers of the staff at my disposal.[102]

This reinforcement also included a group of 7. *Kompanie*, parts of one of the self-propelled anti-tank gun platoons and of the I./501, as they are also mentioned in the list of close combat actions.

At 7:00 p.m. yet another message from Schulz was sent to the division: 'Nagorniy village centre penetrated and occupied, only little fighting there, Grenadier battalion also seems to be advancing.'[103] At this time there were 15 men of the 6. *Kompanie/Grenadier Regiment 396* inside Nagorniy, who arrived together with *11. Kompanie*. *Feldwebel* Wittig and his men fought and worked their way through metre-deep snow to the heights north of Nagorniy, creating a precondition for the subsequent attack on the village. The commander of the bicycle platoon, *Oberleutnant* Dennerlein, was seriously wounded in the fighting. When he was brought to the main dressing station in Smiyevka at around 8:00 p.m., his death was confirmed.[104]

Schulz then ordered Becker to continue the attack on Nagorniy. At about 7:30 p.m. Becker found his old *11. Kompanie*[105] – now consisting of only about 60 men – split up: one platoon on the northeastern edge of Nagorniy on the heights north of the village; another platoon together with a group on the south-western corner on the heights south of the village; parts of the company were about 100 metres inside Nagorniy together with the 15 men of 6. *Kompanie/Grenadier Regiment* 396 facing west. At the north-eastern exit of the village the regimental engineer platoon provided cover to the south and, with about 20 men, the company of *Rittmeister* Erhardt provided cover to the north. In addition, *Oberleutnant* von Oppen was in position there with elements of *14. Kompanie* and on the heights 500

---

101 BA-MA, RH 26-45/62 in BW 57-39: Radio Message of FJR 1 to 45. ID, sent 6:00 p.m., received 7:16 p.m.
102 BA-MA, LV. AK, KTB 36358/4 in BW 57-82: After-action report of Schulz.
103 BA-MA, RH 26-45/62 in BW 57-39: Radio message of FJR 1 to 45. ID, sent 7:00 p.m. received 7:33 p.m.
104 Ancestry/WASt, G-B 221/0964.
105 Becker was commander of this company for the duration of 33 months since its formation in May 1939 until February 1942.

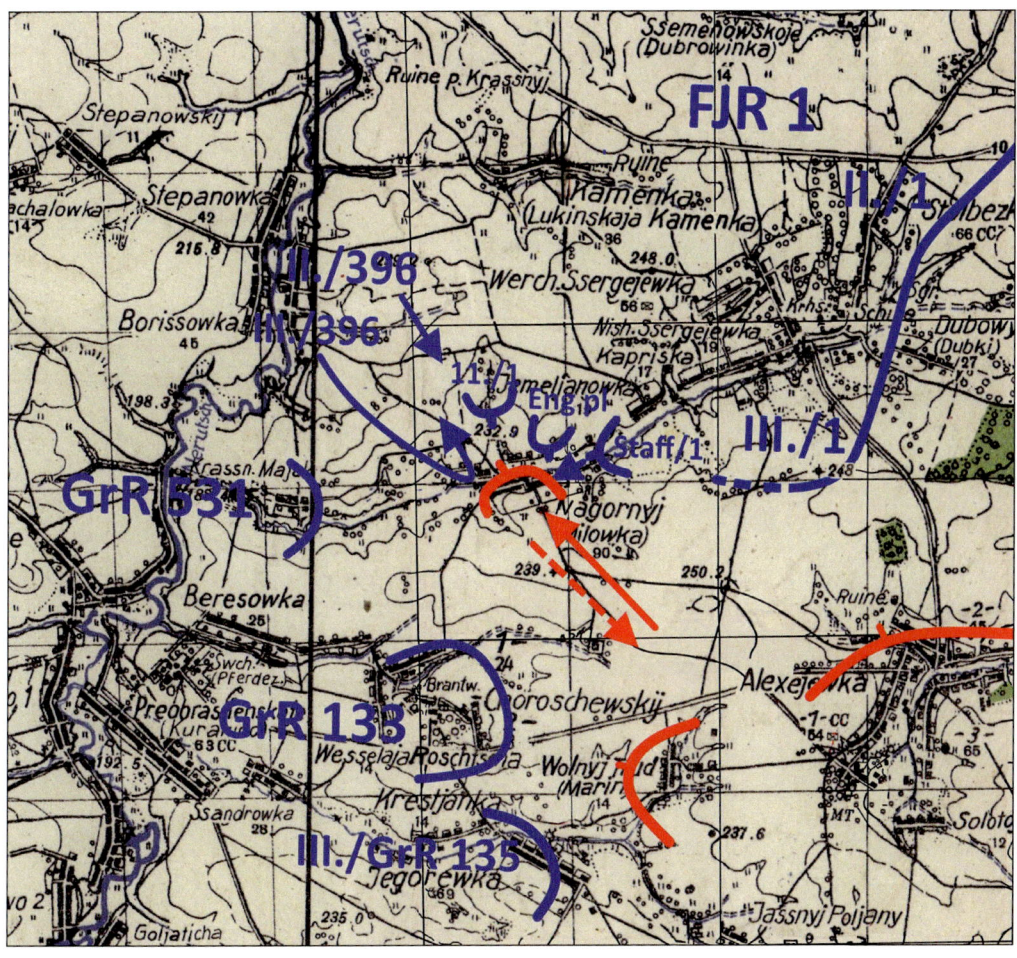

The situation on 19 February 1943, 5:55 p.m.

metres to the north was *Oberleutnant* Fölster with the mortar platoon of *13. Kompanie*.[106] Their field of fire covered only 150 metres in front of their own troops positioned in the village.

This fragmented force had already been through considerable fighting, was short of ammunition, and several machine guns were out of action. *11. Kompanie* for instance had already suffered 12 wounded. Becker knew he had to regroup and asked his commander for reinforcements – which he received. The 60 remaining men of *11. Kompanie* were still under the command of the able *Feldwebel* Wittig, who was soon replaced by the battalion's adjutant, *Leutnant* Behrmann.[107] Behrmann commanded

---

106 Robert von Oppen (Berlin, 6 October 1910–KIA Muravchik, 21 March 1943), *Oberleutnant* of the reserve; Eduard Fölster (Willenscharen, 18 October 1915–KIA Cassino, 13 May 1944), *Oberleutnant*. He commanded the newly formed *III. Bataillon* starting March 1944.
107 Günther Behrmann (1919–1995), later *Oberleutnant* and recipient of the DKiG 1 October 1944.

11. Kompanie ad interim until *Oberleutnant* Werner Heinsen took command. In addition, Becker now received the aforementioned 15 men of *6. Kompanie/ Grenadier Regiment 396* under *Leutnant* Weiß. From his regiment he also received the shock group of *Oberleutnant* Isermann (two officers and 29 men) and *Oberleutnant* Voß (one officer and 22 men). This gave Becker a total of 129 men for the imminent attack. Two Panzer IV F2, equipped with 7.5 cm cannons and two self-propelled anti-tank guns (probably Pusch's platoon), also equipped with 7.5 cm cannons, were helpful additional reinforcements. The remaining groups – the engineer platoon under *Leutnant* Weser and 17 men of *Rittmeister* Erhardt's company – had to cover the attack to the south, under the command of *Oberleutnant* von Oppen. *Oberleutnant* Fölster's mortars were to provide preparatory fire into the village until 10:45 p.m. – the planned start of the attack.

At 8:25 p.m. Schulz's patience obviously ran out and he sent two messages to Kühlwein, which unfortunately did not get through until 11:45 p.m. and 12:15 a.m. respectively: 'Why doesn't grenadier battalion attack Nagorniy, is absolutely necessary.' and 'Nagorniy up to the centre in German hands, grenadier battalion apparently not yet in place. Please hurry them up.'[108]

It was not until 8:30 p.m. that the division learned from a message by *Oberstleutnant* Gnoth that the two battalions of his *Grenadier Regiment 396* had not yet entered the village. They were able at first to advance to the foremost houses south of the stream, but the grenadiers were thrown back across it to the north side.

Leutnant Günther Behrmann the deputy adjutant of *III. Bataillon* who commanded *11. Kompanie* ad interim from 19 February 1943. Later promoted to *Oberleutnant* he was awarded the German Cross in Gold on 1 October 1944. (Private Collection)

> In the village itself, a tank was driving up and down and was constantly inflicting heavy losses on our troops on the opposite side. The enemy had nested on the elevated southern bank of the stream in a row of trees between the row of houses and were firing extremely heavy fire from there with infantry weapons of all kinds.[109]

Oberstleutnant Wirsing reiterated to Gnoth that the order to attack and take Nagorniy was still in effect and had to be followed under all circumstances.

Shortly afterwards, the commander of *Grenadier Regiment 531* (383. ID) reported:

> …that his regiment had failed to enter the village. There were six tanks in the western part of the village whose strong defensive fire prevented them from entering. The regiment intended to

---

108 BA-MA, RH 26-45/62 in BW 57-39.
109 BA-MA, RH 26-45/62: 45. ID, KTB, Attachments vol.2, 1–28 February 1943: After-action report of *45. Infanterie Division* on the taking of Nagorniy on 19 and 20 February 1943, p.4.

withdraw the units that had come close to the edge of the village, and then, after a combined fire of all available artillery batteries, to attack again. However, according to the commander of the artillery battalion, the ammunition situation was a cause for concern since the heavy field howitzer battery only had about 80 rounds left.[110] In several inquiries with the commander of *Artillerie Regiment 98* and the Second Staff Officer of the division (Ib), the ammunition situation was clarified, and preparation was ordered for concentrated fire on the western part of the village.[111]

Sometime before the actual attack, paratroopers of *11. Kompanie* had already entered the village:

We approached the village at night and somehow, we knew there was a Russian tank in there. A non-commissioned officer got the order to blow it up with a sticky charge. He brought a machine gun with him, posted it in the middle of the village street, proceeding quietly and slowly. As he approached the centre of the village, he saw two Russian tanks standing there, a fire burning, and Russian soldiers being busy at the tanks. As he was still considering about how to get close enough, a messenger silently approached him from behind with orders to come back immediately and without a sound. It turned out that all the village houses on both sides of the road they had passed were full of sleeping Russian soldiers, again without guards. We then took up position on a hill to the side of the village.[112]

The night was clear and cold (-25°C) and the light of the full moon reflecting from the snow illuminated the scenery.[113] In three spearheads Becker and his men advanced to the western edge of the long-stretched village – *Gruppe Isermann* on the northern edge, *Gruppe Voß* on the southern edge and the centre of Nagorniy was attacked by the two Panzer IV and the assault group of *Leutnant* Weiß (of *6. Kompanie/GrenadierRegiment 396*). They proceeded quickly, considering that there were still Red Army soldiers hiding in the houses.

The Soviet soldiers in the village fought back fiercely, according to the accounts of two of the participants:

For example, in the middle of the village street there was a General Lee tank, under which an officer had taken cover and stopped our attack with his machine pistol. The only way to get him to crawl forward was to sneak up behind the huts and throw hand grenades in front of and behind the tank track.[114]

The village soon caught fire, and due to the smoke the [crews of the] two German tanks could not see where the Russian ones were. Then *Feldwebel* [recte *Oberjäger*] Bollinger lay down on the outside of the one German tank and shouted orders to fire into it: 'More to the left, yes, stop, a little higher, now fire!' He became half deaf as a result ... Another one of the tanks was then also finished off with a sticky charge, but not by the paratrooper who had tried it at first.[115]

---

110 A battery of 15 cm heavy field howitzer, most probably model 18, the standard model for divisional artillery (sFH).
111 BA-MA, RH 26-45/62: 45. ID, KTB, Attachments vol.2, 1–28 February 1943: After-action report of *45. Infanterie Division* on the taking of Nagorniy on 19 and 20 February 1943, p.4.
112 BA-MA, BW 57-89: Hans Dolezalek, Letter to Günter Behrmann, dated 20 February 1990.
113 BA-MA, RH 26-45/59: 45. ID, KTB 1 January–15 July 1943, p.196.
114 BA-MA, BW 57-89: account of H.K.R., dated 3 September 1990.
115 BA-MA, BW 57-89: Hans Dolezalek, Letter to Günter Behrmann, dated 20 February 1990.

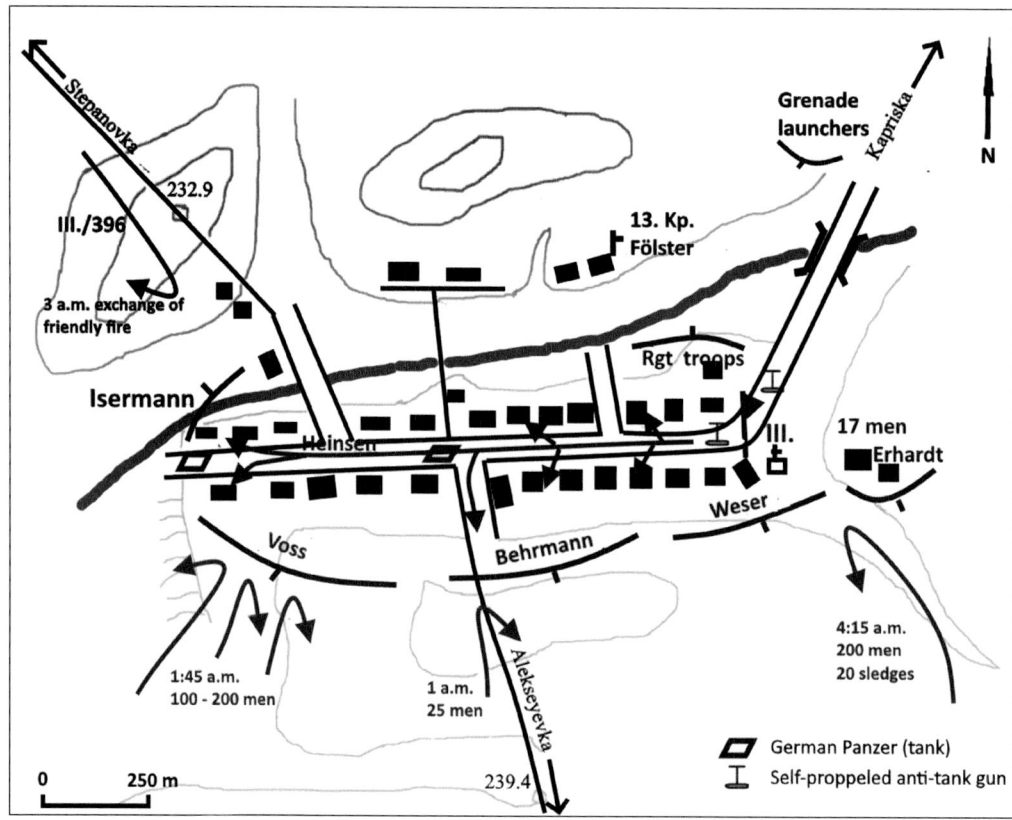

The early morning defence of Nagorniy on 20 February 1943.

The first two groups reached the western edge at midnight, the centre group at 12:30 a.m. Eight Soviet tanks (mainly M3 General Lee, otherwise T-34 and KV-1) were destroyed, 26 prisoners taken, and an estimated 200 Soviet soldiers had fallen.

But the Soviets had no intention of giving in and at 1:00 a.m. they counterattacked from the south and were able to penetrate to the village centre. Once again, the paratroopers combed through the village from east to west with a newly arrived Panzer IV and a 15-man assault group under *Oberleutnant* Heinsen.[116] In the process, 40 Soviet soldiers were killed, and 11 prisoners were taken. A few days later Heinsen took command of *11. Kompanie*.

At 1:45 a.m. the Soviets tried again, this time in battalion strength from the south and southwest, again without success. About 100 died 'in the moonlit snowy landscape'[117] from the defensive gunfire in front of the paratroopers' positions. There was now a brief respite, which was used for the proper seizure of Nagorniy. Every house was searched, every hayloft and every cellar. 'The huts on the village

---

116 Werner Heinsen (Pattensen, 31 December 1914–KIA S.Pietro il Fludo near Ortona, 16 January 1944), *Oberleutnant*. In Italy he was killed in action as commander of *12. Kompanie*.
117 BA-MA, BW 57-89: account of H.K.R., dated 3 September 1990.

road were for the most part in flames. [We] found ... Russians huddled in the cellars, pretending to be dead, and only by kicking them hard could they be brought to life and taken prisoner.'[118] After the battle, a total of 59 prisoners were counted.

At 3:30 a.m. the village was firmly in the hands of Becker's men. By 4:00 a.m. further reinforcements requested by Becker arrived, the last reserves of the regiment: the regimental staff, the music corps, and parts of *III. Bataillon* under *Oberleutnant* Beyer,[119] the orderly officer of the regiment. They arrived at just the right time, for only 15 minutes later a new Soviet attack began. A column of 20 sledges with about 200 men approached from the southeast and tried to reach the southern edge of the village. However, the strong defensive fire of the paratroopers forced the column to turn south, taking at least 20 wounded with them.

Earlier that night, at 11:45 p.m., *45. Infanterie Division* received a report that Gnoth's men of *Grenadier Regiment 396* had meanwhile retreated under of heavy defensive fire from the village and were now one kilometre northwest of Nagorniy. The soldiers were too exhausted to attack again. The staff officers of the division were now thinking of withdrawing the main line of defence and calling off the attack altogether, when at 12:30 a.m. *General* von Roman informed *Generalleutnant* Kühlwein that 'it had been established with certainty that parts of *Fallschirmjäger Regiment 1* are in the village.'[120] Von Roman repeated the order to attack, an order which was immediately passed on to Gnoth.

During the night, the role of Schulz's paratroopers became somewhat clearer to Kühlwein, but the misunderstanding seems to have been only partially cleared up. Kühlwein claims that for a brief moment, at around 2:15 a.m., he was able to communicate with Schulz and be informed of the situation. Only shortly before, at 1:25 a.m., did he receive word from *General* Roman that the paratroopers were in possession of the entire village and that the planned artillery bombardment of Nagorniy, scheduled for 2:00 a.m., was to be cancelled.

The morning report of the division (3:45 a.m.) to the superior *LV. Armee Korps* reads as follows:

> While enemy with tanks was pinned down in Nagorniy by attack *Grenadier Regiment 531* and *396*, a combat group of *Fallschirmjäger Regiment 1* succeeded in penetrating the village from the east and northeast in a surprising, daring advance, destroying six tanks and thus creating the conditions for further action by the grenadier regiments bogged down by heavy enemy fire. Clearing the village of the enemy is under way.[121]

In reality, the village had been completely taken alone by the paratroopers and had been in their hands since 1:00 a.m.

At around 3:00 a.m. there was also an exchange of fire between the paratroopers of *Gruppe Isermann* at the north-western edge of the village and elements of the approaching *Grenadier Regiment 396*, as the latter failed to answer the many identification signals they were firing. A participant recalled: 'When the village was ours, we were attacked by another German unit who didn't know the latest status of the flare signals, which caused some additional casualties.'[122]

---

118 BA-MA, BW 57-89: account of H.K.R., dated 3 September 1990.
119 Günther Beyer (1914-?), *Oberleutnant*.
120 BA-MA, RH 26-45/59: 45. ID, KTB 1 January–15 July 1943, p.196.
121 BA-MA, LV. AK, KTB 36358/3, attachment 2933 in BW 57-82.
122 BA-MA, BW 57-89: Hans Dolezalek, Letter to Günter Behrmann, dated 20 February 1990.

It was not until 5:00 a.m. that *II. Bataillon/Grenadier Regiment 396* under command of *Hauptmann* Grauert, *III. Bataillon/Grenadier Regiment 396* under command of *Hauptmann* Wichert and another battalion of *Grenadier Regiment 531* finally arrived to relieve the paratroopers. Nagorniy was handed over to them at 5:30 a.m. on 20 February 1943, after which the paratroopers left and took up positions in their own section.

In his after-action report, Becker reported 11 dead, including *Oberleutnant* Dennerlein, the commander of the regimental bicycle platoon, 30 wounded and one missing, compared to eight Soviet tanks destroyed, 340 dead and 59 prisoners. Schulz reported 242 enemy dead (only in Nagorniy itself), another 200 in the field outside the village, 58 prisoners and own losses of 11 dead, 38 wounded and four missing. *Rittmeister* Erhardt's group had one dead, 16 wounded and 13 missing. According to the casualty list, the attack and subsequent defence of Nagorniy ultimately cost the regiment 16 killed (seven of whom died of their wounds) and 46 wounded; *11. Kompanie* was the worst hit, with nine killed and 21 wounded.

One of the wounded was *Feldwebel* Wittig, who was awarded the Knight's Cross a year later on 5 February 1944 for his brave conduct and important contribution during this attack and earlier combat operations. Later, on 20 March 1943, Wittig, along with several other paratroopers from the regiment, was awarded the German Cross in Gold for his actions at Velikiye Luki and Gribushino. However, his conduct at Nagorniy was such that *Oberstleutnant* Schulz decided to nominate Wittig for the Knight's Cross as well, his application being dated 18 August 1943.[123] This is remarkable, as only two Knight's Crosses were awarded after the regiment's successful Orel mission, one to *Major* Graf von der Schulenburg (at the suggestion of *78. Sturm Division*) and one to *Feldwebel* Wittig. It was a rare occurrence for an NCO to receive this high decoration.

The perceived failure of *Grenadier Regiment 396* and the poor conduct of the divisional commander, *Generalleutnant* Kühlwein, had consequences, resulting in detailed after-action reports and a justification by him. Kühlwein seems to have been originally a very good troop commander, but by 1943 he was no longer considered fit to lead a division. He is also said to have been extremely pedantic, erratic, and difficult.[124] His pedantry is particularly evident in his meticulous listing of the moments that led him to believe that Schulz's reports were merely observations, as he could not imagine that the regiment had taken Nagorniy far beyond its original order. He stubbornly persisted in his assumption that the objectives and limits of the attack order had been meticulously adhered to, regardless of the changing realities on the ground. Kühlwein still thanked Schulz on 20 February for the successful night attack by the reinforced *Gruppe Becker*.[125]

However, Kühlwein initiated a court martial against the regimental commander of *Grenadier Regiment 396*, *Oberstleutnant* Gnoth. This court martial (if it took place at all) seems not to have hurt Gnoth, as he was awarded the German Cross in Gold on 21 April 1943. Instead, Kühlwein lost command of his division on 29 April 1943.

In particular, the report of *Major* Karl Kaehne,[126] commander of *I. Bataillon/Infanterie Regiment 135* (45. ID), confirms the information given by Schulz and Becker. However, he is the only one to

---

123 Thomas/Wegmann, *Ritterkreuzträger – Fallschirmjäger*, pp.364–365.
124 Hartmann, *Ostkrieg*, p.236.
125 BA-MA, RH 26-45/62, see also BW 57-89: account of H.K.R., dated 3 September 1990.
126 Edgar-Karl Kaehne (Bunzlau, 13 March 1899–Würzburg, 10 July 1969), at the end of the war *Oberst* and commander of *Festungsinfanteriebrigade 954*. He received the Knight's Cross on 2 February 1944. Kaehne, a Nazi-party member since 1929, was accused of complicity in the shooting of German politicians and citizens

note that the paratroopers also fired on the approaching elements of *Grenadier Regiment 396* at around 3:00 a.m., as they failed to respond to the agreed flare signals. There is only one reference to this in Schulz's after-action report: 'upon request the 45. ID stressed that the instruction about the flare signals had taken place (but turned out to be insufficient).'[127]

However, a possible lack of motivation on the part of the men of *Grenadier Regiment 396* is understandable. Parts of the regiment had already come under artillery fire while unloading at Smiyevka on the 18th. Afterwards, the regiment had to carry out an attack on Stepanovsky and Stepanovka and advance further on Nagorniy. After two days of constant fighting the men were simply exhausted and tired; too much had been asked of them. The main 'culprit', however, was probably the poor or non-existent communications. *Fallschirmjäger Regiment 1* had connection problems with the command post of Kühlwein and had to communicate via the radios of *LV. Armee Korps* causing long delays. Additionally, the radios did not function due the cold temperatures and there was no communication at any time to the other attacking units (regiments 396 and 531). *Infanterie Regiment 135*, in turn, could only contact the paratroopers via the *299. Infanterie Division* (XXXV.AK). This resulted in long delays between the writing and sending of a message and its arrival at the addressee, which undoubtedly led to misunderstandings.

In the days that followed, the paratroopers were kept busy in their section east and northeast of Nagorniy by many smaller attacks by Red Army units. The weather was bad, with heavy snow drifts and sub-zero temperatures. Soviet mortars shelled their positions.

From 22 February, *216. Infantry Division* gradually took over the section of *45. Infanterie Division* and took command of its subordinate troops, including the *Fallschirmjäger Regiment 1*. On the 22nd and 23rd, Nagorniy and also other sectors of the German front were attacked, but the attacks were stopped. In the sector of the divisions on the right, the main line of defence was withdrawn in an orderly fashion (the 'Heinrich movement') and Maloarkhangelsk was abandoned. During the night of the 23rd to the 24th, from 1:15 a.m. to about 4:00 a.m., Gröschke's battalion at Stolpetskoye repulsed two company-scale attacks from the direction of Dubovy. From 5:00 a.m. there were again strong attacks on Nagorniy and Khoroshevsky. At midday the Soviet attackers again succeeded in breaking through at Nagorniy, prompting the paratroopers armour-piercing weapons to be used in support to save the situation, which proved successful. The section of the regiment came under Soviet artillery and mortar fire at 2:00 p.m., the regimental radio station was hit, and communications with the command of *216. Infanterie Division* were again severed. Schulz therefore moved his regimental command post to the rear to Kamenka.

On the 25th, further Soviet attacks were launched against the positions of *II. Bataillon*, resulting in close combat with the *7. Kompanie*, and again on the next day, 26 February with *6. Kompanie*. Each of these engagements resulted in losses of dead and wounded.[128]

On 27 February there was movement in front of *II. Bataillon* and it became apparent that heaps of straw near Verkh. Stolbetskoye were in fact camouflaged tanks, which later withdrew after being fired upon by artillery. In the section of *9. Kompanie* an attack on Hill 250.2 resulted in a breach, and the intruders were repulsed in hand-to-hand combat. On the same day, a reconnaissance patrol from the same company had enemy contact south of Kapriska, which also resulted in close combat.

---

    in Altötting, Bavaria, who wanted to hand over the town to the US Army without a fight on 28 April 1945. However, he was later acquitted.

127 BA-MA, LV. AK, KTB 36358/4 in BW 57-82: After-action report of Schulz.

128 25 February: three dead, five wounded; 26 February: five dead, eight wounded.

A successful assault was carried out on Hill 250.2 on 1 March by 20 men of *III. Bataillon* (probably by *11. Kompanie*). In the process, the advanced enemy position was rolled up in close combat without suffering any casualties. The Soviet soldiers must have been completely taken by surprise, because 14 dead, 20 wounded and nine prisoners were recorded. Another assault patrol of *II. Bataillon* reconnoitred Dubovy and found the western part of this hamlet free of the enemy.

The Soviet 48th Army had now become bogged down after an initially successful offensive and was unable to advance on Orel. *Fallschirmjäger Regiment 1* had played an important and considerable part in thwarting this effort.

On 3 March 1943, the order was given to *216. Infanterie Division* to detach *Fallschirmjäger Regiment 1* together with the subordinated I./501 and two platoons of self-propelled anti-tank guns, leaving behind *II. Bataillon* and two anti-aircraft units (two 8.8 cm and three 2 cm guns). The regiment was to be assigned to *XXXXVI. Panzer Korps* under command of *General der Infanterie* Hans Zorn as of 4 March.[129] The paratroopers left for Yeropkino during the course of the day, with the staff quickly reaching Kromy. *III. Bataillon* was relieved by *III. Bataillon/Grenadier Regiment 396*. Again, snowdrifts severely hampered and delayed the transport of the paratroopers.

General der Infanterie Hans Zorn, commanding general of *XXXXVI. Panzer Korps*. (Szukaj w archiwach, 3/2/0/-/12738)

---

129 Hans Zorn (Munich, 27 October 1891–KIA Orel, Krasnaya Rostokha, 2 August 1943), *General der Infanterie*; RK (27 July 1941), Oak Leaves (posthumous 9 September 1943), DKiG (14 June 1942).

20

Schulenburg's *I. Bataillon*, 13–28 February

From 13 February, *Major* Graf von der Schulenburg and his *I. Bataillon* had been reinforcing the left wing of *34. Infanterie Division* near Frolovka, 62 kilometres northeast of Orel. On the 13th the division's *II. Bataillon/Grenadier Regiment 253* repulsed a Soviet attack by two battalions,[1] but as this happened in another section the paratroopers were not directly affected. The next day, 14 February, Soviet attacks by the 3rd Army on the boundary line between *34.* and *112. Infanterie Division* took place early in the morning, with a local break-in at Gorodishche succeeding at around 10:00 a.m. Otherwise, all Soviet attack probes were defeated by the Germans with help of their artillery.

At 12 noon on 14 February, the divisional command received the order that *I. Bataillon/Fallschirmjäger Regiment 1* was to be detached and should immediately follow *II. Bataillon* in the direction of Orel at the disposal of *2. Panzer Armee*, since the situation on the right army boundary which at the moment was defended by *LV. Armee Korps* had worsened. The battalion started moving immediately but progress was very slow. The road towards Mtsensk was impassable and first had to be cleared with only two available motorised snow ploughs. It was not until 11:30 p.m. that this work was finished, and the transport was finally able to leave. But then the telephone rang in the command post of *34. Infanterie Division*: the battalion was to be stopped immediately and should remain as an army reserve in the area of the division. Somehow it was possible to find the transport in the snowstorm, to stop it and to direct it to Voin, a place on the road between Orel and Mtsensk, where the command post of *34. Infanterie Division* was also located. The reason for redirecting the battalion was newly collected intelligence information about a major build-up of strong Soviet motorised forces on the left divisional boundary between *34.* and *112. Infanterie Division*, which gave reason to believe that another attack was to be expected there. However, Voin, which was only about 40 kilometres away by road from Frolovka, could not be reached by the paratroopers until the next day, 15 February, at about 6:00 p.m., which allows corresponding conclusions about the bad weather and road conditions. The battalion now served as an army reserve.[2]

The '*Spieß*' of *3. Kompanie*, *Oberfeldwebel* Wagner, aptly described the hardships to which the soldiers were subjected during this back and forth in a letter to his wife on 14 February:

> After days of travelling we have now arrived at our new section on the southern front. We are now about 50 kilometres northeast of Orel. For three days and nights we drove continuously with trucks,

---

1   NARA, T-315 R-878: 34. ID KTB 6, Attachments 12 January–31 March 1943, Daily report 13 February 1943 of *XXXV. Armee Korps*.
2   NARA, T-315-878: 34. ID, KTB 6, 11 January–31 March 1943.

not an hour's sleep and bitterly cold, in addition to a wild snowstorm that went through all the seams. Vehicles constantly got stuck in deep snow and had to be shovelled out. Other cars drove into the ditch or down the embankment because the drivers were overtired. Fortunately, there were no breakdowns. Never before have such demands been made on the drivers. The worst enemy here, apart from the cold, is sleep. You simply can't fight it. I myself have hardly ever been so tired. But all the stress and sometimes superhuman performances were overcome and mastered by all the men in an exemplary manner. I have seen shining examples of what man can endure and is willing to do for his homeland.

We are currently off the road and are so snowed in that we can't get out without snow ploughs and caterpillar-tracked vehicles. We have found good accommodation here with the artillery in a truly comradely manner. The [3.] *Kompanie* is about 18 kilometres away from us. But they didn't have any food with them because the food truck is here with us. So, we borrowed a small sledge and pulled it with eight men. One kilometre through deep snow took us one hour. We left here at 1 p.m. and arrived at the company at 8 p.m. At midnight we were back again … This current situation even partly surpasses the difficulties of the previous winter 1941/42, with the only difference that all difficulties are being overcome much better than last winter. The situation here does not look hopeless at all …

We have not yet been deployed and are still in reserve. My commander changed during the trip, and we now have *Oberleutnant* [Otto] who already led our company in France for half a year. I get on very well with him. My old boss [*Hauptmann* Gessner] is now in the reserve of our regiment as a potential battalion commander.[3]

But the battalion did not even stay long at Voin. At the boundary between *LV. Armee Korps* (*45. Infanterie Division*) and *XXXV. Armee Korps* (*299. Infanterie Division*) – as described above – a Russian advance towards Smiyevka succeeded, thereby causing a crisis for *2. Panzer Armee*. At 9:00 p.m. on the 15th, *Generaloberst* Schmidt issued a direct order to *299. Infanterie Division* 'to prevent a breakthrough by the enemy under all circumstances,' stressing that 'the fate of the entire front depends on the energetic leadership of the division and the devotion of all members of [it].'[4] To assist in this task, Schulenburg's battalion was to be attached to this division. So, the order went out that very night for the battalion to move off to Stolbetskoye, with the battalion commander to report ahead (at 2:30 a.m.) to the division command post of *299. Infanterie Division*.[5] Again, there were time delays in the transmission of messages. *LV. Armee Korps* was only able to send the telex to *299. Infanterie Division* at 3:25 a.m. The staff now expected the paratroopers to arrive at their destination in the early morning hours of 16 February.

Like the other units trying to reach the front near Smiyevka, *I. Bataillon* also had problems due to snowdrifts on the approach roads. The first parts of the battalion did not reach Smiyevka until noon, causing *Major* von der Schulenburg to report to the command post of *299. Infanterie Division* at 1:50 p.m.[6] Onward transport to the front of the division was repeatedly made difficult as the roads were still clogged by transports of *45. Infanterie Division* flooding back. Formally, the battalion was placed under the command of *299. Infanterie Division* at about 4:00 p.m.,[7] while the battalion only arrived in the Kopanov-Noyavoyka-Kamenka area during the early evening.

---

3 Archive Franz: Wagner, letter dated 14 February 1943.
4 BA-MA, RH 26-299/103: 299. ID, KTB 10, Attachments vol.2; 1–28 February 1943.
5 NARA, T-315 R-153: PzAOK 2, KTB 3, vol.1, 16–28 February 1943.
6 BA-MA, RH 26-299/101: 299. ID, KTB No.10, 1 January–31 March 1943.
7 BA-MA, RH 26-299/103: 299. ID, KTB No.10, Attachments vol.2; 1–28 February 1943.

In a long-distance telephone conversation on 16 February with *Generalfeldmarschall* von Kluge, commander of *Heeresgruppe Mitte*, *Generaloberst* Schmidt complained about the delays:

> Things are not very great at 299 either. This paratrooper battalion, which was scheduled to arrive last night and supposed to be in Yefrasimovka early this morning, only got to Smiyevka at 11 a.m., despite everything having been done to clear the way for it. And only because the commander, although the urgency had been made clear, had stopped somewhere. During this stop the snowstorm blew him over. I hope he will get there now.[8]

The actual reason for the delay or why Schulenburg ordered a halt is not known.

During the sometimes hasty retreat during the previous week *299. Infanterie Division* was severely weakened and had lost most of its artillery.[9] The division had been able to hold the Lipovets line through 15 February, but on the 16th and 17th the Soviet attackers from the 48th Army (Bryansk Front) made deep incursions, which – luckily for the Germans – they were unable to exploit adequately. In this confusing situation, the paratroopers of *I. Bataillon* arrived.

The individual companies of the battalion were distributed in the sector of the division. *1. Kompanie* of *Oberleutnant* Josef Vogler was placed under command of *Grenadier Regiment 528* on the morning of 17 February. Vogler was originally an NCO who became an officer and was promoted to *Hauptmann* after this mission. He originally came from the parachute infantry battalion of the *Heer* and had already participated in the early missions of the paratroopers like Sudetenland 1938 and Poland 1939.[10] His company – in some of the sources called '*Gruppe Vogler*' – had a combatant strength of 123 men (three officers, 37 NCOs and 83 enlisted men) and was armed with 12 MG 34 and two heavy machine guns. The company was deployed on the left divisional wing near the village of Karla Marksa.[11] The paratrooper company made quite an impression on the grenadier regiment: 'We have been assigned a paratrooper company as reinforcement. It's great how these soldiers are equipped with weapons and winter clothing. We feel like soldiers from the poorhouse. One company after the other is taken out [of the front] in rotation as a reserve and can warm up for a while.'[12]

Paratroopers of *III. Bataillon* with their equipment on sledges entering a Russian village. (Private Collection)

---

8 BA-MA, BW 57-82.
9 NARA, T-315 R-153: PzAOK 2, KTB 3, vol.1, 1–15 February 1943.
10 See Janzyk, *Deckname Fall Weiß*, p.68.
11 BA-MA, RH 26-299/103: Radio message 299. ID to GrRgt 530 on 17 February, 7:50 a.m.; BA-MA, RH 26-299/108: Report of changes of the 299. ID to XXXV. AK on 20 February 1943.
12 Hans-Martin Fritsche, *Die Geschichte des Grenadier-Regiment 528* (self-published, 1966) – (by message from Karl Kiel, 8 December 2017).

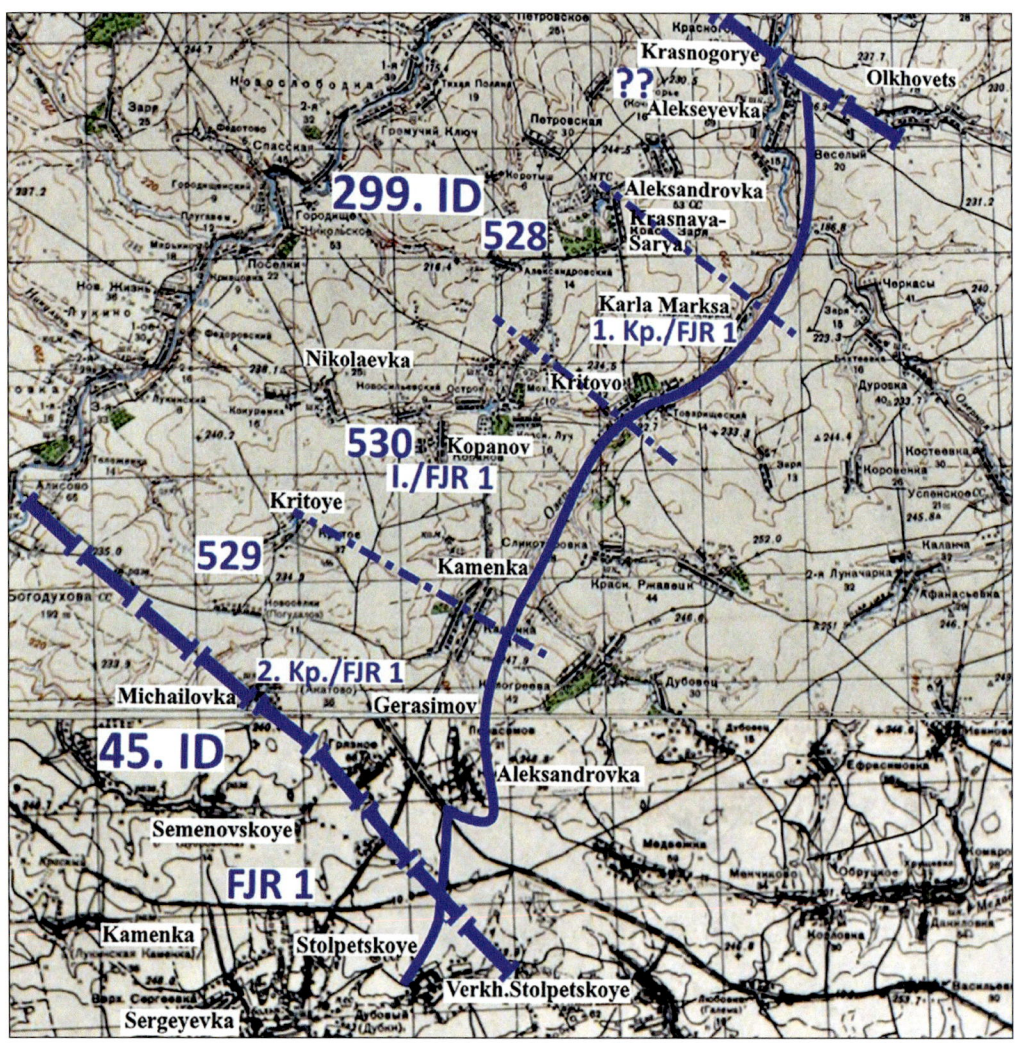

The deployment area of *I. Bataillon* in the section of *299. Infanterie Division* on 17 February 1943.

The company was immediately deployed in the front line and had to fend off attacks for the next few days. On 19 February, for example, the company repelled an attack of about 60 Red Army soldiers.[13] Losses were recorded every day: On 17 February three wounded, of whom two succumbed to their wounds; 18 February one dead and three wounded, of whom one died of his wounds; 19 February one dead, four wounded. After four days of fighting, on 20 February, the company was taken out of the front and remained as a divisional reserve near Krasnaya-Sarya in the sector of *Grenadier Regiment 528*.[14]

---

13   BA-MA, RH 26-299/108: 299. ID, KTB No.10, Attachments vol.7, daily reports 1 January–31 March 1943.
14   BA-MA, RH 26-299/103: 299. ID, KTB No.10, Attachments vol.2, 1–28 February 1943; BA-MA, RH

On 17 February, the previously mentioned Soviet attack at Nagorniy towards Smiyevka took place. Due to this alarming news, *2. Kompanie* commanded by *Oberleutnant* Kissling and subordinated to *Grenadier Regiment 529*, was deployed to provide cover for an artillery group on the southern edge of the village of Mikhailovka on the evening of 17 February. The company had a total combatant strength of 110 men (two officers, 31 NCOs and 77 enlisted men) and was armed with 15 MG 34 machine guns, two heavy machine guns and three light mortars.[15] The rest of the battalion, 337 men, stayed as divisional reserve in the rear at Kopanov, where the divisional command post was also located. The number gives the total strength and not the combatant strength of the battalion without *2. Kompanie* and *14. Kompanie*: 10 officers, 327 NCOs and enlisted men; 22 light machine guns, 10 heavy machine guns, four heavy mortars, two *Panzerbüchsen 41*, three *Nebelwerfer* 10.5 cm.[16]

For the men of *2. Kompanie*, these days were reasonably quiet, interrupted only by reconnaissance activities. On 19 February, for example, a reconnaissance patrol on skis, *Gefreiter* Schneider and *Gefreiter* von Zimburg, were sent out in the early morning hours to determine whether the village of Stepanovka was free of the enemy, which the patrol was able to confirm. These paratroopers – ignorant of that fact – operated in close proximity to their comrades of *Fallschirmjäger Regiment 1*, who were subordinate to the neighbour on right, *45. Infanterie Division* and helped to fight the Soviet incursion (see above).

Meanwhile further north in the sector of *LIII. Armee Korps* on the boundary line to *XXXV. Armee Korps* (*112.* and *34. Infanterie Division*), additional attacks were successfully repelled. On 22 February 1943, a large-scale attack by the Soviet 3rd Army (Bryansk Front) was launched in the area 25–30 kilometres north of Mtsensk and 20 kilometres east of Bolkhov with the aim of capturing the latter and then advancing south towards Orel. At the same time, the Soviet 16th Army (Western Front) intended to support this attack from the north but failed due to the effective defence by *Korps* Scheele.[17] Within three days, the Bryansk Front only managed to establish a bridgehead five kilometres wide and four kilometres deep between Gorodishche and Chegodayevo on the western bank of the Oka. The defending German infantry regiment of *112. Infanterie Division* succeeded in sealing off the breach on 26 February with the help of rapidly supplied reinforcements and artillery support from the neighbouring *34. Infanterie Division*. Counterattacks in the following days gradually reduced the bridgehead, and the Soviet forces were pushed back across the Oka by 12 March.

With the left flank of *34. Infanterie Division* threatened by this incursion and no reserves available, the division received the welcome news on the afternoon of 22 February that *I. Bataillon/Fallschirmjäger Regiment 1* with two companies (*2.* and *3. Kompanie*) and one heavy company (*4. Kompanie*) would be made available for support. However, *1. Kompanie*, which was attached to *Grenadier Regiment 528*, remained behind and was not to be reassigned to the battalion until 28 February. The battalion was due to move out towards Voin at 5:30 p.m.

Accordingly, *2. Kompanie* was ordered back to join the battalion at Kopanov on the evening of 22 February. The same night, the battalion marched to the road Smiyevka-Orel and moved again by truck

---

26-299/101: 299. ID, KTB No.10, 1 January–31 March 1943.
15   BA-MA, RH 26-299/108: Report of changes of 299. ID to XXXV. AK, 20 February 1943; BA-MA, RH 24-35/51: Morning report of 299. ID to XXXV. AK, 18 February 1943, 5:35 a.m.
16   BA-MA, RH 26-299/108: 299. ID, KTB No.10, Attachments vol.7, daily reports 1 January–31 March 1943; BA-MA, RH 24-35/51: Radio message 299. ID to XXXV. AK 17 February 1943, 5:35 a.m.
17   This corps stood under the command of *Generalmajor* Hans-Karl von Scheele. The corps command was created on 8 February by *2. Panzer Armee* and consisted of *Brigade Stab z.b.V. 4*. It took over the sector of *XXXXVII. Panzer Korps* northwest of Orel. The command was dissolved on 28 March 1943, its sector was then taken over by *LV. Armee Korps*.

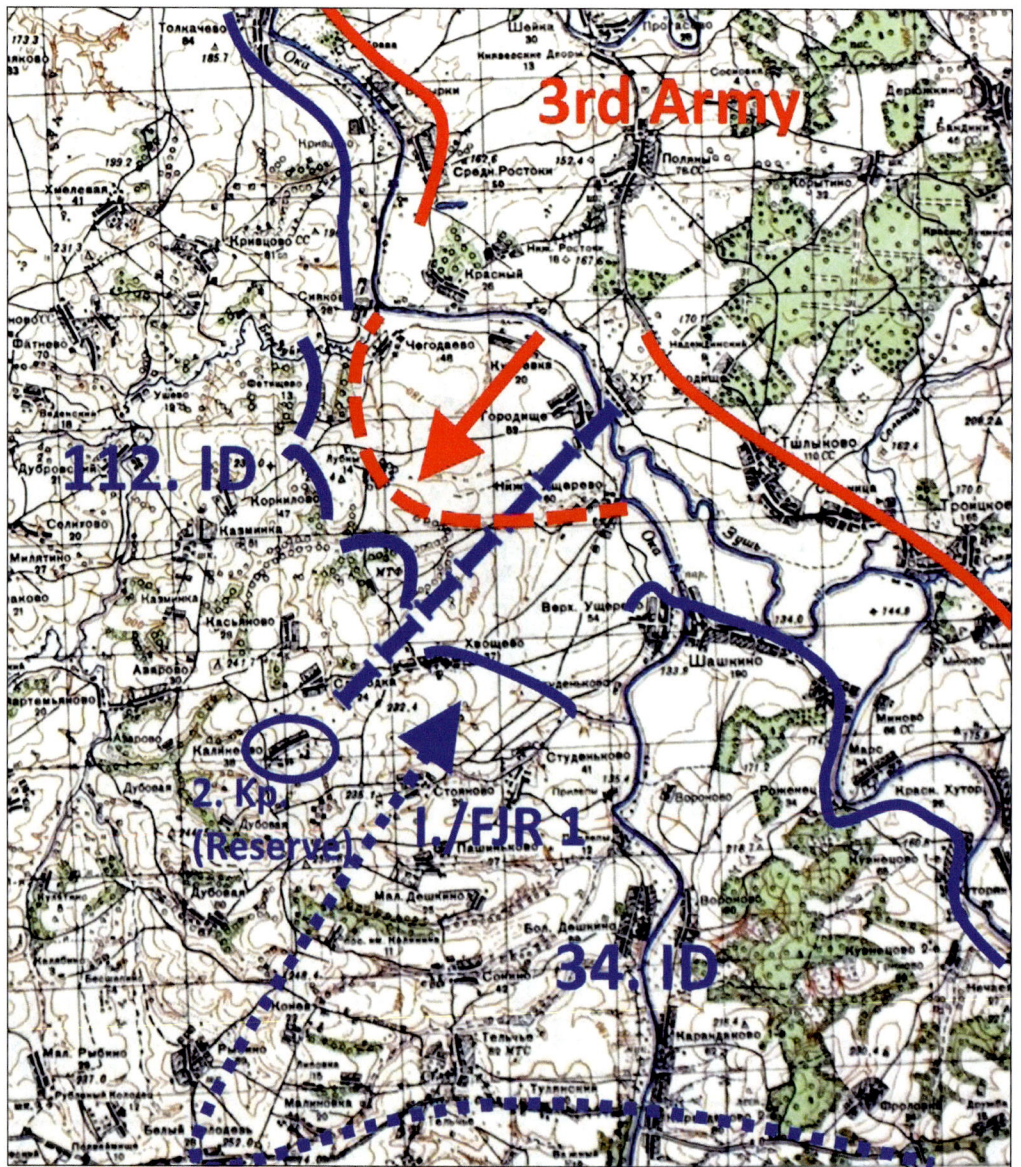

The positions of *I. Bataillon* attached to *34. Infanterie Division* north-east of Orel from 23 until 28 February 1943.

to Voin, just outside Mtsensk. This time there were clearly no delays, and the transport seems to have arrived at Voin, the next day at 1:30 p.m. without any major interruptions. At 5:00 p.m. the battalion was moved from Voin to the area of Belyi Kolodes, which was only a few kilometres west of Frolovka, the last deployment of *I. Bataillon* in the sector of *34. Infanterie Division*. There, the battalion was 'made sledge-mobile' and transported north to the assigned Stoyanovo-Kalinayevo area to intercept a possible Soviet advance to the south or west.[18] This area lay east-southeast of Bolkhov and south of the breach in the front. However, the transport speeds were relatively slow due to bad weather and road conditions. For example, on the 23rd on the Mtsensk-Bely Kolodes road, trucks advanced at six kilometres per hour; from Bely Kolodes onwards, the sledge speed was one and half kilometres per hour. The battalion could only take over its assigned section the next day, 24 February, at 8:30 p.m.[19]

As the situation changed, the defensive section of *34. Infanterie Division* had to be extended to the left. The battalion was now deployed in a defensive position in the front line and was to move into positions in the 'line stream north-eastwards Studenkovo–Khvoshchevo' on the left defensive flank. One company (most likely *2. Kompanie*) was to be detached as a reserve and stay behind the left wing of this defensive line in the Kalineyevo area.[20]

However, the situation in front of *34. Infanterie Division* eased over the next few days, to the effect that on 27 February at 5:30 p.m. the division received order that Schulenburg's battalion was to march off. The situation on the right wing of the army was still tense, reserves were needed there. It was promised that a sufficient number of trucks would be sent to Voin. Sledges were provided at Bely Kolodes. The departure was not expected before 9:00 a.m. the next day, 28 February. Once again, the transport was hampered by poor road conditions. The delay was such, that the staff of *2. Panzer Armee* demanded a report as to why such delays occurred. It turned out that the 25 empty trucks were driving without snow chains thus sliding on the slippery road and getting stuck near Volebuyevo. This blocked other units which were also to be moved. This chaos was worsened by the weather conditions and was further aggravated by the army staff, who was unable to correctly assess the road conditions in its time calculations. Underlining this is a remark in the war diary of *34. Infanterie Division*: 'The speed calculation for winter marches is only possible according to practical experience and does not correspond in any way to an otherwise usual march average.'[21]

The battalion now moved via Orel to Dmitrovsk-Orlovsky,[22] with the last remnants only being able to leave Bely Kolodes at 6:30 p.m. on 28 February.

Oberleutnant Vogler's *1. Kompanie*, which remained in the sector of *299. Infanterie Division*, was at Petrovskaya on the 23rd and still had a combatant strength of three officers and 112 NCOs and enlisted men, 12 machine guns, two heavy machine guns and two anti-tank rifles.[23] Since the battalion had moved off, the company did not suffer any further losses until the end of the month, when it too was detached, and driven to Dmitrovsk on 28 February.

---

18   Glantz, *After Stalingrad*, p.295. BA-MA, BW 57-82: 34. ID KTB 6; individual reports.
19   BA-MA, RH 24-35/52: Message of 34. ID to XXXV. AK.
20   BA-MA, RH 25-34/22: Telex XXXV. AK to 34. ID on 23 February 1943.
21   NARA, T-315 R-878: 34. ID, KTB 6, entry 28 February 1943.
22   This is the correct name of the town at the time. In German sources mostly the shorter Dmitrovsk is used, which is also its name today (since 2005), so the latter form is used in this book.
23   BA-MA, RH 26-299/108: Morning report of 299. ID to XXXV. AK of 23 February 1943.

21

I. Bataillon at Dmitrovsk-Orlovsky

Initial Situation

After the Soviet breakthrough attempts along *2. Panzer Armee*'s front towards Orel had failed, the Stavka changed its plans. The Bryansk Front was now to concentrate on the push towards Orel from the south. The operational objective was announced to General Reyter, commander of the Bryansk Front, on 24 February, which explains the easing of pressure on *112.* and *34. Infanterie Division* at the time of the arrival of *I. Bataillon* in its section. Reyter changed his offensive concept and moved the forces of the 3rd Army from the Bolkhov sector to the south in order to be able to attack Orel from the southeast and south with the concentrated forces of the 48th and 13th Army.

West of *LV. Armee Korps* a continuous German front was forming slowly. The weak German forces tended to be spread out in small strongpoints, defending their ground against the attacking 13th Army where they could. An even more worrying gap, however, presented itself around Dmitrovsk and west of it between *XXXXVI.* and *XXXXVII. Panzer Korps*, among others. The command staff of *XXXXVI. Panzer Korps* had arrived in support of *2. Panzer Armee* on 15 February and had taken over command over several divisions and units deployed around Dmitrovsk. On 4 March it consisted of *20. Panzer Division, 12. Panzer Division, 78. Sturm Division* and *258. Infanterie Division*.

Further south another large gap which had opened between *2. Panzer Armee* and *2. Armee*, was expanded operationally by the Red Army. This gap was also at the boundary line between *Heeresgruppe Mitte* and *Heeresgruppe Süd* as well as between *Luftwaffenkommando Ost* and *Luftflotte 4*.[1]

The Central Front, under the command of General Rokossovsky, moved south of Orel between the Bryansk Front and the Voronesh Front. The front's 2nd Tank Army (Lieutenant General Alexey Rodin)[2] successfully advanced to the west but was also turning north with 65th Army and 70th Army, whose troops were arriving piecemeal in the area of operations. *Generaloberst* Schmidt recognised the danger for his army and the importance of the Dmitrovsk road junction to his position around Orel. The challenge was to build up reserves as quickly as possible and deploy them there, reserves that were not readily available. Troops first had to be withdrawn from other parts of the front, thereby severely weakening their respective sectors. This Soviet advance was ultimately halted by German reinforcements which had been arriving from the northern front of *Heeresgruppe Mitte*, the sector of *Generaloberst* Model's *9. Armee* in the Rzhev salient, in anticipation of the success

---

1   Bergström, *Black Cross – Red Star, Volume 4*, p.214.
2   Alexey Grigoryevich Rodin (17 February 1902–27 May 1955) colonel general; Hero of the Soviet Union. He commanded the army until August that year.

of operation BÜFFELBEWEGUNG – the withdrawal from the Rzhev salient by 1 March 1943. As Model had to release several troop contingents, which were demanded even before the start of BÜFFELBEWEGUNG by *Heeresgruppe Mitte*, the front line of *9. Armee* was dangerously thinned out, so that he even saw the success of the enterprise endangered. However, the very well-planned retreat to shorten the front and to free urgently needed forces turned out to be a resounding success.

In particular, Rokossovsky had been surprised by the unforeseen arrival of *78. Sturm Division*, whose approach had remained hidden and had not been incorporated in the Soviet offensive plans of the Central Front. Zorn's *XXXXVI. Panzer Korps* had orders to throw back the enemy 'who had advanced into the Trofimovka area and to the southwest across the Troyanovo-Lobanovo line.'[3] For this purpose, *78. Sturm Division* under command of *Generalleutnant* Paul Völkers,[4] together with *Gruppe Bornemann (442. Division z.b.V.)*[5] and as strong as possible forces of *12. Panzer Division* on the left (east) of it were to be used. To the west was *SS-Gruppe Zehender*,[6] a battalion-strong battle group around *2. SS-Reiter Regiment* named after its commander *SS-Obersturmbannführer* August Zehender,[7] which was subordinated to *XXXXVII. Armee Korps (General der Artillerie* Joachim Lemelsen).[8] This group was to support the attack, planned for 2 March. This intention – apart from repelling Soviet attacks – was behind all planning for the next few days. But almost hourly crises arising in the division and corps areas during these days partially prevented a success of this plan. The fighting strength of the German soldiers was also severely depleted by the long, arduous marches and the frequent need to bivouac outdoors in the harsh winter conditions.

But the Soviets did not fare better. Let us follow the 193rd Rifle Division under the command of Major General Smekhotvorov,[9] which was nearly annihilated at Stalingrad. The division had been newly established with reserves from the East. According to prisoner interrogations the division consisted of the Rifle Regiments 685, 883 and 895 and the Artillery Regiment 392.[10] On 12 February the division was leaving the area around Saratov to be transported by rail to Yelets where it arrived on the 18th. Now the division had to march in harsh winter conditions on foot 340 kilometres to

---

3 NARA, T-313 R-172: PzAOK 2 KTB 3, Attachments vol.50, Right Flank, frame 7429619: Telex PzAOK 2 to XXXXVI. and XXXXVII. PzK, 1:25 a.m., 1 March 1943.
4 Paul Völkers (Kiel, 15 March 1891–sov. imprisonment, 23 January 1946), *General der Infanterie*; RK 11 December 1942, DKiG 1 April 1942. As commanding general of XXVII. AK he was captured by the Red Army during operation BAGRATION near Mogilev on 9 July.
5 Karl Bornemann (Znoimo, 15 September 1885–Vienna, 20 February 1979), *Generalleutnant*; DKiG (23. February 1943); This was a divisional staff for special purposes and not a division per se.
6 CAMO, 500_12466, file 33, p.23: Telex of PzAOK 2 to HGrM dated 21 February 1943, 11:00 p.m.
7 August Zehender (Aachen, 28 April 1903–suicide Budapest 11 February 1945) *SS-Brigadeführer* and *Generalmajor* of the *Waffen SS*; RK 10 March 1943, Oak Leaves 4 February 1945, DKiG 16 October 1942). His regiment was part of the *SS Kavallerie Division*, which at this time was stationed at Karachev. Zehender was awarded the Knight's Cross on 10 March 1943 for his effective leadership during these days. Later he also was awarded the Oak Leaves on1 February 1945 (CAMO, 500_12466, file 33, p.23; see also <www.lexikon-der-wehrmacht.de>, accessed 15 August 2022).
8 Joachim Lemelsen (Berlin, 26 September 1888–Göttingen, 30 March 1954), *General der Panzertruppe*; RK 27 July 1941, Oak Leaves 7 September 1943, DKiG 15 July 1942. He later commanded *10.* and *14. Armee* in Italy and entered British captivity.
9 Fedor Nikandrovich Smekhotvorov (17 July 1900–26 October 1989), Major General.
10 T-315 R-1101: *78. Sturm Division*, KTB Attachments, Prisoner interrogations 1 March–24 June 1943; prisoner interrogation No. 14.

Kruglaya where Rifle Regiment 685 and 883 arrived on the 27th and 28th. Rifle Regiment 895 reached Kruglaya on 1 March. During the march considerable numbers of men dropped out due to exhaustion and illness, but also quite a lot deserted.[11] At Kruglaya the latter regiment suffered further losses through aerial attacks by the *Luftwaffe*, which very successfully attacked the approaches of the Central Front.[12] Artillery Regiment 392 was unable to reach the area. As the whole of Central Front had only one single approach road,[13] which was in poor condition due to snowstorms and traffic, heavy weapons were generally not moved forward in a satisfactory manner. In addition, fuel shortages severely hampered transport efforts. The access roads were also subject to heavy *Luftwaffe* attacks, when the weather permitted. Initially, morale was good despite some grumbling about food shortages similar to the previous week's march.[14] This later changed due to unsuccessful attacks and lack of food and ammunition.

Arrival of *I. Bataillon* in Dmitrovsk

The battalion was initially placed under the command of *Gruppe Bornemann*, while still en route.[15] Before reaching Dmitrovsk it was placed under the command of *78. Sturm Division* at 2:30 a.m. on 1 March. This formation had just arrived in the area of operations with its first units – *Sturm Regiment 14* and *215* – after a journey of several days. The third regiment of the division, *Sturm Regiment 195* was still on its way.

This division had recently been formed from the remnants of *78. Infanterie Division* at the end of December 1942. It was an attempt to create a new type of division reinforced with heavy weapons, to provide a special strike force. The division lay at rest for refreshment southeast of Smolensk. A printing platoon and the *Volkswagen-Aufklärungsabteilung 178* were added to its command. *Sturm Regiment 14, 195* and *215* initially each received only one assault battalion (*Sturm Bataillon*). The other two battalions were still regular infantry battalions. A second assault battalion is said to have been formed later in March or April. The assault battalion had three assault companies, a heavy company, an infantry gun company, an engineer company, a cavalry platoon and a signals platoon. In addition, *Artillerie Regiment 178* had three battalions of light field howitzers and one battalion of heavy field howitzers, *Panzerjäger Abteilung 178* was supplied with heavy anti-tank guns and self-propelled guns. The signals battalion, *Nachrichtenabteilung 178*, was motorised. A new addition were the motorised *Schweres Granatwerferbataillon 5* with a total of 36 heavy mortars, *Sturmgeschütz Abteilung 178* with 30 assault guns, and *Heeresflak-Abteilung 293* with 18 light and eight heavy 8.8 cm anti-aircraft guns. Furthermore, the regiments were equipped with the newly introduced MG 42 machine gun, medium and heavy mortars, flamethrowers, heavy anti-tank guns, and other weapons.[16]

---

11 T-315 R-1101: *78. Sturm Division*, KTB Attachments, Prisoner interrogations 1 March–24 June 1943; prisoner interrogation No. 22.
12 Bergström, *Black Cross – Red Star, Volume 4*, p.214.
13 Igor Nebolsin, *Stalin's Favorite – The Combat History of the 2nd Guards Tank Army from Kursk to Berlin – Volume 1, January 1943–June 1944* (Solihul: Helion, 2015, reprint 2022), p.27.
14 T-315 R-1101: *78. Sturm Division*, KTB Attachments, prisoner interrogations 1 March–24 June 1943; prisoner interrogation No. 13 and 14.
15 NARA, T-313 R-172: PzAOK 2 KTB 3, Attachments vol.50, Right Flank: Telex PzAOK 2 to XXXV. AK, XXXXVI. and XXXXVII. PzK, dated 27 February 1943.
16 Merker, *78. Sturm Division*, pp.208–209.

The morning of 1 March was not an easy one for *78. Sturm Division*, for the Soviet 65th Army under General Batov attacked on a 20-kilometre wide front with the 69th and later 193rd Rifle Divisions – altogether about 16,500 men.[17] The 149th Rifle Division (6,800 men), which was also deployed shortly afterwards, was still on the march and the 70th Army had not yet arrived in the theatre of operations.[18] At several points they were able to penetrate the German front. For example, at around 7:30 a.m., strong Soviet forces of the 237th Rifle Regiment (69th Rifle Division) attacked the positions of *Sturm Regiment 215* from the forest north of Malo-Bobrovo and occupied Strashnovsky and Krasnovsky. The villages were recaptured despite fierce resistance from the very brave fighting Red Army soldiers, some of whom were slain in their 'machine gun positions…while still at their guns in hand-to-hand combat.'[19] North of Ivanovsky, an independent ski battalion of the 69th Rifle Division overran the weak defences of *Sturm Regiment 14* between Hills 262.3 and 266.0, and occupied the villages of Moshky, Sedlechko, Toporichny and a wooded area north of them. Immediate countermeasures were taken by the Germans and Toporichny was retaken by counterattack. However, the gap could not be closed quickly. Further east, a Soviet attack in battalion strength was launched from a forest south of the village of Uspensky towards the north, which was repulsed by *Sturm Regiment 14*. Soviet reinforcements were constantly observed approaching from the southeast, with about 80 men arriving at Trofimovka every hour. The arrival of eight tanks of 84th Separate Tank Regiment was also reported. The other 26 tanks of the regiment were delayed as they got stuck on the way.[20]

Schulenburg's battalion was assigned the section Pervomaisky via Baldyzh to the northwest.[21] The average strength of the four companies of the battalion was reported as 100 men each.

The paratroopers, arriving company by company, were deployed immediately. Thus, at 12:35 p.m., *4. Kompanie* was deployed against the area west of Pervomaisky and *3. Kompanie* was to attack Promklevo.[22] The village was occupied by parts of the 193rd Rifle Division and was attacked by the company with the help of supporting anti-aircraft guns, whose fire was very accurate. Close combat ensued, in which *Feldwebel* Leonhard Schmidt and his platoon distinguished themselves.[23] Schmidt was awarded the German Cross in Gold for his bravery during the Orel operation, rose to be an officer, led *II. Bataillon/Fallschirmjäger Regiment 1* as *Hauptmann* in Italy and was unofficially awarded the Knight's Cross towards the end of the war.[24] After the war he joined the German border police.[25]

---

17 Pavel Ivanovich Batov (Filissovo, 1 June 1897–Moscow, 19 April 1985), Army General and twice Hero of the Soviet Union. He was later commander of the Soviet occupation zone in Germany (1945 until 1949).
18 Glantz, *After Stalingrad*, p.285. The strengths of the divisions are of 24 February.
19 BA-MA, RH 26-78/52 in BW 57-82: Daily report of 1 March 1943, *78. Sturm-Div.* to XXXXVI. Pz.K.
20 NARA, T-315 R-1101: *78. Sturm Division*, KTB Attachments, prisoner interrogations 1 March–24 June 1943; prisoner interrogation No. 3.
21 Sometimes transliterated in German as 'Waldysch'. However, since with few exceptions in German sources the place is consistently referred to as 'Baldysch' which appears also in modern maps as 'Baldyzh', this version is used in this book to avoid confusion.
22 *4. Kompanie* is not explicitly mentioned, but as *1.* and *2. Kompanie* had not arrived yet, it can only be this company, maybe reinforced by battalion staff personnel.
23 Leonhard Schmidt (Weißenstadt, 9 December 1916– Weißenstadt, 12 August 2006), *Hauptmann*; RK 30 April 1945 as commander of II./FJR 1 (contested); DKiG 24 June 1943; Thomas/Wegmann, *Ritterkreuzträger – Fallschirmjäger*, p.268.
24 *General der Fallschirmtruppe* Heidrich, commanding General of. *I. Fallschirm Korps* in Italy awarded several Knight's Crosses without formal authorisation to some of his paratroopers in the last days of the war. The association of the award recipients, although not legally valid, accepted these awards. See Veit Scherzer, *Ritterkreuzträger 1939–1945* (Bayreuth: Scherzer, 2021), 3rd ed., p.99.
25 DDF (2006), vol.5, pp.40–41.

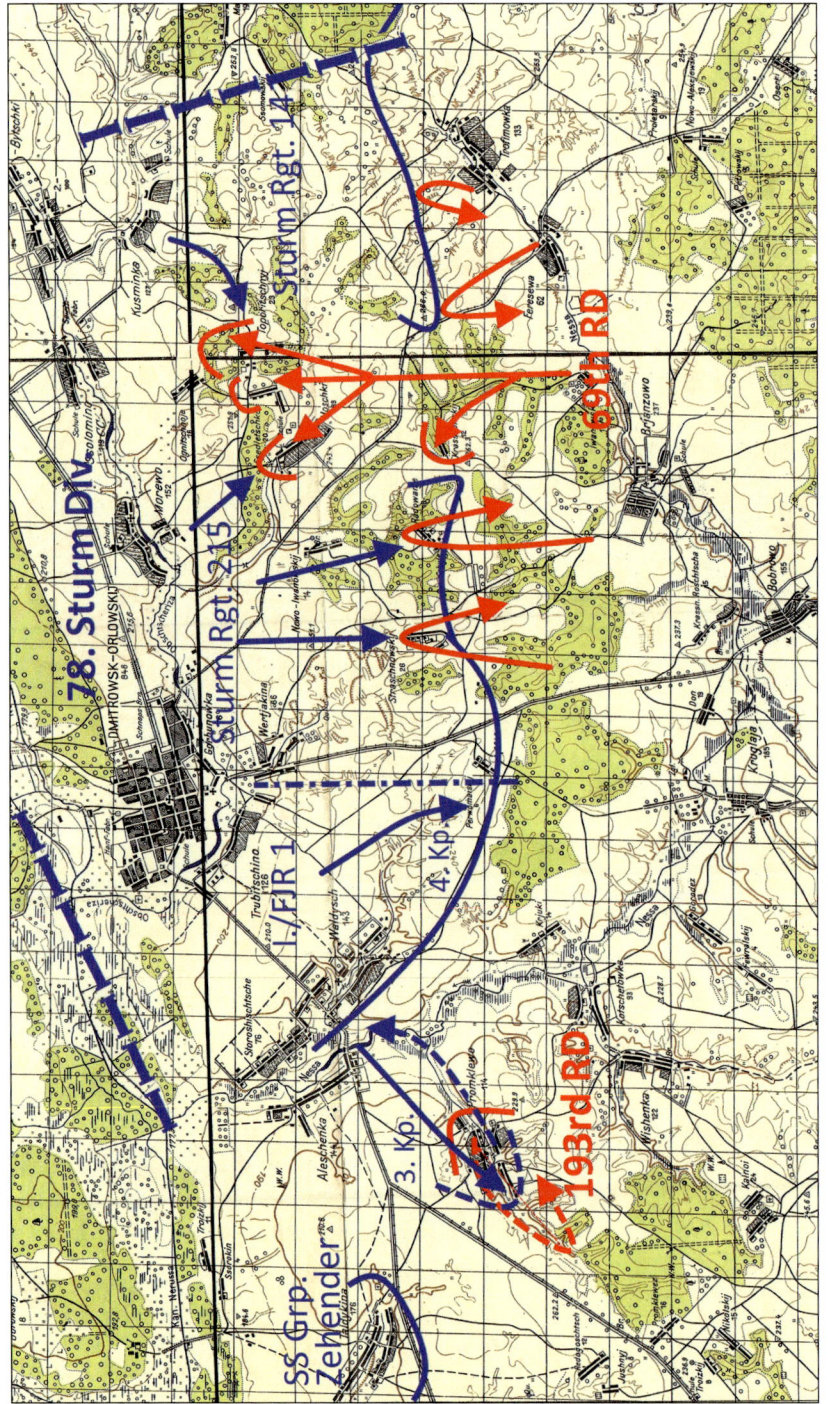

The situation on 1 March in front of 78. *Sturm Division* at Dmitrovsk-Orlovsky.

At 1:10 p.m. Schulenburg reported that the village was in the paratrooper's hands. At 2:55 p.m., he had to report this again, as the division had received contradictory messages in the meantime.[26] *Oberfeldwebel* Willi Wagner described this attack almost euphorically in a letter to his wife:

> We then mounted a surprise attack with our company, and despite fivefold superiority – the Russian was about 500 men strong and sitting in extended positions – put them to flight. In the process, our company, without any heavy weapons support [his bragging towards his wife is forgivable, anti-aircraft guns undoubtedly supported the attack] showed an attacking momentum similar to the first days of the war. The *Waffen-SS* and infantry were completely enthusiastic about the paratroopers. They can still take a leaf out of their book. Our company stormed the Russian-occupied village over a completely open area, and it was such a joy. Afterwards our battalion commander expressed his special appreciation to the chief for the company's courage and attacking spirit. This attack took place after the company had sat in the trucks for 48 hours in the cold and in drifting snow without sleep and had to attack immediately after dismounting. That is the spirit of the paratroopers. Unfortunately, we have had some losses in the process, which are very painful for the company. We buried six good comrades today and some were seriously wounded. In return, however, the Russians had to leave behind many times more dead, so that our losses are small in comparison to the Russians.[27]

The casualties mentioned by Wagner cannot be found in the casualty lists. Nine wounded of which two succumbed to their wounds are listed under the (wrong) date 3 March and (right) place Promklevo.

However, the Soviet side had no intention to give up the village under any circumstances, so the pressure increased, and the exposed company of paratroopers had to retreat to Baldyzh in the evening; *2. Kompanie* was already in position there, having arrived at around 5:00 p.m.

The battalion formed the right wing of *78. Sturm Division*, from the Nerussa Canal to the western edge of Vertyakina and to the western edge of Pervomaisky. On its arrival, *Sturm Regiment 195* was in the adjacent position on the left. On the right there remained a large gap to *SS-Gruppe Zehender*. During the night, the paratroopers were ordered to make contact with the latter by means of reconnaissance patrols. In addition, several reconnaissance patrols were sent out to scout the area in front of their main line of defence; *2. Kompanie* and *4. Kompanie* reconnoitred in the direction of Kochetovka and Kriuki, during which a firefight ensued between these patrols and Soviet troops of the 193rd Rifle Division in Kriuki. The patrol of *2. Kompanie* was led by

IV platoon of *2. Kompanie* is moving into position near Dmitrovsk. (Private Collection)

---

26 BA-MA, RH 26-78/52 in BW 57-82: message by *Oberst* Eckholt, commander of Art.Rgt. 178: 1:45 p.m.: 'Promklevo without a doubt in Russian hands.'
27 Archive Franz: Wagner, letter dated 3 March 1943.

Oberfeldwebel Hoffmeister,[28] leader of IV platoon, one of the highly respected and very capable NCOs who formed the backbone of the regiment. He was awarded the German Cross in Gold after the Orel mission and was later taken into Canadian captivity north of Ortona in January 1944. *Gefreiter* von Zimburg was also part of this patrol:

> On 2 March at 3 a.m. we set off, taking the following weapons with us: a machine gun with three boxes of ammunition in an *Akja* (snow boat/sledge), two rapid-fire rifles and two machine pistols. The two crewmen of the machine gun and the platoon leader each took a carbine. Each man had four hand-grenades in his pockets. I had a machine pistol with me. For clothing we wore the Luftwaffe winter combat suit. We trudged in single file in the darkness through knee-deep snow in the approximate direction of Kriuki. I led the way. Soon we entered the Nessa Valley, where we went downstream along the willow bushes. Suddenly it was light and close by on a slope to our left was Kriuki. The Russians must have spotted us, for we saw that they were putting up a defence. At my suggestion, we retreated into a ravine that ran along a hill to the right, roughly in the direction of Kochetovka. The machine gun was positioned on a small knoll and blocked the Russians from coming through the Nessa valley.
>
> Suddenly we saw a patrol of [*4. Kompanie*] also moving downstream along the road to Kriuki … While the patrol marched under the cover of some bushes to near Kriuki, two Russians went down the same way to the Nessa. When the Russians reached the ridge, they sent a third person, a woman, ahead, who, seeing the…patrol, signalled to the rear. *Oberfeldwebel* Hoffmeister immediately had the riflemen shoot at the woman. The Russians then ran back into the village.
>
> The 4th's patrol retreated to the left behind the ridge and disappeared from our view. After about two minutes Russians broke out of the village in open order in the direction of the ridge. *Oberfeldwebel* Hoffmeister counted about seventy men, but there were certainly over ninety. When they were about 150 metres from the edge of the village, a very small tank (one to two-man tank) also drove behind the Russians but got stuck after only fifty metres and had to turn back. *Oberfeldwebel* Hoffmeister sent *Gefreiten* Hörenberg back to the company as a messenger to call for artillery support for the reconnaissance patrol of *4. Kompanie* …[29]

Hoffmeister's patrol continued its way towards Kochetovka up the hill where they had a good field of observation. 'We could not see any tanks or heavy weapons. *Oberfeldwebel* Hoffmeister asked me to look to the right against the horizon, where a windmill could be seen. I could not believe my eyes. There was a closed column marching from the horizon into Kochetovka (about 4 or 4.5 kilometres), we had seen enough and went back.'[30]

Otherwise, the night was quiet. In the early morning hours of the 2nd, *Oberleutnant* Vogler's *1. Kompanie* finally joined its battalion. Its mission was to link with *SS-Gruppe Zehender* via Aleshenka to Taldykina.[31] Night reconnaissance revealed that Soviet units had established themselves in Mikhailovsky, in the forest east of it, in Promklevo and Kriuki, and were constantly bringing up reinforcements in groups of 100 and 200 men via Vizhenka-Kochetovka. The forest to the east of Kriuki

---

28   Hugo Hoffmeister (1916–?), *Oberfeldwebel*; DKiG 24 June 1943.
29   Zimburg, *Erinnerungen*, pp.84–86.
30   Zimburg, *Erinnerungen*, p.86.
31   Today the name has a slightly different spelling and is called Aleshinka.

was reported to be free of the enemy for the time being, but during the morning the Soviets occupied it to the northeast.[32]

Major von der Schulenburg was now also assigned a company of a *Volkswehr* battalion, 200 Russian volunteers, to provide flank protection along the Nerussa Canal and on both sides of Troitsky towards the south.[33]

The Attack on Kriuki

XXXXVI. Panzer Korps had the task of preventing an advance of the Red Army to the north, while *78. Sturm Division* had to carry out this very task on the right wing of the corps. It was planned that after the arrival of *Sturm Regiment 195* – which would complete *78. Sturm Division* – an attack to the south would be launched into the flank of the Central Front advancing to the northwest. This was expected to tie up enemy forces in order to gain time and bring in reinforcements. The attack was to be carried out on 4 and 5 March. For 3 March it was planned that Schulenburg's battalion should reach a better starting position and take Kriuki and Promklevo. For this purpose, *Kampfgruppe Schulenburg* was formed, which consisted of the following units:

I. Bataillon/Fallschirmjäger Regiment 1,
Staff and *1. Kompanie* of *Bau Bataillon 421*,
2. Kompanie/Bau Bataillon 576,
2. Kompanie/Pionierbataillon 745,
1. Volkswehr-Bataillon,
2. Kompanie/Sturmgeschütz-Abteilung 189,
one heavy anti-tank gun company of *Sturm Regiment 215* (12 guns) and a platoon of *Panzerjäger Abteilung 178* with three self-propelled anti-tank guns.

Artillery support was provided by *Alarm Batterie (mot.) 604 (b)*.[34] At the same time, *Sturm Regiment 215* was to push south and take the woods to the east of Kriuki.

Meanwhile, the division's defensive front was consolidated on the afternoon of 2 March, when *Sturm Regiment 14* succeeded in counterattacking towards the previous day's breach near Moshki and closing the gap in the front.

Schulenburg decided to attack Kriuki with Kissling's *2. Kompanie* and parts of Vogler's *1. Kompanie* as well as other supporting units of the battalion. Schulenburg requested that his attack take place before that of *Sturm Regiment 215* in order to maximise the element of surprise.

I, II and III platoons of *2. Kompanie* formed the main left assault group, which was to attack Kriuki from the east, while the right group, consisting of IV platoon under *Oberfeldwebel* Hoffmeister and a platoon of *1. Kompanie* under the command of *Leutnant* Lorenz,[35] was to attack from the north. The

---

32   BA-MA, RH 26-78/52 in BW 57-82.
33   BA-MA, RH 26-78/52 in BW 57-82.
34   NARA, T-314 R-1086: XXXXVI. PzK, KTB Attachments 1 January–31 May 1943, Subordinated units. There is also an artillery unit mentioned: BA-MA, RH 26-78/50: Divisional order of *78. Sturm-Division*.
35   Hans Lorenz (1921–?), *Oberleutnant*.

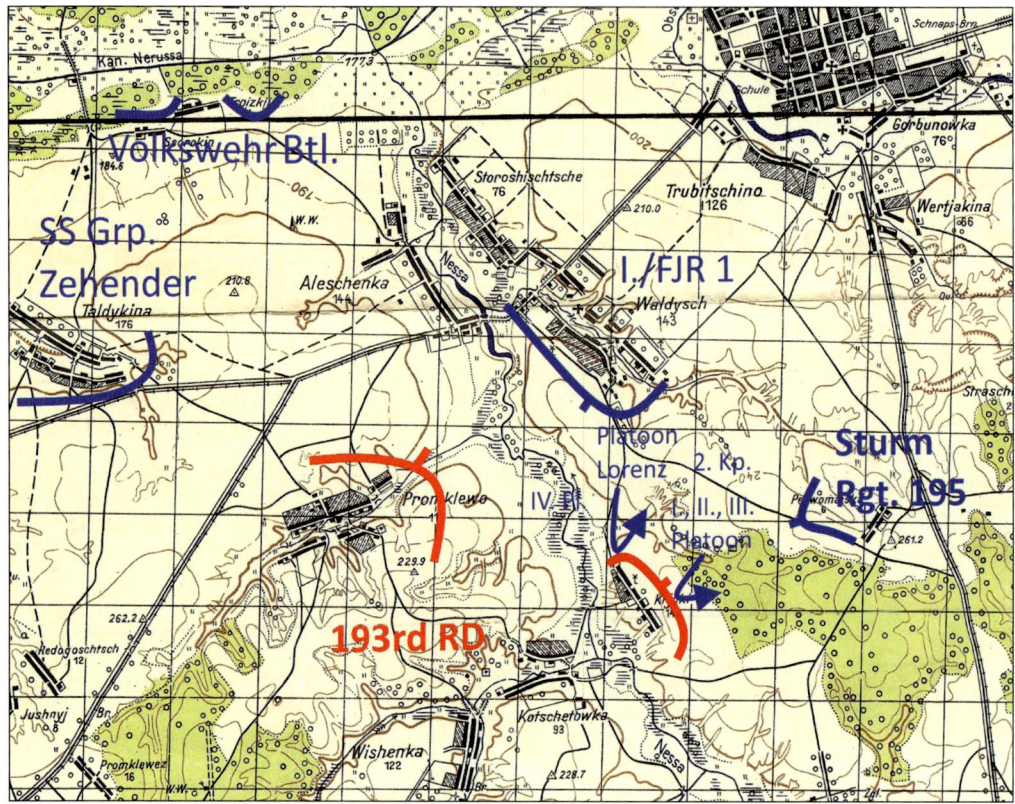

The attack on Kriuki by *2. Kompanie* on 3 March 1943.

heavy machine guns of IV platoon were to provide covering fire. The mortars of *4. Kompanie* provided artillery support.[36]

On the afternoon of 2 March, they began to move into the initial positions. The forest northeast of Kriuki was reached by the assault group during the night. The paratroopers spent the night in the open. During the night it snowed, it was bitterly cold, and a blizzard formed. *Obergefreiter* Thomas Mikolaiewsky, a veteran of the Norway, Crete and Leningrad campaigns remembers vividly:

> We were housed in snow huts and in the evening, we went into attack position in a small wood. There, too, the snow was so high that we already created a shallow foxhole by stomping the ground. With two men in a foxhole, we warmed each other so that we wouldn't freeze to death. But when it came to the attack, it took us a long time to get everyone going.[37]

---

36 Zimburg, *Erinnerungen*, p.88.
37 BA-MA, BW 57-93: Mikolajewski (Hitzfeld) recollections.

Elsewhere, on the Baldyzh-Kriuki road, attached to the platoon of *Leutnant* Lorenz, *Gefreiter* von Zimburg was in position and prepared for a cold night: 'We dug ourselves into a snowdrift, faces downwind, and let the blizzard that had by now begun rage over us.'[38]

In the early morning hours at 6:00 a.m., the main group started its advance to the village from the east. The attack initially stalled, the Soviet defenders fought back tenaciously and seemed to have occupied Kriuki more strongly than expected. 'I [*Obergefreiter* Mikolajewski] know that I was on the right wing with Franz Szugat when strong gunfire hit us. Also, the Russians had snipers there who cleaned everything off in their line of fire.'[39]

The snowstorm prevented communication between the two attacking groups and so the operation was carried out uncoordinated. After a burst of artillery fire, the paratroopers of the left attack group managed to enter Kriuki in close combat, but were unable to hold. Under heavy Soviet pressure, they were forced to withdraw to their original positions around 10:00 a.m. suffering heavy losses, including the company commander *Oberleutnant* Kissling, an officer very much liked and respected by his men.[40]

Gefreiter von Zimburg lay in position on the far right and had to block the Baldyzh-Kriuki road together with *Obergefreiter* Zimmermann with their heavy anti-tank rifle (*2.8 cm Panzerbüchse 41*): 'No one knew what was going on, whether the company was already in the attack or not, where the company was, because there was no contact with it. We stayed about fifty metres in front of our attack position and waited for further orders.'[41]

It was only when *Unterarzt* Dr Bachmann appeared at the right-wing group in search of

These pictures were taken most probably by a soldier of *Sturm Regiment 215* between the village of Morevo and Dmitrovsk on 3 March 1943. They show the snowstorm during which the paratroopers had to perform their attack. (Collection Paul Dekkers)

Oberleutnant Kissling and *Leutnant* Thede in France Summer 1942. In the background on the right *Feldwebel* Steindl. (Archive BDF)

---

38 Zimburg, *Erinnerungen*, p.88.
39 BA-MA, BW 57-93: Mikolajewski (Hitzfeld) recollections.
40 BA-MA, RH 26-78/52 in BW 57-82.
41 Zimburg, *Erinnerungen*, p.88.

A *Fallschirmjäger* warming food, in the background a heavy anti-tank rifle *2.8 cm Panzerbüchse 41*. (BArch, Bild 101I-540-0407-12/Helmuth Pirath)

Oberleutnant Kissling,[42] who had been wounded by a bullet to the head, that this group also started its attack on Kriuki.

> At first we went in short jumps through the over-knee-deep snow. However, the Russian defensive fire became so strong that we could not dare to stand up. So, we crawled up one next to the other. Suddenly, an *Oberjäger* and two men from Lorenz's platoon ran upright to the first house. But all three of them were shot down immediately. Two Russians ran towards them. *Oberfeldwebel* Hoffmeister had guessed the Russians' intention and was able to take out one of them; unfortunately, the second was able to retreat into the house. A medical orderly, *Sanitäts-Gefreiter* Gertenbach,[43] wanted to go forward to the wounded *Oberjäger*, but he fell a few metres in front of us, shot in the head. A runner from the company staff who had a wounded foot, *Obergefreiter* Laimer, a mountain farmer from South Tyrol, had come up in the meantime

---

42 Dr Bruno Bachmann (Innsbruck, 1 June 1912–Wildschönau, 25 January 1990), *Stabsarzt*; DKiG 1944. After the war he worked as a medical doctor in the public health service of Austria in Wildschönau, Tyrol, where he was a founding member of the *Scharfschützenkompanine Wildschönau*, a traditional Tyrolean marksmen association.
43 Martin Gertenbach (Kassel, 21 May 1921–KIA Kriuki, 3 March 1943), *Sanitäts-Gefreiter*. In his WASt-file a shot to his chest is noted. (Ancestry WASt IDNr. G-C 157/0301, accessed 15 June 2021). According to the casualty list he is the only orderly who was killed that day.

with a sled to help transport the wounded. When he heard that we had wounded lying on the edge of the village, he wanted to crawl to them. When he was next to us, he was shot in the thigh. *Gefreiter* Zimmermann, who was closest to him, loaded him into his own sled and took him back where he was handed over to a medic [Zimmermann was also wounded]. We still worked our way to within throwing distance of Kriuki, but could not recover the wounded *Oberjäger*, so we dug shallow covers in the snow and, as far as the snowstorm allowed, fired only precisely aimed shots. In the meantime, our heavy machine guns had set most of the houses on fire. A Russian sniper was still firing at us, although the attic in which he had entrenched himself was already ablaze. Only a precisely aimed burst of fire from one of our heavy machine guns silenced him. The heavy mortars of *4. Kompanie* fired several rounds into the village, but the observer could not give any corrections because of the driving snow [he could not see anything], so they had to stop firing.[44]

The attack was then also broken off on the right wing and the two platoons withdrew. Four men attempted to rescue the wounded *Oberjäger* on the outskirts of Kriuki, but this was unsuccessful as he was shot in the head during the rescue attempt. Another paratrooper of this group also fell.

The Soviet defenders of Kriuki were probably part of Rifle Regiment 895 (of the 193rd Rifle Division) or of Rifle Regiment 120 (of the 69th Rifle Division) – a prisoner statement suggests the latter.[45] They were able to repulse the attack with extremely accurate defensive fire, despite the unfavourable weather conditions. The complete absence of Soviet artillery is also significant, as all the dead were killed by infantry fire; half of the German dead suffered head shots.

The result of this failure was sobering for *2. Kompanie*: two officers, the company commander *Oberleutnant* Kissling and a platoon commander *Leutnant* Thede, as well as several other platoon and group leaders had fallen. The battalion's initial report for *2. Kompanie* of 14 dead, 30 wounded and five missing was subsequently corrected to 23 dead (including two who later died of their wounds), 24 wounded and one missing. *1. Kompanie* had initially reported six dead and three wounded, but as one of the wounded was recorded as killed in action in the casualty list, the total is seven killed and two wounded. The *Leichtgeschütz* platoon (recoilless gun platoon) of *13. Kompanie* had five wounded, including *Leutnant* Lodders,[46] and the signals platoon also had one killed and one officer wounded, *Leutnant* Andres.[47] In total, the battalion had suffered 63 casualties (31 dead/one missing/32 wounded) in this attack. The leadership of *2. Kompanie* was now taken over by the company's only surviving officer, *Oberleutnant* Paul-Ernst Renisch, who had previously led II platoon. In contrast to his predecessor Kissling, Renisch was rather disliked by his men.

Renisch had the unpleasant task of informing the families of the dead and missing and describing the circumstances. One of the missing whose fate is still unknown was *Obergefreiter* Fritz Hansen,[48] the only son of *Luftwaffe Major* Karl Hansen, a pilot during the First World War. Trained as a mechanical engineer, Fritz Hansen joined the paratroopers in 1940. As a member of *3. Kompanie/Fallschirmjäger Regiment 1*, he saw action at Narvik, Crete and Leningrad and joined *2. Kompanie* in the spring of

---

44 Zimburg, *Erinnerungen*, pp.87–89.
45 NARA, T-315 R-1101: *78. Sturm Division*, KTB Attachments, Prisoner interrogations 1 March–24 June 1943; prisoner interrogation No. 14.
46 Wilhelm Lodders (1913–1995), *Hauptmann*; DKiG 1 January 1945.
47 Erich Andres (1919–?), *Oberleutnant*; DKiG 27 June 1944.
48 Karl Friedrich ‚Fritz' Hansen (Mannheim, 17 June 1920-MIA Kriuki, 3 March 1943), *Obergefreiter*.

1942. He was unable to go to Smolensk with his company in October due to illness and did not re-join his company until early February 1943, just in time to be transferred to Orel.⁴⁹

Renisch wrote:

> The attack took place in a heavy snowstorm and cost the company many casualties, including the company commander and a large part of the platoon to which your son belonged. When the casualties were later recovered, your son was not found.
>
> It is almost certain that he died a hero's death and is still buried under the snow. Unfortunately, I cannot be certain, as no surviving member of the company can give any definite information as to your son's whereabouts…
>
> But the company misses a brave soldier, an excellent machine-gunner and a good comrade.⁵⁰

Hauptfeldwebel Wagner mourned his friend *Leutnant* Thede in a letter to his wife:

> I am sorry about Hans. He was a good man. What will his wife now say? Please do not write to his wife before I give you notice as the letter has not been sent yet [by our company]. I will write later to Ms Thede as well. Hans was so looking forward to seeing his boy. His boss [Kissling] was also father of three children. Yes, fate hits some people very hard.⁵¹

As head of the administrative duties of the company the fallen were also Wagner's responsibility: 'Now I still have a lot of work to do with the things of our dead. This work is really no joy. Sometimes it is also quite hard for me when I see all this suffering. It is often difficult not to lose heart when many a good comrade passes away.'⁵²

Fritz Hansen as *Gefreiter* during a visit at his parents' place in Mannheim late 1941 or early 1942. He went missing during the attack on Kriuki. (Collection Paul Dekkers)

Another paratrooper who was killed in action at Kriuki was *Obergefreiter* Werner Teegen, a close friend of Fritz Hansen, pictured in Mamellière, France, in April 1942. (Collection Paul Dekkers)

---

49 Information provided by Paul Dekkers, December 2023.
50 Letter by *Oberleutnant* Paul-Ernst Renisch to the parents of Fritz Hansen, dated 28 March 1943. Collection Paul Dekkers.
51 Archive Franz: Wagner, letter dated 3 March 1943.
52 Archive Franz: Wagner, letter dated 3 March 1943.

Remembrance card of 23 year-old *Oberjäger* Kurt Foss, who was killed during the attack on Kriuki on 3 March 1943. (Private Collection)

The battalion's main line of defence on the 3rd ran from Taldykina (held by *SS Gruppe Zehender*) along the road to Aleshenka, to the southwest edge of Baldyzh, to the southwest edge of the forest east of Kriuki, to Hill 237.3 and one kilometre north of Malo-Bobrovo Hill 262.3.[53] The link to the west with *SS Gruppe Zehender* was maintained by the battalion through strong patrols.

The Defence Against the Soviet Attack on Baldyzh (4 March)

The 193rd Rifle Division was mainly deployed in front of the Dmitrovsk sector of the *78. Sturm Division*. Its right neighbour changed during the day of 3 March as the heavily mauled 69th Rifle Division was replaced by 246th Rifle Division (65th Army). On 4 March the 149th Rifle Division moved into position to the east, opposite the left wing of the *Sturm Division*.[54]

The 193rd Rifle Division for its part, took advantage of the opportunity after the failed German attack on Kriuki and prepared for the attack on Baldyzh and Storoshishche which was to take place in the early morning hours of 4 March. 1st and 3rd battalion (5–600 men) of Rifle Regiment 895 moved

---

53 NARA, T-315 R-1100: *78. Sturm-Division*, KTB 1 January–4 July 1943, Attachments: Protocol of Commanders' meeting.
54 Glantz, *After Stalingrad*, p.320.

Envelope and letter of Willi Wagner to his spouse mourning his friend *Leutnant* Thede, dated 3 March 1943. (Archive Florian Franz)

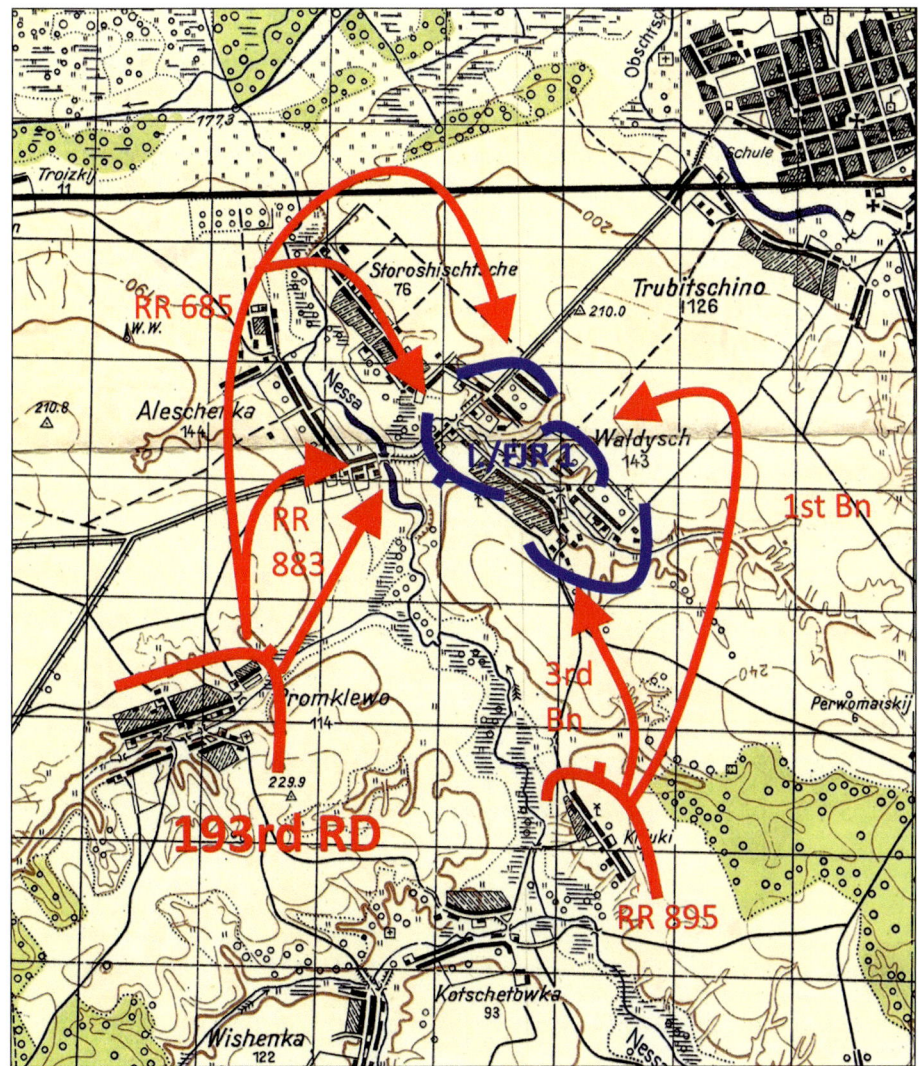

The defence of Baldyzh by *I. Bataillon* on 4 March 1943.

into Kriuki during the day. The 2nd battalion stayed as a reserve in Malo Bobrovo. The 1st battalion was to bypass Baldyzh on the eastern side and attack the village from the east, while 3rd battalion was to attack the village from the south-west. Rifle Regiment 883 was to perform a frontal attack from Promklevo towards Aleshenka and Baldyzh while Rifle Regiment 685 was to bypass Storoshishche on the western side and attack the villages from north and east.[55]

---

55 NARA, T-315 R-1101: *78. Sturm Division*, KTB Attachments, Prisoner interrogations 1 March–24 June 1943; prisoner interrogation No. 13 and 14.

The two battalions of Rifle Regiment 895, which were preparing to attack between 3:00 and 4:00 a.m while it was still dark, were discovered by chance by a patrol of *Oberfeldwebel* Hoffmeister. *Gefreiter* von Zimburg ran back and at the last minute managed to alert the paratroopers of his company, who were lying exhausted and asleep in the village. He was awarded the Iron Cross 2nd Class for this action on 16 March 1943.

The attack was reported by Schulenburg to the division at 3:55 a.m.: 'Enemy is attacking *[2.] Kompanie* located southeast of Baldyzh from the forest northeast of Kriuki'.[56] At the same time the Soviets were advancing eastwards from this forest with reconnaissance patrols towards the German lines. Also, further attacks by the 69th Rifle Division on the front of *78. Sturm Division* on Krasnovsky, Hill 266.0 and eastward of it were carried out at the same time. All of them were repulsed by the Germans.

The attack on Baldyzh widened, as another battalion of the Soviet Rifle Regiment 895 pushed west past the village and broke through to the north between Aleshenka and Taldykina. The situation became increasingly precarious for the battalion. At 5:12 a.m. Schulenburg reported to *78. Sturm Division*: 'Enemy is attacking Baldyzh from all sides, has broken through to the north between Aleshenka and Taldykina and is attacking Aleshenka-Storoshishche from the northeast. The situation is very threatening.'[57] Baldyzh was now also attacked by yet another battalion from the south and also from the east. At around 6:00 a.m., the paratroopers' baggage train was attacked there, which meant that the battalion was surrounded and trapped for a short time. Around 6:25 a.m., however, the crisis was overcome. *Gefreiter* von Zimburg described the end of the fighting:

> Our heavy machine guns had only very few boxes of ammunition left. Then the Russians, who had managed to get very close to our defences, suddenly stood up and surrendered. They ran towards us with their hands up. Russians with the most terrible wounds came along as if nothing was wrong with them. *Oberfeldwebel* Hoffmeister, some *Feldwebel* and non-commissioned officers from *3. Kompanie* and quite a few of us, including myself, made a counterattack without any special order and re-established the connection between us and the troops who had occupied the main line of defence.[58]

This counterattack was conducted by *Feldwebel* Leopold Schmidt with parts of his platoon and the company squad of *3. Kompanie*. They succeeded in bringing in 100 prisoners. As threatening as the situation was, the battalion did not suffer many losses: *2. Kompanie* had four wounded and *3. Kompanie* three dead and seven wounded, among the latter also *Feldwebel* Germer of the company squad.

The Soviets had covered their attack to the east or northeast with a flank guard, which was now attacked and routed by two companies of *Sturm-Regiment 195*. These companies subsequently put the Soviet soldiers who were retreating from Baldyzh under fire.[59]

At around 9:20 a.m. the left section had been cleared and the casualties counted. Thus, of the estimated 500 to 600 attackers of the two battalions of Rifle Regiment 895, 250 lay dead in front of the paratroopers' positions. The two battalions were basically annihilated. The imminent danger for Dmitrovsk had been averted, but the threat remained. The towns of Aleshenka and Storoshishche

---

56 BA-MA, RH 26-78/52 in BW 57-82.
57 BA-MA, RH 26-78/52 in BW 57-82.
58 Zimburg, *Erinnerungen*, pp.92–93.
59 Merker, *78. Sturm-Division*, p.212.

I. BATAILLON AT DMITROVSK-ORLOVSKY 217

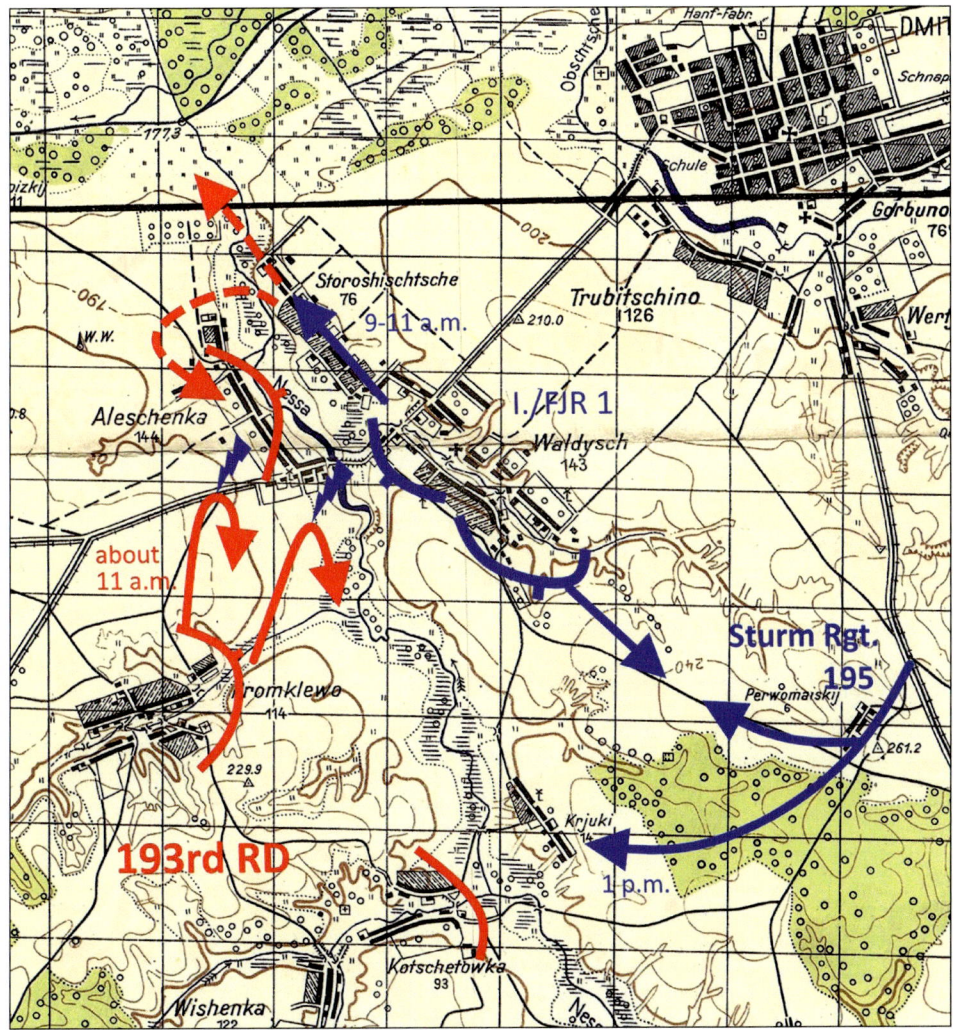

The counterattack of *I. Bataillon* on Storoshishche on 4 March 1943.

adjacent to Baldyzh were still partially occupied by Rifle Regiment 685, the paratroopers being forced to abandon their positions in the villages due to heavy enemy pressure.

The next task for the paratroopers was to retake the lost villages and regain the former main line of defence. First the battalion attacked Storoshishche at around 9:00 a.m. A tough house-to-house fight ensued, which ended in favour of the paratroopers. It is not confirmed which companies took part in this action. Zimburg states that he participated with parts of his company;[60] according to the casualty lists losses were only incurred by the *1.*, *4.* and *14. Kompanie*.

---

60 Zimburg, *Erinnerungen*, pp.93–94.

At this time, around 9:30 a.m., Schulenburg's battalion was placed under the command of *Sturm Regiment 195*, the first parts of which had arrived the day before, and which was given the task of securing the Dmitrovsk section, but mainly to block Storoshishche.⁶¹ This regiment was commanded by *Oberstleutnant* Walter Hollaender. He was a nephew of the composer Friedrich Hollaender. As he was half Jewish, he got a special 'German blood certificate' to be able to follow his military career. In 1944 he went into Soviet captivity and was released only in 1956.⁶²

Meanwhile, the 193rd Rifle Division tried to save the situation for the Soviet side by moving a company into Aleshenka and attacking Baldyzh with another at about 11:30 a.m. These companies came under heavy fire from German 2 cm anti-aircraft guns and artillery at the outset, and were thus prevented from advancing. At 1:00 p.m. Storoshishche was reported clear of the enemy by Schulenburg, and the village was again in the hands of the paratroopers. The fighting of this day in Baldyzh and Storoshishche resulted in considerable losses for the battalion, with 30 killed and 65 wounded.

This picture was taken by *Oberleutnant* Mössinger during the house to house fighting in Storoshchiche. (Private Collection)

Losses of *I. Bataillon/Fallschirmjäger Regiment 1* on 4 March 1943

Unit	Dead⁶³	Wounded
Bataillonsstab	1	1
14. Kompanie	4	3
1. Kompanie	14	33
2. Kompanie		4
3. Kompanie	3	7
4. Kompanie	8	17
Total	30	65

Of the officers of the battalion, Schulenburg's adjutant *Oberleutnant* Hörnig,⁶⁴ a veteran who had participated in the Poland campaign in 1939, who had survived the missions at Oslo, Rotterdam, Narvik, Crete and Leningrad was killed in Storoshishche, the company commander of *1. Kompanie*, *Oberleutnant* Vogler was among the wounded. His company was taken over by *Oberleutnant* Mössinger,⁶⁵ a seasoned veteran of the Poland, Norway, Crete and Shlisselburg campaigns.

---

61 BA-MA, RH 26-78/52 in BW 57-82.
62 Walter Hollaender (Verden, 15 October 1903–Hamburg, 8 September 1974), *Oberst*. RK 18 July 1943; DKiG 18 October 1942. See also Bryan Mark Rigg, *Hitler's Jewish Soldiers: the untold story of Nazi racial laws and men of Jewish descent in the German military* (Lawrence: University Press of Kansas, 2002), pp.18, 39–40, 201–202.
63 Including those who died of their wounds.
64 Peter Hörnig (Bonn, 5 January 1917–KIA Storoshishche, 4 March 1943), *Oberleutnant*.
65 Ernst Mössinger (10 December 1915–22 May 2006), *Major*; DKiG 1 October 1944.

Mein über alles geliebter Mann gab in treuester Pflichterfüllung sein Leben für unser Volk und Vaterland

Peter Hörnig

Oberleutnant in einem Fallschirmjäger-Regt.

Träger des Eisernen Kreuzes I. und II. Kl., des Luftwaffensturmabzeichens, des Narvikschildes und des Verwundetenabzeichens

fiel am 4. März 1943 im Osten, nachdem er den Feldzug in Polen, die Fallschirmeinsätze in Oslo, Rotterdam, Narvik und Kreta und den Feldzug der Fallschirmjäger im Winter 1942 bei Leningrad siegreich miterleben durfte.

Er starb, ohne seinen so sehr ersehnten kleinen Sohn Peter gesehen zu haben.

Stendal, im März 1943
Horst-Wessel-Str. 33

In stolzer Trauer:

Erni Hörnig geb. Jacob
Monika Hörnig
Peter Hörnig
Eltern und Angehörige

Above: *Oberleutnant* Peter Hörnig, the battalion adjutant of *I. Bataillon* who was killed in action during the attack on Storoshishche on 4 March 1943, here pictured as a *Leutnant*. He was married and had a baby son whom he never saw. (Collection Stephan Janzyk)]

Right: Death notice for *Oberleutnant* Hörnig, by his wife Erni. 'He died without having seen his much-longed-for little son Peter.' (Collection Stephan Janzyk)

The graves of two paratroopers from *1. Kompanie* killed in action at Storoshishche on 4 March 1943. The outskirts of Dmitrovsk can be seen in the background. (Private Collection)

Originally from the *Heer,* Mössinger joined the paratroopers in 1938. He is best-known for his brave conduct at Dombås, Norway, in 1940, where he led the remnants of the company when his company commander was badly wounded. Mössinger was later seriously wounded at Monte Cassino in March 1944. Having recovered, he participated in the last battles around Berlin 1945. After the war he became an architect in Frankfurt am Main.⁶⁶

It is not known to what extent the weather conditions – there had suddenly been another heavy frost and snowdrifts – led to further casualties. All units of *78. Sturm Division* reported considerable losses on this day due to illness and frostbite.⁶⁷

However, the Soviet 193rd Rifle Division, which held Promklevo, succeeded in continuing to feed reinforcements into Aleshenka and the area north of it during this time, despite heavy defensive fire from the Germans. The paratroopers' outposts in Aleshenka had to be withdrawn.

In the early afternoon of 4 March, parts of *Sturm Regiment 195,* which had already arrived, managed to advance to the edges of the forest east and south-east of Kriuki. This village, which had been fought over so much the day before, was found free of Soviet soldiers and thereupon burned down so that this place could no longer provide shelter for them. The connection to *Kampfgruppe Schulenburg* was thus established.

Ernst Mössinger as *Oberleutnant* 1942.
(Private Collection)

At hills 266.0, 262.3, and other points that day, *78. Sturm Division* was able to repel attacks and consolidate the defensive line it had reached: 'confluence of the Nessa Canal and Nerussa-Storoshishche-Baldyzh-South edge of the forest north of Kruglaya-to the left as before.'⁶⁸

Aleshenka (5 March)

Generalleutnant Völkers received the order to establish the connection between his *78. Sturm Division* and its left-wing neighbour in Taldykina, *SS-Gruppe Zehender*. He assigned this task to Hollaender's *Sturm-Regiment 195* and Schulenburg's battalion. Early the next morning it was *3. Kompanie*'s turn to attack Aleshenka at about 6:00 a.m. with the help of four assault guns of *Sturmgeschützabteilung 178*. The village was occupied by three previously weakened battalions of Rifle Regiment 685.⁶⁹ The

---

66 See also DDF (2006), vol.4, p.27.
67 BA-MA, RH 26-78/52 in BW 57-82: report of *Sturm Rgt.. 215*; BA-MA, RH 26-78/59 in BW 57-82: daily report of *78. Sturm-Division* 4 March 1943.
68 BA-MA, RH 26-78/59 in BW 57-82: daily report of *78. Sturm-Division* 4 March 1943.
69 NARA, T-315 R-1101: *78. Sturm Division*, KTB Attachments, Prisoner interrogations 1 March–24 June 1943; prisoner interrogation No. 22.

lead platoon of the German attackers was commanded by *Feldwebel* Schmidt.[70] The fight was fierce but not long-lasting, the Soviet soldiers retreated across the open area to Troitsky and may have then tried to regroup north of this village to join partisans operating in the area. Around 10:00 a.m., *2. Kompanie* also advanced in an arc towards Troitsky, which was already free of Soviet soldiers. Liaison was established with Kühlwein's *45. Infanterie Division* in Taldykina which had, in the meantime replaced, *SS-Gruppe Zehender*. That this still exhausted division had to be deployed so shortly after it was so heavily mauled, also emphasises the desperate situation of Schmidt's *2. Panzer Armee*. The attack was supported by *2. Artillerie Abteilung* of *Artillerie Kommando 101*, which fought 'in combined fire [against enemy] movements in Promklevo, from Kruglaya to the north as well as deployments for attack north of Pereseva and also an attack from Malo-Bobrovo to the north'.[71] In the process, 3,133 shells were fired. The Soviet side, on the other hand, did not have any significant heavy artillery in support, only mortars, anti-tank and infantry guns. The Soviet artillery was only able to fire 88 rounds of disruptive fire into the southern part of Dmitrovsk.[72]

A Sturmgeschütz III near Orel. (Collection Peter Bedenk)

Once again, the paratroopers suffered considerable losses. The casualty list mentions a total of 21 casualties, 16 dead and five wounded.[73] The leadership personnel of *3. Kompanie* were hit hard this time: *Oberleutnant* Nagel fell, *Leutnant* Daum succumbed to his wounds,[74] and two officer candidates were wounded or killed. The only surviving officer of this company was its commander, *Oberleutnant* Otto.

---

70 Thomas/Wegmann, *Ritterkreuzträger–Fallschirmjäger*, p.268.
71 NARA, T-314 R-1086: XXXXVI. PzK, KTB Attachments, corps units, 1 January–31 May 1943.
72 NARA, T-314 R-1086: XXXXVI. PzK, KTB Attachments, corps units, 1 January–31 May 1943.
73 Staff: two dead, one wounded; 1. Kp.: one wounded; 3. Kp.: nine dead, three wounded; 4. Kp.: five dead.
74 Ulrich Daum (Schneideml.,18 November 1922–KIA Aleschenka, 5 March 1943), *Leutnant*.

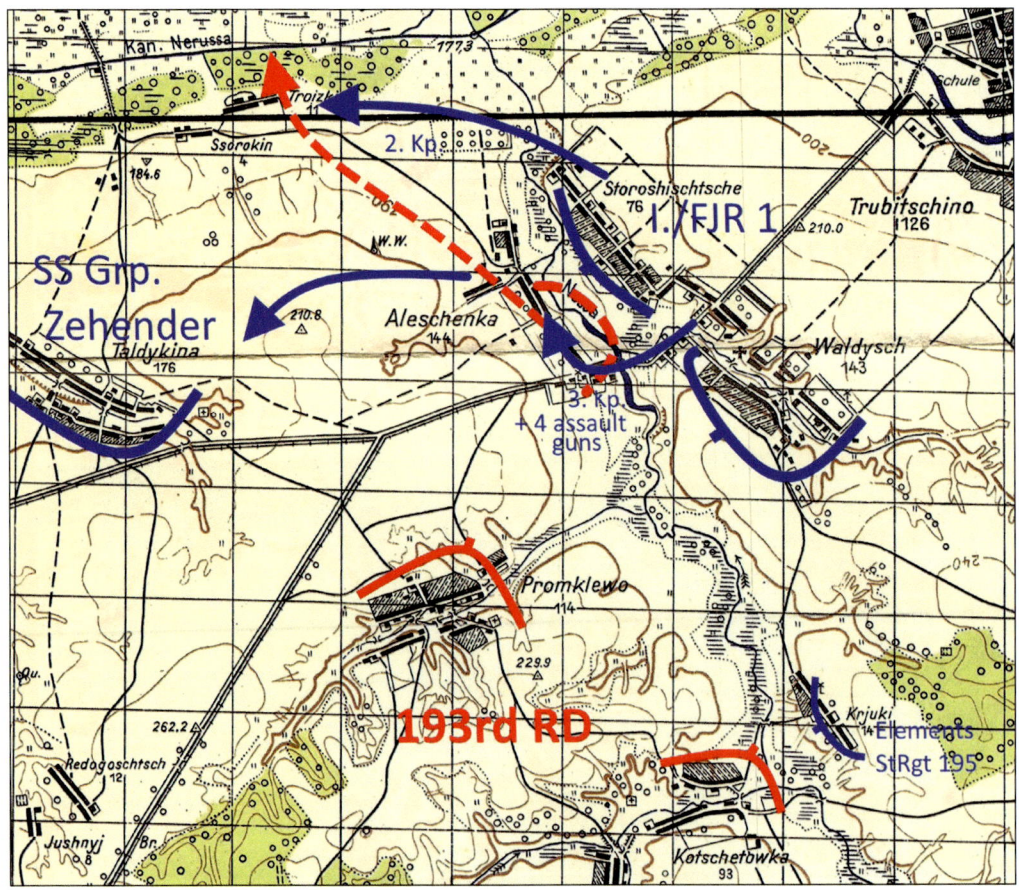

The counterattack on Aleshenka on 5 March 1943.

Generalleutnant Völkers now ordered that combat-ready reconnaissance patrols were sent to Promklevo and Kochetovka. They detected that the villages were occupied by strong Soviet forces. The ruins of Kriuki were now occupied by an outpost of *Sturm Regiment 195*. The line reached that day was 'Hill 210.8–road-junction two kilometres southwest of Aleshenka-south edge of Aleshenka-from Baldyzh to the left as before.'[75]

The worn-out battalion of paratroopers was now moved to Dmitrovsk as a reserve, where they could get some rest. During the previous three days it had lost 68 dead and 102 wounded.

On 5 March, the *78. Sturm Division* had considerable supply problems, because Dmitrovsk could only be reached with difficulty by tracked vehicles from Kromy, as heavy snowdrifts hindered the transports. The next day, *Sturm Regiment 195* retook Promklevo. The paratroopers were not involved in this attack. After the fighting of 4 until 6 March, Rifle Regiment 685 was virtually annihilated as Lieutenant Polubotkov confirmed in his prisoner interrogation. He was an officer

---

75 BA-MA, RH 26-78/59 in BW 57-82: daily report of *78. Sturm-Divison* of 5 March 1943.

in the machine-gun company of the 2nd battalion of Rifle Regiment 685 and was captured at Aleshenka on 6 March.[76]

The other units of *Fallschirmjäger Regiment 1*, which had been transferred from *LV. Armee Korps*, were now also in Dmitrovsk – even if only for a short time (for its deployment during these days, see below).

Barely arrived, *Fallschirmjäger Regiment 1* was alerted on 7 March and assigned to the section of *12. Panzer Division*, the left neighbour of *78. Sturm Division*, as a crisis was imminent there. However, as the situation was quickly saved with the support of *Sturm Regiment 14* and *Artillerie Abteilung 178*, Schulenburg was halted in Lubyanki during the movement and ordered back to Dmitrovsk, and back to *78. Sturm Division*. The rest of the regiment remained in Lubyanki as a corps reserve, but was primarily at the disposal of *78. Sturm Division*. For the paratroopers 7 March was otherwise a rather quiet day.[77]

Hauptfeldwebel Wagner must have been physically and mentally exhausted as he wrote only a very short letter to his wife, not mentioning the fighting in detail but remarked: 'It is good for all of you that you do not have to see all this. Even watching it would make some people sick.'[78]

The Defence of Hill 266.0 (8 to 10 March 1943)

By closing the gap between *XXXXVI.* and *XXXXVII. Panzer Korps*, the attempt to surround the German defensive positions around Dmitrovsk by General Batov's 65th Army was thwarted. The arrival of the remaining parts of *78. Sturm Division* sufficiently reinforced the section. An assembly of more Soviet divisions of the Central Front in front of the corps was observed. The 65th Army was now reinforced by the slowly arriving 70th Army, which was inserted to its right, the village of Trofimovka being the left section boundary belonging to the 70th Army. Both armies were ordered to push north. Bryanzovo, Trofimovka and Malo-Bobrovo especially were constantly reinforced. However, there was no real waiting for a concentration of troops, but rather the units attacked piecemeal as soon as they arrived.[79] On 8 March the following Soviet formations were positioned in front of *78. Sturm Division* from west to east: opposite *Sturm Regiment 195* was still the 193rd Rifle Division, then slightly to the east opposite *Sturm Regiment 215* was the 149th Rifle Division (65th Army). Adjacent, from Trofimovka onwards, from west to east, lay the 102nd (NKVD) Rifle Division, the 140th and 175th Rifle Divisions, all of which belonged to the 70th Army. The 102nd was partly in front of *Sturm Regiment 14* and the rest in front of *12. Panzer Division*.[80] The soldiers of 70th Army were well trained and highly motivated but lacked combat experience. They mostly came from former NKVD units, mainly used for policing, border protection and overseeing prison and labour camps.

---

76 NARA, T-315 R-1101: *78. Sturm Division*, KTB Attachments, Prisoner interrogations 1 March–24 June 1943; prisoner interrogation No. 21.
77 BA-MA, RH 26-78/52 in BW 57-82.
78 Archive Franz: Wagner, letter dated 8 March 1943.
79 Glantz, *After Stalingrad*, p.342.
80 Glantz, *After Stalingrad*, p.343; NARA, T-315 R-110: *78. Sturm Division*, KTB, *Tätigkeitsberichte Ic* 1 November 1942–20 April 1943: *Feindnachrichtenblatt* of *78. Sturm-Division* dated 16 March 1943. In a sketch of enemy positions of 7 March 1943 mistakenly 246th RD was thought to have been in front of *Sturm Regiment 14*, on 8 March even additionally 120th RD and rightly the 102nd (NKWD) Rifle Division.

The afternoon of 8 March saw a series of Soviet attacks on key points of *78. Sturm Division*'s front.[81] Mainly they were directed at Hills 266.0 and 262.3, which had already been attacked several times. These attacks were carried out from Trofimovka by the 102nd Rifle Division; Hill 266.0 changed hands several times. Both hills were in the sector of *Sturm Regiment 14* which was commanded by *Oberst* Ernst Kaether.[82]

The positions of *Sturm Regiment 14* were on high ground about 30 to 40 metres above and north of the Nessa valley. From Hill 266.0 Trofimovka, at about 220 metres high, lay little more than a kilometre southeast and from Hill 262.3 about the same distance to the southwest. During the night it was possible for the Soviets to get closer to the positions in the hills through some shallow ravines which could not be easily observed in the darkness by the Germans who were in positions covering each other behind the ridge of the hill.

At about 3:00 p.m., two companies of the 102nd Rifle Division attacked Hill 266.0 and at the same time another company attacked Hill 262.3. The latter attack stopped 500 metres short of the main line of defence of *Sturm Regiment 14*, but the former came close to the regiment's own positions, where more and more Soviet forces from Trofimovka arrived as reinforcements. Finally, at 5:00 p.m., the situation became so serious that *Oberst* Kaether requested *I. Bataillon/Fallschirmjäger Regiment 1* to be moved forward to Moshki, a village behind Hill 266.0. His wish was granted. As tanks were also observed in the vicinity of Trofimovka, an additional tank company was requested by the division.[83]

At 6:10 p.m. *General* Zorn rejected the additional deployment of *III. Bataillon/Fallschirmjäger Regiment 1* to this area, as he felt that his last reserve might be needed elsewhere. A mortar company of *Schweres Granatwerfer Bataillon 5 (mot.)* was also sent to Moshki, as an increased need for artillery support was expected to help repel the intensifying attack. *Luftwaffe* air reconnaissance confirmed the infantry's observation reports: Soviet forces were advancing towards the division's left wing.[84] Zorn also promised that *III. Abteilung/Panzer Regiment 21* would arrive in Moshki in the early morning hours.[85]

The situation at Hill 266.0 had become highly critical at 6:20 p.m. as the defensive line of *Sturm Regiment 14* was only thinly manned. Kaether was now authorised to bring forward *2. Kompanie* of the paratroopers as support to Hill 266.0 and to hold back the rest of the battalion as a counter-attack reserve.[86] But the paratroopers were not on site yet. They had been alerted after 5:00 p.m. and left Dmitrovsk, where they were billeted, to Moshki at about 7:00 p.m.

Although the pressure on Hill 266.0 had eased at about 8:00 p.m. an imminent threat remained. The Soviet soldiers were just 50 metres in front of the German positions directly on the main line of defence, which plainly indicated that a continuation of the attack could be expected in a matter of minutes. The paratroopers arrived at the command post of *Sturm Regiment 14* at 9:00 p.m. At 10:00 p.m. *Oberleutnant* Renisch's *2. Kompanie*, together with the battalion commander *Major* Graf von

---

81   For Rokossovsky's attack orders see Glantz, *After Stalingrad*, pp.338–342.
82   Ernst Kaether (Aachen, 25 September 1903–Puchheim, 11 August 1999), *Oberst*; RK 10 December 1942. He commanded the regiment from June 1942 until August 1943, after which he was transferred to OKH. In April 1945 Kaether was briefly commander of the defence area Berlin and fell into Soviet captivity to be released in 1955.
83   BA-MA, RH 26-78/52 in BW 57-82.
84   BA-MA, RH 26-78/52 in BW 57-82.
85   BA-MA, RH 26-78/59 in BW 57-82.
86   BA-MA, RH 26-78/52 in BW 57-82.

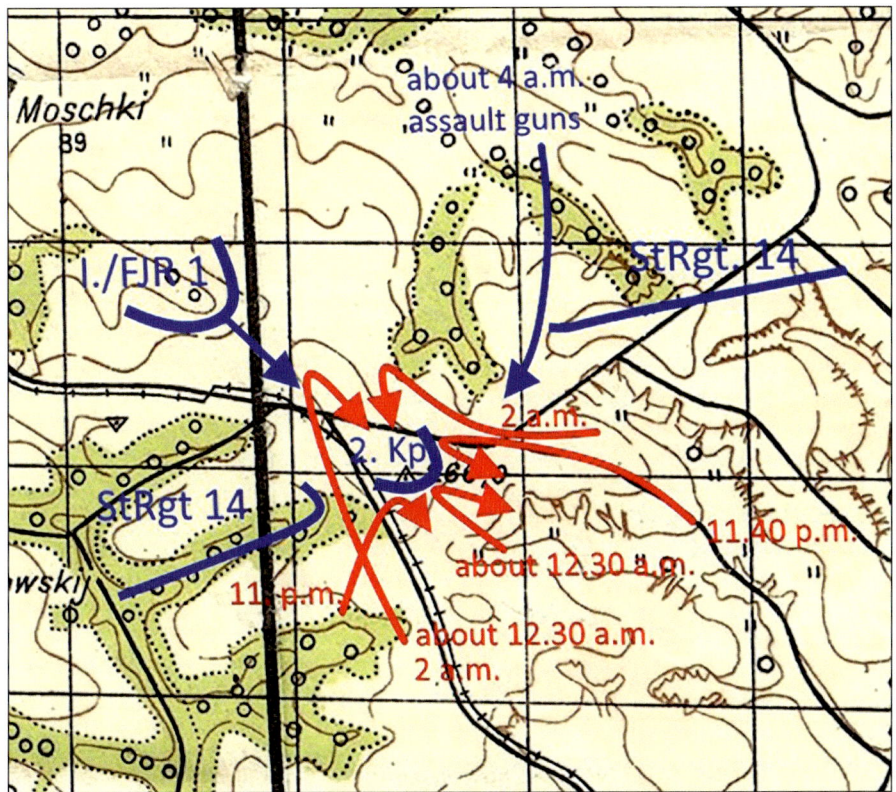

The defence of Hill 266.0 by *2. Kompanie* during the night of 8 to 9 March 1943.

der Schulenburg, had arrived at Hill 266.0 and had been assigned to their positions. The rest of the battalion took up a blocking position south of Moshki.

It did not take long before the first of many attacks that night on the paratroopers' shallow positions in the snow was launched at around 11:00 p.m. It was brought to a halt south of the heights. Again, two Soviet companies formed up and attacked the hill from the east. Thus, until the early morning hours attack after attack hit the paratroopers of *2. Kompanie* and the remnants of three companies of *Sturm Regiment 14* defending this section.

Gefreiter von Zimburg, who participated in the defence of Hill 266.0 described the events:

> The relief [of the infantry] was not quite finished on the right wing when heavy machine gun fire started from both sides. At first, we thought the infantry were firing their remaining ammunition, but found out that the Russians were attacking our right wing. They were shouting and screaming like a bunch of lunatics. After twenty minutes the attack died down and the clamour of voices moved forward to the middle of the heights and from there came closer again. When the Russians were closest, our machine guns started firing like mad. Again, the Russians failed to capture even one snow hollow or snow castle. The shouting died down and then came again from the left, where they broke through the infantry and tried to surround us. *Oberfeldwebel* Hoffmeister used the two heavy machine guns in such a way that the Russians were thwarted in

this attempt. This attack also subsided. In the meantime, there was a severe shortage of ammunition. It was radioed back that we urgently needed ammunition, otherwise we would not be able to hold our position. The Russians attacked again from the front and from the right. This time they succeeded in penetrating the infantry positions on our right and firing at us from the rear. Again, *Oberfeldwebel* Hoffmeister's heavy machine guns fired into the night in such a way that the Russians had to retreat.

But the company was now surrounded. An artillery observer who was with 2. *Kompanie* directed the [artillery] fire [most probably of *Schweres Granatwerferbataillon 5*] very accurately and to our advantage. During a small lull in the fighting, two sledges loaded with ammunition were able to break through to us. When I was not running messages to the individual machine guns, I helped to recover the wounded and dead, who were immediately brought back by the sledges.

Unfortunately, two friends of mine were hit: During the first attack, *Obergefreiter* Hörenberg received a kidney shot. He died during the transport to the dressing station. During the attack from the right, *Gefreiter* Wiedl was wounded by a shot to the stomach and had to be transported back to the field hospital.

After a short lull in the fire, the Russians broke through again, first on the left and then on the right, so that we were completely cut off. (2 a.m.). The Russians fired with weapons unknown to us so far (spade mortars), whose 3.7 cm calibre projectiles burst like spray. So, a continuous firefight raged until dawn. When daylight came, the Russians retreated to their assault positions, as they were too exposed to our fire. For us it was like target practice on the firing range.

At 4:15 a.m. tanks appeared on the hill to the north-east of us. At first, we thought they were Russians, but then to our greatest relief we realised that they were our own assault guns [of *Sturmgeschützabteilung 178*], rolling up the Russian lines from the side. When they reached us, everyone who was still alive and in one piece stood up, and with cheers they went after the Russians who were trying to escape. Machine gunners shot at the Russians from the hip. Only a few of them managed to retreat into the forest. Only now were we able to determine the numbers of Russians who had attacked during the night. At least 600 dead [most probably of Rifle Regiment 6 of 102nd Rifle Division] lay around Hill 266. During the night attack our artillery, thanks to the good observer, had fired so accurately that the shells hit right into the middle of the attacking Russians with corrections of fifteen and twenty metres. This artillery observer was in one of our machine gun positions.[87]

The positions of 2. *Kompanie* on Hill 266.0 in the early morning of 9 March 1943. The dramatic events of the night are underlined by the bodies of the fallen Soviet soldiers right in front of the position. (Private Collection)

---

87 Zimburg, *Erinnerungen*, pp.98–100.

Paratroopers in front of the positions of *2. Kompanie* surrounded by fallen Soviet soldiers on Hill 266.0 in the early morning of 9 March 1943. The tanks of *Sturmgeschützabteilung 178* and a destroyed Soviet tank can be seen in the background. (Private Collection)

In a blocking position behind *2. Kompanie*, *3. Kompanie* also had work to do, for at least one Soviet unit of undetermined strength that had broken through the defensive line was destroyed by *Feldwebel* Schmidt in the course of a counterattack carried out on his own initiative.[88] In addition, *2.* and *3. Kompanie*, but also the self-propelled anti-tank gun platoon of *Leutnant* Brammer and parts of *13. Kompanie*, were all involved in close combat fighting that night. At 8:00 a.m. the main line of defence was once again in German hands.

The toughness of this night battle in front of the section of *Sturm Regiment 14* and the paratrooper company located there is reflected in the counted losses of the attacking Soviet formations of 2,200 dead and 389 prisoners. The losses of *2. Kompanie*, which was already weakened after the attack on Kriuki, were 12 killed and 18 wounded, three of whom went to hospital due to severe frostbite. *3. Kompanie* also lost two killed and five wounded. With the loss of one man each in *13.* and *1. Kompanie*, the total number of casualties added up to 39 men. The fact that this number was not higher and that the hill could be successfully defended was only possible due to the effective German artillery support fire and the almost complete lack of it on the Soviet side.

Rokossovsy blamed Major General Tarasov,[89] the commander of 70th Army for not having done enough to ensure availability of artillery.[90] Tarasov had already previously proved his military failings and had been relieved of command of the 41st Army, which was unsuccessful in operation MARS against Model's *9. Armee* (see above). Apart from the failures of Tarasov, there were few roads on which the artillery of the Central Front could be brought forward in time. Its movements were additionally hampered by the weather conditions, fuel shortages and frequent *Luftwaffe* aerial attacks.

The command post of *1. Kompanie* was underneath this knocked out T-34. (Private Collection)

---

88 Thomas/Wegmann, *Ritterkreuzträger – Fallschirmjäger*, p.268.
89 German Fiodorovich Tarasov (29 March 1906–19 October 1944), Major General. He lost his command again after the failure of this offensive.
90 Glantz, *After Stalingrad*, p.384.

Paratroopers of *1. Kompanie* in their positions around Dmitrovsk. (Private Collection)

Oberleutnant Mössinger with an *Oberjäger* in front of the command post of *1. Kompanie*. (Private Collection)

Oberleutnant Mössinger in the early hours of the morning, exhausted from the previous night's fighting. (Private Collection)

Recognition for this German defensive success followed promptly, *General* Zorn expressed his special thanks to the division and the paratroopers by arranging the following announcement in the *Wehrmacht* report:

> Due to the toughness and defensive readiness of an assault regiment under the leadership of the Knight's Cross holder *Oberst* Kaether in the formation of a Baden-Württemberg division, the mass attacks of four Soviet elite divisions failed after nine hours of fierce night fighting and in the counterattack with one paratrooper battalion and one tank unit, 2,200 enemy casualties were counted; 389 prisoners remained in own hands. Over 200 automatic weapons were captured; the numbers of prisoners and booty are still rising.[91]

On the evening of 9 March, *2. Kompanie* was pulled out of its positions and moved to Dmitrovsk, where the paratroopers were able to rest until 13 March. The rest of the battalion remained in Moshki.

As early as 10 March, Völkers' order to his *78. Sturm Division* mentioned that Schulenburg's battalion should be reunited with its regiment as soon as possible. Two companies of the regiment were therefore to move without delay to the left divisional boundary and support *Sturm Regiment 14*. Beyond the divisional boundary, *Fallschirmjäger Regiment 1* was attached to *12. Panzer Division*. During the day of 13 March, *2.* and *3. Kompanie* arrived at Somovsky. The latter relieved two companies of *Panzer Pionier Bataillon 32* on the right wing of *Fallschirmjäger Regiment 1* on that day, while the former relieved a company of *Sturm Regiment 14* on the left wing of *78. Sturm Division* on the following day, the 14th.

Those parts of *14. Kompanie*, which were attached to the battalion, and *4. Kompanie* seem to have remained in Moshki, because on 15 and 16 March wounded from these companies are recorded there.

---

91 BA-MA, BW 57-82: Telex of XXXXVI. PzK to *78. Sturm-Division* dated 9 March 1943, 10:30 p.m.

Left: A *Feldwebel* or *Oberjäger* with the initials HH (possibly Hans Homberg of *9. Kompanie*) and a paratrooper called Schöpp, both from *III. Bataillon* are transported back to the dressing station to Kusminka with minor wounds or frostbite. (Private Collection)

Right: *Gefreiter* Josef Sailer and *Gefreiter* Heinz Peter Pedvaidic of *2. Kompanie* in front of the dressing station at Somovsky. Neither of them survived the war: Sailer was killed in action on 11 September 1943 at Castellaneta and Pedvaidic on 11 February 1944 at Cassino. (Private Collection)

Above: *Major* von der Schulenburg awards the Iron Cross 2nd Class to *Oberjäger* Seewig of *2. Kompanie*. In the background is a 'Finnzelt' (Finnish tent), a prefabricated plywood hut used as a command post by *Oberleutnant* Renisch. From left: *Oberleutnant* Renisch, *Major* Graf von der Schulenburg, unknown, *Oberjäger* Seewig, *Gefreiter* Fischer. (Private Collection)

Left: *Oberjäger* Adolf Kunert, leader of the company staff squad of *2. Kompanie* in front of the dressing station at Somovsky. He was later killed in action in Italy, between Rimini and Cesenatico, on 24 September 1944. (Private Collection)

Another photo of the award ceremony on 16 March 1943 at the command post of *2. Kompanie*. From left: *Oberleutnant* Renisch, *Oberjäger* Seewig, *Gefreiter* Fischer, *Major* Graf von der Schulenburg, *Gefreiter* von Zimburg, *Obergefreiter* Schneider, unknown. (Private Collection)

Major Koller-Kraus,[92] the First General Staff Officer (Ia) of *78. Sturm Division* took stock of the period from 28 February to 15 March of the hard fighting that had taken place under difficult conditions on 16 March. The front could be stabilised and consolidated by counterattacks; the mission was fulfilled. The number of Soviet casualties of approximately 5,500 mentioned in this report is very high, while the losses suffered by the Germans amounted to 310 killed and 76 missing, plus 682 wounded and 141 cases of frostbite.[93] Weather conditions had started to change as Spring slowly made itself felt. During the day temperatures started to rise, and it started to thaw, while at night freezing temperatures prevailed. As a result, the soldiers got wet during the day and had to take care not to get frostbite during the night.

---

92 Heinz-Michael Koller-Kraus (27 May 1909–22 April 1993), *Oberst*; DKiG 4 February 1943. He was later a brigadier general of the German *Bundeswehr*.
93 NARA, T-315 R-1100: Report about the deployment of the *78. Sturm Division* between 27 February and 15 March 1943, dated 16.3.1943.

I. Bataillon was gradually reassigned to *Fallschirmjäger Regiment 1* until 17 March. Only *2. Kompanie* remained subordinated to *Sturm Regiment 14* until 22 March, while other individual units, probably of *4.* and *14. Kompanie*, did not leave the section of *78. Sturm Division* until 24 March.[94]

Everything became more organised. Renisch's command post was in a prefabricated makeshift hut – a so-called Finnish tent.

> These huts were produced in plywood factories; they were constructed in such a way that they could be easily transported and erected. They consisted of a circular floor plate with a diameter of five metres; a 120 cm high plywood wall was placed around the edge; a stove was placed in the middle and plywood panels were used as a roof. In the middle came a stove and on top were plywood panels as a roof.[95]

---

94 BA-MA, RH 26-78/52 in BW 57-82: Daily report of *78. Sturm Division* of 24 March 1943.
95 Zimburg, *Kriegserinnerungen*, p.108.

22

Fallschirmjäger Regiment 1 in the sections of *12. Panzer* and *216. Infanterie Division*

The Soviet Situation (Bryansk and Central Front)

By 6 March, the offensive of General Reyter's Bryansk Front was considered a failure. The forward movements of the 48th and 13th Armies came to a standstill, the soldiers were exhausted, demoralised and weakened from almost three months of continuous fighting. The German *LV.* and *XXXV. Armee Korps* managed to stabilise the defensive line and prevent a breakthrough towards Orel, supported by reinforcements such as *Fallschirmjäger Regiment 1*.

Rokossovsky's Central Front, operating to the south and south-west, appeared to be more successful at this point, advancing far to the west with its 2nd Tank Army, thus widening the gap between the German *2. Armee* and *2. Panzer Armee* to a depth of 140 kilometres and a width of 100 kilometres. However, the northward push of Central Front's 65th and 70th Army was stopped at Dmitrovsk by *78. Sturm Division* and *12. Panzer Division* – both subordinate to Zorn's *XXXXVI. Panzer Korps* – and by *XXXXVII. Panzer Korps* with the help of the last reserves; the still weak *45. Infanterie Division* and *72. Infanterie Division*. West of Batov's 65th Army, Rodin's 2nd Tank Army was to take the Lokot area but encountered severe logistical problems.[1] Rodin's efforts were also thwarted by *2. Armee*, which managed to push back the far advanced Soviet units, slowly pushing the front back to the east. Without reinforcements, neither Front was able to make much progress before the onset of the mud season.[2]

At this point, Manstein's success in the south at Kharkov, which fell into German hands on 14 March, made itself increasingly felt. The Stavka's strategic reserves of four armies were not fed to the Central Front as planned but were instead redirected to the south as of 28 February. Nevertheless, the offensives against Schmidt's *2. Panzer Armee* continued. Rokossovsky was only allowed to bring in the 21st Army as reinforcement, which was en route from Stalingrad. He had it gathered in the area of Fatezh, in order to be able to deploy them with their concentrated force. Lead elements arrived there on 5 March, with the rest only arriving slowly.[3]

---

1 See Nebolsin, *Stalin's Favorite*, vol.1, pp.45–65.
2 Glantz, *After Stalingrad*, pp.318–319.
3 Glantz, *After Stalingrad*, p.320.

A 5 cm Pak 38 anti-tank gun of *12. Panzer Division* near Trossna. (Private Collection)

The armies of the Central Front were now focussing on their objective – Orel. Batov's 65th Army was to take Dmitrovsk and attack further towards Kromy and Orel.[4] Tarasov's 70th Army, in cooperation with the 13th and 48th Army of Reyter's Bryansk Front, was now to smash the German front between Trossna and Malo-Arkhangelsk.[5] Rokossovsky ordered on 8 March that the 70th Army continue its offensive in the direction of Orel on the next day in the morning. The left border of the army was at Trofimovka, and its righthand neighbour was the 13th Army at Chern. These attacks also came to a halt, not least because the 21st Army, which was supposed to attack north through the lines of the 13th Army on 10 March, was not yet ready for action due to transport delays. In the end this army could not be deployed in this sector at all but was to stem the German advance on the southern side of the now forming Kursk bulge.[6]

On 10 March the following units of the 70th Army were facing the Germans in the Dmitrovsk sector: 102nd, 140th, 175th and 106th Rifle Divisions, with the 182nd and 162nd Rifle Divisions and the 19th Tank Corps behind them.[7]

Due to these failed attempts to break through towards Dmitrovsk and Kromy, the Stavka decided on 11 March to disband the Bryansk Front as of 12 March, with the 3rd, 13th and 48th Armies now being part of the Central Front.[8] This regrouping gave the paratroopers a few relatively quiet days.

Rokossovsky also had to deal with increasing pressure from the German *2. Armee* from the south and southwest, but nevertheless he urged Tarasov to continue his efforts to break through *12. Panzer Division*'s front towards Orel.

---

4 Glantz, *After Stalingrad*, pp.340–342.
5 Glantz, *After Stalingrad*, pp.339–340.
6 Glantz, *After Stalingrad*, pp.339–340.
7 Glantz, *After Stalingrad*, p.344.
8 Glantz, *After Stalingrad*, p.354.

Fallschirmjäger Regiment 1 at **Dmitrovsk-Orlovsky**

In order to support the German forces in the Dmitrovsk sector, *Oberstleutnant* Schulz's *Fallschirmjäger Regiment 1* was detached from *LV. Armee Korps* on 4 March 1943 and assigned to *General* Zorn's *XXXXVI. Panzer Korps* as a reserve. It was to be reunited with Schulenburg's battalion and deployed on the west wing of the corps in such a way that *78. Sturm Division* could be concentrated in a smaller area for a planned attack.[9] The regiment was initially attached to this division. To speak of a regiment, however, is misleading. At the outset *Fallschirmjäger Regiment 1* consisted only of its staff, parts of *13.* and *14. Kompanie*, parts of *I./Flak Regiment 501*, the two platoons of Brammer's and Pusch's 7.5 cm self-propelled anti-tank guns, and the remnants of *III. Bataillon* – altogether about 650 men. Gröschke's *II. Bataillon*, which had been badly mauled during the failed attack on Alekseyevka had remained at Stolbetskoye in the command area of *LV. Armee Korps* while *I. Bataillon* was still attached to *78. Sturm Division* and thus had no formal direct link with its own regiment.

The order to release the regiment arrived at *LV. Armee Korps* at around 10:30 a.m. on 3 March. However, the transport had to be organised by the receiving *XXXXVI. Panzer Korps*. This caused delays because means of transport first had to be found and sent to Smiyevka. As a result, the regiment did not report to the Volobuyevo area until 5 March.[10] On the 6th it finally reached Dmitrovsk, where Schulenburg and his staff were also located at the time. Barely arrived, the regiment was alerted by order of *XXXXVI. Panzer Korps* at 3:20 a.m. on 7 March,[11] because the Soviet 70th Army had succeeded in breaking three kilometres deep into the front of *12. Panzer Division* north of Chern.

The panzer division was under the command of *Generalmajor* Wessel until 27 February,[12] when *Oberst* Erpo Freiherr von Bodenhausen took over.[13] The division consisted mainly of *Panzer Regiment 5* (*Oberst* von Müller),[14] *Panzer Gernadier Regiment 25* (*Oberst* Lemke), *Panzer Regiment 29* (*Oberst* von Heimendahl), *Panzer Regiment 2* (*Oberst* Decker), *Kradschützen Bataillon 22* (*Hauptmann* Noeske),[15] *Panzerjäger Abteilung 2* (*Major* Lutterbeck) and *Panzer Pionier Bataillon 32* (*Hauptmann* Marufke).[16] Prior to this deployment the division had been resting in the area north of Nevel where it had almost been restored to target strength. For example, *Kradschützen Bataillon 22* had a strength of 951 men (14 officers, 170 NCOs and 767 men).[17] However, the level of training of the fresh recruits sent from Germany left a lot to be desired. Von Bodenhausen would have liked to have had three more weeks

---

9   NARA, T-313 R-172: PzAOK 2 KTB Ia, Attachments vol.50: Radio message of Ia of PzAOK 2 to LV. AK and XXXXVI. Pz.K. on 3 March 1943, 10:35 a.m.
10   BA-MA, RH 21-2/452: daily report of XXXXVI. PzK 5 March 1943.
11   BA-MA, RH 26-78/59 in BW 57-82: conversation Ia XXXXVI.PzK. with Ia 78. Sturm-Div.
12   Walter Wessel (Weßel) (Lautental, 21 April 1892–Morano, Italy (car accident), 20 July 1943), *Generalleutnant*; RK 15 August 1940, Oak Leaves 17 February 1942.
13   Erpo Freiherr von Bodenhausen (Castle Arnstein, Witzenhausen, 12 April 1897–Grobin, suicide, 9 May 1945); *Generalleutnant*, RK 17 December 1943; DKiG 31 Jauary 1942. He commanded the division until April 1945 and took over command of L. AK in the Kurland cauldron. To escape Soviet captivity, he committed suicide.
14   Dietrich von Müller (Malchow, 16 September 1891–Hamburg, 3 January 1961), *Generalleutnant*; RK 3 May 1942, Oak Leaves 16 August 1943), Swords 20 February 1945; DKiG 21 February 1942. Von Müller was taken prisoner of war by Czech partisans and handed over to the Red Army, he was released in 1955.
15   Hubertus Noeske, *Oberstleutnant*; DKiG 20 July 1943.
16   Joachim Marufke (Meseritz, 10 January 1913–?), *Major* (1 July 1943), was commanding the engineer battalion from January until 31 December 1943.
17   Gerd Niepold, *12. Panzerdivision (2.Inv.Div.) Pommern 1921–1945* (Koblenz: private print, 1988), p.65.

General Zorn briefs *Oberstleutnant* Schulz and *Hauptmann* Becker on the situation upon arrival of the regiment (left to right): Schulz, Becker, Zorn, unknown. (Private Collection)

for training, which was not possible due to the dire situation in the south. The division had been set in motion in the direction of Orel only shortly after Schulz' paratroopers left Smolensk. Alerted on 13 February, leaving Nevel on 14 February and arriving after four days of travel, the division – subordinated to *XXXXVI. Panzer Korps* – had to hold off attacks of Pukhov's 13th Army, which had broken through in the south and was now turning north. The division succeeded in reaching the line Uspenskiy-Khalseyeva-Solotnoye Dno-north of Chern in hard fighting until 27 February – days of combat which inflicted severe losses. The fighting continued and the division had to be supported by various other reserve units, including *Fallschirmjäger Regiment 1*.

On 6 March, attacks by the 70th Army took place in front of the entire 26.5 kilometre wide divisional section starting from 11:00 p.m. Only a few hours later, at 3:20 a.m. on 7 March, the order had already been given to *Fallschirmjäger Regiment 1* to move to Lubyanki. *Oberstleutnant* Schulz was to go ahead eastward to the command post of *12. Panzer Division* at Topkovo.[18]

At 4:30 a.m., a platoon of self-propelled anti-tank guns of *Fallschirmjäger Regiment 1* was ordered directly by *XXXXVI. Panzer Korps* to Sergeyevka.[19] At 7:50 a.m., the guns were brought forward to Topkovo. At around 10:00 a.m. it was still planned to have the regiment attack in the direction of Nezhivka, if this should still be necessary.

---

18 BA-MA, RH 26-78/52 and RH 26-78/59 in BW 57-82.
19 BA-MA, BW 57-82: Telephone conversation Ia of XXXXVI. PzK with platoon leader of self-propelled anti-tank gun platoon of FJR 1.

It was not until 10:45 a.m. that Schulenburg's battalion, as the last unit of the regiment, left Dmitrovsk for Lubyanki. But in the meantime, *12. Panzer Division* managed to clear the situation on its own and closed the breach thereby trapping the Soviet units in a cauldron.

Since *I. Bataillon* was therefore no longer needed by *12. Panzer Division*, Schulenburg was immediately ordered back to the section of *78. Sturm Division*. However, the regiment itself, *III. Bataillon* together with the regimental staff, remained in Lubyanki for the time being. On that 7 March, moving troops on the roads between Lubyanki, Dmitrovsk and Aleshenka proved difficult and time consuming because of snowdrifts and a worsening weather situation in the afternoon, culminating in a heavy snowstorm. Therefore *I. Bataillon* arrived back at Dmitrovsk only around 5:00 a.m. on 8 March. The battalion did not participate in the successful attack of the division to close the remaining gap to the *XXXXVII. Panzer Korps*.

As the situation was under control on the evening of the 8th, all parts of the regiment within the command area of *XXXXVI. Panzer Korps* were again directly subordinated to it, whereby *Generalleutnant* Völkers had the prerogative to call up this reserve, but also had to provide for its rations. The regiment (without *I.* and *II. Bataillon*) had assembled in Lubyanki as a corps reserve, the platoon of self-propelled anti-tank guns was assembling there as well.

Around midnight of the night from 8 to 9 March, strong Soviet attacks again hit the section of *78. Sturm Division* and the right wing of *12. Panzer Division*. The 102nd Rifle Division managed to penetrate the front of *12. Panzer Division* at Khalseyeva and Uspenskiy. One push succeeded even in reaching a point beyond the village of Muravchik. To intercept this advance unit, Becker's *III. Bataillon* was requested by *12. Panzer Division* to move to Ignateyeva, a few kilometres northwest of Muravchik. At 9:30 a.m. two anti-tank guns of *Panzer Regiment 5* were ordered to the right wing of the same place to seal off the area together with a platoon of *III. Bataillon*. At 11:00 a.m. the regiment was placed under command of *12. Panzer Division*, whereby *Hauptmann* Becker received the order to deploy his battalion between *Panzer Pionier Bataillon 32* and *Kradschützenbataillon 22* at Uspenskiy and while moving forward to clear the forest northwest of the village of enemy soldiers.[20] Forward elements of the Soviet push had even reached Mai, a village two kilometres north of Uspenskiy.

This deployment seemed essential to *Oberst* von Bodenhausen, as his forces had been severely depleted during the previous days' fighting and there was a danger that this section could no longer be held.

A counterattack by *Kradschützenbataillon 22* was successful: The battalion was able to reoccupy the old positions in the morning hours and retake Uspenskiy. Becker's advance established a safe connection between Uspenskiy and *Panzer Pionier Bataillon 32* in the early afternoon.[21] On this occasion, Becker also briefly took command over the latter as well as over the self-propelled anti-tank gun platoon of *Leutnant* Brammer, who had only two operational guns.[22] Due to the lack of records, it is not possible to follow exactly the actions of the battalion, but at least *9.* and *10. Kompanie* were involved in the advance on Uspenskiy as these companies suffered two killed and five wounded. One of the latter was *Leutnant* Adelsheimer,[23] a platoon leader in *10. Kompanie*. At least parts of the *11.*

---

20   NARA, T-315 R-633: 12. PzDiv., KTB No. 4, entry 9 March 1943.
21   BA-MA, RH 27-12/37 in BW 57-82 and NARA, T-315 R-633: 12. PzDiv., KTB No. 4, attachments vol.2: Daily report of 12. PzDiv to XXXXVI. Pz.Korps, 9 March 1943.
22   Brammer, 'Kriegstagebuch', p.110.
23   Ludwig Adelsheimer, (Häslach, 17 April 1919–KIA Villa San Nicola near Ortona, 9 January 1944), *Oberleutnant*; DKiG 16 January 1944 (post mortem).

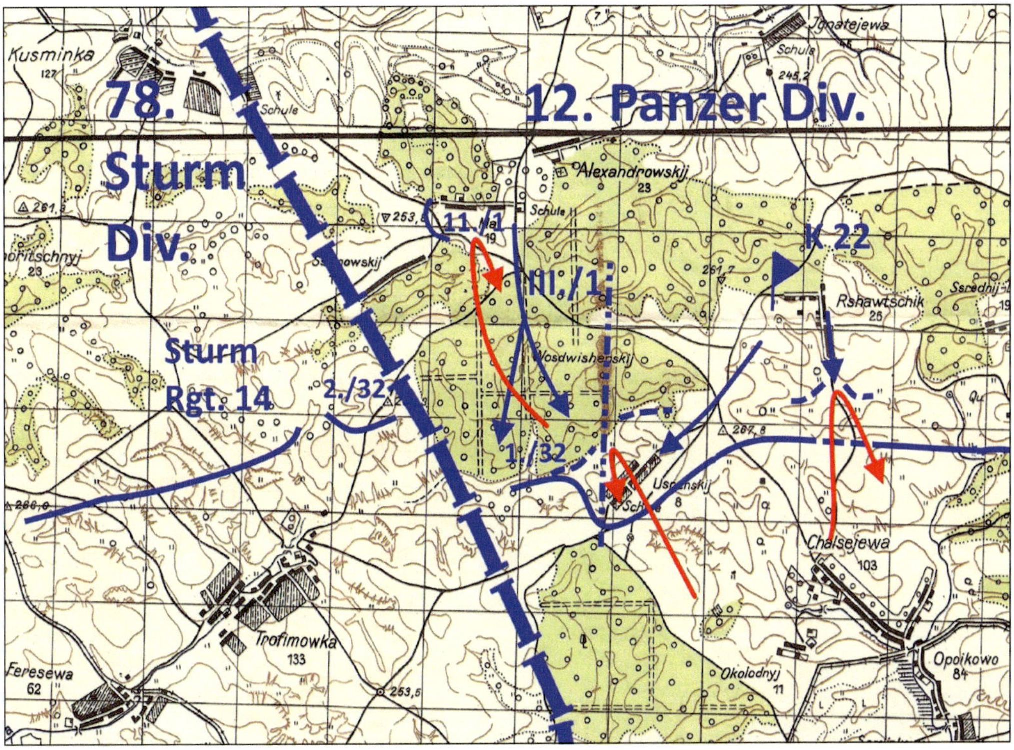

III. Bataillon's push towards Uspenskiy on 9 March 1943.

Leutnant Ludwig Adelsheimer was wounded at Uspenskiy on 9 March 1943. Later promoted to *Oberleutnant*, he was killed in action at Villa San Nicola near Ortona on 9 January 1944. For his bravery he was awarded the German Cross in Gold posthumously on 16 January 1944. (Collection Stephan Janzyk)

The self-propelled anti-tank gun 'Max' and its crew in its position waiting for the next mission. (Private Collection)

A depression behind the front is used to safely bring in supplies by sledge. (Private Collection)

Kompanie were in reserve at Mai, where they seem to have fought with scattered Soviet soldiers, as the casualty list shows one dead and three wounded.

The following deed by *Obergefreiter* Fritz Arndt of *Panzer Pionier Bataillon 32* gives an idea of how dramatic the situation must have been in the forest north of Uspenskiy.[24] Arndt, after all his group of comrades defending the position had fallen, defended it alone with his machine gun. In a mad fight for survival, in which he captured enemy weapons which he immediately put to use, he succeeded in taking out two Soviet heavy machine guns with a crew of eight, and killing and wounding a further nine opponents. 'By this act, he enabled a paratrooper company to proceed through the forest near Mai.'[25] Arndt was not only awarded the Iron Cross 1st Class on 10 March, but also the Knight's Cross on 31 March 1943 for this action, a rare distinction for an ordinary soldier (he later even received the Oak Leaves).

---

24 Fritz Arndt (Zehdenick, 1 June 1910–Mildenberg, 12 March 2003), *Oberfeldwebel*; RK 31 March 1943, Oak Leaves 9 December 1944 (678).
25 NARA, T-315 R-633: 12. PzDiv, KTB No. 4, Attachments 2, 1 February–20 March 1943: Daily report 12. PzDiv. to XXXXVI. PzK, dated 10 March 1943.

On the evening of the same day, at about 7:45 p.m., *XXXXVI. Panzer Korps* sent a telex to *78. Sturm Division*, *12. Panzer Division* and *Fallschirmjäger Regiment 1*, placing the paratroopers entirely under the command of von Bodenhausen. Now the first parts of Schulenburg's battalion were reassigned to the regimental section. On 11 March, at about 10:30 p.m., *Oberleutnant* Otto's *3. Kompanie* relieved *1.* and *2. Kompanie* of *Panzer Pionier Bataillon 32* and was now subordinated to *III. Bataillon*. The battalion itself was under command of *Gruppe Heimendahl* (staff of *Panzer Regiment 29*), the heavy weapons belonging to *78. Sturm Division* were to stay in the sector for the time being.[26]

The lull in fighting made further reorganisations possible. The regiment now took command of its own defence section from *Gruppe Heimendahl* on 12 March at 6:00 p.m.:

> Boundary to the right (at the same time divisional boundary to *78. Sturm Division*) was the line of middle of Bychki School-about 400 m west of Hill 262.3 past-Kharlanovo;
> Boundary to the left to *Kradschützenbataillon 22* ('*Gruppe v. Müller*') was Uspenskiy, which belonged to *Fallschirmjäger-Regiment 1*.

At this point Schulenburg's battalion was still not completely in the section of the regiment. It was intended, after arrival of these parts, to extend the section of the regiment eastwards to the road Rzhavchik-Khalseyeva, which never happened.

On 12 March Schulz reported the combatant strength of his regiment that can be found in the table below.[27]

Combatant strength FJR 1 (without I. and II. Bat.) on 12 March 1943

Unit	Officers	NCOs	Men	Total
Staff (incl. engineer and bicycle platoon)	10	31	125	166
III. Bataillon	8	74	156	238
13. Kompanie	2	18	85	105
14. Kompanie	1	5	22	28
4./Fallsch.Fla.MG Abt. '*Pakzug Wagner*'	1	8	20	29
1./Fallsch.Pz.Jg. Abt. (platoon Brammer)	1	3	11	15
4./Fallsch.Pz.Jg.Abt. (platoon Pusch)		3	7	10
I./Flak-Rgt. 501	4	11	71	86
3. Kompanie	1	22	46	69
4. Kompanie (one platoon)		3	12	15
Total	28	178	555	761

Significant are the low numbers of *III. Bataillon* with a total of only 238 men. The strength of *I. Bataillon* was not reported but must have been at about the same strength, if not weaker.[28] In terms

---

26   NARA, T-315 R-633: 12. PzDiv, KTB No. 4, Attachments 2, 1 February–20 March 1943: Radio message of 12. PzDiv to PzRgt 29, PzRgt 5 and FJR 1 on 11 March 1943, 7:00 p.m.
27   NARA, T-315 R-633: 12. PzDiv, KTB No. 4, Attachments 2, 1 February–20 March 1943: combatant strength of 12. PzDiv on 12 March 1943.
28   On the 17th the strength of these two battalions was reported as average. NARA, T-315 R-633: 12. PzDiv, KTB No. 4, Attachments 2, 1 February–20 March 1943: combatant strength of 12. PzDiv of 17 March 1943.

of heavy weapons Schulz reported four of the regiment's own 5 cm anti-tank guns and six of the regiment's own 7.5 cm self-propelled anti-tank guns (Brammer's and Pusch's platoons), as well as four 2 cm anti-aircraft guns and three 8.8 cm guns at his disposal. Schulz also tried to bring Gröschke's battalion back to his regiment, with *Panzerarmee Oberkommando 2* (PzAOK 2) expressing its support to *Flieger-Division 7* (but ultimately achieving nothing of the sort).[29]

During the night of the 12th to the 13th, the paratroopers repelled an attack of a Soviet reconnaissance in force. Otherwise, things remained relatively quiet in front of this section. However, there were increasing signs that something might happen soon. One could hear that, for example, vodka was being distributed in Kucheryayevka, reconnaissance patrols were trying to scout the German positions, and prisoner testimonies also supported this assumption.

On 15 March von Bodenhausen issued orders for 17 March, wherein a company of Schulenburg's battalion was supposed to relieve the last remaining company of *Panzer Pionier Bataillon 32*. The staff of the battalion was also to be deployed in the regimental sector. The new boundary between *Fallschirmjäger Regiment 1* and *Gruppe von Müller* (*Kradschützenbataillon 22*) was Hill 267.8. The intention to extend the section of the regiment to the east to the road Rzhavchik-Khalseyeva after bringing in another company of *I. Bataillon* remained.[30]

The anti-tank gun resources of the regiment changed on 16 March compared to the report of four days before: four 5 cm guns, five self-propelled 7.5 cm guns (one less), and two 7.5 cm guns (from *4. Kompanie/Sturm Reg. 14*).[31] Where the rest of the regiment's guns were, is not clear. The next evening parts of *I./Flak Regiment 501* with two 8.8 cm guns and nine 2 cm guns were to arrive.

Around Uspenskiy, something happened almost every day, including on the 16th in the late afternoon, when a Soviet reconnaissance in force of about 50 men was repulsed. There were again increasing signs of a larger attack the next day including loud singing of apparently drunk Soviet soldiers, which was usually a strong indicator.

The Defence Against the Major Soviet Attack of 17 March 1943

The expected Soviet attack of the 70th Army hit *12. Panzer Division* with full force in the early hours of 17 March. Five rifle divisions were attacking from west to east: the remnants of 102nd, 140th, 175th, 106th, 162nd.

Oberstleutnant Schulz's after-action report titled 'Repulse of repeated enemy attacks in front of the regimental section and capture of Sredniy Log and Muravchik'[32] dated 20 March, provides detailed information on the paratroopers' combat that took place from 17 to 18 March.

The first half of the night of 16 to 17 March was initially quiet. When, at 1:30 a.m., the sound of tanks and logging – apparently trees were being felled to clear the way for the tanks – could be heard at Hill 258.4, it was clear that an attack was imminent. What followed was an almost classic preparation: from 3:00 a.m. on, the positions of the regiment were hit with sporadic mortar (60 rounds) and

---

29   NARA, T-313 R-172, PzAOK 2, KTB Nr. 3 Attachments vol.50 'Right Flank' 14 February–15 March 1943.
30   BA-MA, RH 27-12/37 and NARA, T-315 R-633, 12. PzDiv, KTB No. 4, Attachments 2, 1 February–20 March 1943: Radio message of 12. PzDiv to FJR 1, PzPiBtl 32, PzGrRgt 5 on 15 March 1943, 2:15 p.m.
31   NARA, T-315 R-633, 12. PzDiv, KTB No. 4, Attachments 2, 1 February–20 March 1943: Anti-tank gun situation report of 12.PzDiv to XXXXVI. Pz.K, 16 March 1943.
32   BA-MA, RH27-12/37 in BW 57-82.

anti-tank gun (30 shells) fire, which suddenly intensified at 6:00 a.m. Within half an hour, about 400 anti-tank and 250 mortar rounds hit the ground. This was accompanied by intensified machine gun and rifle fire. The telephone connection from *Oberstleutnant* Schulz's command post in Alexandrovskiy to Becker's was disrupted and the latter could not be reached for a while.

The regiment readied itself for battle, the reserves – the engineer platoon, bicycle platoon (together 53 men), company staff squad and II platoon of *14. Kompanie* – were alerted. At 6:40 a.m. a forward observer of *I. Batterie/Panzer Artillerie Regiment 2* reported enemy gathering and preparing themselves for an attack in a depression northwest of Khalseyeva.[33]

At the same time, Becker reported by radio – the telephone connection was not yet re-established – an attack from Uspenskiy or from the wooded area at Hill 258.4 with a strength of about 350 men. His battalion had now a strength of slightly more than 344 men (including 84 men of *3.* and parts of *4. Kompanie*) and had to defend a strip of about four kilometres. Ten minutes later Schulz again received an uncoded message from Becker that since 6:45 a.m. another attack, albeit a weaker one, of 60 men was underway from the direction of a hollow northeast of Trofimovka on the positions of *3. Kompanie*. Around 8:00 a.m., the all-clear was given from this sector for the time being, as the attacks were not determined and were repelled. However, it was observed that further enemy forces were approaching from the direction of Trofimovka.

The situation was completely different at the left-hand neighbours further to the east: At around 7:00 a.m., the attackers managed to break through the positions of *II. Bataillon/Panzer Grenadier Regiment 5* with a company and two tanks. Between the positions of the paratroopers and the breach were the positions of *Kradschützenbataillon 22*, which was subordinated to *Panzer Grenadier Regiment 5 (Gruppe von Müller)*. At the same time, the village of Muravchik was under heavy Soviet fire. Individual tanks were sighted at Hill 260.2 and at the top of the forest at Hill 258.4. There was now a wide-ranging incursion of a width of about 10 kilometres into the front of *12. Panzer Division*. Schulz's paratroopers were involved in securing the right or western edge of this incursion, thus contributing strongly that the front did not crumble, and the attack could be stopped.

Schulz could now see that a hard day of fighting lay ahead and Mössinger's *1. Kompanie*, which was still in reserve in Dmitrovsk, was alerted. Mössinger was supposed to form the regimental reserve, but only had 40 men left to fight. Pusch's platoon with three 7.5 cm self-propelled anti-tank guns, was also alerted and had to get ready for action. It was located at the regimental command post in Alexandrovskiy as an intervention reserve.

Muravchik and the left wing of *Kradschützenbataillon 22* were attacked in regimental strength. This village together with the village of Sredniy Log, is believed to have fallen at around 9:00 a.m. Counterattacks by *Gruppe von Müller* were unsuccessful and a dive bomber attack on Muravchik was requested by von Bodenhausen.

At the same time, the positions of *III. Bataillon* were attacked by eight tanks and 250 accompanying infantry while under heavy mortar and anti-tank gun fire; *9. Kompanie* reported two tanks in front of its positions.

To fight against the incursion on the left, which was apparently to be extended northwards by the enemy, von Bodenhausen gave Schulz the order to attack the hamlet of Sredniy Log via Rzhavchik with all available reserves at 9:20 a.m. and to throw the enemy back again. At the same time, *Kradschützenbataillon 22* was subordinated to the regiment. A task force of the division (*II. Bataillon/Panzergrenadier Regiment 25, Gruppe Jähde*) was to support the attack from the east in order to close

---

33 Today Khalsevo.

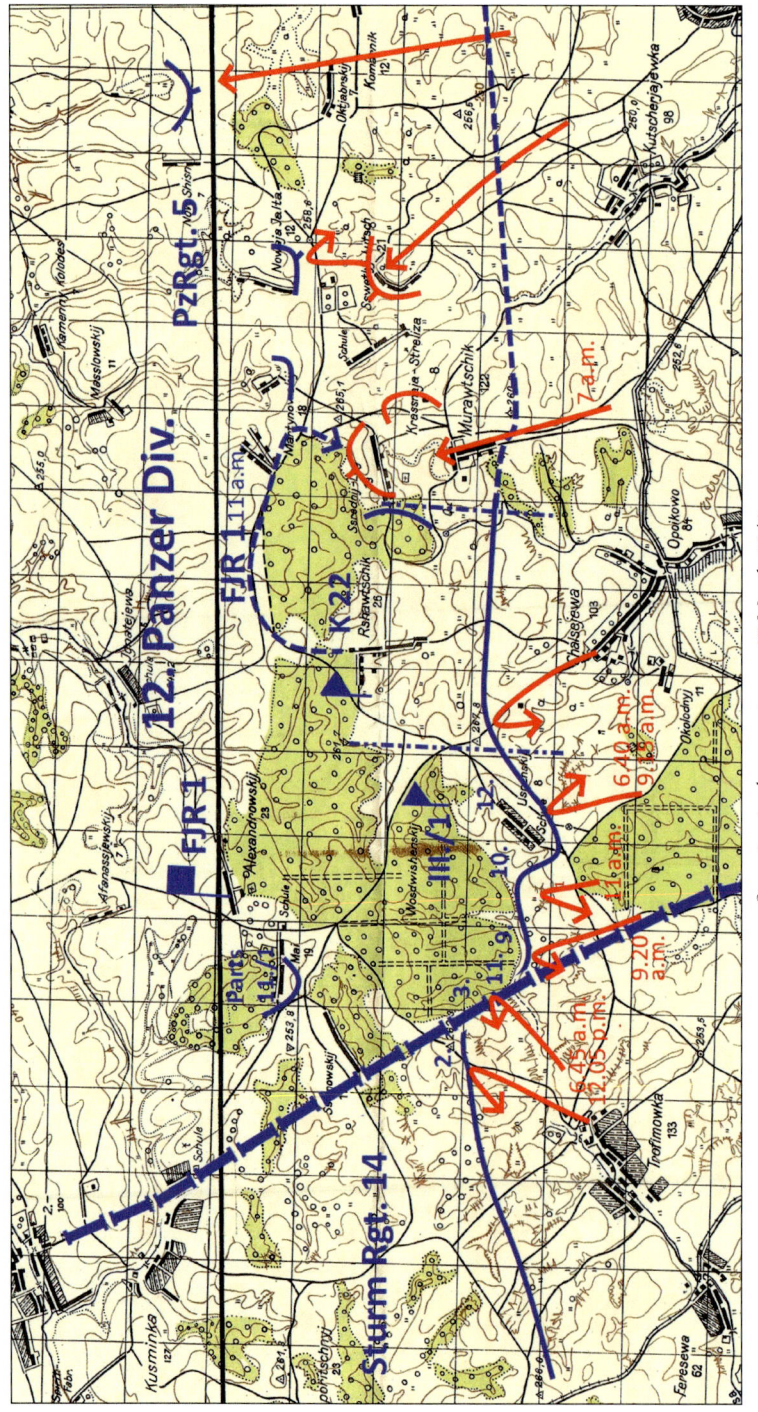

Situation in the morning on 17 March 1943.

Platoon Brammer getting their self-propelled anti-tank guns ready for attack. (Private Collection)

the gap, as well as to seal it off to the south. Schulz decided to lead this counterattack personally. The reserves he had at his disposal for this task were: the regimental engineer platoon, a group from the regimental bicycle platoon, company staff squad and II platoon of *14. Kompanie* (*Oberleutnant* von Oppen), the latter meeting the attack group at Rzhavchik at 11:10 a.m. Schulz had thus a total of two officers and 55 men, plus the guns of *Oberfeldwebel* Pusch at his disposal. In addition, he ordered the heavy machine gun platoon of *4. Kompanie*, which was with *III. Bataillon*, to Rzhavchik.

At 9:30 a.m., Becker reported over the restored telephone line that the Soviet infantry attack supported by eight tanks (four T-34s and four KV-1s) was beaten off. One T-34 was knocked out by *Leutnant* Brammer's gun. However, the attack was resumed, with Brammer hitting and disabling another four tanks by 10:22 a.m. A sixth Soviet tank hit a mine and was also destroyed. Six tanks, three T-34s and three KV-1s were burning in front of *III. Bataillon*, the remaining two tanks preferred to call off the attack and withdrew. Shortly afterwards, a gun of Brammer's platoon knocked itself out due to a burst barrel. Additionally, one man of Brammers platoon got killed and two were wounded by Soviet anti-tank gun fire.

Schulz left his command post at Alexandrovskiy at 10:00 a.m. with *Oberfeldwebel* Pusch's guns. The other men at his disposal, the company staff and II platoon of *14. Kompanie* (*Oberleutnant* von Oppen) and a group of the regimental bicycle platoon with a total of 31 men (one officer, six NCOs and 24 men) immediately followed. Arriving from the nearby hamlet of May, the engineer platoon (1 officer, 27 men) joined the attack group.

While preparations for the next Soviet attack were being observed in front of *III. Bataillon* at 10:45 a.m. and heavy weapons were being brought into position by the enemy, Schulz arrived in Rzhavchik with the bulk of his forces. Here he met the commander of *Kradschützenbataillon 22*, *Hauptmann* Noeske, who briefed him on the situation. Due to the enemy incursion, the latter had to withdraw his left wing to protect his flank to the east. He was no longer in contact with *II. Bataillon/Panzer Grenadier Regiment 5*, his neighbour on the left. After only 10 minutes, Schulz sent out a reconnaissance patrol to the eastern edge of the forest near Sredniy Log and on to Martinovsky to reconnoitre the situation. At the same time, the regimental medical officer, Dr Eiben,[34] arrived in Rzhavchik to organise

---

34 Dr Adolf Eiben (26 September 1903–4 February 1991), *Oberfeldarzt*; DKiG 22 July 1943.

medical care and the transport of the expected wounded. He was a very respected medical doctor who participated in the attack on Crete and was awarded the German Cross in Gold for his bravery after this mission in Russia. He later became doctor of *1. Fallschirmjäger Division* and of *I. Fallschirm Korps* in Italy and was promoted to *Oberfeldarzt* (lieutenant colonel) the highest possible rank for a medical doctor of the reserve. After the war he became a respected medical doctor in Aurich.[35]

The first objective of Schulz's counterattack was Sredniy Log, so he gave the order:

> The attack group of *Fallschirmjäger Regiment 1* gains Hill 265.1 via Martinovsky and attacks Sredniy Log from there [Schulz had to choose this way as the more direct way from Rzhavchik to Sredniy Log through the woods was impassable for the self-propelled guns of Pusch]. The left wing of the *Kradschützenbataillon* [22] will stand by on the eastern edge of the woods to the east of Rzh[avchik] and join the attack of the northern group as soon as it recognises from the noise of the battle that its attack will be effective. Liaison by white flares and by radio. After the capture of Sredniy Log, the *Kradschützenbataillon* shields to the south to hold off the enemy counterattack. Continuation of the attack will then be ordered.[36]

The regimental surgeon *Stabsarzt* Dr Adolf Eiben in 1943. (Private Collection)

During this time requested dive-bomber attacks were also carried out in several waves on Sredniy Log and Muravchik. Soviet fighter squadrons were also in the air, so that a fight with *Luftwaffe* fighter pilots ensued.

Schulz subordinated himself two more tanks equipped with machine guns and a 2 cm cannon and was with his attack group in Martinovsky at 11:10 a.m. At the same time, it was observed that further Soviets reinforcements of about 600 men were on their way towards Muravchik.

Meanwhile further to the west, Becker counted 100 dead attackers in front of the positions of *III. Bataillon*, which had to repel another attack by 200 Red Army soldiers.

Schulz reached a wooded area south of Martinovsky, where he encountered a scattered leaderless group of about 100 men of *Panzer Grenadier Regiment 5*. The soldiers, 'who made an indecisive and frightened impression',[37] were members of *6.* and *7. Kompanie* of this regiment, who had arrived at the front as replacements only the day before and for the most part had no combat experience at all.

---

35 Anon., 'Abschied von Dr. Eiben' in DDF (1991), vol.2, p.26.
36 BA-MA, RH 27-12/37 in BW 57-82: After-action report of *Oberstleutnant* Schulz.
37 BA-MA, RH 27-12/37 in BW 57-82: After-action report of *Oberstleutnant* Schulz.

Schulz also took command of these men and used the remnants of *6. Kompanie*, led by an NCO called Oremek, to cover the attack from Hill 265.1, which had to be held at all costs. A welcome reinforcement appeared in the form of four *Panzer IV lg* of *Panzer Regiment 29* under command of *Leutnant* Laubach, which Schulz gratefully incorporated into his attack force.[38]

This tank group was originally held in reserve at Krasnaya Strelitsa, a village to the south-east of Sredniy Log, were it defended the village together with units of *Panzer Grenadier Regiment 5* against the broken through Soviet units. In the process, four T-34s and two heavy anti-tank guns were knocked out. After the hamlet had to be abandoned due to enemy pressure, *Leutnant* Laubach retreated to the forest corner near Martinovsky.

Schulz now deployed two tanks to safeguard Hill 265.1, while one tank remained with the actual attack group. The last tank was unfortunately out of fuel and therefore not ready for action.

The commander of *II. Bataillon/Panzer Grenadier Regiment* 5, *Hauptmann* Mossmann, who had no further knowledge of the enemy situation, showed up, and tried to sort out the remnants of his battalion, which had been completely scattered by the Soviet attack. As soon as this was done, they were to join Schulz as reinforcements for the attack group as soon as possible.

Soviet reinforcements moving into Muravchik were constantly observed, for example, at 11:50 a.m. six tanks moved into the village, at 1:00 p.m. another five tanks with two guns attached and mounted infantry arrived.

The reconnaissance patrol sent out earlier reported back at 12 noon; the forest was free of enemies up to the eastern edge. A second patrol was to reconnoitre the enemy strength at Sredniy Log. Schulz used the waiting time well, put his attack group in order and created a combat group under command of *Oberleutnant* von Oppen consisting of II platoon of *14. Kompanie*, the company staff squad, the regimental engineer platoon and a group of the bicycle platoon.

Schulz's western flank was still covered as Becker reported at 12:05 p.m. that two Soviet companies were advancing through the hollow between *3.* and *11. Kompanie* but were repelled with machine gun and mortar fire. At 12:30 p.m., another battalion-sized attack was repulsed there. The rest of the afternoon remained quiet in this section.

Martinovsky was also the position of *2. Batterie/Panzer Artillerie Regiment 2*, from whose command post Schulz had contact with the division. He reported his attack plan from there at 12:30 p.m. and learned about the situation previously not known to him:

> … that the enemy had attacked on a broad front from Trofimovka, the forest at 258.4 Khalseyewa, Kucheryayevka, Gorki and Chern and had broken through the main line of defence of *Panzer Grenadier Regiment 5*. The newly formed main line of defence ran roughly along the supply route of *12. Panzer Division* from Zolotoye Dno via Hill 251.1 in the direction of Hill 267.3. West of the latter hill there was a gap through which the enemy had already advanced to Pokhvisnevo.[39]

Schulz's plan of attack, which was to begin at 1:15 p.m. and supposed to continue towards Muravchik, was approved by von Bodenhausen. *Major* Keibel, commander of the artillery in Martinovsky promised Schulz artillery support, which was easily possible as he had just got supplied with ammunition.

Shortly before the start of the attack, Schulz noticed that Hill 265.1, which was supposed to be occupied by *6. Kompanie* of *Panzer Grenadier Regiment 5* was deserted. The men were found leaderless

---

38 NARA, T-315 R-633, 12. PzDiv, KTB No. 4, Attachments 2, 1 February–20 March 1943.
39 BA-MA, RH 27-12/37 in BW 57-82: After-action report of *Oberstleutnant* Schulz.

north of it – the *Unteroffizier* Oremek had disappeared. They had retreated because seven Soviet tanks were said to have approached. It turned out that there were only two Soviet tanks, one of which was knocked out immediately. Schulz was very annoyed and also made the appropriate report to have *Unteroffizier* Oremek court-martialled. A *Leutnant* of the grenadier regiment took command of the group and reoccupied Hill 265.1.

The start of the attack was delayed. At 1:30 p.m., the commander of *Panzer Grenadier Regiment 5*, *Oberst* von Müller, arrived at Schulz's command post, who agreed with the attack plan as well as with the subordination of his battalion.

In the meantime, *Major* Graf von der Schulenburg, arrived at the regimental command post in Alexandrovskiy and was briefed on the situation by the regimental staff left behind. He had to form the regimental reserve with his battalion staff, *1. Kompanie* and the signals platoon. Schulenburg's group had previously been in reserve in Dmitrovsk with *78. Sturm Division*, but from now on it remained in the regiment's section with the units mentioned above. Only *2. Kompanie* and some groups of *4. Kompanie* remained with *78. Sturm Division*.

Finally, at 1:50 p.m. the heavy machine gun platoon of *4. Kompanie* under command of *Oberfeldwebel* Einhäupl arrived from Rzhavchik and was sent also to Hill 265.1 to support the attack.[40]

The attack on Sredniy Log began at 2:00 p.m.: three *Panzer IV lg*, one 2 cm gun tank and one machine gun tank (perhaps VK 18 and VK 16 – see below), three 7.5 cm self-propelled anti-tank guns and one heavy mortar (also self-propelled) together with von Oppen's company set out to march on Sredniy Log from their starting position immediately north and northwest of Hill 265.1. Arriving on the heights, the attackers received mortar, machine gun and rifle fire, but continued to advance under the covering fire of the German tanks, artillery (an observer of the artillery regiment accompanied the attack) and the heavy machine gun platoon, as Einhäupl had taken up position at 265.1. On the left wing, parts of the *6.* and *7. Kompanie/Panzer Grenadier Regiment 5* joined this attack and at the same time covered the open flank of the attack group to the left.

The paratroopers entered the burning village from the north and west (2:45 p.m.) together with the alarm company of *Kradschützenbataillon 22*, with which they had been in direct contact since 2:30 p.m. The Soviet soldiers were seen fleeing in the direction of Muravchik.[41]

This first attack, which lasted less than an hour, was a complete success, Sredniy Log being taken with only minor losses of four wounded. A T-34 was knocked out by one of the German tanks on the northern edge of Sredniy Log.[42] According to Schulz, this determined attack also resulted in the withdrawal of up to 2,000 Soviet soldiers from Muravchik, a number which seems somewhat exaggerated.

The following short pause in the fighting was used by Schulz to reorganise his own forces. *Kradschützenbataillon 22* moved up behind the retreating enemy and prepared for the attack on Muravchik. After a meeting of the attack group leaders, the continuation of the attack was set to begin at 4:20 p.m. The resistance in Muravchik was expected to be low.

After an artillery barrage the group was to attack from the jump off position south of Sredniy Log towards Muravchik. On the left the grenadiers together with tanks and self-propelled guns moved

---

40 Fritz Einhäupl (Altenburg, 28 June 1909-KIA, east of Maierhöfen near Wiesenfeld, Austria, 23 April 1945), *Leutnant*. He was killed in action as leader of the *8. Kompanie/Fallschirmjäger Regiment 30*.
41 BA-MA, RH 27-12/37 in BW 57-82: After-action report of *Oberstleutnant* Schulz; NARA, T-315 R-634, 12. PzDiv. KTB 4 Attachments 3: After-action report of *Kradschützenbataillon 22*, *Hauptmann* Noeske.
42 *Feldwebel* Nippraschk, of the tank group of *Leutnant* Laubach, PzRgt 29. NARA, T-315 R-633, 12. PzDiv. KTB 4, Attachments 2.

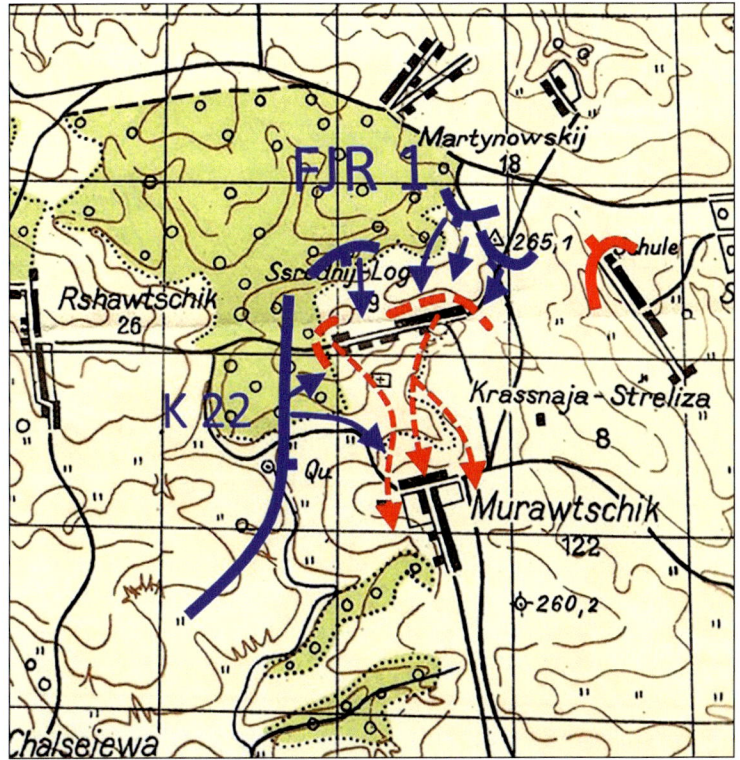

The attack on Sredniy Log on 17 March 1943.

Paratroopers mounted on a *Panzer IV*. (Private Collection)

forward, in the middle von Oppen with his men and on the right units of the *Kradschützenbataillon 22*. Covering fire was given by the heavy machine guns of Einhäupl from a hill southeast of Sredniy Log.

> 4:20 p.m. start of attack: Initially unseen by the enemy, *Kompanie* von Oppen works its way towards Muravchik in hollow terrain. The village and the snow positions on the adjacent ridges are under friendly artillery and heavy machine gun fire. Since this fire is placed very close to their own right wing, the *Kradschützen* do not advance any further at first. At the same time as the tanks and self-propelled anti-tank guns, the *Panzer Grenadiere* advance on the left wing.
>
> At 5 p.m. von Oppen's company is the first to win the outskirts of Muravchik and, after clearing the northern part, advances further south, taking the Russians fleeing in the direction of Khalseyeva under effective fire. Shortly afterwards, the grenadiers attacking on the left wing also reached the village and the ridge east of it. The tanks accompanying the attack destroyed another T-34 which tried to escape to the southwest in the hollow southeast of the village.
>
> The *Kradschützen* on the right wing pushed past the western edge of the village at about the same time; the supply-train company Hotzel which followed behind the paratroopers throws the enemy out of the small wood southwest of Muravchik and retakes the position (main line of defence) of the 6. *Kompanie/Pz.Gren.Rgt. 5*. The 4. *Kp./Kradschützenbtl. 22*, advancing on the right of it in the hollow of the stream, has reached and occupied its old position again at 5 p.m.[43]

At 5:10 p.m. the counterattack was successfully completed, and the old main line of defence was occupied again. Schulz gave orders to secure this line and to defend against possible new Soviet attacks. It remained quiet, however, and Schulz was able to return to his command post in Alexandrovskiy. Individual units of the paratroopers, under the leadership of *Oberleutnant* von Oppen, remained behind at Muravchik to provide cover.

German losses in these two attacks were light. The paratroopers had only six wounded – two of whom later succumbed to their wounds – the *Kradschützenbataillon 22* lost one dead and 15 wounded. Specific losses of *Panzer Grenadier Regiment 5* are not known but should also have been small. The estimated number of Soviet soldiers killed, at least 300, shows that the attack was not a walk in the park. Nine prisoners were taken, and three tanks were destroyed.

By comparison, the engagements of *III. Bataillon*, described only in passing in Schulz's detailed report, were much harder if one compares the figures. Here 440 enemy dead were counted in front of the positions and six tanks were destroyed; their own casualties were 12 killed and 42 wounded.

Not only *III. Bataillon* but also parts of *I. Bataillon* were directly involved in the defensive battles of 17 March 1943. *Oberleutnant* Otto's *3. Kompanie* was assigned to *III. Bataillon* and was positioned between it and *2. Kompanie*, which was adjacent on the right. During the day's fighting, the company suffered losses of two killed and seven wounded.[44] It is not known exactly where the other parts of *13.* and *14. Kompanie* and of *4. Kompanie* were deployed. Based on the location information in the casualty lists, the latter was probably still in Moshki (three wounded), while *13. Kompanie* was mainly in the sector of *III. Bataillon*. Some elements of these companies were also still attached to *78. Sturm Division*.

---

43 BA-MA, RH 27-12/37 in BW 57-82: After-action report of *Oberstleutnant* Schulz.
44 NARA, T-315 R-633, 12. PzDiv. KTB 4, Attachments 2, p.381 and Attachments 5, maps and sketches.

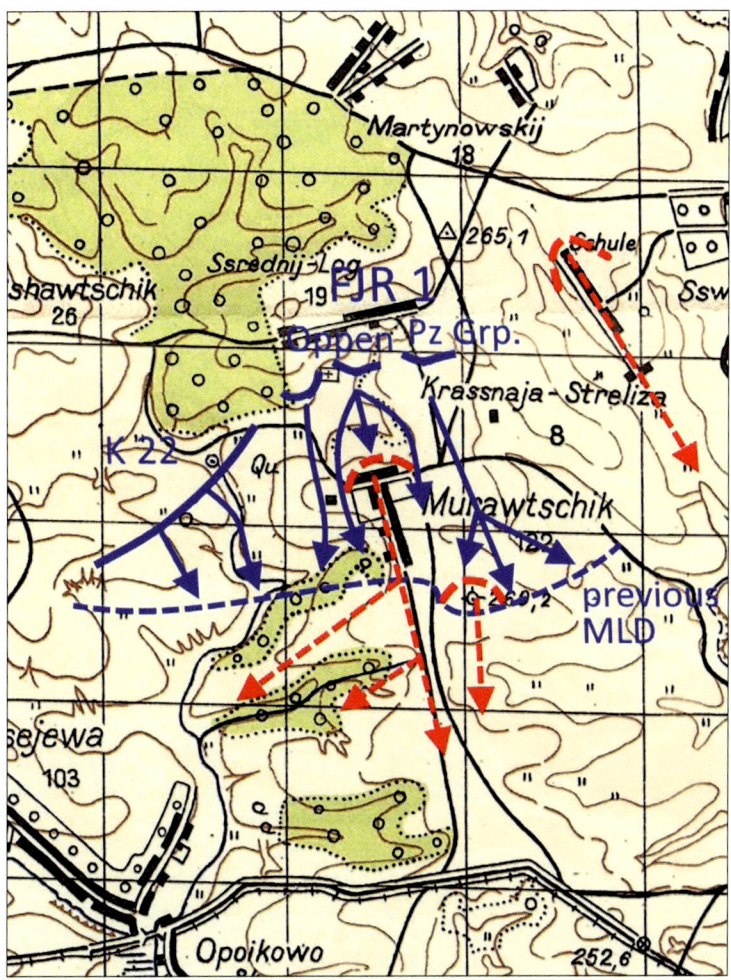

The attack on Muravchik on 17 March 1943.

Oberleutnant Renisch's *2. Kompanie* was still stationed in the sector of *Sturm Regiment 14*, directly on the divisional boundary to *12. Panzer Division*, with its neighbour *3. Kompanie/Fallschirmjäger Regiment 1*. The company was located around Hill 262.3, which was in the same attack direction of the Soviet units as *III. Bataillon* and it also had to endure a hard defensive fight with quite a few casualties – two dead and four wounded. The main dressing station of *2.* and *3. Kompanie* was at Somovskiy.

The company was released from the command of *Sturm Regiment 14* on 23 March. This was done by simply shifting the divisional boundary line to the west, the company remained in its positions at Hill 262.3.

On 17 and 20 March the combatant strengths of some the individual companies can be found in the table below.[45]

---

45 NARA, T-315 R-633, 12. PzDiv. KTB 4, Attachments 2, report of combatant strength and Attachments 5, maps

Combatant strength FJR 1(without I. and II. Bat.) on 17 and 20 March 1943

Unit	Officers	NCOs	Men	Total
Staff (incl. engineer, bicycle platoon) (20 March)				155
3. Kompanie (incl. a grenade launcher group of 4. Kompanie)	1	25	58	84
9. Kompanie	1	19	30	50
10. Kompanie	2	12	30	44
11. Kompanie		18	37	55
12. Kompanie	2	10	41	53
13. Kompanie (20 March)				83
14. Kompanie (20 March)				76
1./Fallsch.Pz.Jg. Abt. (20 March)				10
4./Fallsch.Pz.Jg.Abt. (20 March)				13
I./Flak-Rgt. 501(20 March)				84
4./Fallsch.Fla.MG Abt. '*Pakzug* Wagner' (20 March)				29
Total				736

Kradschützenbataillon 22 remained under command of *Fallschirmjäger Regiment 1* for the time being. On the same day, parts of I./501 with their 8.8 cm guns arrived in Kromy and were reassigned to the regiment during the night.

The intensity of the defensive battles of Zorn's *XXXXVI. Panzer Korps* on 17 March 1943 is evidenced by the casualty figures of *12. Panzer Division* alone: 114 dead (5/20/89), 298 wounded (7/42/249) and 206 missing (3/23/180), a total of 618. It is not clear whether these figures include or exclude the casualties of the paratroopers mentioned above.[46] In terms of Soviet losses, the Ic of the division initially estimated 1,120 dead, later raising this to 2,155 and adding 106 prisoners and six defectors. For the 18th, 690 dead, 20 prisoners and five defectors were added, later corrected to 1,140 dead, 101 prisoners and four defectors. On both days a total of 41 Soviet tanks were destroyed in front of the division.[47]

On the 18th, the regiment did not have to face any major battles, but there were nevertheless dead and wounded again at Uspenskiy: *Leutnant* Wenderoth of *13. Kompanie* was seriously wounded and died the next day,[48] another soldier of the company was wounded and one of *9. Kompanie* was killed. At Muravchik, *14. Kompanie* and the engineer platoon each had one dead, *4. Kompanie* one dead and five wounded. The exact location of the units of *4. Kompanie* cannot be determined exactly as in the casualty lists Rzhavchik is noted as place of death for the fallen and the two wounded, for the others it is 'near Dmitrovsk'.

On this day, 18 March, *12. Panzer Division* managed to clear the incursions into its front and establish a defensive line which was nearly the one before the Soviet attacks, despite several counterattacks from the Soviets. The division had only 35 of its own tanks available on a front width of 35 kilometres. On the 17th and the 18th of March alone, 35 Soviet tanks were destroyed, five of them by artillery.[49]

---

and sketches.
46 Niepold, *12. Panzer-Division*, p.68.
47 NARA, T-315 R-634, 12. PzDiv. KTB 4, Department Ic, Attachments 2 to Activity Report 4, pp.66, 75: Radio message Ic 12. PzDiv. to XXXXVI. PzK. Dated 19 March 1943, 3:30 p.m.
48 Karl-Heinz Wenderoth (Oberscheden, 5 August 1916–Main Dressing Station, Lubyanki, 19 March 1943), *Leutnant*.
49 Niepold, *12. Panzerdivision*, p.68.

Hauptfeldwebel Wagner of *3. Kompanie* was so busy at the time that he even forgot his wedding anniversary. He apologised to his wife in a letter and enjoyed the first signs of spring:

> Yes, darling, spring is coming with giant steps here too, the sun is already shining quite warmly, but the cold and snow still doesn't want to go away. Now I would so like to go on holiday and spend the beautiful spring days outside with you and the boy. Spring brings new courage and strength here too. I don't know yet when our relief will come. Hopefully quite soon. I'd still like to think that we'll be coming to Germany soon.[50]

Final Engagements

Further attacks to reach the old main line of defence in the centre and left section of the division were planned for 19 March but had to be postponed until the 20th. Schulz's regiment was not directly involved. At 11:00 a.m. on the 20th, however, a Soviet counterattack on Muravchik took place. There was still a combat group of paratroopers under the command of *Oberleutnant* von Oppen in the village, which was subordinated to *Panzergrenadier Regiment 5*. Six Soviet tanks attacked Muravchik from Hill 256.6 after an artillery barrage and were able to break through. However, the Soviet infantry attack following the tanks could be repulsed with the help of *Kampfgruppe von Oppen*. The tanks that penetrated the line of defence were destroyed by the self-propelled guns of the paratroopers. Two more Soviet attacks followed at 1:30 p.m. and 4:30 p.m. The first one could be beaten off by parts of *Panzergrenadier Regiment 5* probably together with *Kampfgruppe von Oppen*. However, the Red Army, most probably the 175th Rifle Division, kept the pressure on Muravchik. At 5:20 p.m. *12. Panzer Division* reported: 'No more reserves.' The defence against this attack was now assigned to *Oberstleutnant* Schulz. For this purpose, the deployment of the last reserves of *Kradschützenbataillon 22*, *Gruppe Hotzel*, and parts of the *Panzerspähkompanie* was also ordered.

Schulz reacted immediately. At 6:00 p.m. he put *Gruppe von Oppen* and *6.* and *7. Kompanie* of *Panzergrenadier Regiment 5*, which had been stationed at Muravchik, under the command of *Kradschützenbataillon 22*. *Hauptmann* Noeske, as the officer closest to the events, was to clarify the situation. *Gruppe Hotzel*, with one officer, four NCOs and 39 men from the battalion's supply train, was set in motion towards Muravchik. Two tanks (a VK 18 and a VK 16) from the division's armoured reconnaissance company were also deployed. This is a remarkable and seldom documented use of these lightly armed reconnaissance tank prototypes, probably from *1. Kompanie/ Panzerabteilung z.b.V. 66*, which was attached to *Panzer Regiment 29* of *12. Panzer Division*. The *Versuchskampfwagen 18* (VK 18) was armed with two MG 34 machine guns and weighed 20 tonnes. It was a successor to the Panzer I, possibly an example of the version F, of which only 30 were produced. The *Versuchskampfwagen 16* was a Panzer II version J with a 5 cm gun and weighing 21.6 tonnes, of which the division received seven units and of which only a small number were produced.[51]

---

50 Archive Franz: Wagner, letter dated 18 March 1943.
51 <www.achtungpanzer.com/panzerkampfwagen-ii.htm#panzer2>, accessed 20 January 2018 and email of Ingo Apel, April 2021.

Hauptmann Noeske found the following situation in Muravchik:

II.[Bataillon]/[Panzer Grenadier Regiment] 5 has abandoned Hill 260.2. 6. *[Kompanie]*/5 has contact with 4./K. 22, which is still in the old positions until far south of Muravchik, then in front of the eastern edge of the village is 7./5. Both companies are interspersed with elements of the now fully deployed paratroopers. *Oberleutnant* von Oppen (14./FJR 1) has now taken command of the whole section. On the left there is a gap to the 5./5, which is in front of Krasnaya Strelitsa. Hill 260.2 is occupied by the enemy. In the bright moonlight entrenchment work could be clearly observed there. From 260.2 Muravchik could be dominated and the main line of defence could be flanked far into the section of K. 22, so that hill could not remain in enemy hands. In order to regain the heights during the night, the alarm platoon Hotzel with the two tanks was deployed. The commander [of K. 22] discussed with *Hauptmann* Mossmann, commander II./5, that the driver's platoon of II./5 would now also be brought forward to close the gap between 7. and 5./5.[52]

Hauptmann Noeske consulted with *Panzerartillerie Regiment 2*, which was to support the planned attack, and then reported to *Oberstleutnant* Schulz.

At 11:30 p.m., after a short artillery barrage, supported by the self-propelled anti-tank guns and two heavy machine guns of the paratroopers, Hotzel's platoon attacked and recaptured Hill 260.2. It was then reoccupied by *II. Bataillon/Panzer Grenadier Regiment 5*. Schulz observed the attack from Muravchik. During this attack, *Oberleutnant* von Oppen was killed by grenade shrapnel in the back in the early morning hours, probably around 1:00 a.m. on 21 March near Muravchik.[53] A doctor and friend of von Oppen's, probably *Stabsarzt* Dr Eiben, who arrived immediately but could do nothing to save his life, later wrote to von Oppen's widow: 'We always have to accept that brave men have to give up their lives in this war, but sometimes this dying touches us particularly hard. This is true of the death of *Hauptmann* [*Oberleutnant*] Robert von Oppen, who was taken from us in the first hour of the first day of spring.'[54] He was a popular officer with his men and the other officers of the regiment. In 1940, he volunteered for the paratroopers, but a knee injury prevented him from participating in the mission in Crete. In civilian life he was a lawyer and farmer and had married Jutta von Waldhausen shortly before the Russian campaign in 1942.

The paratroopers of *14.* and *4. Kompanie* and the engineer platoon in this section suffered losses of eight dead, including *Leutnant* Otto Weser of the engineer platoon, and 17 wounded between 20 and 21 March. *Oberleutnant* von Oppen was the regiment's last casualty to be killed in combat during the winter campaign in Russia.

Oberst von Bodenhausen, who had taken command of *12. Panzer Division* on 27 February, complained about his division's lack of fighting morale. The division had suffered heavy casualties during the winter in the Rzhev salient while repelling the Soviet operation MARS in the Bely area. The short period of rest, which was used to refresh the division with replacement troops, was not enough to properly train the newly arrived and inexperienced soldiers. Von Bodenhausen went on to say that

---

52 NARA, T-315 R-634, 12. PzDiv. KTB 4, Attachments 3: after action report of *Kradschützenbataillon 22* for 20 March 1943, dated 23 March 1943.
53 Ancestry/WASt: G-A 677/0134.
54 Message from the von Oppen family.

...only where the officer or senior non-commissioned officer has a direct influence on the troops can one speak of an attacking spirit. In other places, however, due to a lack of officers and non-commissioned officers, a complete failure has occurred in some cases, which has already led to the point that in some places the men could only be driven to attack or held in their positions by force of arms.[55]

Despite these criticisms, the division had managed to repel the strong Soviet attacks, largely because of the destruction of many tanks, effective artillery fire and – weather permitting – *Luftwaffe* support.

There were reasons why the Soviet side abandoned the villages of Muravchik and Sredniy Log without any significant resistance and fled: The Soviet attackers were demoralised. According to Anton Savisko – a defector from the 142nd Rifle Regiment – all the rifle regiments (RR 15, 126 and 142) were scattered in panic and routed after the attack at Muravchik had failed. He doubted that the remnants could still be motivated to any further attack.[56] The Soviet soldiers' rations were poor, so the mood was not good. In addition, they were poorly trained or had been forcibly recruited from the civilian population of the liberated areas only a short time before (eight to 14 days). The lack of fighting morale on the Soviet side was also confirmed by *Oberst* von Bodenhausen, who observed this behaviour throughout the front of his division, with the paratroopers only responsible for part of the defensive success:

The enemy's attacking force was broken and the situation turned to the Russian's disadvantage when the mass of the attacking tanks was finished off. The defence in depth of our own anti-tank defence proved its worth … The Russian infantry, even if it has broken through deeply with the help of the tanks, is no longer a difficult opponent once its tanks have been dealt with.[57]

The decisive contribution and higher combat value of Schulz's paratroopers is emphasised by the fact that of the 33 tanks destroyed on 17 March, six tanks were attributed to *Leutnant* Brammer's 'tractor' alone and that the breach on the left wing was sealed by Schulz's energetic counterattack with comparatively weak forces. The regiment was already badly weakened in numbers, but it consisted of well-trained and experienced soldiers, led by capable NCOs and officers.

The worn-out *12. Panzer Division* was relieved by *7. Infanterie Division* on 21 and 22 March. The paratroopers remained in position for the time being and were now subordinate to this division.

Gröschke's *II. Bataillon* during March 1943

After Schulz had left for Dmitrovsk with his staff units and Becker's battalion, Gröschke remained in the command area of *LV. Armee Korps* with his still considerably weakened *II. Bataillon*. It was attached to *Grenadier Regiment 396* on 4 March and remained in its positions near Stolbetskoye. The Soviet units in front of the battalion had dug in near Dubovy and were constantly harassing the

---

55 Niepold, *12. Panzerdivision*, p.69.
56 NARA, T-315 R-634, 12. PzDiv. KTB 4, Department Ic, Attachments 2 to Activity Report 4, p.55: prisoner statement 31 of Anton Savisko, machine gun company, II. Battalion/142 Rifle Regiment of the 'Ural Division' dated 18 March 1943.
57 Niepold, *12. Panzerdivision*, p.69.

The crew in front of their Marder II 'Max': *Obergefreite* Brenner, Oheim and Seitz at the end of their mission at Orel end of March 1943. (Private Collection)

paratroopers by shelling and anti-tank gun fire. *Obergefreiter* Heinkelein, who had received the Iron Cross 1st Class for his conduct at Alekseyevka, described the un-enviable situation of the paratroopers:

> After the end of our big attack, without a breather, we lay in the freezing cold and deep snow for over three weeks, in shallow snow holes in the open terrain, not even a few metres away from the Russians, with only a few men still able to fight … Daily attacks by the Russians and reconnaissance. We couldn't move or be seen during the day. We had to relieve ourselves lying down.[58]

There were no large-scale attacks by the Soviets until the end of March, but several paratroopers fell victim to artillery fire, smaller skirmishes, and almost daily assault and reconnaissance activities. From 4 March, when the remainder of the regiment had departed, the battalion suffered losses of five killed or succumbed to wounds sustained, and 13 wounded. The number of casualties due to illness or frostbite are not known.

On 16 March, *LV. Armee Korps* received the order that all parts of *Fallschirmjäger Regiment 1* still in the corps area were to be transferred to *XXXXVI. Panzer Korps*, but this was not carried out.

Position of a machine gun squad of 6. Kompanie near Stolbetskoye after the attack on Alexeyevka. (Private Collection)

---

58   Heinkelein, *Recollections*.

23

The Failed Offensive of the Central Front

After the Bryansk Front's offensive against *2. Panzer Armee* had run out of steam, it was up to Rokossovsky's Central Front to defeat it. But in the end, he also failed to reach his objective. The Soviet losses were horrendous: Glantz estimates 300,000 casualties for the period from mid-February to mid-March, of which 90,000 were dead, missing or captured, and 210,000 wounded.[1] The losses of Tarasov's 70th Army were particularly high – 8,849 men between 8 and 17 March alone.[2] Glantz's figures also correspond with the German ones. *2. Panzer Armee* and *2. Armee* together reported 78,178 enemy casualties and 9,480 prisoners and defectors for the period 14 February–21 March 1943.[3]

The failure of Rokossovsky's Central Front offensive had many causes and many contributing factors. One important point was certainly that Stavka's planning was too ambitious and optimistic. It did not take into account the time factor or the overstretched transport and supply lines. The forces deployed did not have time to gather and create a critical mass that would have allowed them to form a sufficiently strong attacking force that the weak German forces would hardly have been able to counter. Boris Sokolov openly criticised the withdrawal of the Don Front forces to the Orel salient, saying that it would have been wiser to leave them in the Kharkov area, as Manstein's operation would then not have been successful or could not have taken place to the same extent.[4]

An important reason for the failure was that the Don Front's road-building machines and work units had remained behind in Stalingrad, making it almost impossible to build vital roads for the transport of artillery and supplies.[5] It was above all the lack of heavy artillery on the Soviet side that made the German defensive success possible.

In the absence of other means of transport, units had to march on foot from their unloading stations at Yelets and Livny 150 to 200 kilometres to the front. Kursk could not be used as a supply centre, because its railway station was subject to heavy *Luftwaffe* air raids and passable roads were lacking.[6] Because of the time pressure, units were sent into battle as soon as they arrived. Often these units were not even fully formed, so that they had to forcibly recruit their missing personnel from the population

---

1 Glantz, *After Stalingrad*, p.375.
2 Glantz, *After Stalingrad*, p.375.
3 CAMO, 500_12454, file 680: Files of Ic of *Heeresgruppe Mitte*: reports 20 to 25 March 1943, p.123.
4 Boris Sokolov, Richard Harrison (trans.), *Myths and Legends of the Eastern Front – Reassessing the Great Patriotic War* (Barnsley: Pen & Sword, 2019), p.153.
5 Sokolov, *Rokossovsky*, p.236.
6 Sokolov, *Rokossovsky*, pp.236–237.

of the newly liberated areas. In some cases, losses were also compensated for in this way. These forced recruits were neither properly equipped – there were no uniforms – nor trained and therefore could not form a strong force. Prisoner testimonies taken by the intelligence unit of *12. Panzer Division* unanimously show that the attacking divisions were poorly resourced with personnel. The replacements from the population were not trained, and hardly any rations were issued to them. Individual soldiers had to rely on the help of the local population, who had little food of their own, so that morale among the attackers was low. This is illustrated by excerpts from the interrogations recorded in the activity report of the responsible staff officer (Ic) of *12. Panzer Division*:

> 5 March 1943: Soldier Ivan Nikolaevich Makarov (Rifle Regiment 914), defected 4 March to *Kradschützenbataillon 22*: He left by train from Grisovka on 10 February and reached an unknown station near Yelets on 15 February. From there his unit marched about 230 kilometres on foot to its present area of operations, where it arrived on 3 March in the area of Khalyeyeva. The only rations he received during the march was a warm soup every day, bread was only sometimes given to him by the civilian population.[7]
>
> 7 March 1943: '…132nd Rifle Division: has been replenished only from [Russian] civilians from the areas vacated by us [the Germans], some of whom have only been with the troops for two or three days and without any training; hence huge losses. Often only platoon or company commanders are trained soldiers.' The conscripted civilians were each given a rifle with 40 to 100 rounds of ammunition, but no uniform. Those who could not go on due to overexertion were shot by the officers and commissars walking behind the ranks.[8]
>
> 8 March 1943: 'Further prisoner interrogation confirms the composition of Rifle Regiment 498 [of the 132 RD] almost exclusively of newly conscripted civilians from the cleared areas.'[9]
>
> 9 March 1943, Lieutenant Vasily Salevsky (7th/IIIth/149th RR of 175th RD): 'During times of poor rations quite bad mood and little fighting spirit …'[10]
>
> 10 March 1943, Ivan Ivanov (9th company/III Bn 126th RR): 'During the march no rations were received, people had to take from the population. … Even communists … are said to have stated that they would die or starve here anyway. Allegedly, very many want to defect, but they are always told that German captivity is worse than death.'[11]
>
> 17 March 1943, Sub-Lieutenant Ivan Lopatkin (1st company/I. Bn/RR 498 of the 132 RD): 'The entire replacement of the regiment is composed of recruited civilians from Fatesh', the mood was 'depressed. The recruited civilians have to be pushed forward by force and are trying to defect.'[12]

---

7   NARA, T-315 R-634, 12. PzDiv. KTB 4, Department Ic, Attachments 2 to Activity Report 4, p.13: prisoner statement 14, dated 5 March 1943; Anti-tank rifle platoon of I./RR 914, attached to 1st company.
8   NARA, T-315 R-634, 12. PzDiv. KTB 4, Department Ic, Attachments 1 to Activity Report 4, p.12 and Attachements 2, p. 23. Prisoner statement 16, dated 7 March 1943.
9   NARA, T-315 R-634, 12. PzDiv. KTB 4, Department Ic, Attachments 1 to Activity Report 4, p.12; Attachments 2, pp.24,25: prisoner statements 17 and 18 dated 8 March.
10 NARA, T-315 R-634, 12. PzDiv. KTB 4, Department Ic, Attachments 2 to Activity Report 4, p.26: prisoner statement 19, dated 9 March 1943.
11 NARA, T-315 R-634, 12. PzDiv. KTB 4, Department Ic, Attachments 2 to Activity Report 4, p.29: prisoner statement 21, dated 10 March 1943.
12 NARA, T-315 R-634, 12. PzDiv. KTB 4, Department Ic, Attachments 2 to Activity Report 4, p.49: prisoner statement 27, dated 17 March 1943.

Another prisoner reported that a lot of equipment had broken down during the transport. For example, out of 33 new tanks of the 202nd Tank Brigade, only 14 T-34s had arrived in the theatre of operations during the night of 15 to 16 March. The defective tanks were said to have been British Matilda IIs.[13]

It is also worth noting that the Soviet attackers had no heavy artillery at their disposal due to the lack of suitable access roads. Although there appear to have been sufficient mortars and anti-tank guns on the Soviet side, the lack of artillery was painfully obvious, especially as the corps artillery of *XXXXVI. Panzer Korps* had enough ammunition to support the defenders with between 1,000 and 5,000 shells fired daily.[14]

An additional complication for Rokossovsky was that Manstein's counter-offensive in the south tied up Soviet troops that were intended for his Central Front.[15] The 21st Army, fully assembled at Fatezh and ready to attack northwards, was taken away from Central Front on the 11th, dealing a blow for Rokossovsky's chances of success. In the end, he was unable to achieve the strength he had planned for and needed to break through to the north.

Another factor was Major General Tarasov, the commanding general of the 70th Army, which faced the *12. Panzer Division* and parts of the *78. Sturm Division*, including *Fallschirmjäger Regiment 1*. He was (probably rightly) declared incompetent and also used as a scapegoat for Rokossovsky's own failures, a tactic not unknown to others as well, Zhukov and Konev did the same.[16] Tarasov had shortly before commanded the 41st Army, whose offensive at Bely had failed, so he was relieved of his post there as well. Rokossovsky severely criticised him in a long decree of 4 April 1943:[17]

> The unsuccessful offensive operations by the 70th Army for the seizure and retention of the Svetlyi Luch, Novaia Ialta, Rzhavchik, Muravchik, and Hill 260.2 regions and the heavy losses in personnel (8,849 men) and equipment suffered during them are explained by the unsatisfactory preparations for these operation on the part of the Military Council and, first and foremost, by the commander of the army, Major General Comrade Tarasov; the weak organisational role and unsatisfactory control on the part of the staff; and the perfunctory attitude of the commanders of the formation and units to the organisation of combat.[18]

In his letter Rokossovsky goes on to list the following points of criticism:

- There was no proper reconnaissance of the enemy forces.
- The Military Council had not taken enough measures at the beginning of the operation (8–12 March) to bring sufficient ammunition to the front and had not organised artillery support.
- After the setbacks at Rzhavchik and Muravchik and the heavy losses suffered, the right conclusions were not drawn, and the same mistakes were made in the attempts to take these villages from 18 to 28 March with high losses. In particular, the planning and coordination of the field

---

13 NARA, T-315 R-634, 12. PzDiv. KTB 4, Department Ic, Attachments 2 to Activity Report 4, p.54: prisoner statement 30, dated 17 March 1943, Lieutenant Kiril Iwanow (202. Tank Brigade, XIX Corps).
14 NARA, T 314 R-1086: XXXXVI. PzK, KTB Attachments, 31 January-31 May 1943, corps units.
15 Sokolov, *Rokossovsky*, p.238.
16 Buttar, *Meat Grinder*, p.131.
17 For the complete text in English see Glantz, *After Stalingrad*, pp.383–386.
18 Glantz, *After Stalingrad*, p.384.

commanders, tank units, and artillery was carried out superficially, without the participation and control of the commanding general Tarasov. Explicit rules and regulations had been violated on the part of the Military Council and the divisional commanders, with the commander of the 278th Rifle Division, Colonel Sedlovsky, sending his entire cadre forces to the front into battle, resulting in a complete breakdown of the command structure. This led to the loss of 224 military and political leaders in the 175th Rifle Division in the last days of the battle. In addition, insufficient care was taken to ensure that military equipment did not fall into enemy hands in the event of a retreat. Thus, on 30 March, the 70th Army was short of 7,802 rifles, 2,145 heavy machine guns, 20 4.5 cm cannons, 44 8.2 cm mortars, 93 5 cm mortars and 240 anti-tank rifles.

- Rokossovski also blamed Tarasov for the lack of supplies: He had not seen to it that the roads were also paved until the beginning of the Rasputitsa, so that the necessary supplies did not get forward and reach the troops. All this would have led to severe states of exhaustion among the soldiers. Not infrequently, soldiers died as a result.

All these accusations led to Tarasov's dismissal, although it is evident that he was not responsible for all of them. In his defence, it must be noted that the 70th Army was predominantly made up of border guards whose officers had no experience in combined arms fighting.[19]

The Costs of a Successful Defence

It was a successful defence for the Germans but not a victory. *Generaloberst* Schmidt's *2. Panzerarmee* was instrumental in achieving this success and in preventing the collapse of *Heeresgruppe Mitte*'s front. Ultimately, this was only possible because of the reserves sent south by the *Heeresgruppe* which were released by operation BÜFFELBEWEGUNG, the targeted use of artillery, and more or less functioning supply routes. The *Luftwaffe* successfully supported these efforts. Without Manstein's achievements in the south, this success would probably not have been possible. Although the Red Army had suffered a setback, the *Wehrmacht* had been further weakened.

For the period 1–10 March 1943 alone, PzAOK 2 reported an average of 2,000 casualties per day, including the sick and wounded (a total of 20,000 casualties in 10 days), while in the same period it claimed to have inflicted enemy losses of 15,000 dead or, including the wounded, a total of 60,000 casualties. In addition, 2,130 Soviet prisoners were taken.[20]

On 16 March 1943, the war diary of *2. Panzer Army* put its own 'bloody' losses – those inflicted in combat operations – at 41,000 since the beginning of the defensive battle,[21] while *Generaloberst* Schmidt in his later report on the winter battles, put this figure at 45,000 including losses up to the end of March.[22]

For February 1943, *Panzer Armee Oberkommando 2* recorded losses of 22,314 men. Of these, 157 officers and 4,881 NCOs and enlisted men were killed in action and 26 officers, and 1,939 NCOs and enlisted men were reported missing. It is not clear whether these figures include losses due to illness

---

19 Sokolov, *Rokossovsky*, p.239.
20 NARA, T-313 R-153, PzAOK 2, KTB 3, part 2, entry 10 March 1943.
21 NARA, T-313 R-153, PzAOK 2, KTB 3, part 2, entry 16 March 1943, p.3.
22 CAMO, 500_12454, file 680: documents of Ic of *Heeresgruppe Mitte*: current reports (20–25 March 1943)

or not. As the report explicitly states 'own losses in the heavy defensive battles' the latter should be assumed.[23]

By way of comparison, *Heeresgruppe Mitte* had recorded total losses from combat of 170,513 during the period December 1942–1 July 1943, with estimated casualties of 143,399 added. In numerical terms, these are the highest losses of any German army group on the Eastern Front during this period – except for the total loss of the 6th Army at Stalingrad (178,505).[24]

Comparing these figures, it is easy to assess the severity of the fighting in which *2. Panzer Armee* was involved.

Fallschirmjäger Regiment 1 suffered heavy losses. Schulenburg's battalion was the worst hit while Becker's, already weakened, was comparatively better off. The losses among the officers were high during this period: A total of 27 officers were among the casualties, 10 killed, and 17 wounded, of which two later succumbed to their wounds. Worst hit was *I. Bataillon* with four dead and three wounded, of which one later succumbed to his wounds, and *II. Bataillon* with three dead and six wounded. The regimental staff suffered three killed and three wounded, one of whom died in hospital, *III. Bataillon* suffered six wounded officers.

NCOs suffered 53 casualties: 11 dead, and 42 wounded, of which four later succumbed to their wounds. Again *I.* and *II. Bataillon* had highest losses with 19 and 17 casualties each.

Casualties of FJR 1 February–March 1943

Unit	Dead	Wounded	Missing	Total
Staff	40	123	0	163
I. Bat.	92	187	1	280
II. Bat.	60	197	4	261
III. Bat.	32	117	2	151
Total	224	624	7	855

---

23 NARA, T-313 R-153, PzAOK 2, KTB 3, vol.2, 1 March–31 May 1943: entry 2 March 1943, p.4.
24 Liedtke, *Whirlwind*, p.311.

24

The Last Days on the Eastern Front

A Final Attack on *Flieger-Division 7*

The withdrawal of *Flieger Division 7*, which had been planned since January 1943, was again ordered by the *Oberkommando des Heeres* on 19 March 1943.[1] The division was to be pulled out of the front north of Smolensk in an accelerated manner so that it could be transported to the West by the end of the month. *Heeresgruppe Mitte* gave Model the order to begin with the withdrawal of the division on 21 March. This news caused some consternation as *Flieger Division 7* was the only division of *9. Armee* still considered to be fully operational for an attack. The remainder of *9. Armee* consisted of weak divisions: seven divisions were 'limited suitable for attack', 13 divisions were 'suitable for defence' and two divisions were 'limited suitable for defence'.[2]

Feldwebel Gaunersorfer of *7. Kompanie/Fallschirmjäger Regiment 4* observes the enemy. (BDF Archive)

---

1 CAMO, 500_12454, file 633.
2 CAMO, 500_12454, file 675: combat value of the divisions in the sector of *Heeresgruppe Mitte*, dated 1 March 1943.

The opinion of the staff of *9. Armee* was:

> Even if the surrender of this division with high fighting power, which had been created for the war of aggression, had been expected, it is still considered regrettable that the disengagement has now been ordered so suddenly and at such short notice. In this way the divisions destined for disengagement, which have covered the entire BÜFFELBEWEGUNG, would not enjoy a day of rest if they can arrive at all in the sector of the 7. Fl.Div. [*Flieger Division 7*] in the time prescribed by H.Gr. [*Heeresgruppe Mitte*]. A request Ia [of] 9 [*Armee*] to Ia. H.Gr. at 8:20 p.m. for a postponement of the relief (in favour of the 206. ID) has, in the opinion of H.Gr., little chance of success. H.Gr., for its part, is of the opinion that the removal could at least be started in time with the non-deployed parts of the 7. Fl.Div.[3]

Fallschirmjäger of the *Fallschirm Panzerjäger Abteilung* bring an anti-tank gun into position, 27 February 1943. (Private Collection/Dahm)

But this plan was interrupted by a long-awaited Soviet attack on the section of *Flieger Division 7* on 20 March 1943. Following several small-scale attacks during the night, the pressure by the attacking three Soviet rifle regiments, supported by some 50 tanks, on the positions of *III. Bataillon/Fallschirmjäger Regiment 4* and *I. Bataillon/Luftlande Sturm Regiment* grew. The attacks were repulsed except for a local incursion southeast of Lake Ryta, at the positions of *III. Bataillon/Fallschirmjäger Regiment 4*. The positions of *12. Kompanie* on 'Knobloch Hill', named after the former commander of *12. Kompanie*, *Hauptmann* Fritz Knobloch,[4] were taken by the Soviet attackers around 2:30 p.m. and the company

---

3   NARA, T-312 R-308, KTB 7 AOK 9, Entry 19 March 1943.
4   Fritz Knobloch (11 January 1916– ?), *Major i.G.* Originally from *Fallschirmjäger Regiment 2*, he was commander of *12. Kompanie/Fallschirmjägerregiment 4* until 3 December 1942, after which he was transferred to the staff of *Brigade Häring*. In March 1943 he was with *Flieger Division 7* as chief intelligence officer (Ic). At the end of the

destroyed in the process. Also, parts of the positions of *11. Kompanie* were taken. To contain this breach the division sent all available reserves and alarm units to the aid of *Kampfgruppe Walther*. The fighting continued on 21 March, after which the attacking pressure eased, and the breach was sealed.[5]

As part of BÜFFELBEWEGUNG, the right wing of *Flieger Division 7* had folded in, *III. Bataillon/ Fallschirmjäger Regiment 3* under command of *Hauptmann* Kratzert, which held the former positions of *Fallschirmjäger Regiment 1,* was thus freed. It had been transferred to the left wing during the night of 22 to 23 March and placed under the command of *Kampfgruppe Walther* as a reserve. The battalion had a combatant strength of 11 officers and 464 men.[6]

Generalmajor Heidrich ordered the retaking of the lost positions. A difficult task as the last 400 meters of the lines of approach were without any cover and visible to the enemy on 'Knobloch Hill'. Therefore, it was decided to carry out the attack during the night.

Thus, during the night of 25–26 March, Kratzert's men carried out the planned counterattack with two main attack groups. *10. Kompanie* was to attack on the right while *11. Kompanie* was to do the same on the left. *9. Kompanie* was held in reserve while *12. Kompanie* supported the attack with its machine guns together with artillery from various units.

The attacking groups reached their jump-off positions undetected by their opponents around 9:45 p.m., while the reserve units of *9. Kompanie* and the battalion staff reached theirs around 10:00 p.m.

After an artillery barrage the men attacked the Soviet soldiers in the former trenches of *11.* and *12. Kompanie/Fallschirmjäger Regiment 4*. Due to heavy resistance Kratzert's men were only able to take their objective by around 6:00 a.m. on 26 March. They found the trenches destroyed by the artillery fire of the previous days, so that they offered little cover. They were filled with the bodies of paratroopers from *Fallschirmjäger Regiment 4* and Soviet soldiers on top of them. They were also muddy and grew shallow because of the thawing snow. The paratroopers had to dig new trenches as there was practically no cover left. Having suffered comparatively few casualties during the attack, Soviet artillery fire and several counterattacks now inflicted heavy casualties on the battalion. Further Soviet attacks the following day were also unsuccessful. Kratzert's losses were seven killed and 35 wounded in the attack, while holding the positions cost him a further 50 killed, eight missing and 144 wounded.[7] Some of the dead – and missing – paratrooper's bodies from both regiments were only discovered underneath Russian bodies several metres underground by Russian detector enthusiasts between 2007 and 2008.[8]

As a result of this fighting, the division suffered 917 casualties between 21 and 27 March 1943: 15 officers killed and nine wounded; 220 NCOs and enlisted men killed, 636 wounded and 47 missing.[9] *Fallschirmjäger Regiment 4* lost 134 killed (10 officers), 14 missing and 305 wounded (six officers) between 20 and 22 March.

Many a veteran blamed Heidrich for a considerable part of the losses as he insisted on the counterattack on 25 and 26 March, which was by many considered not to be necessary, so shortly before being

---

    war, he was chief of operations (Ia) of *10. Fallschirmjäger Division*.
5   For details see BA-MA, RL 33/70: KTB 2 of FJR 4.
6   BA-MA, RL 33/57: After action report of *Hauptmann* Kratzert, dated 1 June 1943.
7   A detailed account can be found in Donth, *Fallschirmjäger Regiment 4*, pp.39–53.
8   See the very interesting thread '9./Fallschirm.Jg.Rgt. 3' in the Fallschirmjäger Forum at <wehrmacht-awards. com>.
9   Attachment to the after-action report of *Kampfgruppe Walther* by *Flieger Division 7*, dated 31. March 1943 BA, BW 57/39.

Counterattack of *III. Bataillon/ Fallschirmjäger Regiment 3* under the command of *Hauptmann* Kratzert during the night of 25 to 26 March 1943 (after the original sketch in Kratzert's after-action report).

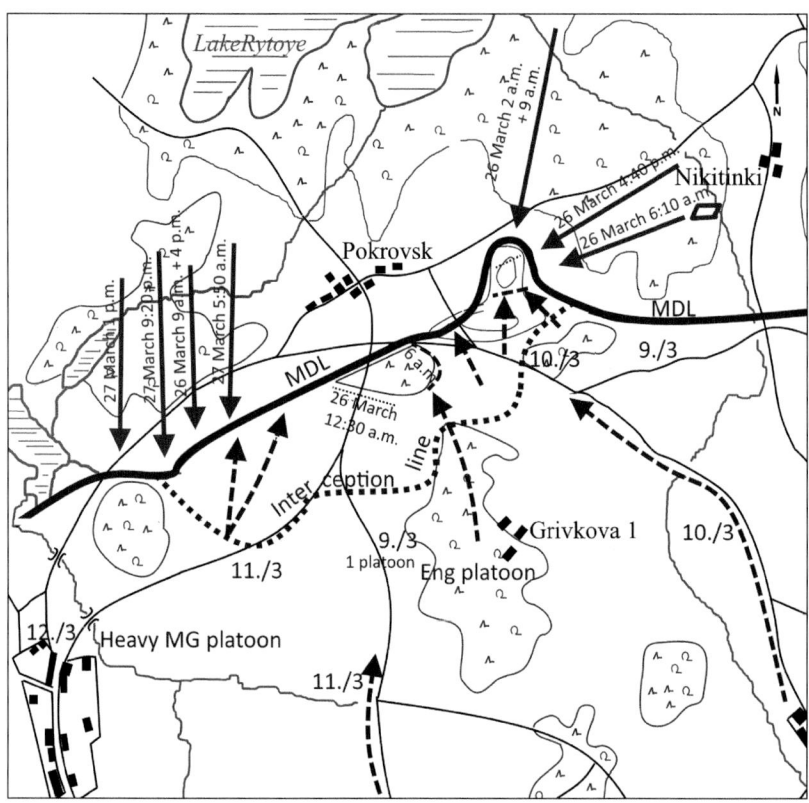

Fallschirmjäger during the counterattack on 25–26 March 1943. (Private Collection/Gross)

relieved. They may have a point, apparently this was a matter of principle and prestige for Heidrich. His theory of the rubber band that must snap back was implemented, regardless of whether it made tactical or strategic sense.

Kratzert also observed weaknesses: 'Nervous breakdown of *Leutnant* Skupsch and here and there unauthorised leaving of the main line of defence (MLD),[10] the first very deplorable signs of decay also in our force! Heated confrontations with Walther over this.'[11]

Despite these battles, *Heeresgruppe Mitte* did not abandon its plan to withdraw the division by 31 March.

The Journey to France

On 25 March, after the successful completion of BÜFFELBEWEGUNG, Model handed over the section of *9. Armee* to *4. Armee* and *3. Panzer Armee*, with *VI. Armee Korps* being subordinated to the latter. On 29 March, the relief of the elements of *Flieger Division 7* started and the journey back to France began. The division was transported by 26 trains from Smolensk (mainly FJR 3), 14 and half trains from Rudnya (mainly divisional staff, engineer battalion, supply train) and 24 trains from Vitebsk (mainly FJR 4, *MG Bataillon* and *Panzerjäger*).

This return journey was described as 'adventurous' because the roads were muddy and slowed down movements considerably. Some units only left Smolensk 10 to 14 days later, with elements of *Fallschirmjäger Regiment 4* not leaving Vitebsk until 2 May.[12] The trip was not uneventful for some. The transport of the *Fallschirm MG Bataillon* hit a mine laid by partisans after Minsk on 3 April:

> Around 7 p.m. past Minsk, then endless swamps and wastelands, vast forests. Just as we were about to hang up our stretchers to sleep, a detonation, the smell of gunpowder, splinters of wood and coal. The train stops. Lights out and out with our weapons. The mine detonated behind the wagon, tearing it apart. From the first platoon, Ebert was badly hit, Bader, Reichert, Schuster, Stolpke and Gumpoltsberger lighter. We cordon off the area and secure it. We use the locomotive to fetch engineers. Luckily, a hospital train is just coming to take our wounded.[13]

The division was transferred to Normandy in France, where it was refitted, reorganised and renamed *1. Fallschirmjäger Division* on 1 May 1943. At the beginning of June 1943, the division was transferred to Avignon in southern France to serve with the newly formed *2. Fallschirmjäger Division* as an 'intervention reserve of the OB West in the event of an enemy landing.'[14]

---

10   Ernst Skupsch (1910-?), *Oberleutnant* and commander of *10. Kompanie/FJR 3*. As a result, he seems to have been transferred away from the paratroopers, as he is no longer with the regiment in July 1943 (Christian Unverzagt, *Sizilien – Kämpfe des Fallschirmjäger Regiments 3 vom 12. Juli-16. August 1943* (Hamburg: self published, 1977), p.21.
11   Kratzert, *Vom k.u.k. Offizier zum Ritterkreuzträger*, p.87.
12   Ernst H. Simon, *Meine Kriegserlebnisse 1940–1945*, Chapter 9 (<ewnor.de>, accessed 5 November 2017). Simon was in *13. Kompanie/Fallschirmjäger Regiment 4*.
13   Pöppel, *Himmel und Hölle*, p.116.
14   Percy E. Schramm, (ed.), *Kriegstagebuch des Oberkommandos der Wehrmacht 1943 – vol.3, part 1* (Augsburg: Weltbild, 2005), p.254.

The Disengagement of *Fallschirmjäger Regiment 1*

On the night of 24 March at 10:50 p.m., *7. Infanterie Division*, which had relieved *12. Panzer Division*, received a telex from *XXXXVI. Panzer Korps* stating that *Fallschirmjäger Regiment 1* (including the subordinate units of *I./Flak Regiment 501*) was to be disengaged during the night of 29–30 March in such a way that the regiment would arrive in Orel on 1 April.[15] It was then to be transported back to Smolensk to join *Flieger Division 7*. This plan seems not to have been carried out as the paratroopers were sent directly back to the West. The regiment was to be relieved by *Gruppe Kaellner*, which was transferred from the sector of *XXXXVII. Panzer Korps* and consisted of Kaellner's staff, *Jägerbataillon 10* and *11*, an assault gun battery as well as three light artillery batteries.

The order was quickly carried out and Renisch's men of *2. Kompanie* moved out during the night of the 26th to the 27th. The disengagement of the regiment went according to plan.

Gröschke's battalion, which had remained in the section of *LV. Armee Korps* was relieved by *I. Bataillon/Grenadier Regiment 396* late in the evening on 28 March. The task was completed by 1:30 a.m. the next day. The battalion was transferred to Orel, where it joined the rest of the regiment.

The tension of the last few weeks fell away from the soldiers. They were deloused and could recover a little from their exertions. The relief can also be felt in the recollections of *Gefreiter* von Zimburg. After his company was pulled out of the front, he was able to visit a field cinema in Orel where a light-hearted musical movie was shown. 'After such a long time – since Braunschweig – once again in a cinema. We had to laugh so much at every little thing that the other spectators were already complaining loudly.'[16]

On 31 March 1943, the first transports took place. Gröschke's men left Orel for France, which must have lifted their spirits the most. *Hauptfeldwebel* Wagner was happy to leave Orel with *I. Bataillon* on 2 April, but was saddened by the fact that the transport passed through Germany on its way to France without giving him the opportunity to see his wife.[17]

The regiment's departure was not uneventful; *13. Kompanie* suffered seven wounded, two of whom later died, during a Soviet bombing raid on a railway station near Bryansk on 6 April 1943. *I. Bataillon* also suffered a tragic incident on its way west:

> At 10 a.m. on 3 April 1943[18] our battalion was transported to Bryansk and from there to Gomel. At 10.30 p.m. we were suddenly awakened by a terrible jolting of the carriage (we were in a cattle wagon, sleeping on the floor). The train stopped with a bang, rifle shots were heard and when we opened the door, we noticed that it was as bright as day. At first, we thought we had been attacked by partisans, but it soon turned out that we had had a train collision. The impact knocked over the stove in our wagon – it was the fourth behind the locomotive. A fire was prevented by a cool-headed paratrooper, who was standing next to the stove and threw it out of the door. He burned both his hands terribly. The railway accident happened as follows: an infantry transport was heading to the front and left our track for a secondary one. Our train, however, had not been stopped by a signal and rain straight into the other train, which was just with its middle on the

---

15 BA-MA, RH 26-7/46; XXXXVI. AK, 37551/3 in BW 57-82.
16 Zimburg, *Erinnerungen*, p.114.
17 Archive Franz, Wagner letters dated 18 March and 6 April 1943.
18 Zimburg might have gotten the date wrong, as *Hauptfeldwebel* Wagner mentions in his letter to his wife dated 6 April 1943 that the battalion left on the 2nd.

The road Dmitrovsk-Orel, which the *Fallschirmjäger Regiment 1* had to use, was next to impassable because the mud season had started. (Private Collection)

switch. Four or five wagons were knocked over, unfortunately on the side where the sliding doors were. In winter, the second doors were nailed shut and only had a small hole for the stove exhaust. When the wagons were turned over, the stoves fell down and set fire to the straw. By the time the thick planks of the cattle wagons were hammered down, many of the comrades inside had already been burned and suffocated. The fire also caused boxes of handgrenades to explode, which again cost the lives of several soldiers. Altogether there were 31 dead, 50 seriously injured and 20 slightly injured. Our unit had only one casualty, a soldier who had been riding on the locomotive for fun and tried to jump off but was crushed in the process. The boiler man and the locomotive driver, who were unable to jump off, were only slightly injured.[19]

This snapshot was taken by a paratrooper of the regiment during the transport to France in April 1943. The tactical sign of *Flieger Division 7* is clearly visible on the right mudguard of this *Kübelwagen* Wanderer, probably type W 26. (Private Collection)

Praise by Higher Command

The commanders of the armies, corps and divisions to which *Fallschirmjäger Regiment 1* was attached had nothing but praise for the paratroopers.

Generaloberst Schmidt, the commander of *2. Panzer Armee* thanked the regiment in a handwritten letter to *Oberstleutnant* Schulz for their service in his section: 'I express my gratitude and appreciation for the commitment of your paratroopers. You have sealed off the enemy's incursions and destroyed the enemy units that had broken in, your paratroopers were the salvation of Orel. You have saved *2. Panzer Armee* from heavy losses.'[20]

General der Infanterie Zorn, commanding general of *XXXXVI. Panzer Korps*, particularly emphasised the efforts of Schulenburg's battalion, which:

> ... performed outstandingly in attack and defence in the period from 28 February to 3 March 1943, as well as in the defence against the heavy enemy attacks from 17 to 19 March 1943, where the *Fallschirmjäger Regiment 1* ... not only held the defensive positions, but through effective neighbourly assistance contributed to driving the enemy out of Muravchik and holding the village as a pillar against the deep enemy incursion further east. In this way, *Fallschirmjäger Regiment 1* played an essential part in the great defensive success of the corps, which frustrated the enemy's large-scale attempt to encircle and destroy our forces around Orel.[21]

---

19 Zimburg, *Erinnerungen*, p.116.
20 BA-MA, BW 57-89: copy of the letter of *Generaloberst* Schmidt dated 2 April 1943.
21 BA-MA, BW 57-89: Letter dated 30 March 1943.

In his special order of 17 April 1943, Schulz proudly summed up the entire mission, praising his soldiers, including the motormen, medics and troopers, for their efforts throughout, and, of course, giving them all the highest praise.²²

The second and last deployment of *Fallschirmjäger Regiment 1* on the eastern front was over.

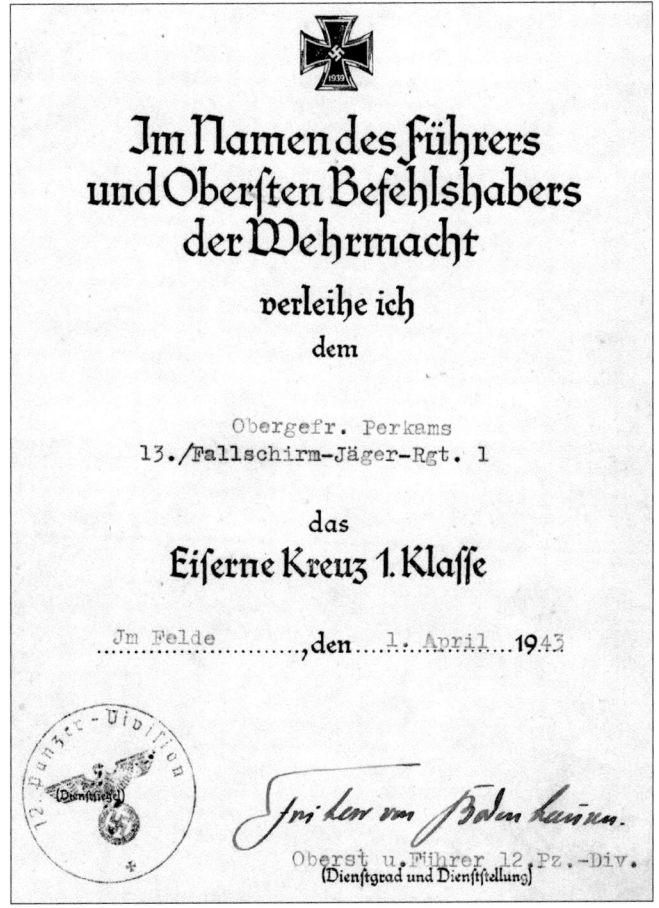

Obergefreiter Otto Perkams of *13. Kompanie* was awarded the Iron Cross 1st Class at the end of the campaign on 1 April 1943 by the commander of *12. Panzer Division*, *Oberst* Freiherr (Baron) von Bodenhausen. He had been previously awarded the Iron Cross 2nd Class on 15 December 1941 for his bravery at Leningrad during the previous winter. (Collection Stephan Janzyk)

---

22 BA-MA, BW 57-84: special order of *Oberstleutnant* Schulz, 17 April 1943.

25

Losses

Flieger Division 7

On 1 November 1942 *Flieger Division 7* had an actual strength of 19,649 men. The combatant strength of the division – at that time the numerically strongest division of *9. Armee* – was given as 6,846 men on 27 December 1942, which does not include the men of *Fallschirm Artillerie Regiment 1*, the *Fallschirm Panzerjäger Abteilung*, divisional troops (staff, *Kradschützenkompanie*), as well as the regimental troops (staff, bicycle platoon, signals platoon and engineer platoon, *13.* and *14. Kompanie*).

The following table is a compilation of the overall losses of *Flieger Division 7* for the winter of 1942/43 is based on the daily casualty reports of the *Luftwaffe* and the casualty lists of *Fallschirmjäger Regiment 1* for the period February to March 1943.[1] It is probably the most comprehensive account. The numbers are broken down into officers and then other ranks).

Flieger Division 7 Casualties

Month	Killed in Action	Wounded	Missing	Total
October 1942	3/39	1/63	1	4/103
November 1942	6/157	12/477	2/101	20/735
December 1942	2/126	12/386	9	14/521
January 1943	7/137	9/527	34	16/698
February 1943	10/269	26/835	21	36/1,125
March 1943	25/584	29/1,399	42	54/2,025
Total	53/1,312	89/3,687	2/208	144/5,207

Missing from this list are the absences due to illness, which totalled 2,560 men (including 75 officers).[2] Many of the slightly wounded remained with their units and sometimes did not even appear on the casualty lists, many were able to return after a short recovery; the same can be assumed of the losses due to illness and frostbite. Some of the losses could be compensated for in the first phase by replacements from the *Fallschirmjäger Ersatz-Regiment*. However, this regiment was transferred to France relatively early, at the beginning of February.

---

1   BA-MA RL 2III/903-907 in BW 57: D.R.d.L.u.Ob.d.L., GenSt.GenQu. 6.Abt., daily loss reports. See also Stimpel, *Fallschirmtruppe – Osten und Westen*, pp.87–88, who refers to the same source.
2   BA-MA, BW 57-39: AOK 9,KTB, attachments to activity report of section IIa/b, 1 October–31 December 1942 dated 22 March 1943 and 1 January–20 March 1943 dated 27 March 1943.

As if the figures were not high enough, it should be pointed out that between 1 January and 20 March 1943, *Flieger Division 7* suffered the highest losses of all the divisions of *9. Armee*. The deployment of *III. Bataillon* at Velikiye Luki, the constant aggressive reconnaissance patrols and attacks, as well as the fighting between 20 and 27 March led to these high figures.

Regimental Losses

Fallschirmjäger Regiment 1 had an actual strength of 3,684 men on 8 November 1942, whereas the corresponding lower combatant strength of its battalions on 14 November was 1,941 men (I.Bat. 644; II. Bat. 635, III. Bat. 662 men). If one adds the combatant strength of the regimental staff troops (bicycle platoon, engineer platoon, *13.* and *14. Kompanie* etc.) with an estimated 350 men, one arrives at a combatant strength of the regiment of 2,300 men. The total number of casualties in the winter of 1942–1943 of 1,444 men is in any case high in relation to the combatant strength. The regiment suffered heavy losses, with 427 dead, missing or dying of their wounds, and a further 1,017 were wounded. These figures include 18 officers killed in action or dying of wounds, and a further 24 wounded. The loss of NCOs was also high, with 24 killed, and 62 wounded. No information could be found on absences due to illness and frostbite, but these were a major problem. The number of wounded who were unfit for service after recovery is also unknown.

It is hardly surprising that *III. Bataillon* was particularly hard hit, with the number of casualties – including those wounded who later succumbed to their wounds – roughly equal to that of *I. Bataillon*.[3] However, the number of wounded differs greatly. This suggests that it was not always possible to recover the wounded of *I. Bataillon* during the confusing battles of 1–9 March at Kriuki, Baldyzh and Aleshenka. Some of the wounded could not be brought to medical attention in time and probably froze to death. The more difficult and the fiercer the battle, the more the ratio of 1:4 between the dead and the wounded, which was otherwise the norm in the *Wehrmacht*, shifted. *I. Bataillon* had a ratio of 1:2, *II. Bataillon* 1:3 and only *III. Bataillon* had almost 1:4.

Unit	Dead	Wounded	Missing	Died of Wounds	Total Dead & Missing	Total
Reg. staff	43	151	0	18	61	194
I. Bataillon	107	247	1	20	128	355
II. Bataillon	68	261	7	21	96	336
III. Bataillon	93	404	13	25	131	510
Others	1	9	1	1	3	11
14./FJR 5	4	34	0	4	8	38
Total	316	1,106	22	89	427	1,444

---

3   The wounded of the casualty lists of *Fallschirmjäger Regiment 1* were matched via the database of <volksbund.de> and so those who died of their wounds were determined. The results were then compared with the Ancestry/WASt. database. The number of cases (died of their wounds) not shown in these databases makes the overall number certainly somewhat higher.

Losses were highest during February (attack on Alekseyevka) followed by March (Kriuki, Baldyzh, Hill 266.0, Nagorniy) and January (Velikiye Luki).

Losses of *Fallschirmjäger Regiment 1* by Month

Month	Dead	Wounded	Missing	Died of Wounds	Total
November 42	9	59	0	3	68
December 42	19	102	3	4	124
January 43	64	321	12	28	397
February 43	102	335	5	29	442
March 43	122	289	2	25	413
Total	316	1,106	22	89	1,444

Losses of Officers

Unit	Dead	Wounded	Missing	Died of Wounds	Total
Reg.Stab	3	3	0	1	6
I. Bataillon	4	3	0	1	7
II. Bataillon	4	7	0	0	11
III. Bataillon	3	15	0	2	19
Total	14	28		4	43

NCOs (*Feldwebel* upwards) Losses

Unit	Dead	Wounded	Missing	Died of Wounds	Total
Reg.Stab	1	7	0	1	8
I. Bataillon	7	16	0	3	23
II. Bataillon	5	21	0	1	26
III. Bataillon	5	23	1	0	28
Total	18	67	1	5	85

A comparison of the casualty figures of *Fallschirmjäger Regiment 1* and *4* shows that the supposedly quieter period on the front north of Smolensk was far from it, due to the Soviet attack on 20 March 1943 and the subsequent counterattacks. Both regiments suffered similar losses. Losses due to exhaustion, frostbite and illness are also not included, nor are those who died of their wounds.[4]

Losses of *Fallschirmjäger Regiment 4* by month

Month	Dead	Wounded	Missing	Total
November 42	45	279	1	325
December 42	64	225	4	293
January 43	37	96	1	134
February 43	26	104		130
March 43	170	426	15	611
Total	342	1,130	21	1,493

4　BA-MA, RL 33/69 and 70; Donth, *Fallschirmjäger Regiment 4*, p.53 – uses slightly different figures.

Losses of *Fallschirmjäger Regiment 3* were considerably fewer. The woods in front their main line of defence were not suitable for large scale attacks. The numbers in the table are taken from the war diary of the regiment.[5]

Losses of *Fallschirmjäger Regiment 3* by month

Month	Dead	Wounded	Missing	Total
October 42	3	8	0	11
November 42	13	60	2	75
December 42	19	82	0	101
January 43	13	52	4	69
February 43	15	74	0	89
March 43	67	204	7	278
Total	130	480	13	623

The most casualties were suffered by Kratzert's *III. Bataillon* during the fighting 25 until 27 March and 224 cases of illness were recorded in this war diary among them typhoid fever and hepatitis.

The total numbers which are found in the after-action report of *Fallschirmjäger Regiment 3* are higher from those given above, perhaps because the casualties from the company which was transferred to the ski battalion might have been included. Over the period of the deployment, four officers were killed in action, a fifth was as a platoon commander with the ski battalion, while 16 were wounded.[6]

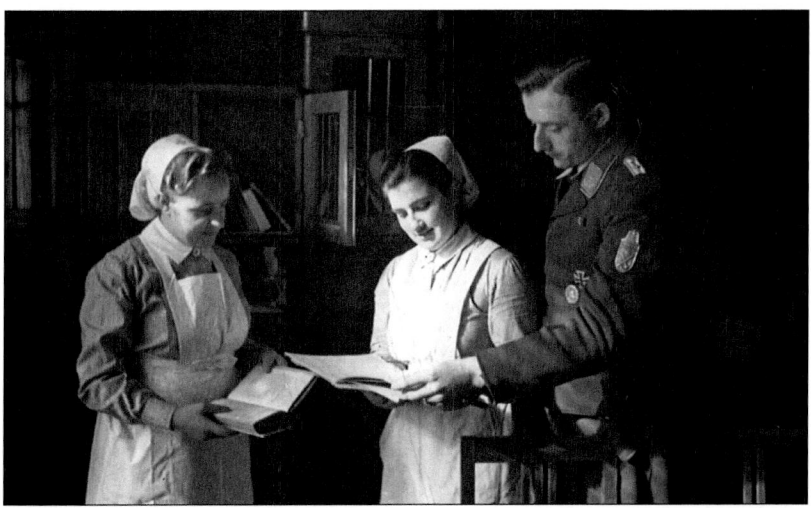

A number of paratroopers, both officers and enlisted men, fell ill or suffered frostbite during the mission and were hospitalised for some time. As a rule, these were not included in the casualty lists. *Oberleutnant* Mössinger of *1. Kompanie* pictured in hospital in Orel, recovering from an illness. The Narvik shield is clearly visible on his left upper arm. (Private Collection)

---

5   BA-MA, RL 33/54.
6   BA-MA, RL 33/57.

Losses of *Fallschirmjäger Regiment 3* (Officers/NCOs & enlisted men)

Period	Dead	Wounded	Missing	Total
1 November 1942–1 April 1943	141 (5/136)	501 (16/485)	19	661 (21/640)

All these figures prove only one thing: a special unit, trained for offensive operations and with a high combat value, was deployed in an area to which it was not accustomed to and not trained for, as infantry training was still somewhat lacking. The consequence was that this unit suffered above-average casualties, also because it had also fought particularly offensively – and successfully – in defence.

26

Conclusion

The deployment of *Fallschirmjäger Regiment 1* in the section of *Flieger Division 7* north of Smolensk from November 1942 to the beginning of February 1943 was comparatively uneventful. The expected large-scale attack on Starina with a thrust towards Dukhovshchina and Smolensk as part of the Soviet operation MARS did not take place, *Flieger Division 7* could not influence the overall events. From this point of view, both intelligence gathering on the enemy and resulting situation assessments had led to a deployment in the wrong place, which, however, had not had a negative effect in the overall picture. Operation MARS was a failure, Model's *9. Armee* was able to achieve a defensive success. Nevertheless, the aggressive reconnaissance activities, the many tactical raids and attacks carried out, as well as the defence against the like from the opposing side led to significant losses.

The command structure between the *Luftwaffe* and the *Heer* which resulted in constant conflict between the two and had a negative effect on Model's countermeasures, did not help either.

The men of the other regiments of the division felt similarly about the mission. Only the attack on 20 March 1943 is mentioned in memoirs and recollections, along with the many reconnaissance patrols and tactical raids. The new divisional commander, *Generalmajor* Heidrich, used the time to shape the division according to his ideas and he succeeded. He became a respected but also feared commander because of his strictness. During the formation of *1. Fallschirmjäger Division* in France, which followed this deployment, he was able to further develop the character of his division.

For the paratroopers of *Fallschirmjäger Regiment 1*, the deployment of the winter of 1942/1943 was a particularly difficult and trying one. The regiment suffered most from the unpopular 'lending out' to other units. The subordination of *II.* and *III. Bataillon* to *197. Infanterie Division* was of little importance, as Heidrich was able to maintain a physical link within his division and soon had the whole units reassigned to him.

However, he could not prevent the detaching of first *III. Bataillon* and then the entire *Fallschirmjäger Regiment 1*. The fighting at Velikiye Luki decimated *III. Bataillon* considerably. This, together with the regiment's almost two-month deployment near Orel, determined the narrative of the winter campaign.

The battalion commanders – Schulenburg and Becker – were able to prove their leadership qualities during the longer independent operations at Velikiye Luki, the attack on Nagorniy and the defence of Dmitrovsk. On the other hand, attack operations ordered by higher army commands were rarely successful. The frontal attack on Alekseyevka failed spectacularly, effectively disabling *II. Bataillon* for major deployments for the remainder of the operation. Given the situation, the attack should not have taken place. In contrast, the attacks on Nagorniy and Muravchik, in which the regimental commander Schulz proved himself, were a complete success, as here the paratroopers' strengths of acting quickly, independently and adapting to changing situations could be played out. Becker also demonstrated these qualities when he broke off the futile attack on the citadel of Velikiye Luki and the next day saved the situation at Gribushino with heavy losses. The attack on Kriuki was also a failure, but this was due to the bad weather and the surprisingly strong garrison there. Schulenburg showed nerves of steel and leadership when he repulsed the attack on Baldyzh shortly afterwards and then helped to clear the situation. In defence, the paratroopers proved to be strong nerved and successful at all locations. They never lost sight of the big picture in critical situations and their ability to launch quick, aggressive counterattacks was well utilised.

One of the regiment's advantages at Orel was that it was well equipped with heavy weapons, something that was usually a point of criticism of paratrooper units. Rarely could a regiment rely on a sufficient number of effective anti-tank weapons such as 8.8 cm anti-aircraft guns and 7.5 cm self-propelled anti-tank guns. The soldiers' personal equipment was also much better than in the previous winter. Winter clothing, boots and gloves were finally available in sufficient quantities.

The lack of transport capacity was problematic, which considerably limited the regiment's mobility.

In the end, the regiment's performance was praised by all its superiors, but it became apparent that the fighting had severely depleted the regiment's strength. The regiment suffered a total of 1,444 casualties, of which 427 were killed, missing or had succumbed to their wounds, which alone is equivalent to the combatant strength of a battalion.

The fact that the regiment had by far the most spectacular missions of the division during this campaign is evidenced by the awards. A total of two Knight's Crosses and some 39 to 41 German Crosses in Gold (DKiG) were awarded to *Flieger Division 7* for this operation on the Eastern Front, with both Knight's Crosses and 22 German Crosses in Gold going to members of *Fallschirmjäger Regiment 1* alone (see Appendix II). Looking at the distribution of casualties within the division, however, the burden was relatively even between *Fallschirmjäger Regiment 1* and *4*, while *Fallschirmjäger Regiment 3* suffered considerably fewer casualties, as it defended a section of the front unsuitable for large scale attacks.

The next few months in France were used to reorganise the division, while constant infantry training continued as *Generalmajor* Heidrich did not want his division to be idle. The division was renamed *1. Fallschirmjäger Division* per 1 May 1943. *Fallschirmjäger Regiment 4* received the *Ski Bataillon* as *II. Bataillon*, the divisional engineer and anti-tank battalion as well as others received new numbers, '1' instead of

Paratroopers of the *Ski Bataillon* leave the front line at the end of March 1943. (BDF Archive)

'7'. *I. Bataillon/Luftlande Sturm Regiment* was sent to France as well and became later the nucleus of the newly formed *4. Fallschirmjäger Division*. Soldiers were allowed to go on leave, while others returned from sick leave.

Although weakened by the losses sustained during the campaign in Russia, the division was now a coherent unit, the soldiers of the companies, platoons and groups were bound by their shared combat experience. Replacements were quickly integrated and learned from their battle-hardened comrades. The soldiers knew they could rely on each other. The division was ready for its new deployment in Sicily and Italy, where it fought until the capitulation of the German forces in Italy on 2 September 1945. The division was regarded as one the best formations in Italy by both its own and opposing Allied commanders. The experience gained during the winter in Russia was therefore crucial to the paratroopers' successes, such as at Monte Cassino.

Appendix I
Combatant Strengths

Combatant strength of *Fallschirmjäger Regiment 11*

Unit	Date	Strength (Officers/NCOs/Soldiers)
Regimental staff (incl. bicycle, engineer platoon)	12 March 1943	10/31/125 = 166
Bicycle and engineer platoon (without regt. staff)	17 March 1943	1/5/117 = 123
Regimental staff (incl. bicycle, engineer platoon)	20 March 1943	155
I. Bataillon/FJR 1	29 November 1942	599
	27 December 1942	573
	31 January 1943	572
	abt. 10 February 1943	579
1. Kompanie	23 February 1943	3/112 = 115
	1 March 1943	approx. 100
2. Kompanie	1 March 1943	approx. 100
3. Kompanie	1 March 1943	approx. 100
	12 March 1943	1/22/46 = 69
(inkl. GrW von 4./1)	17 March 1943	1/25/58 = 84
II. Bataillon/FJR 1	20 October 1942	22/782 = 804 (actual)
	29 November 1942	578
	27 December 1942	591
	3 January 1943	555
	17 January 1943	437
	31 January 1943	544
	7 February 1943	443
	Circa 10 February 1943	approx. 580
7. Kompanie	12 December 1942	2/113 = 115

---

1 The figures were compiled from the following sources: NARA, T-315 R-633, 12. PzDiv KTB 4, Attachments 2, p.371: report of combatant strengths; p.412: weekly situation report of 12. PzDiv to XXXXVI. PzK.; T-315 R-634, 12. PzDiv, KTB vol.4, Ia, attachments 5, maps and sketches, 1 January–16 June 1943; T-312 R-307, AOK 9 KTB Nr. 6, Attachments IV (26 November – 31 December 1942); T-312 R-308, AOK 9 KTB 7 Attachments IV (1 January–12 February 1943); BA-MA, RH 26-78/52: Report of I./FJR 1 to 78. Sturm-Div; RH 26-299/108: Morning report of 299.ID to XXXV. AK. BA-MA: BW 57-84. CAMO, 500_12454, file 637.

Unit	Date	Strength (Officers/NCOs/Soldiers)
III. Bataillon/FJR 1	21 October 1942	25/178/942 (actual)
	29 November 1942	604
	27 December 1942	562
	10 January 1943	516
	7 February 1943	192
	Circa 10 February 1943	402
	12 March 1943	8/74/156 = 238
9. Kompanie	17 March 1943	1/19/30 = 50
10. Kompanie	17 March 1943	2/12/30 = 44
11. Kompanie	17 March 1943	0/18/37 = 55
12. Kompanie	17 March 1943	2/10/41 =53
13. Kompanie	12 March 1943	2/18/78 = 98
	20 March 1943	83
14. Kompanie	12 March 1943	1/5/22 = 28
	20 March 1943	76

Combatant Strength of Subordinated Units at Orel[2]

Unit	Date	Strength (Officers/NCOs/Soldiers)
Platoon 'Brammer' 1. Kompanie/Fallschirm Panzerjäger Abteilung	12 March 1943	1/3/11 = 15
	20 March 1943	10
Platoon 'Pusch' 4. Kompanie/Fallschirm Panzerjäger Abteilung	12 March 1943	0/3/4 = 7
	20 March 1943	13
I./Flak-Rgt. 501	12 March 1943 (1 Batterie)	4/11/71 = 86
	20 March 1943 (1 Batterie)	84
Platoon 'Wagner' 1. Kompanie/ Fallschirm-Fliegerabwehr-MG-Btl.	12 March 1943	1/8/20 = 29
	20 March 1943	29

---

2 Compiled from the following sources: NARA, T-315 R-633, 12. PzDiv. KTB 4, Attachments 2, p.371: report of combatant strengths; p.412: weekly situation report of 12. PzDiv to XXXXVI. PzK.

Appendix II
Awards

Knight's Cross of the Iron Cross 1939 (RK)

Wolf Werner Graf von der Schulenburg, *Major*, leader *I. Bataillon* (20 June 1943)
Karl Hans Wittig, *Feldwebel,* platoon leader, *11. Kompanie* (5 February 1944)

Major von der Schulenburg receives the Knight's Cross from his divisional commander, *Generalmajor* Heidrich, in France on 20 June 1943. (BDF Archive/Dahm)

German Cross in Gold (DKiG)

As far as could be determined, 22 soldiers of *Fallschirmjäger Regiment 1* received this award for their conduct during the Winter Campaign 1942–1943. In comparison FJR 3 received eight to 10 DiKG (Höseler, Lange, Lauk, Peiser, Rau, Sassen, Scholz, Schwarz, Stephan [the latter two maybe for Sicily]), FJR 4 four (Hübner, Graßmehl, Koch, Meyer), other divisional battalions altogether five (Mertins, v. Nordheim, Sander, Schramm, Tappe).[1]

---

1   Compiled from Klaus Patzwall, Veit Scherzer (eds), *Das Deutsche Kreuz 1941–1945 – Geschichte und Inhaber – Volume 2* (Norderstedt: Patzwall, 2001), and Schmitz, Thies, Wegmann, Zweng (eds), *Die Deutschen Divisionen 1939–1945* (Osnabrück: Biblio, 1994), vol.2, p.95.

Name	Date	Unit
Dr Eiben, Adolf, *Stabsarzt*	22 July 1943	Regimental Staff
Hoffmeister, Hugo, *Oberfeldwebel*	24 June 1943	I. Bataillon, 2. Kompanie
Otto, Johann, *Oberleutnant*	24 June 1943	I. Bataillon, 3. Kompanie*
Germer, Ernst, *Feldwebel*	24 June 1943	I. Bataillon 3. Kompanie
Jahn, Max, *Feldwebel*	24 June 1943	I. Bataillon, 3. Kompanie
Schmidt, Leonhard, *Feldwebel*	24 June 1943	I. Bataillon, 3. Kompanie
Gröschke, Kurt, *Major*	21 June 1943	II. Bataillon
Poppele, Erwin, *Oberleutnant*	28 April 1943	II. Bataillon, 5. Kompanie
Hartmann August, *Feldwebel*	20 March 1943**	II. Bataillon, 5. Kompanie
Büsche, Otto, *Feldwebel*	28 April 1943	II. Bataillon, 6. Kompanie
Mootz, Helmut, *Feldwebel*	22 July 1943	II. Bataillon, 6. Kompanie
Nollen, Willi, *Feldwebel*	28 April 1943	II. Bataillon, 6. Kompanie.
Oppelt, Otto, Feldwebel	20 March 1943**	II. Bataillon, 6. Kompanie
Schneider, Willi, *Feldwebel*	1 August 1943	II. Bataillon, 6. Kompanie.
Abratis, Herbert, *Oberleutnant*	15 March 1943	II. Bataillon, 7. Kompanie.
Schon, Georg, *Oberfeldwebel*	20 March 1943	II. Bataillon, 7. Kompanie
Dietrich, Bruno, *Oberfeldwebel*	20 March 1943**	II. Bataillon, 8. Kompanie
Merkordt, Fritz, *Oberleutnant*	20 March 1943	III. Bataillon, 9. Kompanie
Wöstmann, August, *Oberjäger*	20 March 1943	III. Bataillon, 9. Kompanie
Schulze, Georg, *Oberleutnant*	24 June 1943	III. Bataillon, 10. Kompanie
Wittig, Karl Hans, *Feldwebel*	20 June 1943**	III. Bataillon, 11. Kompanie.
Isenberg, Werner, *San.-Feldwebel*	20 March 1943**	III. Bataillon, 11. Kompanie

*   *1. Kompanie* wrongly given in Schmitz, Thies, Wegmann, Zweng, *Die Deutschen Divisionen*, Vol.2, p.95.

** In Patzwall/Scherzer, *Das Deutsche Kreuz in Gold* the year is incorrectly given as 1944. As with Wittig and Isenberg, this has been corrected in other publications to 1943. Oppelt, Dietrich and Hartmann could not be verified, but their rank and events undoubtedly point to the year 1943.

Appendix III

Approved Close Combat Actions of *Fallschirmjäger Regiment 1* during Winter 1942–1943 at Smolensk, Velikiye Luki and Orel

Date	Action	Unit
18 November 1942	Reconnaissance in force at Solovyevka	1. Kompanie
21 November 1942	Reconnaissance in force at Durnevo	9. Kompanie
24 November 1942	Reconnaissance in force at Ovsyankina	2. Kompanie
28 November 1942	Reconnaissance in force at Sh.-Deshnaya valley	10. Kompanie
1 December 1942	Reconnaissance in force at Vishenki	6. Kompanie
4 December 1942	Reconnaissance in force north of Vishenki	7. Kompanie
14 December 1942	Defence against an enemy attack with counterattack	3. Kompanie
15 December 1942	Reconnaissance north of Mushitskaya	7. Kompanie
16 December 1942	Reconnaissance in force at Soshno	12. Kompanie
18 December 1942	Reconnaissance in force at south of Ovsyankina	1. Kompanie
18 December 1942	Reconnaissance in force south of Gavrovo	11. Kompanie
19 December 1942	Reconnaissance in force at the river Arshat	2. Kompanie
20 December 1942	Reconnaissance in force north of Gorki	9. Kompanie
21 December 1942	Reconnaissance east of Vervishche	6. Kompanie
14 January 1943	Tactical raid on strongpoint 'Russian path'	II. Bataillon
16 January 1943	Attack on heights south of Gribushino	III. Bataillon
17 January 1943	Attack on hills eastwards of Ivantseva	III. Bataillon
15 February 1943	Attack on Alekseyevka	II. Bataillon, engineer platoon, self-propelled anti-tank gun platoon Pusch
16 February 1943	Reconnaissance towards Khoroshevsky and Volny Trud	9. Kompanie
17 February 1943	Defence at Alekseyevka	III. Bataillon, 13. Kompanie (elem.), self-propelled anti-tank gun platoon Pusch

Date	Action	Unit
17 February 1943	Defence at Stolbetskoye	II. Bataillon 13. Kompanie (III platoon) 14. Kompanie (elem.)
17 February 1943	Tactical raid on Stepanovka	11. Kompanie
18 February 1943	Defence of Kastritsa with tank battle	self-propelled antitank gun platoon Brammer
18 February 1943	Attack on Stepanovka	14. Kompanie (elem.) 1. Batterie/501
18 February 1942	Crossing of the river Neruch and reconnaissance near Stepanovka	11. Kompanie 14. Kompanie (elem.) 1. Batterie/501
19 February 1943	Attack on Nagorniy	III. Bataillon (elem.) Regimental units 7. Kompanie (a group) Self-propelled anti tank gun platoon (elem.) I./Flak Regiment 501
25 February 1943	Defence at Stolbetskoye	7. Kompanie
26 February 1943	Defence at Stolbetskoye	6. Kompanie
27 February 1943	Break-in and close combat at Hill 250.2	9. Kompanie
1 March 1943	Reconnaissance south of Kapriska	11. Kompanie
1 March 1943	Attack on Promklevo	3. Kompanie
3 March 1943	Attack on Kriuki	1. Kompanie (elem.) 2. Kompanie
4 March 1943	Defence against major attack on Baldyzh	1. Kompanie (elem.) 2. Kompanie 3. Kompanie 4. Kompanie
4 March 1943	Attack on Aleshenka	Staff/I. Bataillon Signals platoon 3. Kompanie 4. Kompanie
8 and 9 March 1943	Defence and counterattack southeast Dmitrovsk	2. Kompanie 3. Kompanie
9 March 1943	Tactical raid on Mai	10. Kompanie
17 March 1943	Defence southeast of Dmitrovsk	2. Kompanie 3. Kompanie
17 March 1943	Defence against a Soviet tank attack at Uspenskiy	10. Kompanie 2. Kompanie 13. Kompanie (elem.) Self-propelled anti-tank gun platoon
17 March 1943	Attack on Sredniy Log and Muravchik	Stabskompanie (elem.) 4. Kompanie (platoon Einhäupl) 14. Kompanie Self-propelled anti-tank gun platoon
20 March 1943	Attack on hill at Muravchik	Regimental staff units (elem.) 14. Kompanie (II platoon)
22 March 1943	Tactical raid south of Uspenskiy	10. Kompanie (elem.)

Appendix IV

Subordinations

Subordinations of *Fallschirmjäger Regiment 1* (without I. Bataillon) during the Orel Mission (February until March 1943)[1]

Unit	Subordination	Date
FJR 1	LIII. AK (PzAOK 2)	12–13 February
FJR 1 (w/o *I. Bataillon*)	LV. AK (PzAOK 2)	14 February
FJR 1 (w/o *I. Bataillon*)	45. ID (LV. AK)	15 February
FJR 1 (w/o *I. Bataillon*) + 2 platoons FschPzJg Abt. +1 platoon Fsch FlaMgBtl. + I./Flak Rgt. 501	216. ID (LV. AK)	24 February
II. Bataillon/FJR 1	216.ID (LV. AK)	24 February until 31 March
FJR 1 (w/o I. Bat., II. Bat.) Only regt. staff, train and III. Btl.	XXXXVI. PzK (PzAOK 2)	4–30 March
FJR 1 (like above)	78. Sturm Div. (XXXXVI. PzK)	4 March
FJR 1 (like above) + SFL platoon	12. PzDiv (XXXXVI. PzK)	7–8 March
FJR 1 (w/o I. and II. Btl.) regt. staff, III. Btl., I. Flak Rgt 501	XXXXVI PzK (PzAOK 2)	8 March
FJR 1 (staff and III.Btl.)	12. PzDiv (XXXXVI. PzK)	9 March
I.Btl./FJR 1	FJR 1 (12.PzDiv)	17 March (from *78. Sturm-Division*)
FJR 1 (w/o II. Bat.)	12. PzDiv (XXXXVI. PzK)	18 March
FJR 1 (w/o II. Bat.)	7. ID (XXXXVI. PzK)	20 March (23 March?)
2. Kompanie	I. Btl./FJR 1 (7. ID)	22 March (from Sturm Rgt. 14)
FJR 1	*Flieger Division 7*	31 March

---

1   Compilation in BW 57-82.

Subordinations of *I. Bataillon/Fallschirmjäger Regiment 1* during the Orel Mission (February until 17 March 1943)[2]

Unit	Subordination	Date
I. Bat./FJR 1	34. ID (XXXV. AK)	12 February
I. Bat./FJR 1	PzAOK 2	14 February (10 p.m.)
I. Bat./FJR 1	XXXV. AK (PzAOK 2)	16 February (2.30 a.m.)
I. Bat./FJR 1	299. ID (XXXV. AK)	16 February (3.55 p.m.)
1. Kompanie	GrRgt 528 (299. ID)	17 (8.25 a.m.) until 28 February
2. Kompanie	GrRgt 529 (299. ID)	18 February (5.35 a.m.)
I. Bat./FJR 1 (w/o 1. Kp.)	34. ID (XXXV. AK)	23 February
I. Bat./FJR 1	*Kampfgruppe Bornemann* (XXXXVI PzK)	28 February
I. Bat./FJR 1	78. Sturm Div. (XXXXVI. PzK)	1 March
I. Bat./FJR 1	Sturm-Rgt. 195 (78 Sturm Div.)	4 March
2. Kompanie	Sturm-Rgt.14 (78 Sturm Div.)	8–22 March
I. Bat./FJR 1 (w/o 2. Kp.)	78. Sturm Div. (XXXXVI. PzK)	8–17 March
I. Bat./FJR 1 (w/o 2. Kp.)	FJR 1 (12.PzDiv.)	17 March

---

2 Compilation in BW 57-82.

Bibliography

Archives and Online sources

Ancestry.com. Deutschland, im Kampf gefallene Soldaten, 1939–1948 online database. Deutsches Bundesarchiv Kartei der Verlust- und Grabmeldungen gefallener deutscher Soldaten 1939–1945 (–1948), Bundesarchiv B 563-2 Kartei. Berlin, Deutschland (Digitised card file)

Bundesarchiv-Militärarchiv Freiburg: FJR 3 and FJR 4 (RL 33), 45. ID (RH 26-45), 197. ID (RH 26-197), 299. ID (RH 26-299), VI.AK (RH 24-6), LIX. AK (RH 24-59), Archiv des Bundes Deutscher Fallschirmjäger (BW 57)

German-Russian Project for digitizing German documents in Central Archives of the Ministry of Defence of the Russian Federation (CAMO): stock 500, finding aid 12454 (*Heeresgruppe Mitte*); 12455 (situation maps of *Heeresgruppe Mitte*) 12466 (*Panzerarmeen*); 12472 (AOK files); 12474 (corps files). (www.germandocsinrussia.org).

German War Graves Commission: Database of more than 4.8 million war dead and missing (www.volksbund.de)

National Archives, Washington DC (NARA): AOK 9 (T312 R-307, R-308, R-310, R-317 and R-320); PzAOK 2 (T-313 R-153 and R-172); LV. AK (T-314 R-1376 and R-1377); XXXXVI. PzK (T 314 R-1086); 12. PzDiv (T-315 R-633 and R-634); 34. ID (T-315 R-878); 78. Infanterie-Division (T-315 R-1100 and R-1101)

Österreichische Nationalbibliothek, ANNO – Historical Newspapers and Journals (www.anno.anb.ac.at)

Other internet sources:
    www.lexikon-der-wehrmacht.de
    www.forum-der-wehrmacht.de
    forum.axishistory.com
    libraries.indiana.edu/cyrillic-index-cyrillic-topographic-maps
    www.tracesofwar.com
    www.wehrmacht-awards.com
    www.wii-microfilm.blogspot.com
    Henry L. deZeng IV and Douglas G. Stankey, Luftwaffe Officer Career Summaries www.ww2.dk/lwoffz.html

Unpublished or Self-Published Manuscripts, Chronicles and Memoirs

Anon., *Geschichte des III./Fallschirmjäger-Regiment 1* (self-published)
Anon., *Rot scheint die Sonne – Eine Kompanie schreibt ihre Geschichte Fallschirm-Transport-, Kradschützen- und Aufklärungskompanie* (self-published)
Donth Rudolf, *Chronik der 2. Kompanie Fallschirmjäger-Ski-Bataillon* (BA-MA, BW 57-41)
Donth, Rudolf, *Geschichte des FJR 4*, (Schongau: self-published)
Fricke Walter, *An die Gewehre! An die Gewehre!* (BA-MA, BW 57-89)
Germer, Ernst: Tagebuch (typewritten copy and excerpt, BA-MA, BW 57-81)
Heinkelein, Walter: *Recollections* (Manuscript, Estate of Walter Heinkelein, Stadtarchiv Crailsheim)
Heilmann, Ludwig, *Memoirs* (Hoover Institution Library & Archives, Box 1)
Jacob, Gerhard, *Der letzte Befehl ist heilig!* (self-published)
Klitzing, G., *Die Geschichte des Fsch.MG.Btl/Fsch.Gr.Werferbtl. 1* (self-published)
Müller, Dr. Ludwig, Oberstarzt a.D., *Damals* (Würzburg: self-published, 1981)
Niehaus, Heino (ed.), *Chronik der Fallschirm-Panzer-Jäger-Abteilung 1, 1939–1945* (Bremerhaven: self-published, 1996)
Niepold, Gerd, *12. Panzerdivision (2.Inf.Div.) Pommern 1921–1945* (Koblenz: self-published, 1988)
Rohsen, Franz (?) *Chronik 1. Fallschirmjäger-Division – Italien 1943–1945* (self-published, 1961)
Unverzagt, Christian, *Sizilien – Kämpfe des Fallschirmjäger Regiments 3 vom 12. Juli-16. August 1943* (Hamburg: self-published, 1977)
Wanderwitz, Alfons: *11. Kompanie/Fallschirm-Jäger-Regiment 1* (without place, self-published, 1978)

Articles, Journals, & Pamflets

Anon., 'Karl-Heinz Becker – ein Fünfzigjähriger', *Der Deutsche Fallschirmjäger*, (1964), vol.1, p.7
Anon., '"Schwarzer" Becker – 70 Jahre', *Der Deutsche Fallschirmjäger*, (1984) vol.6, pp.5–6
Anon., 'Nachruf Kurt Gröschke', *Der Deutsche Fallschirmjäger* (1996), p.25
Boerger, Eberhard, 'Nachruf auf Karl Heinz Becker', *Der Deutsche Fallschirmjäger*, (2000) vol.6, p.12
Brammer, Bruno, 'Kriegstagebuch', *Traditionsgemeinschaft Fallschirmpanzerjäger Abteilung 1*, (1983), vol.16, pp. 108–111
Heeresgruppe Mitte (ed.)., *Der Kampf um Welikije Luki vom 24.11.1942–16.1.1943* (Heeresgruppe Mitte, 1943), CAMO, 500_12454, file 653
Helmecke, Chris, 'Generaloberst Schmidt – Denken und Handeln im Vernichtungskrieg', *Militärgeschichte* (2017), no. 1, pp.14–17
Heidrich, Richard, 'Mein Soldatenleben', *Der Grüne Teufel – Mitteilungsblatt der deutschen Fallschirmjäger* (1951), December, pp.2–4
Kretschmar, Heinz, 'Von Mal zu Mal sich übertroffen – Aus der Geschichte der 11./Fallschirmjäger-Regiment 1', *Der Deutsche Fallschirmjäger*, (1976), vol.5, pp.14–16
Kretschmar, Heinz, 'Die Kameraden herausgeholt – Das III./FJR. 1 im Kampf um Welikije Luki Anfang 1943', *Der Deutsche Fallschirmjäger*, (1979) vol.3, pp.16–17
Kretschmar, Heinz, 'III./Fallschirmjäger-Regiment 1 – Blitz-Einsatz Welikije Luki Januar 1943', *Der Deutsche Fallschirmjäger*, (1991) vol.1, pp.8–11
Stain, Walter, 'Kriegstagebuch', *Traditionsgemeinschaft Fallschirmpanzerjäger Abteilung 1* (1983), vol.16, pp.89–107
Schenkel, Franz, 'Unser Graf', *Der Deutsche Fallschirmjäger*, (1957) vol.7, p.11

Scherzer, Veit, 'Unbekannte Deutsche-Kreuz Träger-Archivfunde und neue Nachrichten', *Ritterkreuz Archiv*, (2010), vol.2, pp.28–34
Schütze, 'Kurt Gröschke', *Der Deutsche Fallschirmjäger*, (1996) vol.3, p.25
Wanderwitz, Alfons, *Treffen der 11./Fsch-Jg-Rgt. 1* (Neustadt a.d. Aisch: Wanderwitz, 1976)
Wittig, Karl-Hans, 'Der rettende Stoßtrupp von Durnewo – Ein Glück, daß die Elfte im Zuschauerraum saß', *Der Deutsche Fallschirmjäger*, (1968) vol.1, pp.7–10.

Books

Ailsby, Christopher, *Hitler's Sky Warriors – German Paratroopers in Action 1939–1945* (Barnsley: Pen & Sword, 2011)
Austermann, Heinz, *Von Eben Emael bis Edewechter Damm – Fallschirmjäger, Fallschirmpioniere* (Holzminden: Fallschirmpionier-Gemeinschaft, 1971)
Bergström, Christer, *Black Cross – Red Star, Air war over the Eastern Front, Volume 4 – Stalingrad to Kuban* (Eskilstuna: Vaktel, 2019)
Bernhard, Paul (ed.), Gerhard Broder, *Guerre Mondiale contre moi* (Dornstedt: Hess, 2013), 3rd ed.
Buchner, Alex, *Waffen und Ausrüstung der deutschen Fallschirmtruppe 1935–1945*, Waffenarsenal Sonderband 37 (Friedberg: Podzun-Pallas, 1995)
Böhmler, Rudolf, *Fallschirmjäger – Bildband und Chronik* (Bad Nauheim: Podzun, 1961)
Busch, Erich, *Die Fallschirmjäger Chronik 1935–1945* (Friedberg: Podzun-Pallas, 1983)
Buttar, Pritt, *Meat Grinder – The Battles for the Rzhev Salient 1942–43* (Oxford: Osprey, 2022)
Christensen, Ben, *The 1st Fallschirmjäger Division in World War II – Volume One: Years of Attack* (Atglen: Schiffer, 2007)
Denzel, Egon, *Die Luftwaffen-Felddivisionen 1942–1945* (Neckargemünd: Vonwinkel, 1976), 3rd expanded ed.
Fritsche, Hans-Martin, Oberst a.D., *Die Geschichte des Grenadier-Regiment 528* (self published, 1966)
Fritz, Steven G., *Ostkrieg – Hitler's War of Extermination in the East* (Lexington: University Press of Kentucky, 2015)
Forczyk, Robert, *Velikiye Luki 1942–1943 – The Doomed Fortress* (Oxford: Osprey, 2020)
Gerasimova, Svetlana, *The Rzhev Slaughterhouse: The Red Army's Forgotten 15-Month Campaign Against Army Group Center, 1942–1943* (Solihull: Helion 2013)
Glantz, David M., *After Stalingrad – The Red Army's Winter Offensive 1942–1943* (Solihull: Helion, 2009)
Glantz, David M., *From the Don to the Dnjepr: Soviet Offensive Operations, December 1942–August 1943* (London: Cass, 1991)
Glantz, David M., *Zhukov's Greatest Defeat – The Red Army's epic disaster in Operation Mars, 1942* (Lawrence: University Press Kansas, 1999)
Glantz, David M./House Jonathan M., *When Titans clashed – How the Red Army stopped Hitler* (Lawrence: University Press Kansas, 2015)
Jukes, Geoffrey, *Stalingrad to Kursk – Triumph of the Red Army* (Barnsley: Pen & Sword, 2011)
Golla, Karl-Heinz, *The German Fallschirmtruppe 1936–41* (Solihull: Helion, 2013)
Großmann, Horst, *Rshew – Eckpfeiler der Ostfront* (Bad Nauheim: Podzun, 1962)
Gschöpf, Dr. Rudolf, *Mein Weg mit der 45. Inf.-Div.* (Linz: Oberösterreichischer Landesverlag, 1955)
Hammel, Klaus, *Krieg in Italien* (Bielefeld: Osning, 2017), 2nd ed.

Harrison Richard W. (ed.), *Rollback – The Red Army's Winter Offensive along the Southwestern Strategic Direction 1942–43* (Soviet General Staff) (Solihull: Helion, 2015)

Hartmann, Christian, *Wehrmacht im Ostkrieg* (Munich: Oldenburg, 2010) 2nd ed.

Hartmann, Christian, Hürter, Johannes, Lieb, Peter, Pohl, Dieter (eds), *Der Deutsche Krieg im Osten 1941–1944, Facetten einer Grenzüberschreitung* (München: Oldenbourg, 2009)

Haupt, Werner, *Heeresgruppe Mitte 1941–1945* (Dorheim: Podzun, 1968)

Haupt, Werner, *Die Schlachten der Heeresgruppe Mitte 1941–1944 – Aus Sicht der Divisionen* (Eggolsheim: Nebel-Dörfler, year unknown)

Gerhard Herm, *Hitler, Göring und ich – Ein Fallschirmjäger im Dritten Reich* (Crailsheim: Baier Verlag, 2005)

Hildebrand, Karl Friedrich, *Die Generale der Deutschen Luftwaffe 1935–1945* (Osnabrück: Biblio, 1991) vol.2

Hürter, Johannes, *Hitlers Heerführer – Die deutschen Oberbefehlshaber im Krieg gegen die Sowjetunion 1941/42* (Munich: Oldenburg, 2007)

Husen, Martin, *Die Deutsche Fallschirmtruppe – Ärzte und Sanitätsdienst im Zweiten Weltkrieg* (Munich: Grin, 2022)

Janzyk, Stephan, *Deckname Fall Weiß – Deutsche Fallschirmjäger im Polenfeldzug 1939* (Herne: VS-Books, 2015)

Jenner, Martin, *Die Geschichte der 216./272. Infanterie-Division* (Eggolsheim: Nebel-Dörfler, year).

Kamann, Willi, *Der Weg der 2. Fallschirmjägerdivision* (München: Schild, 1998), 3rd ed.

Klietmann, Kurt-G., *Auszeichnungen des Deutschen Reiches 1936–1945* (Stuttgart: MotorBuch, 1994)

Kratzert, Rolf, *Vom k.u.k. Offizier zum Ritterkreuzträger* (self published, 1991)

Kühn, Volkmar, *Deutsche Fallschirmjäger im II. Weltkrieg – Grüne Teufel im Sprungeinsatz und Erdkampf 1939–1945* (Stuttgart: MotorBuch, 1974)

Kunz, Andreas, *Wehrmacht und Niederlage: Die bewaffnete Macht in der Endphase der nationalsozialistischen Herrschaft 1944 bis 1945* (Munich: Oldenburg, 2007), 2nd ed.

Kurowski, Franz, *Die Heeresgruppe Mitte 1942/43* (Bad Nauheim: Podzun-Pallas, 1989)

Liedtke, Gregory, *Enduring the Whirlwind – The German Army and the Russo-German War 1941–1943* (Solihull: Helion, 2016)

Lucas, James, *Storming Eagles – German Airborne Forces in World War II* (Edison: Castle, 2004)

McNab, Chris, *German Automatic Rifles 1941–1945* (Oxford: Osprey, 2013)

McMeekin, Sean, *Stalin's War – A New History of World War II* (New York: Hachette, 2021)

Mehner, Kurt, *Die Geheimen Tagesberichte der deutschen Wehrmachtsführung im zweiten Weltkrieg 1939–1945* (Osnabrück: Biblio, 1989) vol.6, 1.12.1942–31.5.1943

Merker, Ludwig, *Das Buch der 78. Sturmdivision* (Tübingen: Kameradenhilfswerk d. 78. Sturm-Division e. V., abt.1955)

Nebel, Gerhard, *Unter Partisanen und Kreuzfahrern* (Stuttgart: Deutscher Bücherbund, without year), reprint of 1950 edition.

Nebolsin, Igor, Britton, Stuart (ed. and transl.), *Stalin's Favorite – The Combat History of the 2nd Guards Tank Army from Kursk to Berlin* (Solihull: Helion, 2015) vol.1: January 1943–June 1944, reprint 2022

Pahl, Magnus, Wagner, Armin (eds), *Hitlers Elitetruppe? – Mythos Fallschirmjäger* (Dresden: Militärhistorisches Museum, be.bra, 2021)

Pahl, Magnus, *Monte Cassino* (Paderborn: Brill, 2021)

Patzwall, Klaus and Scherzer, Veit (eds), *Das Deutsche Kreuz 1941–1945 – Geschichte und Inhaber* (Norderstedt: Patzwall, 2007and 2001), vol.1 and 2

Peters, Klaus J., *Fallschirmjägerregiment 3 – Eine Chronik in Bildern* (San José: Bender, 1992 and 1995), vol.1 and 2

Hönscheid, Johannes (ed.), Pöppel, Martin, *Himmel und Hölle – Das Kriegstagebuch des Fallschirmjägers Martin Pöppel* (Munich: Internationaler Kulturdienst, 1985)

Quarrie, Bruce, *Deutsche Fallschirmjäger 1935–45* (Königswinter: Brandenburgisches Verlagshaus, 2013)

Queen, Eric, *Red Shines the Sun – A Pictoral History of the Fallschirm-Infanterie* (San Jose: Bender, 2002)

Ramcke, Hermann Bernhard, *Fallschirmjäger – Damals und danach* (Oldendorf: Schütz, 1973)

Von Roon, Arnold, *Die Bildchronik der Fallschirmtruppe 1935–1945* (Friedberg: Podzun-Pallas, 1985)

Rigg, Bryan Mark, *Hitler's Jewish Soldiers: the untold story of Nazi racial laws and men of Jewish descent in the German military* (Lawrence: University Press of Kansas, 2002)

Scheibert, Horst, *Die Träger des Deutschen Kreuzes in Gold Kriegsmarine, Luftwaffe, Waffen-SS* (Friedberg: Podzun-Pallas, without year)

Scherzer, Veit, *Ritterkreuzträger 1939–1945* (Bayreuth: Scherzer, 2021), 3rd ed.

Schlaug, Georg, *Die Deutschen Lastenseglerverbände 1937–1945 – Eine Chronik aus Berichten und Tagebüchern* (Stuttgart: MotorBuch, 1985)

Schmitz, Thies, and Wegmann, Zweng, (eds), *Die Deutschen Divisionen 1939–1945* (Osnabrück: Biblio, 1993), vol.1

Schmitz, Thies, and Wegmann, Zweng (eds) *Die Deutschen Divisionen 1939–1945* (Osnabrück, Biblio, 1994), vol.2

Schramm, Percy E. (ed.), *Kriegstagebuch des Oberkommandos der Wehrmacht 1942* (Augsburg: Weltbild, 2005), vol.2, part 2

Schramm, Percy E. (ed.), *Kriegstagebuch des Oberkommandos der Wehrmacht 1943* (Augsburg: Weltbild, 2005), vol.3, part 1

von der Schulenburg, Tisa, *Ich hab's gewagt – Bildhauerin und Ordensfrau – Ein unkonventionelles Leben* (Husum: Husum, 2013)

Sokolov, Dr Boris, Stuart Britton (ed. & trans.), *Marshall K.K. Rokossovsky – The Red Army's Gentleman Commander* (Solihull: Helion, 2015)

Sokolov, Dr Boris, Richard Harrison (trans.), *Myths and Legends of the Eastern Front – Reassessing the Great Patriotic War* (Barnsley: Pen & Sword, 2019)

Stein, Marcel, *A Flawed Genius – Field Marshal Walter Model – A Critical Biography* (Soilhul: Helion, 2010)

Stimpel, Hans-Martin, *Die deutsche Fallschirmtruppe 1942–1945 – Einsätze auf Kriegsschauplätzen im Osten und Westen* (Hamburg: Mittler, 2001)

Götzel, Hermann (ed.), Student, Kurt, *Generaloberst Student und seine Fallschirmjäger* (Friedberg: Podzun-Pallas, 1980)

Sutherland, Jon, and Canwell, Diane (eds), *Fallschirmjäger – Elite German Paratroops in World War II – Rare Photographs from Wartime Archives* (Barnsley: Pen&Sword, 2010)

Thomas, Franz, and Wegmann, Günter (eds), *Die Ritterkreuzträger der Deutschen Wehrmacht 1939–1945, Teil II: Fallschirmjäger* (Osnabrück: Biblio, 1986)

Tress, Karl, *Das Infanterie- und Sturm-Regiment 14 im Zweiten Weltkrieg* (Konstanz: Der Seehase, 1959)

Vetter, Fritz, *Die 78. Infanterie- und Sturm-Division 1938–1945 in Bildern* (Friedberg: Podzun-Pallas, 1981)

Wachsmuth, Werner, *Ein Leben mit dem Jahrhundert* (Berlin: Springer, 1985)

Wegner, Bernd, 'Der Krieg gegen die Sowjetunion 1942/43' in Horst Boog, Werner Rahn, Reinhard Stumpf, Bernd Wegener (eds), *Das Deutsche Reich und der Zweite Weltkrieg* (Stuttgart: DVA, 1990) vol.6, pp.761–1102.

Yerger, Mark C., and Fiorenza, Leslie, *Honouring those they led – Decorated Field Commanders of the Third Reich: Command Authorities, Award Parameters, and Ranks* (Solihull: Helion, 2016)

Zimburg Albrecht (ed.), Zimburg, Rüdiger, *Kriegserlebnisse eines Fallschirmjägers* (Salzburg: Milizverlag, 2018)

Zweng, Christian, *Die Truppen und Verbände der Deutschen Wehrmacht 1939–1945* (Osnabrück: Institut für deutsche Phaleristik und Militärgeschichte, 2015), vol.3c